TUNE TO WIN

WWW.CARROLLSMITH.COM

"Very often, a considerable lack of understanding is apparent between 'mathematicians' and 'engineers'. Their abilities and tasks are basically different and there are only a few men who can master both theoretical research and practical application."

S.F. Hoerner

"The racing car is an inanimate object; therefore it must, eventually, respond to reason."

Unknown

TUNE TO WIN

*THE ART AND SCIENCE OF RACE CAR
DEVELOPMENT AND TUNING*

CARROLL SMITH

ADDITIONAL INFORMATION AND REORDER
OF ALL CARROLL SMITH TITLES AT
WWW.CARROLLSMITH.COM

First Published in 1978
Carroll Smith Consulting Incorporated
P.O. Box 2851, Rolling Hills Estates, CA 90274
Csci1@msn.com

Cover design by Curved Space Creative

Disclaimer of liability:
The information in this book is true and complete to the best of our knowledge. All recommendations are made without any guarantee on the part of the author or publisher, who also disclaim any liability incurred in connection with the use of this information.

Library of Congress Catalog Card Number: 78-73549
ISBN 978-0-879-38071-7

Printed and bound in the U.S.A.

DEDICATION

Since none of my friends who promised to write forewords came through in time—and since we have allotted space for one and it's too late to change now—there will be no foreword. Instead, I would like to dedicate this one to my wife Jane, who has put up with a quarter of a century of gypsy existence so that I could race—and to my children Dana and Christopher, who have, I hope, enjoyed a somewhat unusual childhood.

PREFACE

In the preface to PREPARE TO WIN I threatened that, if the book were successful, it would be followed by TUNE TO WIN.

Thanks to you, the readers, PREPARE TO WIN has been a modest success—modest enough so that I have not thrown away my stop watches and drafting tools but successful enough to motivate me to get started on TUNE TO WIN.

I do so with a certain amount of reluctance. I am constantly reminded of Eric Broadley's reply to a serious inquiry as to why no designer has written anything resembling a comprehensive study of racing car design—"Probably because no one is willing to expose the depths of his ignorance to public view." Too true!

I am fully aware that much of what I have to say in this book is subjective. I wish that my knowledge and wisdom were such that this were not so. Many readers are going to disagree with my interpretations, conclusions and recommendations. I offer no apology. In each case I will put forth my personal best shot on the subject at the time of writing. I reserve my right to change my thinking at any time.

Our knowledge of any field whose title includes the word dynamics should be constantly expanding. This is because, particularly in motor racing, we approach a complex subject from a base of abysmal ignorance and also because, in a field defined by compromises, knowledge gained in one area can and does modify our thinking in related areas.

What follows is not intended to be a step-by-step instruction manual for decreasing the lap times of a racing car. Rather it is intended to be a mind-opening exercise—admittedly in a narrow field. If, at the end, the reader has gained a better understanding of vehicle dynamics and a fuller appreciation of the problems of control and response at high force levels, my primary purpose will have been reached. If the reader is then able to apply this knowledge to enhance his enjoyment of motor racing and/or increase his success at it, the book will be a success.

TABLE OF CONTENTS

STATEMENT OF NON-LIABILITY

Our society has reached the point where I am advised that, in order to protect myself from possible lawsuits, I should include a statement of non-liability in this book. Since I believe that the human being is wholly responsible for his own actions, I strongly object to this necessity and to the morality that has spawned it. However, I would object even more strongly to being sued—so here it is.

The price of man in motion is the occasional collision. Motor racing is dangerous. In order to be competitive in this business it is necessary to operate at the outer edges of the performance envelope. The closer we come to the edge, the greater the risk of falling off becomes. This book is about improving the performance of the racing car and its driver— particularly with respect to the roadholding department. It deals with the deliberate exploration of the outer limits of traction. The closer the racing car approaches its potential in this department, the less forgiving it becomes and the greater the chances of paying a sudden stop type penalty become when an error in judgment occurs.

If, while attempting to apply any of the ideas, procedures or advice contained in this book, you should come unstuck, you will have done so through your own conscious decision. I disclaim responsibility for your actions—and for your accident.

CHAPTER ONE

VEHICLE DYNAMICS — WHAT'S IT ALL ABOUT?

Before we can do anything intelligent with any piece of machinery we had better figure out the exact function of the piece—"if all else fails, read directions." In the case of the racing car that function is deceptively simple. The racing car exists *only* to allow one man to negotiate a certain fixed distance in less time than any other combination of man and machine present on that day. Whether the distance happens to be the 440 yards of a drag strip, 200 laps of Indianapolis, 14 laps of the Nurburgring or 1000 miles of Baja landscape is immaterial. The racing car is not a technical exercise. It is not an art object. THE RACING CAR IS SIMPLY A TOOL FOR THE RACING DRIVER. Our objective in this book is to learn how to provide our driver with the most effective tool possible within the framework of our limitations—human, financial and temporal.

What this book is going to be about is Basic Vehicle Dynamics—a term that most people find somewhat frightening. The term dynamics brings to mind groups of confusing diagrams accompanied by strings of obtuse formulae. It doesn't have to be that way. Vehicle Dynamics is simply the study of the forces which affect wheeled vehicles in motion and of the vehicle's responses, either natural or driver induced, to those forces. In many cases it is sufficient to understand the cause and effect of the forces and responses without establishing finite values or magnitudes. Since we are interested only in the racing car we can and will ignore many aspects which concern the designers of passenger cars.

For our purposes vehicle dynamics can be conveniently broken down into a few inter-related fields:

LINEAR OR STRAIGHT LINE ACCELERATION

The ability to accelerate faster than the next car is the single most important factor in race car performance. It is more important than cornering capacity and infinitely more important than top speed. Basic factors which govern the vehicle's ability to accelerate include:

Net power available at the driving wheels
Tractive capacity of the driving tires
Gross vehicle weight
Aerodynamic drag
Rolling resistance
Component Rotational Inertia

LINEAR DECELERATION OR BRAKING CAPACITY

Braking is simply acceleration turned around. It is governed by exactly the same factors as acceleration with the power of the braking system substituted for net engine power. In this case the power of the braking system is transmitted to the road surface through all four of the tires instead of through the driving wheels only. The vehicle's ability to stop is relatively less important than its ability to accelerate because much less time is spent braking than is spent accelerating. We stop faster than we accelerate.

ACCELERATION OR CORNERING POWER

Except for Drag Cars and Bonneville cars all race cars are required to go around corners. Obviously the faster that a given car can go around the type of corners which it is called upon to negotiate, the less its lap time will be—for two reasons. The first reason is simply that the faster the vehicle is traveling the less time it will take to cover a given section of race track, either straight or curved. The second reason is equally obvious, although less understood. It is perhaps more important. The car that exits a given corner at say eighty miles per hour is going to get down the ensuing straight in less time than the car which exits the same corner at seventy miles per hour. It will do so simply because it doesn't have to waste time accelerating from seventy to eighty miles per hour—it is already there and so has a head start. Factors which determine the cornering power of a given race car include:

Cornering capacity of the tires, which is influenced by:
    Suspension geometry
    Vehicle load transfer characteristics
    Vehicle downforce
    Size and characteristics of the tires
Vehicle gross weight
Height of the vehicle center of gravity

TOP SPEED

In most forms of racing top speed is nowhere near so important as it would appear to be. Unless the corners can be taken at top speed both cornering power and acceleration capacity are much more important. How often does the losing Drag Car come up with the highest trap speed? Elapsed time is the name of the game that we play—don't ever forget it. Given the opportunity to gain significant engine torque and area under the power curve in the engine's operating range at the expense of peak horsepower—do it. When you find that your lap times are better with enough wing on the car to cut down the top end - don't worry about it.

Factors controlling top speed include:
    Net power at the driving wheels
    Aerodynamic drag
    Rolling resistance

CONTROLLABILITY AND RESPONSE

If we could design and build a Can Am car with the acceleration of a AA Fueler, the top end of a Bonneville Car and the braking and cornering power of a Formula One Car it would avail us nought if it lacked adequate controllability and response characteristics. The racing car must be capable of being driven—and driven consistently hard—in traffic. As you would expect, this is the difficult part. There are very few factors which do not affect controllability and response but the most important are:

Center of gravity height
Load transfer characteristics
Suspension geometry and alignment
Polar moment of inertia
Chassis and suspension link rigidity
Differential characteristics
Slip angle versus coefficient of friction curves of the tires
Aerodynamic balance

COMPROMISES AND TRADE OFFS

By now it should be becoming obvious that it is just not possible to combine maximum acceleration, maximum cornering force, maximum top speed and optimum controllability and response characteristics in any one vehicle You don't take a drag car to Indianapolis Motor Speedway because it won't go around the corners. It won't go around the corners because it was designed and developed for maximum acceleration. It has a very narrow track, a very long wheelbase and an enormous concentration of weight on the rear wheels. It has tiny front tires and no suspension. It just doesn't want to know about corners—but it surely does accelerate. By the same token, A.J. had best not bring his Coyote to Irwindale. Even if it had enough power it won't transfer enough weight to the rear wheels, the fat front tires will slow it down, etc., etc. This much is pretty obvious. What is not so obvious is that the same type of trade off and compromise affects the performance of every racing car on the circuits that it was designed for. If we can gain corner exit acceleration at the expense of corner apex speed—or maybe vice-versa—we may be able to improve our lap time. Or if we can gain corner apex speed at the expense of top end—or whatever. Just to make things a little more complex we must also realize that the optimum set up for a given car at Long Beach, with its predominance of slow corners, is going to be less than brilliant at Mosport where the corners are very fast indeed. Add to this the fact that no two drivers like their cars set up exactly the same and the hope that our knowledge of vehicle dynamics is constantly growing, and we begin to understand why this is not a simple business.

There is a school of thought, particularly prevalent among those new to racing, that the way to ensure success is to purchase whatever chassis is winning, bolt in the best engine that money can buy, install a super-driver and start collecting first place checks. WRONG!

Assuming that enough spares, support equipment and competent mechanics are included in the package and that a good manager is around to make the decisions and run the operation, this is a good way to consistently finish third or fourth. But it will not win. It will not win because someone else is going to take an identical chassis, an identical engine, an equal driver, a lot of hard work and a whole bunch of knowledge—tune on the whole package—and blow your doors off. That's just about what tuning adds up to—the difference between first and third.

So in order to become competitive and in order to stay competitive we're going to have to tune on the package. The main reason has to do with the very nature of vehicle dynamics—there are so many compromises and trade offs involved that we can never realize the optimum possible performance. Because the opposition can be depended upon to keep improving, we must also. But there is another reason and this one involves the natural limitations built into any race car that you can buy.

LIMITATIONS OF THE AS-BOUGHT RACE KAR

All race cars are full of design compromises. The bought "kit car" has more than the "works car." The obvious reason is cost. The kit car manufacturer is vitally concerned with his costs. He is engaged in one of the shakiest possible business ventures and spends all of his time walking the thin line between beans and bankruptcy. Even if he has brilliant concepts, he often can't build them because he hasn't got the funds for new tooling and/or he is terrified of pricing himself out of the market. Also he cannot afford to take a giant step forward that might not work—remember the Lola T400?

That's part of the problem. Another part of it is the simple fact that most of the manufacturers do not race a works team of cars. The successful professional racing teams don't build customer cars because it is a pain in the ass, it doesn't make very much money and it inevitably dilutes the racing effort. The kit car manufacturers don't race because they can't afford to. Since they can't sell very many cars without racing successes to boast about they usually give some sort of support to carefully chosen racing teams in the hope that these "works supported" teams will win and, in so doing, create a demand for the product. The team does all of the testing and development and supposedly passes the word on to the factory for the ultimate benefit of the customer. Good Luck! The race team is guaranteed to display considerable reluctance at passing on their hard won tweaks for the immediate benefit of the opposition. What does trickle down does so just as slowly as the racers can arrange it.

Further, at some cut off date before work is actually begun on a batch of customer cars, the design must be frozen or they will never get built. After that time the best you can hope for is the opportunity to buy expensive update kits.

The last bit has to do with operating conditions, tire characteristics and driver skill. Development may well have been done on circuits totally different to those that you will race on and/or with tires of different characteristics. It may also have been done by a certified hero driver whose skill and experience requires a much less forgiving car than your rookie driver is ready for.

TUNING

Anyway, what you can buy is a starting point. In a really competitive class of racing it is unlikely to be capable of winning races out of the box. Development is up to you. You will do it by tuning.

My definition of tuning is simply any intentional modification to any component of the total race car system made for the purpose of increasing the probability of winning a motor race. The removal of unnecessary weight is tuning. So is increasing effective power output, improving cornering power, reducing drag and just about anything else that we can do to our machines to make them faster, more controllable or more reliable—although reliability has more to do with preparation than it does with tuning.

WHAT'S HAPPENING OUT THERE

Since the publication of PREPARE TO WIN I have received many ego inflating comments. To date no one has disagreed or even found fault with any of the factual material, procedures or recommendations put forth. This will not be true this time! The actual preparation of a race car, an aircraft or a machine tool is merely the compilation and sorting out of what has been learned by those who have operated similar equipment under like conditions. Experience and judgment is necessary but the field is pretty much a black and white area. Someone, somewhere, can answer correctly—virtually any question that comes up.

None of the above is true of tuning—at least of tuning on the racing car or virtually any part thereof. Tuning is like designing in that, if it were a precise science, all of the cars campaigned by competent organizations would exhibit no faults or vices, drivers would have nothing to bitch about, every modification and demon tweak would work and the cars would go like stink all of the time. None of this happens. We spend most of our professional lives in one quandary after another—wondering why our bright ideas don't work—and searching for our very own Holy Grail. Once in a while we make a breakthrough and think that we have gained a tenuous hold on the handle of the grail. Inevitably we then find that whatever bit of knowledge we have just learned merely lets in enough light to allow us to see a whole new series of problems. The visibility at the best of times is liable to be a bit hazy due to clouds of ignorance.

The basic problem, as usual, is very simple. We just don't know enough about what we are doing.

This is not to imply that racers are stupid, or ignorant or lazy. To the contrary—a more clued-in and dedicated group of individuals has never trod the earth. For reasons having to do with "the lacks"—lack of money, lack of time and lack of communication—NO ONE has yet defined in detail just what is happening, in the vehicle dynamics sense, as the racing car is driven around the race track at high force levels.

How can this be? After all, high performance aircraft are much more complex than race cars, they operate at vastly higher speeds and they are defying the law of gravity to start with. They have nonetheless been developed to a rare state of perfection and, with minor but exciting exceptions, can pretty much be depended upon to operate to design objectives straight off the drawing board and out of the wind tunnel. Why have we failed to achieve this level with our relatively simple devices?

There are several reasons. Physically, the foremost is that aircraft operate in one medium only—the air—and they have freedom of rotation about all three of their axes—roll, pitch and yaw. Except when leaving or returning to the earth, they are free of ground effects. Normally a pilot finding himself in trouble near the ground has the saving option of going up. At those times when this option is not available both the pilot and the designer are a lot more interested in stability than absolute performance so that the aircraft will be operating well inside the limits of its performance envelope. Crop Dusters, Fire Fighters and Close Ground Support Pilots, forgive me—your game doesn't count in this discussion.

In extremis, if the aircraft designer, builder, tuner or pilot has really screwed up, the driver of the high performance aircraft normally has one final option—he can jump out of the thing. This becomes rather more difficult in the case of the racing driver and, with the notable exception of Masten Gregory, has seldom been attempted with success. Even Masten got tired of it after while.

Among high performance machines the racing car is a rather unique projectile. It operates ON one medium—the earth—and IN another medium—the air. It receives simultaneous, and sometimes conflicting, inputs from each. It has only two dimensional freedom of rotation, and even that is severely limited. While full rotation about the yaw axis is not uncommon it is also not desired. Nothing good has ever been reported about the full rotation of a race car about either its pitch or roll axis. The machine operates in tenuous contact with the earth while passing through the air with instantaneously varying values of velocity, yaw and pitch. It is forever being upset by inputs from the ground, the air and the driver.

The driver has control of three thrust inputs to the ground —acceleration, deceleration and turning—but only up to the limit of tire traction in each case. After that the immutable laws of physics take over and, while the behavior of the vehicle can be modified to some extent after that point has been reached, the laws are indeed immutable. The driver has no control over the inputs received from either the ground or the air. He must anticipate and/or react to these inputs with control responses in order to prevent disaster. He has no direct aerodynamic control over his vehicle. Just to make sure that he doesn't become bored, if he is going fast enough to be competitive, he will constantly combine turning with either acceleration or deceleration—all of them at the limit of adhesion and in very close proximity to other vehicles. "If you have complete control over the damned thing, you're not going fast enough."

For some years now it has been technically feasible to quantitate much of what is actually happening in various areas as the race car is hurled around. Jim Hall pioneered the field. Ford did some instrumentation work during the late lamented Le Mans program. Donahue and Penske did a lot more, and now Ferrari, McLaren and Tyrell are well into it. I doubt that it is entirely coincidental that each of these operations has won more than its statistical fair share of races.

Having quantitated what is *actually* happening as opposed to what the engineers *think* should happen and what the driver *feels* is happening, it should then be possible to study the accumulated data and, by modifying hardware, change the vehicle's dynamic responses in the direction of optimum performance. To my knowledge no one has yet gone all the way with instrumentation evaluation programs. There are no governments and precious few giant corporations in motor racing, and the finances required for such a program are beyond the resources of individual race teams. We are not going to concern ourselves with extensive instrumentation as it is very unlikely that the reader will have access to it.

This is not necessarily all bad. Motor racing, so far, remains a field where the informed improviser—the try it and see tuner—will usually beat the conventional engineer. This is simply because the conventional engineer will be required to operate in the absence of many of the inputs with which he has been trained to work. He will also usually underestimate the importance of the driver in the performance equation and over estimate the importance of aerodynamic drag. In this over organized world there are too few technical endeavors where the maverick can succeed. Motor Racing, if the maverick thinks clearly enough and works hard enough, remains one of them.

So what do we tune on—and how do we decide in which direction and in what order to proceed? That's why it is an art rather than a science. We tune on just about everything from the driver's head (usually the most productive, but outside the scope of this book) through the tread pattern of the rain tires to the power output of the engine (usually the least productive). Hopefully we will do so from the firm base of as broad an understanding of vehicle dynamics as we can muster. We will do it in logical fashion and we will prioritize our efforts so as to gain the most amount of performance per dollar spent and per hour invested. For certain we will proceed one step at a time. Equally for certain we will attempt to avoid the common human tendency to get all hung up on one particular area—be it aerodynamics, unsprung weight, track width or whatever. The racing car is a system and each component of the system contributes the performance of the whole—although not equally so. More to the point, each area of performance interacts with all other areas, and it is necessary to view the effect of a given change on total performance. If this principle is engraved firmly on our minds we may achieve maximum success with minimum grief. If we allow ourselves to lose track of it success may still come our way—but only by chance.

SMALL INCREMENTS OF LAP TIME

Now is perhaps the time to speak of the importance of tiny increments of lap time. Every racer is willing to admit that one second of lap time is both a real and a significant interval. Indeed any real racer will sell his mother and rent out his lady to gain an improvement of one clear second per lap. After all, one second per lap at Riverside is forty seconds at the end of the race—and when was the last time that anyone won Riverside by forty seconds? Now try to convince this same racer that one tenth of a second has significance. I'm going to let you in on a secret! One tenth of a second per lap is four seconds at the end of a forty lap race

—and that IS a normal winning margin.

The biggest single mistake that racers make is in looking for the super tweak that will produce one large chunk of lap time. Assuming that the equipment is both good and sorted out, that tweak does not exist.

In the days when we still had a Formula 5000 series—before an inexplicable wave of insanity passed through Denver—the reason that Mario Andretti was two seconds faster than the second place qualifier—and four or five seconds faster than the tenth place qualifier—was not because of his engine, or his tires or his basic chassis was that much faster. It wasn't because his driving skill was that superior—although, in this case, I must admit that driving skill was a larger than normal part of the picture - I'm a Mario admirer. The real difference was in the accumulation of a lot of tiny little increments of lap time—a tenth here and a hundredth there painfully gained through endless hours of testing and tuning. Once the car is basically sorted out that's all you are going to gain by tuning—tenths and hundredths. It's enough.

In the chapters that follow I intend to explore the more critical areas of vehicle dynamics as they relate to the racing car. I will attempt to do so in logical and simple fashion, utilizing a minimum of mathematics and formulae. The book is not meant to be a design manual; nor is it intended to be a "follow me book" which tells the reader in several thousand words that if he reduces the diameter of the front sway bar he will reduce understeer. Rather it is intended to say, "this is the way it works and these are the options by means of which we can modify its behavior—in this direction."

We will discuss the various forces that affect the racing car and the vehicle's responses to those forces. Then we will get into the specifics of how to tailor or modify the responses by tuning. We will not discuss Drag Cars because I know nothing about them. We will basically be concerned with Road Racing Cars although virtually everything will also apply to Circle Track Cars at least on paved tracks. I also know nothing about Dirt Tracks or about Off-Road Racing. It is, however, my firm conviction that these areas are also subject to the laws of vehicle dynamics and that much of the material which follows must be applicable—with modification to suit the operating conditions. The principles involved remain constant, but we must weigh our applications of them in the light of expected conditions. Science always lives. It is only our interpretation and application of science that gets a little shaky.

By definition the racing car spends all of its real time flirting with the edge of tire adhesion. If it is not doing so then either it is momentarily on a part of the circuit where adhesion is not a factor (i.e. on a straight long enough that available torque is not sufficient to upset the car) or it is not being driven hard enough. This being the case we had better start with a look at the factors which influence and govern that adhesion. We are not and will not be interested in the lower eighty-five percent of the performance envelope.

CHAPTER TWO

THE RACING TIRE

The Formula Ford that finishes dead last at the East Nowhere SCCA Regional has one vital factor in common with the Indianapolis or Grand Prix winning machine—it is connected to the race track only by the contact patches of its four tires. Through these tenuous interfaces are transmitted all of the accelerations and thrusts that propel the car, decelerate it and change its direction. Through them also are reacted all of the driver's control actions and from them comes most of the sensory information which allows the driver to maintain—or to regain—control at high force levels.

Any discussion of vehicle dynamics must begin with an examination of the operating characteristics of the pneumatic tire—more specifically the racing tire. The subject is complex and imperfectly understood. We will discuss the basics of what we need to know and leave the more esoteric aspects for the magicians in Akron.

VERTICAL LOAD OR NORMAL LOAD

Vertical or normal load is the amount of force applied to an individual tire in the direction perpendicular to the road surface. It is expressed in pounds or kilograms and is the instantaneous sum of that portion of total vehicle weight and aerodynamic downforce which is acting on the individual tire at any given moment. Since vehicle weight is constantly being transferred from one tire to another, and since downforce varies with the square of road speed, the vertical load on any given tire is subject to continuous change. It is important to note that the word "normal" in this case is used in the perpendicular sense and does not refer to the "usual" load on the tire. To avoid confusion we will use the term vertical load.

COEFFICIENT OF FRICTION

When Issac Newton defined the laws of friction, the pneumatic tire had not been invented. When it was invented everyone assumed that the tire would obey Newton's laws and that therefore no tire could develop a force, in any direction, that would exceed the load applied to it. You may recall that, for many years, the experts categorically declared that Drag Racing top speeds and elapsed times would be limited to those that could be produced by a constant acceleration of one gravity—which would correspond to each tire of a four wheel drive dragster transmitting an accelerative thrust equal to its share of the total weight of the vehicle. The experts forgot to tell the Drag Racers who just worked away at going faster and faster until they broke through the "barrier" as if it weren't there. It wasn't.

The racing tire does not follow Newton's Laws of Friction—which are for friction between smooth bodies. It can, and does, generate forces greater than the loads applied to it. Further, it can develop an accelerative force, a decelerative force, a side force or a combination of either an accelerative force and a side force or a decelerative force and a side force. In the case of combined lateral and longitudinal forces, the sum can be considerably greater than the maximum force that can be developed in any one direction.

At the present state of the art a road racing tire on dry concrete with a vertical load of 500 pounds can generate, under ideal conditions, a force of approximately 800 pounds. The ratio of the force that the tire is capable of generating to the vertical load applied to it is termed that tire's "coefficient of friction." In this hypothetical case the 800-pound force divided by the 500 pound vertical load gives a coefficient of 1.6. This means that under ideal and steady conditions the tire could accelerate or decelerate at the rate of 1.6 g or could develop a cornering force of 1.6 g—which is enough to make your neck sore.

It is important to realize that the coefficient of friction is dimensionless. It is an indication of the maximum force which can be developed by one tire when compared to another tire under the same conditions. We need to understand its meaning as a concept in the study of tire dynamics, and the tire designers use it as one of the factors in predicting the performance and handling characteristics of different tire designs.

If you should somehow find out that the tires you are using have a coefficient of 1.5, don't expect your car to corner at 1.5 g. It won't—for several reasons—some of which have to do with tire and vehicle dynamics and some of which are related to the frictional characteristics of the road surface involved. The important thing to remember is that the force that can be developed by any tire is the product of the instantaneous vertical load applied to the tire and the tire's maximum coefficient of friction under the existing conditions. Naturally both of these factors change constantly with variations in road speed, load transfer, track condition, tire temperature and a host of other variables. In the lateral sense we will refer to this generated force as the tire's Cornering Power which is just another term for centrifugal acceleration capability. In the longitudinal sense we will use the term Traction Capacity. For our purposes we will consider the tire's traction capacity to be equal in both directions.

SLIP

Slip is probably the most discussed and least understood of the basic tire characteristics. Much of the confusion stems from the term itself. Slip implies slide and most people seem to believe that in order for a tire to operate in a slip mode it must be sliding. This is not so.

There are actually two distinct types of tire slip—transverse and longitudinal. In the transverse plane slip is referred to as "slip angle" and affects the generation of the tire's cornering forces. In the longitudinal plane slip is referred to as either "slip ratio" or "percentage slip" and affects acceleration and braking. We will look at slip angle first.

SLIP ANGLE

The slip angle of a pneumatic tire is defined as "the angular displacement between the plane of rotation of the wheel (the direction in which the rim is pointing) and the path that the rolling tire will follow on the road surface." This path is made up of the successive footprints of the contact patch laid down as the tire rolls. In order for the vehicle to change direction, regardless of road speed or the radius of curvature, each of the vehicle's tires must assume some value of slip angle. Now let's see why this is true and how it happens.

The existence of the slip angle phenomenon is due to the fact that the pneumatic tire is elastic in twist—i.e. when the tire is turned, that portion of the tread which is in contact with the road surface will resist the turning moment due to elastic friction between the rubber and the road. The tread in the vicinity of the contact patch, since it is elastic, will distort and therefore will not turn as far as the rim does. This being the case, the contact patch—and therefore the tire's rolling path over the road surface—will lag behind the plane of rotation of the wheel by some value of angular displacement. Since the tire is rolling, the contact patch is constantly renewed—if we visualize a single particle of tread rubber as the tire rolls it spends most of its time not in contact with the road. When the particle in question does roll into contact with the road it progresses from the leading edge of the contact patch, through the center, to the trailing edge. The actual elastic deformation takes place during the time that the rubber is in contact with the road. However, since each molecule is attached to the rest of the tread, the displacement actually starts before the tire to road intersection as the portion of the tread not yet in contact is pulled sideways by the portion undergoing deformation. This is a gradual process. When the molecule rotates past the contact patch the rubber "unstretches" and returns to its normal position. Rubber being rubber, this trailing deformation or energy release is much more rapid than the leading deformation. The drawings in Figure (1) are attempts to visualize slip angle in different ways. Figure (1A) also illustrates leading and trailing deformation. It is important that we do not confuse slip angle with steering angle, which is the angular difference between the tire's plane of rotation and the straight ahead position.

Next we are going to take a brief and admittedly incomplete look at what actually takes place at the rolling interface between the rubber and the road.

THE NATURE OF STICK

The racing tire develops friction with (or grip on) the track surface by a combination of mechanical gripping of road surface irregularities by the elastic tread compound and by transient molecular adhesion between the tread surface and these thousands of tiny contact areas. This molecular adhesion only comes into play at very high loads and coefficients and is the reason why we are able to leave impressive black marks on the track when we are neither spinning nor locking the wheels nor sliding the vehicle. I make no claim to understanding the physics involved. For those readers with the ability and inclination I recommend *The Unified Theory of Tire and Rubber Friction* by H. W. Kummer and W. E. Mayer, and *The Physics of Tire Traction*, edited by D. F. Hays and A. L. Brooke. The former is more comprehensive and the latter more comprehensible.

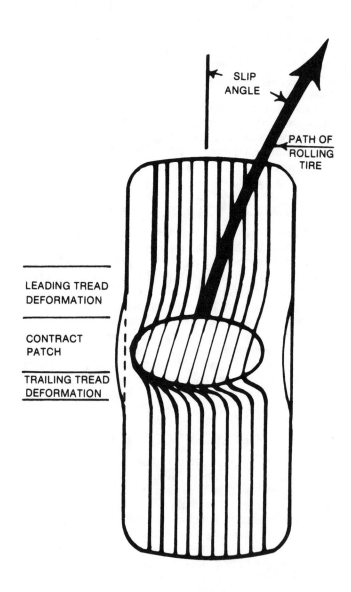

Figure (1A): Tire slip angle viewed from the road with successive tread particle paths depicted on tire tread surface.

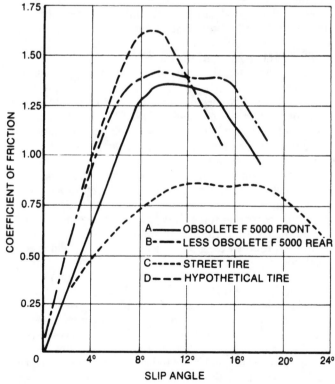

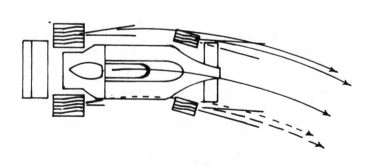

Figure (1B): Tire slip angle with tread particle paths projected on to road surface.

Figure (1C): Tire slip angles and tire paths on road in plan view.

THE RELATIONSHIP BETWEEN SLIP ANGLE, COEFFICIENT OF FRICTION AND CORNERING FORCE

Coefficient of friction varies with slip angle. Therefore cornering force varies with slip angle. The coefficient—and the cornering force—increases with increasing slip angle until, at some given slip angle, it reaches its maximum value. After this maximum value of coefficient has been reached, any further increase in slip angle will result in a decrease in coefficient, and a corresponding decrease in cornering force—the tire "breaks loose" or loses traction. If we make a graph of coefficient of friction vs. slip angle we end up with something like Figure (2) which shows a typical—if idealized—curve for racing tires plus one for a street tire.

The maximum value of coefficient reached on the curve will determine how much cornering power the tire can generate. The shape of the curve will influence vehicle controllability at high force levels. What we need (and what Akron gives us) is a curve in which the coefficient increases rapidly and almost linearly with increasing slip angle until quite high values have been reached (say 80% of the maximum coefficient). This will allow the driver to build cornering force quickly and with confidence as he enters the turn. After this point the slope of the curve must flatten. The curve should remain reasonably flat for a considerable slip angle distance on each side of the maximum coefficient value so as to give the driver a reasonably wide tightrope on which to balance the car on the edge of adhesion. This flat area at the top of the curve, where increasing the slip angle will not increase cornering force, is called the threshold range. When the coefficient inevitably begins its downward plunge it

Figure (2): Tire coefficient of friction vs slip angle curves.

should start off reasonably gently so that when the driver does exceed the maximum he will not necessarily fall off the road as he falls off the top of the slip angle curve. This characteristic curve makes possible smooth and efficient transitions between the various tire functions of braking, cornering and accelerating. If, for example, the curve looked like Figure (2-D), then human limitations would prevent the most skillful and daring driver from utilizing the maximum potential of his tires, and we would have a very inefficient race car which would do a lot of sliding—but not much sticking.

What is actually happening to the tire as we build increasing cornering force with increasing slip angle is that the elastic deformation of the contact patch is steadily increasing. As we approach the maximum value the rolling contact patch is beginning to run out of its elastic capability and some actual sliding starts. We now have a combination of elastic friction and sliding friction at the contact patch. If we increase the slip angle further, the portion of the patch which is sliding increases while the area which is still in the elastic mode decreases until eventually the whole thing is sliding. At some point between where sliding begins and where it becomes complete the coefficient reaches its maximum value. At any point, if we stabilize the slip angle, the coefficient and the cornering force will also stabilize and the tire will enter into a steady state cornering mode at that value of cornering force.

The contact patch itself is roughly eliptical in shape. Due to compression of both the tread and the sidewall the unit pressure over its area varies and so does the contribution made to cornering force by each portion of the patch. This unit pressure is near zero at the leading edge and builds to a maximum somewhere just ahead of the trailing edge. It also varies in the lateral sense, depending on side force and camber angle. When the contact patch begins its transition from elastic friction to sliding friction it does so at the most heavily loaded portion of the footprint and, as the slip angle increases, the transition spreads progressively across the patch toward the more lightly loaded areas. The point where sliding friction first begins corresponds to the end of the linear portion of the slip angle curve. The point where the whole footprint slides corresponds to the point on the curve where the flat top starts downhill and things go to hell in a hurry.

It is important to note that even when we have exceeded the slip angle capacity of the tire and therefore have gone beyond the point of maximum stick, the tire is still generating cornering force. It doesn't suddenly lose all of its grip on the road—regardless of what it may feel like. When the tire has totally exceeded its elastic capability and is completely sliding, it still has considerable cornering force and, if we can somehow reduce the slip angle, we will regain the lost grip. We'll go into this in more depth later.

It is also important to realize that, although we have been talking about generating slip angles by steering the front wheels, a slip angle is generated every time a tire is subjected to a side load of any description. In entering a turn the normal sequence is for the driver to initiate the turn by steering the front wheels in the direction of the turn. After a very short delay the front tires develop slip angles and the vehicle starts to turn. The centrifugal force developed by the initia-

tion of the turn applies side forces through the chassis to the rear wheels which then develop their corresponding slip angles and cornering forces and the vehicle, after some minor hunting, steadies into the turn. Side forces and slip angles are also caused by road irregularities (one wheel or diagonal bumps), side winds, uneven power to the driven wheels, uneven braking and the striking of curbs and/or other cars.

So far, for simplicity's sake, we have been considering the tire under investigation as a single entity with its load constant and vertical to the track surface. In reality, of course, that tire is one corner of the vehicle and is subject to all of the constantly changing loads and forces that occur in real life. Don't worry about it—we'll get to the confusing parts soon enough.

Surprisingly enough, racing tires operate at smaller slip angles than passenger car tires. Of course the corresponding values of coefficient and cornering force are much higher. There are two reasons for this. First, over the past fifteen years or so (Mickey Thompson started the fat tire revolution about 1962), we have gradually decreased the aspect ratio of the racing tire (length of the contact patch divided by width) to the point where the footprint is now many times broader than it is long. Passenger car tires have been moving in the same direction, but at a much lesser rate. Intuition tells us that it is not going to be possible to hold a tire with its major axis in the transverse direction at as high a slip angle as a tire with its major axis oriented fore and aft. This is why Formula Fords go through the slow turns at higher vehicle yaw angles than Formula One Cars and why the old Formula One Cars assumed larger angles to the road than the present generation does—nowhere near as fast—but more sideways.

There is, however, another reason. High slip angles generate more heat than low slip angles. Heat, beyond that necessary to get the tread up to optimum temperature, costs power, deteriorates the tire and does not contribute to performance. The racing tire is designed to run at a given temperature and is efficient over a limited range of temperatures. The lower the tire designers can keep the slip angles for a given coefficient, the more thermally efficient the tire will be and the softer the rubber compound that can be used. The softer the compound the stickier the tire will be and the more force it will be able to generate. Naturally this gets all mixed up with sidewall stiffness, vehicle weight, available power, track characteristics and God knows what else. Also, the slip angle at maximum coefficient must be of sufficient magnitude to allow the generation of a usable curve. As I said, this is a complex subject.

Just to put some numbers on quantities, a Formula 5000 or Can-Am rear tire of a few years ago (no access to current information) reached its maximum coefficient of about 1.4 at a slip angle of approximately 10 degrees, and the curve was very flat from 9 degrees to 14 degrees. This is, of course, one of the curves shown in Figure (2).

Every vehicle and every driver assumes some value of tire slip angle each time that the vehicle is displaced from straight line motion. A.J., Nikki and Mario on their way to fame and fortune deliberately assume very high slip angles indeed—and operate at these values constantly and consistently. Aunt Maude on her way to the Senior Citizen's Center also assumes slip angles—infinitely lower and much less consistent—but slip angles nonetheless. Genius consists not of operating the race car at high values of tire slip angle but of balancing the vehicle consistently at the slip angles that will produce maximum useful total tire thrust.

SLIP RATIO OR PERCENT SLIP

In the fore and aft sense slip ratio or percent slip bears the same relationship to the tire's traction capacity as slip angle does to the tire's cornering power in the transverse sense. The mechanics of friction between the tire and the track surface are the same in each case—a combination of mechanical gripping and transient molecular adhesion that build up until the whole footprint begins to slide. As with slip angle, any given tire will develop its maximum coefficient and therefore its maximum traction capacity at some value of slip ratio. After that value is reached both coefficient and traction capacity will decrease. Again this does not mean that the tire must be visibly spinning in order to develop maximum acceleration—or locked to develop maximum breaking. In fact, visible wheelspin—or brake lock up—are evidence that the maximum has been exceeded and more torque is being applied than the tire is capable of transmitting under the prevailing conditions. In both acceleration and retardation, maximum traction is developed just short of visible spin or lockup. At this point considerable sliding friction is taking place but adhesion still has the upper hand. The slip ratio vs. coefficient of friction curve (Figure 3) is similar to the slip angle curve but it is steeper and the flat area at the top of the curve is somewhat broader. If we can keep the slip ratio on the top of the curve we will be able to realize the maximum acceleration possible. Naturally this is a problem only when available torque exceeds the traction capacity of the driven wheels—as in coming out of relatively

slow corners. It is just a bit difficult to achieve with any degree of consistency. Just watch the exit of any slow corner at a Can Am or Formula One race. The corner doesn't have to be really slow—just slow enough so that available engine torque exceeds the rear tire's traction capacity. The fastest corner exit will always result from just a taste of rear wheelspin—but the fastest drivers will get no wheelspin more often than they will get smoking excess. The slowest corner exit will belong to the man who confuses wheelsmoke with speed—first cousin to the King of The Late Brakers.

VERTICAL LOAD—AGAIN

A tire's coefficient of friction decreases slightly with increasing vertical load. However, up to the design limit of the tire, its traction capacity—its ability to actually transmit force to the road, as opposed to the dimensionless coefficient of friction, increases with vertical load.

This apparent contradiction works like this: As the vertical load on a given tire increases, the area of the rolling contact patch remains virtually constant, and so the unit pressure of the footprint must increase. As the unit loading rises the rubber has less resistance to frictional shearing forces and so the coefficient decreases. This is illustrated by Figure (4). However, the curve is so gentle that the increase in vertical load overpowers the decrease in coefficient. The result is a curve of increasing traction (either transverse or fore and aft) with increasing vertical load. Figure (5) illustrates.

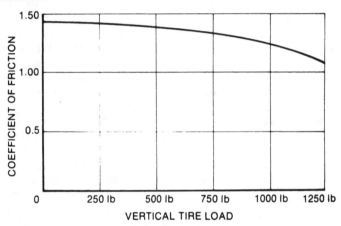

Figure (4): Coefficient of friction vs vertical tire load.

In simple arithmetic, if each rear tire of a car were to support a load of 500 pounds and if the tires had a coefficient of friction of 1.35, then the pair of tires could generate a force of (1.35 x 500) x 2 = 1350 pounds. However, if we add 100 pounds per wheel of rearward load transfer, we find that, although the coefficient has been reduced to 1.33, we now have a traction capacity of (1.33 x 600) x 2 = 1596 pounds. If we now bolt the rear wing on and get the vehicle going fast enough to generate 400 pounds of total rear wheel downforce we end up with a coefficient of only 1.26, but (1.26 x 800) x 2 = 2016 pounds of traction capability—which is why we wear wings in the first place. We will see later that it's not quite that simple, but the point is that increasing the vertical load on any given tire will increase the traction capacity of that

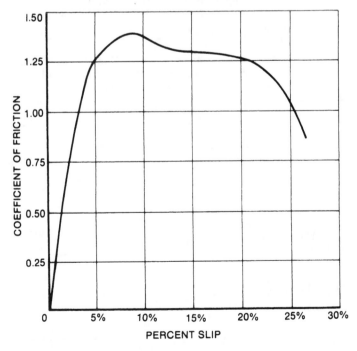

Figure (3): Tire coefficient of friction vs percent slip.

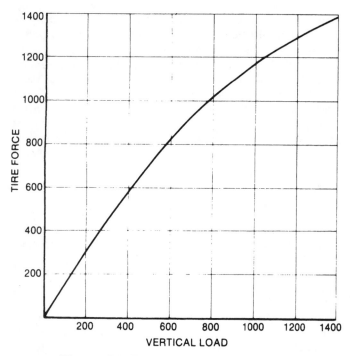

Figure (5): Tire force vs vertical load.

tire. Conversely a decrease in vertical loading will lead to a decrease in traction. This is why dragsters are designed to transfer great gobs of weight to the rear and why we don't object violently to rearward load transfer on corner exit in our road racers.

This relationship is a curve, not a straight line, and it must be noted that when we consider the case of a pair of front or a pair of rear wheels, the vertical load on each of the pair will be affected by lateral load transfer during cornering. We'll get into the nature of this lateral transfer with its causes and effects later. For now we will state that under lateral acceleration a portion of the load on the inside wheel is transferred to the outside wheel. The curve of Figure (5) assures us that, even though the total load on the pair of wheels under lateral acceleration remains constant, a pair of wheels with lateral load transfer between them is not capable of generating the same amount of cornering force that the same pair of tires could if they were equally laden. Referring again to Figure (5) with the assumption that each front wheel of the vehicle in question supports a vertical load of 400 pounds, then the maximum cornering force that can be generated by this pair of wheels is (1.4 x 400) x 2 = 1120 pounds and, if the vehicle's total cornering force is limited by front wheel adhesion, the car could corner at 1120 pounds divided by 800 pounds or 1.4 g in a steady state condition.

However, if we assume an eighty percent lateral load transfer, which is not unusual for the front wheels, then the outboard tire will have a load of [400 lb + (400 lb x .80)] = 720 lb, while the inside tire's load will be only 80 lb. Re-entering the graph we find that, under these conditions, the outside tire can now generate 936 lb of cornering force and the inside 120 pounds. The pair of tires can now develop 1056 lb of cornering force and the vehicle can corner at 1.32 g.

So either lateral or longitudinal load transfer will always increase the traction capability of the more heavily laden tire

or pair of tires. Lateral load transfer between a pair of tires will, however, always result in a decrease in the total capacity of the pair.

Eventually the curve of traction vs. vertical load will peak and fall off—if the tire doesn't blow out first. Under normal conditions, assuming that the tire is designed for the type of vehicle on which it is mounted, we don't have to worry about this eventuality. It is, however, possible to get into trouble on those tracks which feature high banks. If you are going to Daytona or Pocono, check with the tire company first.

CAMBER AND CAMBER THRUST

Coefficient and cornering power vary with camber angle, relative to the surface of the road—not to the chassis. Invariably, maximum cornering force will be realized at some small value of negative camber. This is due to "camber thrust" caused by the straightening out of the arc of the contact patch as the tread of a cambered tire rolls over the ground. If the tire is cambered in the negative sense, this force acts in the direction of the center of curvature and increases cornering power. If the tire is cambered in the positive direction, it acts away from the center of curvature and decreases cornering power. Figure (6) applies. Another way to visualize this effect is to push a standard rubber eraser across a wooden surface with the eraser held vertically, then try it with the eraser held in a negative camber position. This is another elastic deformation phenomenon, and we don't need to know much more than that.

What is important to realize is that with a wide and flat tire, if we allow much camber to develop, we are going to be riding on one edge of the tread and lifting the other off the track. This will both reduce the total footprint area and radically change the pressure distribution. It will not do anything good. This is unfortunate because, as we will see, at the present state of our art we can't control dynamic camber very well and we have to live with some degree of adverse camber change—usually about the time that we really don't need it. Fortunately the tire designers realize this and have gone to very clever carcass construction with controlled but floppy sidewalls so that the footprint stays on the ground

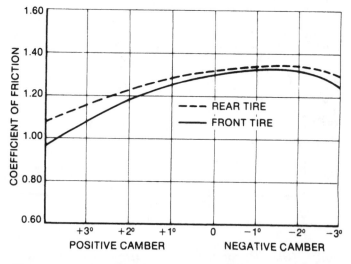

Figure (6): Camber angle vs coefficient of friction.

most of the time. In other words the tire engineers have been forced to compensate for the inadequacy of suspension system design. They have done a superb job of it. The amount of sidewall deflection that the modern racing tire will accommodate is amazing—as witness Figure (7). Of course, like everything else, we pay for it. We pay for it in the knowledge that when we do finally get too much camber on the tire we lose our grip in a big hurry, and we pay for it with tire judder under a combination of hard cornering and hard acceleration. We first ran into judder in the late sixties when drivers of Can Am and Indy cars began to report really severe rear end vibration coming off of corners. As usual we had no idea what was happening and went through a typical witch hunt looking for suspension or drive shaft deflection, faulty shocks and other such ills. Finally, after everybody had about decided to place the blame on Pete Weismann and his differential, it was discovered that under certain combinations of very heavy lateral loads and very high acceleration the tire was assuming a dirty great wave shape ahead of the contact patch and the release of all that stored up energy at the trailing edge was enough to rattle the driver's eyeballs. Only the best drivers were into the problem because only the best were capable of extracting the maximum corner exit performance from the tires. The high speed photos of these antics were enough to make a man think seriously about changing professions.

By modifying the construction of the tire the judder has been reduced to more or less manageable proportions. In fact we now use it as a sort of a yardstick. If the rears aren't juddering on corner exit then either the chassis isn't set up to take full advantage of the tires or the driver isn't doing his job. On the other hand, if the judder begins with throttle application and continues until either the car is going straight or we have run out of available torque, then everything is just fine. The power required to achieve judder limits it to Can Am, Indy and Formula One cars, so don't expect it in your Formula Ford.

Naturally all of this judder and vibration doesn't do the wheels, drive shafts or crown wheels and pinions any good at all, which is why the really quick drivers are hard on those parts. I guess that it is part of the price of speed.

TIRE TEMPERATURE

The next factor which influences tire performance is temperature. Any process that involves friction produces heat. Additionally, a portion of the energy involved in compressing and distorting the tread at the contact patch is not restored to the tire when the tread straightens out at the trailing edge but is converted into heat. Some of the heat so produced is radiated into the airstream but some of it is stored in the tire. If all goes well the tire temperature will raise until a thermal balance is achieved and will then stabilize. Of course the temperature will vary considerably at various points on the track depending on what the tire is doing—or what is being done to it—at the time. With open wheeled cars the driver can actually see the change in surface appearance as the front tires heat up on corner entry.

Most road racing tires are designed to produce maximum traction with tread temperatures between 190 and 220 degrees Fahrenheit. Rain tires, with their softer compounds,

Figure (7): Sidewall deflection

reach their maximums at 140 to 160 degrees while stock car tires are designed to operate at much higher levels. If the tire is operating much below its designed temperature range, it will lack stick. If it is operating very far above it, it is in danger of blistering or chunking due to local destruction of the rubber compound's internal cohesion from excessive heat. If you continue to run on a blistered or chunked tire it will come apart. You will not enjoy the experience.

So two things are important in the tire temperature picture—first to be sure that your tires are operating at a temperature of at least 175 degrees Fahrenheit and, second, to be very sure that you do not exceed the compound limit. You will only exceed the compound limit if you:

(1) run too much negative camber and burn out the inside edge of the tire.

(2) run too low an inflation pressure or run with a slow leak.

(3) run too soft a compound for the track or run rain tires on a dry track—which amounts to the same thing.

If the tires are designed for the type of car on which they are installed and they are not reaching operating temperature, it usually means that the driver is not going hard enough. Seldom, if ever, will this be due to intent. In most cases the driver involved lacks either the skill or the experience to use all of the chassis and tire at his disposal. The only cure is an honest appraisal of the situation, more car time and a really serious effort to improve.

Occasionally the ambient temperature and the frictional characteristics of the track will both be so low that no one can get their tires up to temperature. This is one of those "everybody in the same boat" situations. It is also a situation where the team that can effect an improvement will have at least a temporary edge over the rest. Assuming that a softer tire compound is not available—and it probably won't be—the tires can be heated by dropping inflation pressure to the allowable minimum and by increasing the static toe-in to a pre-determined figure that will not cause the car to dart. An increase in negative camber may also help. If the day warms up or the track gets enough rubber down to bring the temperatures up, remember to change back. Usually these conditions only exist early in the morning on the first day of practice and go away very rapidly as the day warms up and the rubber is laid down.

TIRE PRESSURE

In the days of skinny tires and high tread crowns the coefficient of friction increased with tire pressure, and notable performance increases could be realized by raising the tire pressure to the point where the decreased compliance with the road balanced out the increased tire capacity. Most of us didn't have a lot of power in those days—nor brakes. The pressure to run was very much a function of surface roughness and driver preference. Actually, tire pressure was one of the few methods we had for the adjustment of the understeer/oversteer balance of the car.

This is no longer true—none of it! The present generation of racing tires depends upon inflation pressure to achieve the designed (and necessary) tread arc profile, and we don't get to play the pressure game much of any except with skinny tires, and I don't have any recent experience with rims less than ten inches wide.

It has been my experience, not necessarily agreed to by the tire companies, that operating on the low side of the safe tire pressure range pays off in lap time—probably due to better compliance. Eighteen psi hot is about as low as I am prepared to go—even with safety studs. The low limit is normally reached when the tire temperature at the center of the tread is five to ten degrees F. hotter than the cooler edge. In no case do we want the inside cool. Since the optimum temperature pattern in this respect varies with the construction of the tire, long conversations with selected tire technicians are in order here. Anyway, too much pressure leads to too much crown and reduced compliance, and too little gives sloppy response, reduced footprint effective area and too much tread temperature.

For sure the ever popular idea that the hot tip is to run hard tire pressures at circuits with long straights is a fallacy. You won't pick up enough top speed to read on the tach, and your elapsed time is going to suffer seriously due to decreased bite and compliance. Cornering power, acceleration and braking will all go to hell in a hurry with artificially high pressures.

There are a couple of points to bear in mind about tire pressure. The first is that racing tires tend to leak a lot. The sidewalls have just about enough rubber to stick the cords together—and no more. Cast wheels are porous to some extent, and the life saving wheel safety studs will leak if given half a chance. Each time that a tire is mounted it is absolutely necessary to first check visually that the beads are fully seated and then to check the whole assembly for leaks.

The quick way is to spray a complete covering of Fantastik or 409 cleaner on the tire and rim and look for bubbles. Tiny leaks in the sidewall are not a cause for concern, but any leak in the wheel means that you must either seal a porous area or scrap the rim due to a crack. Obviously there cannot be any leaks on the tread or from the safety studs. Next, time permitting, inflate the tire to some reasonable pressure and write both the pressure and the time of day on the tire. Recheck in an hour. If it leaks down more than about 3 psi per hour, you are not going to be able to race on it. You can, however, practice on it if the leak rate is less than 5 psi per hour. Just keep checking it and pumping it up. Before knocking off for the night, inflate all tires to the same pressure and check them in the morning. Before you return to the manufacturer a new tire that is leaking badly, find the leak and make damned sure that it is in their tire and not in your rim. It pays to check the valve core for tightness yourself, daily, and it is essential to run a valve cap—preferably a metal cap with a rubber seal. It seems that the centrifugal force associated with tire rotation tends to push the valve open.

All air is not the same—some contains more water vapor. This can be due to ambient conditions, lack of moisture traps in the compressor lines or to somebody forgetting to blow the compressor down. The more water vapor contained in the air which you use to inflate your tires, the more pressure buildup you will get at a given tire temperature. Sometimes, if enough moisture is present, the difference can be notable. Since you are looking for a given hot pressure (cold pressure is meaningless, except as a starting point), you must determine, at each track, what cold starting pressure

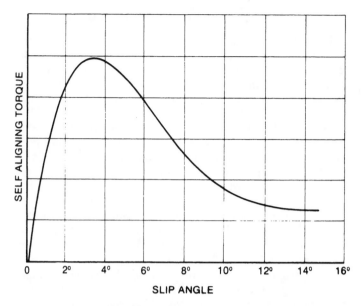

Figure (8): Self aligning torque vs slip angle.

will result in the desired hot running pressure. Again, the tire companies don't necessarily agree with this and usually recommend a cold pressure for the fronts and one for the rears and say to leave it at that. The cold pressure necessary to achieve a given hot reading won't vary more than a pound or two from one track to another but can easily vary by three or four pounds due to moisture in the air. Dry nitrogen solves this little problem but it's a pain to carry around, expensive and not necessary.

I usually set the tires a couple of pounds higher than I think I need and bleed them down the first time the car comes in hot. If the pressures were set evenly left to right the outside tires will have higher hot pressures. This is normal and is due to load transfer and to the predominance of corners in one direction. I almost always run equal left side and right side hot pressures which means that I have to make note of four starting pressures. My thinking is that we are looking for optimum tire usage, and every little bit that we can do is going to help.

SELF ALIGNING TORQUE

When we apply a side force to a rolling tire the point of resistance to turning (the effective center of the contact patch) is actually located at some distance outboard and to the rear of the geometric center of the footprint. This is due to the elastic deformation of the rubber and is referred to as "pneumatic trail." Since the side force generated by the tire acts through this dynamic center, the actual trail distance is a moment arm, and the tire's resistance to turning through this moment arm becomes a torque which tends to return the tire from the direction in which we are trying to turn it back to the direction in which the tread is actually rolling. Pneumatic trail is part of the "self aligning torque" picture. The other parts are positive castor and scrub radius which will be covered later. The three are additive so far as steering resistance is concerned. However, scrub radius is a constant, and castor almost is, while self aligning torque, as shown by Figure (8), is a variable function of slip angle. The initial resistance to turning builds very quickly but starts to

decrease rapidly about half way up the slip angle curve towards maximum coefficient of friction (refer back to Figure (2) which is for the same tire). Trail reaches its minimum value just about the same time that the coefficient starts to drop off. Through the steering wheel this decreasing pneumatic trail gives the driver perceptible warning of front tire breakaway and is the reason why understeer breakaway is often described by the neophyte driver as, "It went all light and funny."

CONSTRUCTION AND COMPOUNDING

Although we cannot do anything about the construction or the compounding of our tires, we should be aware that varying the carcass construction is one of the methods used by the designers to change the characteristics of the tire. The carcass must be strong enough to withstand the loads, both vertical and horizontal, that will be imposed on the tire. It must keep the tread from expanding and/or distorting its profile with centrifugal force of rotation and it must hold air pressure. It must also provide adequate puncture and abrasion resistance. On the other hand, it must be flexible enough to accommodate the distortions—lateral, radial and circumferential—that are necessary for the development of accelerative and side forces. At the same time it must provide adequate stability and response. None of this happens by accident.

The cords that actually provide the structural strength of the tire may be arranged in any fashion the designer fancies and may be of virtually any material. Presently all racing tires are constructed with nylon or similar synthetic cords which offer excellent strength, flexibility, resistance to heat and are light in weight. If the cords are arranged radially the tire will provide the softest ride possible with maximum self dampening but will have virtually no lateral stability. This is why radial tires require circumferential belts, preferably of steel. Racing tires, at the time of writing, cannot accept either the weight or the rigidity of the belts. On the other hand, if the cords were arranged circumferentially the tire would have excellent lateral stability, a very harsh ride and it would be impossible to hold the profile shape. So, borrowing a page from the tailors' and sailmakers' books, the cords of the racing tire are arranged on the bias, thus providing strength in three planes simultaneously. Racing tire cord angles are closer to the circumferential than passenger car bias tires in order to provide smaller slip angles for a given cornering force and a more efficient tire—as well as to provide more support for the wide profile.

The minimum number of plies necessary to provide the required strength and stability are utilized, and tread depth is also held to the minimum. This is in the interest of reducing heat generation. Sidewall construction is a compromise between radial and lateral stiffness which gives lateral stability and flexibility which allows the tread to conform to the road surface despite load transfer and attendant change of camber and also allows the circumferential distortion necessary for the development of high traction forces.

It is necessary to avoid sharp corners and/or heavy tread shoulders lest we build up enough heat in these already overloaded areas to cause the shoulder to chunk.

Last, but far from least, the designer must so arrange his

cord angles, spacing and intersections so that the inflated tire will have the desired profile, so that the profile will not be destroyed by centrifugal force and so that the tread area will resist the hernia type injuries caused by running over stones and such.

Tied in with carcass construction is the tread compound. Racing tire compounders are the late twentieth century equivalent of the medieval alchemists. By varying the chemical ingredients and percentages of the rubber compound, the compounder seeks to provide the most grip that will safely survive the punishment that the tire is going to take. Ideally, I suppose that a different compound and construction would be developed for each circuit—or at least for groups of similar circuits. The same, of course, can also be said for suspensions, engines and aerodynamics. Thank God it hasn't quite come to that—yet. In tires, however, at the top levels of racing, we do find tires for tracks—depending on prevailing turn speed, vertical load and the track surface mix. Unless you are running USAC Champ Cars, Formula One or NASCAR's Grand National Circuit, you won't run into this. The rest of racing gets a standard tire with excellent compromise performance characteristics that is safe anywhere.

The basic tools of the alchemist include styrene butadiene rubber which is the primary ingredient. It has good abrasion resistance, bonds well to the cords and has very high hysterisis or energy absorption characteristics. Carbon black is used to improve tensile strength and wear properties and to color the rubber for resistance to ultraviolet light. The third basic ingredient, believe it or not, is oil. The more oil in the compound, the softer and stickier it will be and the less it is going to be upset by oil on the track. There are also a bunch of chemicals to assist the vulcanization process and then more magic ingredients about which no one outside of the compounding fraternity knows anything—which is just as well as we wouldn't understand it anyway. When the tire man tells you that they have changed the compound or the construction of a tire he is not talking about a minor deed.

WIND UP—OR TANGENTAL SPRING

Drag Racers talk about "getting the car up on the tire." We have all seen photos of drag tires all wrinkled and funny in the sidewall as the car leaves the line. We have also witnessed, at least on the tube, the remarkable sight of the rear end of the dragster raising about six inches straight up just before it comes out of the hole. For a long time I had a lot of trouble believing what was happening there, but they finally convinced me that it was all desirable and even planned. What happens is that, when the power is applied, the axle and wheels start to turn but the tread compound is so sticky and the sidewall has so much tangental spring built into it that the tire lags behind. This stores up a whole bunch of energy, just like stretching the rubber in a slingshot. Eventually this energy is released and literally catapults the car out of the hole. Believe it or not, road racing tires are now designed to do the same thing—to a much lesser extent—and that is what Ongais is talking about when he says that you have to get it up on the tire coming out of slow corners. The human being can be a marvelously sensitive device.

THE APPEARANCE OF THE TIRE

The racing tire that is giving all that it has to give will have a characteristic texture and appearance which we should learn to read. The color will be a very dull black with no shiny areas—if there is a shiny area it will normally appear on the inside shoulder and tells us that we are overloading the inside edge. Unless the driver had done a cool off lap there should be no "pick-up" evident on the tread surface; if there is, the driver isn't working hard enough. If the tire is working—or being worked—as hard as it should be, the tread surface will show a very slight wavy grained texture. Ideally this texture should be uniform over the width of the tire. In practice it will probably be more pronounced inboard. This texture is the beginning of "rolling" or "balling," a condition which tells us that the tire is getting too hot. We want to keep the tire just at the edge of the tread rolling condition.

If the front tire shows more signs of abuse than the rear, it is telling us that the car has too much understeer—regardless of what the driver says. Conversely, tortured rear tires signal excessive oversteer. Tire temperatures significantly higher at one end of the car than the other are another indication of chassis imbalance.

Excessive camber, or camber change—in either direction—can be better detected by the tire wear pattern than by temperatures across the tread. It is normal to wear the inside a bit (say ten to fifteen percent) more than the outside. More than that says "too much negative." Less than that says "too much positive—or not enough negative."

We can tell a lot by just looking at things . . .

TIRE DIAMETER

It is very important that the left side tires on your racer be the same diameter as those on the right side. If they are not, then the static corner weight and the load transfer characteristics will not be what you have planned. More important, under power and, to a lesser extent, under the brakes the thrust will be unbalanced and the car will not proceed naturally in a straight line—assuming a limited slip differential or a locked rear end. It will also affect the understeer/oversteer balance of the vehicle—a larger diameter outside rear promoting understeer. It is true that we deliberately use tires of slightly different diameter to alter the balance of the car (changing the stagger), but that comes later. For now we want to avoid spending hours chasing an apparent chassis problem only to find out that it was a tire diameter problem all along.

Despite everyone's best intentions and efforts, all supposedly identical racing tires of the same size, construction and compound are not created equal in diameter. Unfortunately the only way that you can tell is to mount them and measure their circumference—at equal inflation pressures. To compound the misery Goodyears are directional, so, once they are mounted on the rim, you can't switch them from one side of the car to the other. At the front I will accept a maximum difference (in diameter, not circumference) of two tenths of an inch, and I would strongly prefer less. At the rear what you can live with is a function of what type differential you are using and how much power you have. With a spool or a Weismann locker, unless you are intentionally running stagger, you don't want much more than one tenth of an inch difference, and the big tire must be outside. With a cam and pawl or a clutch pack you can live with more, and with an open diff it probably doesn't make a lot of difference except from the corner weight point of view.

Anyway, this problem of stagger can lead to the mounting and dismounting of rather a large number of tires until you end up with a set that is within your tolerance. This is very liable to make the tire busters cranky. It is possible to stretch a tire's diameter by two or three tenths of an inch by overinflating it ten pounds and leaving it in the sun for an hour.

Not only do we have to check the diameter of the tires when they are first mounted, but we also have to check them again after they have been run. All tires increase in diameter when they are first run but some increase more than others. To our good fortune the outside tires usually grow more than the insides. The whole diameter bit is a pain, but there is no alternative.

SHAPE OR PROFILE

Very rarely a racing tire slips through inspection that does not assume the proper tread profile when it is inflated. This will be visible as either excessive crown or, more frequently, as a depression in the center of the tread. Check all of your tires when they are first mounted. As I said, this is unusual, but it does happen. Nothing that you can do will make the tire work, and, if you have run it before you notice it, you own it. The tire company, rightly, is not going to take back a used tire.

SPRING RATE

Every pneumatic tire has its very own spring rate and its own self dampening characteristics. Except for drag racing tires the spring rate is pretty high (1000 pounds per inch and up) and they dampen themselves pretty well. It is just as well that they do, because the shocks can't do it for them. We don't have to worry about this rate as we cannot do anything to alter it other than to adjust the inflation pressure. Higher tire pressure gives a higher spring rate, less dampening and less compliance. Since the tire's ride rate is so much higher than that of the suspension it doesn't really enter into any of our play areas.

THE RAIN TIRE

Slick racing tires don't work very well on a damp race track. The wider they are the less well they work. They do not work at all—even a little bit—on a really wet track. The reason is that the design has no provision to allow the water to be squeezed out from between the rubber and the track. The water has no place to go so the tire rides on a film of water with little—if any—actual contact with the track surface, and the car is totally out of control. For a given vehicle weight, the wider the tire the worse this condition will be. The condition is called "aquaplaning" and is no fun at all—at any speed.

In order to avoid the aquaplaning phenomenon, the tread of the rain tire is designed with circumferential drainage grooves and connecting side sipes. The whole idea is to give the water someplace to go so that it will not be trapped between the footprint and the road. Since it doesn't rain

much in American Road Racing and since USAC and NASCAR don't race in the rain, we have tended to lag behind the English in rain tire design and development. As near as I can tell we are just about even in compounds, but our tread patterns don't drain well. The judicious use of a grooving iron can work wonders. Basically the tread must be divided into a number of circumferential bands separated by generous channels into which the water will be forced. The idea is that the bands stay in contact with the track surface while the water runs in the channels. In order to be effective the channels should be at least three eighths of an inch wide and as deep as practical. The tread bands should be no more than one and one half to two inches wide. In order to allow sideways drainage at the contact patch the circumferential channels must be inter-connected with open transverse sipes at least three sixteenths of an inch wide. They must completely connect adjacent channels and should be no more than two inches apart.

To my surprise and delight it now looks like all of this may have changed. 1977/1978 Goodyear rain tire tread pattern looks like being a very good one. I have not yet run it, but those who have say that it is magic. Maybe I can throw away my grooving iron! I will not, however, delete the foregoing paragraphs.

What we think happens at the contact patch on a wet track is that the leading one third of the footprint forces the mass of the water out of the way and into the channels, the center one third squeegees the contact area dry and the trailing one third provides all of the grip.

If the circumferential channels are not connected by transverse sipes, or if the sipes are too far apart, then the middle third of the footprint cannot effectively do its squeegee bit because the channels are already full and the water under the tread band has nowhere to go. This is the area where the American rain tires need help.

Because the rain tire is going to be very effectively water cooled and because the friction will be drastically reduced by the presence of lubricating water, the tread compounds are very soft. This means that you cannot run them in the dry. They will disintegrate.

When the rain clouds appear the racer gets to make a lot of decisions—not just about tires. We'll cover racing in the rain in a separate chapter later on.

TIRE BALANCE

Due to the care taken in construction and to the very thin tread, the racing tire is a lot more round and a lot closer to being inherently in balance than the average passenger car tire. It must still be balanced after it has been mounted and before it has been run. It is not absolutely necessary to dynamically balance racing tires—again the light construction and extreme care in manufacture saves us—but it is definitely preferable. At our very high rotational speeds a very small imbalance off the rim centerline can become many pounds of force. However, there is seldom a dynamic balancer available at the track. We therefore get to use a static bubble balancer and, in almost all cases, a good static balance is adequate. It helps to split the weights evenly between the inboard and outboard rims. It is necessary to clean your own rims and to mount and tape your own weights—if you don't want them to come off. Clean the area for at least two inches around where the weight is going to live with acetone and Scotchbrite, stick the weight on, and secure it with a cross of racer's tape. Inspect frequently.

If a tire checks out on the static balancer but is out of balance on the car, either you have a dynamic balance problem, a bent rim, a tire that is out of round or a tire that is out of true (tread band not on straight). This does happen. The only way that you are going to isolate the problem is to either mount it on a spin balancer, where the condition will stick out like a sore thumb, or spin it on the car and indicate it. The tire companies will take back out of round and out of true tires, but you must prove to their satisfaction that they are out.

When a spin balancer is available at the track I pay the difference and dynamically balance my tires. I also stand there myself and watch each tire for out of round or out of true. Finding them on the car is going to cause a lot of misery and cost a lot of time. This is one more reason why you cannot race on a tire that has not been run on the car while mounted on the rim it is presently mounted on.

BREAK IN

New tires, like new anything else, require a break-in period before they will function at maximum efficiency. The reasons are two. First, in order to separate the tire from the mould in which it was made, release agent is applied to the mould. This leaves a very thin coating of slippery release agent on the surface of the tire. The coating must be worn off before the tire will stick. Second, it is necessary to "roughen" the surface of the tire so that we have those thousands of tiny contact patches mentioned earlier and to round off the sharp edges—which shouldn't be there to start with. We used to have to wear them enough to get them "camber cut" or patterned but that isn't necessary these days. However, if you are changing the position of a tire on the car, it will take a few laps for it to wear in and get happy in its new location.

It used to take several laps to scrub in new tires. Present compounds come in after one or, at the most, two laps. It is all downhill from there—although the decrease in capability is very slow indeed. For qualifying you need all of the help you can get and a set of brand new tires is a real advantage.

Do not punish a new tire for the first lap—build the heat up gradually—the tire will last longer. Above all, do not start the race on new tires. If you do, you will be faced with two choices—either go slow on the first lap to scrub them (disheartening and embarrassing) or run a very real risk of falling off the road when the tires don't stick.

THE CARE AND FEEDING
OF THE RACING TIRE

The modern racing tire is a very delicate animal indeed. To get the best out of them a fairly extensive list of "don'ts" must be adhered to:

Don't drive—or push—your racer through the stony paddock on race rubber—especially not on hot race rubber. It can go to and from the pits on rain tires which are not so puncture sensitive. Besides, since the rain rubber will be cold, it won't pick up every stone and bottle cap on the way.

Don't leave the pits until your tires have been cleaned of whatever stones, pop rivet nails and scraps of metal they may have picked up.

Don't transport your car, or even leave it overnight, on race rubber—it flat spots easily. A set of tow wheels from the junkyard mounted with trash rubber may require a little ingenuity but they are worth it.

Don't store race tires in the sun or, if possible, at temperatures over 70 degrees F. Dunlop ships their tires in a black plastic drawstring bag to protect the compound from ultraviolet light—neat idea.

Don't get oil, fuel or solvent on the tread—the compound will deteriorate.

Don't store tires overinflated.

Don't try to clean the tread surface with your bare hand. An old hacksaw blade works just fine, or a rag will get the job done. If you do it with your hand, sooner or later you will gash yourself to the bone on a sharp bit of metal imbedded in the tread.

Don't try to qualify on worn tires. You will be one half to one second slow. The second and third laps that a set of road racing tires do will be the fastest laps of their life.

There is a somewhat shorter list of "does":

Do cultivate the acquaintance and ask for the help and advice of the trackside tire engineers. These are very knowledgeable people, and they are there to help you. Human nature being what it is, unless you are running up front, they are not going to come to you—you have to go to them.

Do learn to say thank you to the tire busters—and to get your clean rims to them in plenty of time.

Do inquire as to the availability of used tires in excellent condition. In those classes of racing where some teams are supplied free tires, some of those teams, in an apparent effort to kill the goose that laid the golden egg, take advantage and turn back tires with ridiculously low mileage.

These can usually be purchased (legally) at vastly reduced rates from the dealer servicing the race. Make sure that they are not *old* used tires.

Once you have scrubbed a set of tires, do use them up as quickly as practical. They die in storage and will be stone cold dead two months after they have been scrubbed. Keeping them away from sun and high temperatures helps, but it is best to use them up.

THE TRACTION CIRCLE

We have seen that the racing tire is capable of generating almost equal force in acceleration, deceleration or cornering. If we plot the maximum forces that a given tire can develop in each of these directions we end up with Figure (9)—often referred to as the "traction circle." Mark Donahue used to call it "the wheel of life." Contrary to current opinion, neither the concept nor the visualization is new. It is not a circle due to the fact that the tire's longitudinal capability is slightly in excess of its lateral capability. We'll consider it to be a circle anyway.

Looking at the diagram, two things become obvious:

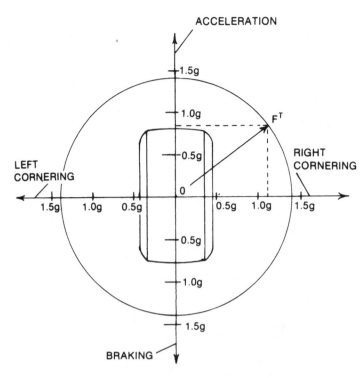

Figure (9): The traction circle—showing vehicle accelerating while turning right.

(1) The tire can generate either 1.4 g of acceleration thrust or 1.4 g of cornering force (we can substitute braking thrust for acceleration thrust). It cannot, however, develop 1.4 g of both at the same time. If a tire is generating both a longitudinal thrust and a cornering force, it must develop a lesser amount of each than it could of either one singly. This is illustrated by the vector marked FT which shows the tire generating a cornering force of 1.1 g while accelerating at 0.8 g with a resultant force vector FT of 1.4. Due to the geometry of the traction circle and of the resolution of vectors, the tire can and does generate forces in each direction the sum of which is greater than the total g capacity of the tire. In other words, the tire can simultaneously generate an amount of braking thrust and an amount of cornering force which, added together, will total more force than the tire is capable of developing in any one direction.

(2) If we are going to utilize all of the performance potential designed and built into our tires, then we must keep the tire operating at very high combined force level at all times while the car is turning. We must "ride the rim of the traction circle" by balancing the brakes, cornering force and throttle so as to keep the tire's resultant line of force just inside the boundary of the circle.

If we follow the prehistoric dictum, "Do all of the braking in a straight line, go through the corner at maximum corner-ing force, then accelerate in a straight line," we are going to waste a lot of our tires' potential and a lot of lap time.

What we need to do—and what every racing driver instinctively does—is to continue our braking well into the corner entry phase so that, while the tires are in the process of building up cornering force they are still contributing braking thrust—we don't have to give up much cornering force in order to develop meaningful amounts of braking thrust—and the resultant tire line of force follows the boundary of the traction circle. We must also start to open up our exit line from the corner—or to "release the car" early so that we will have excess rear tire capacity available for early hard acceleration. Never forget that he who gets the power down first—and is able to keep it down—will arrive first at the other end. If you are using all of the rear tires' capability in cornering force, there is none left over for acceleration—it is that simple.

All of this calls for some pretty careful choices of lines and some reasonably delicate control on the part of the driver. The task is not simplified by dynamic load transfer, changing aerodynamic loads, available torque, variations in the road surface or traffic. The full use of the potential of all four tires is probably not humanly possible—at least not consistently. This is especially true in the case of race cars with very high power to weight ratios in slow corners—which is why we are treated to a fair old bit of pedal stabbing and frantic steering when the Formula One circus comes to Long Beach each spring, but see a lot less of it at Watkins Glen in the fall. The corners at the Glen are faster, so available torque is less and the fast way around is smoother. This is also why a Monza is smoother through a hairpin than a Can Am Car.

Figure (10) is an effort to show what should be happening to the tire forces as a race car progresses through a typical corner. For simplicity's sake we will consider the traction circle to represent the sum of the efforts of all four tires. The forward direction, or acceleration, is always at the top of the traction circle. The large traction circle inset into the diagram shows the results of three ways of taking the corner. The line which nearly follows the rim of the circle represents what Mario and A.J. are doing and is labled "possible." The line marked "probable" is the resultant of the efforts of a very good club driver. The heavy line marked "classic" is the old way of braking, cornering and accelerating in three distinct phases. It is pretty obvious what we have to aim for.

CONCLUSION

This chapter has been mainly devoted to the whats, the hows and the whys of tire dynamics with little time spent describing what we can do with the tires in a practical sense. This has been deliberate. We'll discuss what we can do to help tire performance as we go along. There is precious little that we can do with the tire directly other than to not abuse it.

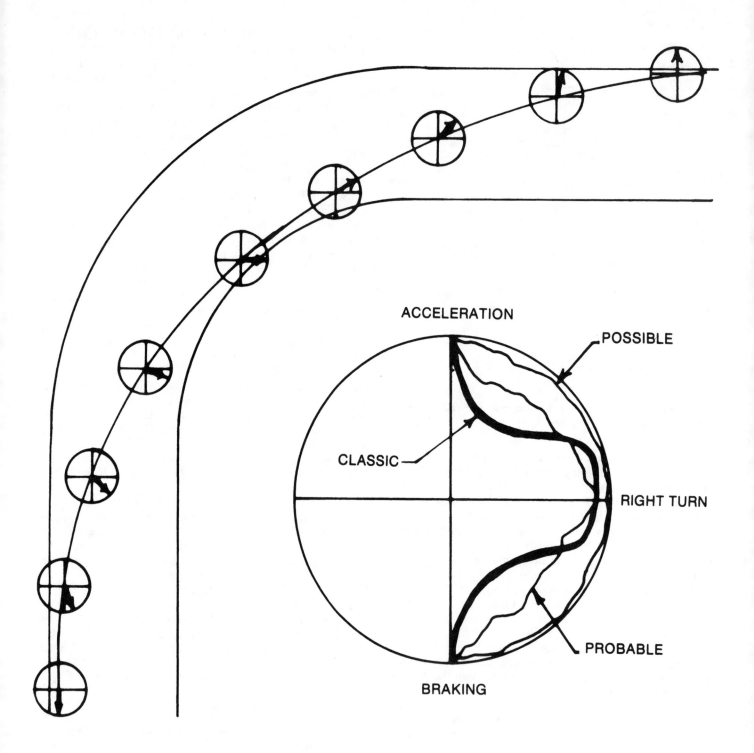

Figure (10): The traction circle and the tire force vector as the vehicle progresses around a corner.

CHAPTER THREE

WEIGHT, MASS LOAD AND LOAD TRANSFER

Despite the older efforts of Detroit's copy writers, those of us who are addicted to the high performance automobile are aware that weight, per se, is a Giant No No in terms of vehicle performance. In Chapter One we determined that virtually every aspect of vehicle performance is dependent on one form of acceleration or another. All acceleration is governed by Newton's first Law of Motion: "Force is equal to mass times acceleration." Transposing we find that the rate of acceleration of a body is equal to the force acting on the body divided by the mass of the body, and it becomes evident that, for a given amount of force, less mass will result in a higher rate of acceleration. For our purposes we will normally use the term "weight"—the force with which a body is attracted to the earth by gravity—rather than "mass"—the measure of the amount of matter in a given body. Weight is expressed in pounds while mass is expressed in slugs. Let's examine again the accelerative functions of the racing car—this time from the weight point of view.

LINEAR ACCELERATION

If we momentarily ignore the effects of drag and play around a bit with Mr. Newton's Formula we find that the rate of acceleration of our racer will be equal to the net force available for acceleration divided by the gross weight of the vehicle. The net available force is usually defined as "engine output torque in pounds feet times final drive ratio times drive line efficiency all divided by the rolling radius of the driven tire in feet." The result will be pounds of thrust available at the driven tire contact patch in a given gear at a given engine rpm. As an example, let's consider a Five Litre Can Am Car exiting a slow corner at 4800 rpm in second gear. At 4800 rpm the engine puts out 380 lb/ft of torque; we are using a 20/35 second gear and a 9/31 crown wheel and pinion, giving a final drive ratio of:

$$\frac{35}{20} \times \frac{31}{9} = (1.75 \times 3.44) = 6.03:1$$

Drive line efficiency is 85 percent and we are using a 26 inch rear tire with a rolling radius of 1.1 feet. Gross vehicle weight is 1900 pounds. Plugging these numbers into the formula, we come up with:

$$\text{Acceleration thrust} = \frac{380 \text{ lb/ft} \times 6.03 \times .85}{1.1 \text{ ft}} = 1770 \text{ lb}$$

This means that, given sufficient rear tire capacity for forward traction, the car can accelerate at the rate of:

$$\frac{1770 \text{ lb thrust}}{1900 \text{ lb weight}} = 0.93 \text{ g.}$$

If we somehow reduce vehicle weight to 1800 lb, the situation becomes:

$$\text{rate of acceleration} = \frac{1770 \text{ lb thrust}}{1800 \text{ lb weight}} = 0.98 \text{ g.}$$

In order to achieve an acceleration rate of 0.98 g with the original weight of 1900 lb we would require an engine output of 400 lb/ft of torque.

Whether or not we can actually achieve this rate of acceleration depends on whether or not the driven wheels are in a dynamic condition to transmit the force to the road surface. We have seen that this will depend on the coefficient of friction between the tires and the track surface, the vertical loads on the rear wheels, camber and how much of the tires' potential is being used up in cornering force. If the 1800 lb car had a static weight distribution of 60% on the rear wheels and 40% on the front wheels, this would give a static load of 1080 lb on the pair of rear wheels. If there were no load transfer, no camber effect, and no aerodynamic downforce involved, the rear tires would require a forward acceleration capability of 1770 lb or a coefficient of

$$\frac{1770}{1080} = 1.64$$

to achieve our theoretical rate of acceleration of 0.98 g. This is unlikely. Under these conditions, if the driver applies full throttle, the result will be wheelspin, and the vehicle's rate of acceleration will be "traction limited." If the rear tires were indeed capable of transmitting the 1770 lb of thrust then full throttle would not produce wheelspin and the acceleration rate would be "thrust limited." From the standpoint of lap time we want the vehicle to be traction limited up to as high a road speed as possible. Wild wheelspin can be avoided by the skillful driver, but if the thrust is not there, then rate of acceleration will be limited by something we cannot do anything about. We don't want to achieve this state by limiting the capacity of the tires—that would be self defeating. This leaves us with four choices—get more torque out of the engine, use a numerically higher gear ratio, increase the drive line efficiency, or put vehicle and/or driver on a diet. All four are valid tuning areas, although we can't normally do much about drive line efficiency. For now we're concerned with weight—the less of it you have, so long as the vehicle and all of its parts are structurally strong enough, the better off you are going to be. Trouble is, pulling weight off the race car is just like pulling it off your body—difficult, expensive and it comes off an ounce at a time. The easiest of the lot is probably removing weight from the driver.

ROTATIONAL INERTIA

This conventional view of the importance of vehicle weight in the linear acceleration picture is valid as far as it goes—but it doesn't go far enough. The limitation lies in the assumption that the engine's torque output, as observed on the dynomometer and corrected for ambient temperature, barometric pressure and drive line efficiency is available to drive the rear wheels. It is not.

We are all familiar with the frictional and heat losses that occur within the engine, the gearbox and the differential. They have been accounted for in our basic equation by using actual corrected dyno torque and by using a drive train efficiency factor. We have not, however, taken into our account the energy required to accelerate the rotating parts of the engine, the drive train and the wheels. The engine on the dyno is operating at constant rpm—it is not accelerating. In order for the race car to accelerate the engine must accelerate. In order for the engine to accelerate the rotational speed of every moving part—as well as the linear speed of each reciprocating part—must increase. The same is true of the components of the gearbox, differential, drive shafts, wheels, brake discs and tires. The only energy available to accelerate this conglomeration of parts comes from the engine itself and an astounding proportion of total engine torque must be used to overcome all of this inertia— especially at high rates of vehicle and component acceleration. As road speed increases the vehicle rate of acceleration decreases due to the effects of aerodynamic drag—which increases as the square power of road speed. As the vehicle's rate of acceleration falls off so does the rate of component rotational inertia. In low gear the energy required to accelerate the racing engine components can approach thirty percent of the engine's dyno output—trailing off to something less than eight percent in high gear. Because the speed of rotation is much slower, the inertial requirement of the wheels, tires and brake discs is considerably less— typically six percent of engine output in low gear and three percent in top. This is roughly the same percentage required by the gearbox, differential and drive shafts. So what does it all mean? It means that as much as forty percent of the engine torque that you assume is going to rocket your Can Am Car out of a slow corner is not, and will not, be available at the rear wheels. The loss fails to somewhat less than twenty percent for a Formula Ford because the rate of vehicle acceleration is that much less but it remains a significant figure in any race car.

So what do we do about it? Not a hell of a lot. Within the bounds of sanity, the biggest single improvement that can be made in this department is to reduce the mass and the moment of inertia of the flywheel and clutch assembly. Since we will be concerned with moments of inertia from time to time we'll digress for a moment in order to discuss the subject.

Any body will resist rotation with its inertia. Bodies of identical mass and basic dimensions can exhibit different amounts of rotational (but not linear) inertia, due to varying moments of inertia. The moment of inertia is simply the linear distance from the body's center of rotation to its center of mass. The further the center of mass is located from the center of rotation the more energy will be required to accelerate the body and the greater tendency it will have to keep rotating once it has started. For example, the gyroscope has a very high moment of rotational inertia. On the other hand, a quick look at one of Mr. Hewland's gears will reveal that its moment of inertia has been intentionally reduced by turning away much of the mass of steel between

the central hub and the gear teeth—leaving a web of sufficient strength to avoid disaster.

Since the designers of passenger automobiles are vitally interested in smooth engine running at low engine speeds they tend to use rather massive flywheels with high moments of inertia in order to encourage same. Since they are also interested in cost they tend to use cast iron for material. For the same reasons they use enormous clutches. The proprietary racing clutches in this country are all made to fit flywheels and, while they will all hold gobs of engine torque, their moments of inertia are ridiculous. Messrs. Borg and Beck have fortuitously provided us with a range of seven and one quarter inch diameter clutches featuring the lowest practical moment of inertia. They make a clutch that will hold anything from a Formula Ford to an Indy Car. Regulations—or regulation enforcement—permitting, there is no excuse for using anything else. The same is true of the flywheel—use the smallest diameter wheels that you can fit a starter to and use aluminum—but not cast aluminum. Flywheels of minimum inertial moment to match the **B & B** clutches are available from B & B's U.S. Distributor, Tilton Engineering, El Segundo, Calif.

Unfortunately, having said that much, I've just about said it all. Our efforts to decrease component moments of rotational inertia are very limited, either because the people who designed and built our racing equipment have already thought about it or because the parts are not practically modifiable. Just keep in mind when you are selecting engine components that all of that stuff has to be accelerated—and it costs.

LINEAR DECELERATION

Everything that I have said about weight and moment of inertia in acceleration holds true under the brakes.

CENTRIFUGAL ACCELERATION

Lateral or centrifugal acceleration in cornering has to do with weight also. The basic equation for cornering force:

Force =

$$\frac{mass \times (velocity)^2}{radius\ of\ curvature}$$

assures us that—all other things, especially tires being equal—a light car will go around a given corner at a greater road speed than its heavier counterpart. It will also be more responsive, easier to control and will permit the use of softer suspension springs and lighter structure. Rather than overworking the formula let's equate our race car, in a steady state cornering situation, to a rock tied to a string. If we whirl the rock around in a circle, restrained by the string, and if we steadily increase the speed of rotation—or the rate of centrifugal acceleration—then sooner or later the load on the string is going to exceed the strength of the string. At this point the string will break and the rock will fly off at a tangent to the circle that it has been describing. If we use the same string but a lighter rock, we will achieve a higher rock speed before the string breaks—at the same load or centrifugal force. In the case of the race car the vehicle is the rock and the string is replaced by the cornering force of the four tires. The operating principle remains the same and the lighter race car will go around a given corner at a higher road speed at the same rate of centrifugal acceleration.

Since acceleration, deceleration, cornering, response and controllability comprise about ninety-eight percent of vehicle performance and, since weight plays a critical part in each of these areas, it becomes obvious that the minimization, placement and control of the various weighty items which make up the racing car form a major part of the designer's and the tuner's tasks.

The realization of this fact has enriched the language of the enthusiast. Terms such as power to weight ratio, sprung and unsprung weight, static weight distribution, dynamic weight transfer and polar moment of inertia are heard wherever bench racing is practiced. As in so many cases, the terms may flow glibly from the tongue, but the understanding of the factors and principles involved and their effect on the vehicle and the driver is liable to be both incomplete and imperfect. It is time to look at the whats, whys and hows of various aspects of vehicular weight and its control as related to performance.

A few definitions are in order:

UNSPRUNG WEIGHT is that portion of the total weight of the vehicle which is not supported by the suspension springs. It is comprised of the wheels, tires, hubs, hub carriers, and brakes (if mounted outboard) plus approximately fifty percent of the weight of the suspension links, drive shafts and springs and shocks (if mounted outboard). Since this unsprung weight is what the shock absorbers must attempt to control—in the bump direction—in order to keep the tires in contact with the road, the less of it there is, the better it can be controlled.

SPRUNG WEIGHT is that portion of the total vehicle weight which is supported by the suspension springs. This includes the chassis, engine, driver, fuel, gearbox, etc.—in other words—most of it.

THE RATIO OF UNSPRUNG TO SPRUNG WEIGHT is simply the proportion of sprung to unsprung weight. To my mind this is a more useful concept than the absolute amount of unsprung weight. Personally, I think—but cannot prove—that we have reached the point of diminishing returns in the reduction of unsprung weight and that, while we should always bear it in mind, the potential rewards to be gained by small decreases in this area do not merit the expenditure of large amounts of time and money. For instance, I do not consider the complica-

tions and total weight of inboard front brakes to be worthwhile. On the other hand, I do use inboard rear brakes because the drive shafts are already there—but I don't think that is a big thing. This is true in road racing and in circle track racing because we have already succeeded in reducing the unsprung weight to a very reasonable proportion. It is definitely not true in fields such as off road racing where there is still a lot to be gained.

POWER TO WEIGHT RATIO, expressed in pounds per horsepower, is a very rough indication of a particular vehicle's linear acceleration capacity. It is obtained by dividing the vehicle's gross weight—including fuel and driver—by its maximum horsepower. The performance indication is only approximate because it does not take into account several vital factors—the characteristics of the engine's power curve, the effective gearing of the vehicle, the ability of the suspension and tires to put the power on the road, the aerodynamic properties of the vehicle and the inertial resistance involved.

THE CENTER OF GRAVITY of any body is defined as that point about which, if the body were suspended from it, all parts of the body would be in equilibrium—i.e. without tendency to rotate. It is the three dimensional balance point of the race car. All accelerative forces acting on a body can be considered to act through the center of gravity of that body. We want our race car's cg to be just as low as we can get it.

THE MASS CENTROID AXIS is related to the cg— sort of. If we were to slice the car into a series of transverse sections—like a loaf of bread—each section would have its own center of gravity, or centroid. If, in side view, we were then to draw a line joining each of these centroids, we would have the mass centroid axis. Figure 11 applies. This axis will not be anything that resembles a straight line, even if we were to go to the considerable trouble of calculating it. However, a reasonable straight line approximation can be intuitively arrived at that will give an indication of the distribution of the vehicle's mass in the vertical plane. This will be useful later.

THE ROLL CENTER of a suspension system is that point, in the transverse plane of the axles, about which the sprung mass of that end of the vehicle will roll under the influence of centrifugal force. It is sort of a geometric

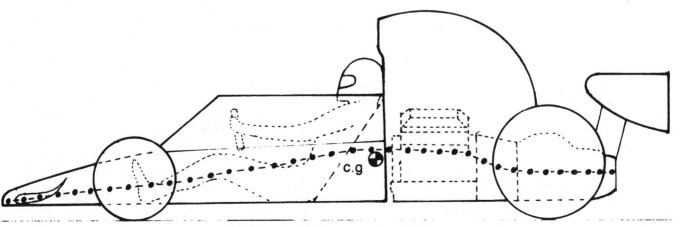

Figure (11): Mass centroid axis.

29

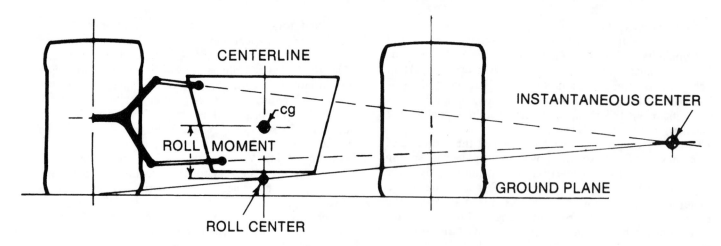

Figure (12): Determination of roll center and roll moment arm.

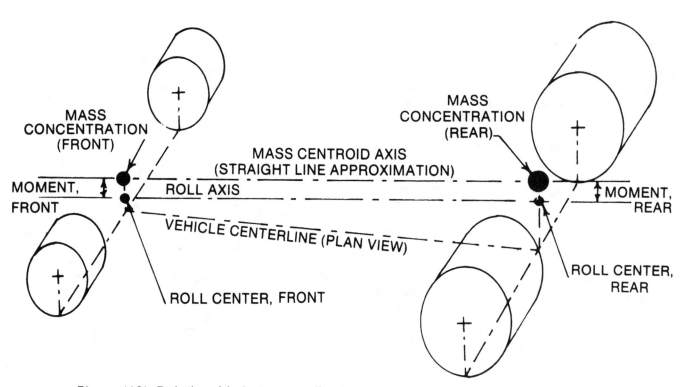

Figure (13): Relationship between roll axis, mass centroid axis and roll moments.

balance point. It is also the point through which the lateral forces transmitted from the tire's contact patches act upon the chassis. As shown in Figure (12) the roll center is found, with the usual four bar link independent suspension system, by extending the suspension link axes until they intersect to form an instantaneous center. A straight line is then drawn between the instantaneous center and the contact patch center of the tire. The intersection of this line and the vehicle centerline is the roll center. It is normally depicted as remaining on the vehicle centerline and moving up and down with wheel deflection. When we get into suspension geometry we will find that

the roll center is much more elusive than is commonly realized—it moves all over the place, both vertically and laterally.

THE ROLL AXIS is the straight line joining the front roll center with the rear roll center.

THE ROLL MOMENT is the linear distance between the roll center at one end of the vehicle and the concentration of mass at that end of the vehicle. For the vehicle as a whole the roll moment is the linear distance between the roll axis and the vehicle center of gravity measured in the transverse plane at the center of gravity. Figure (13) applies.

30

POLAR MOMENT OF INERTIA—We have seen that a body with a low moment of inertia is one with a low resistance to rotational acceleration. A vehicle with a low polar moment of inertia is one which displays fast steering and cornering response—i.e. a maneuverable vehicle. We achieve this desirable feature by concentrating the mass of the vehicle within the wheelbase and as close to the longitudinal location of the cg as possible.

Ergo the mid-engined racing car with minimum overhung mass. Again I feel that we have just about reached the point of diminishing returns with the present generation of road racers, although there is plenty of room for improvement in other fields of racing.

STATIC WEIGHT DISTRIBUTION—It is important to differentiate between polar moment of inertia and static weight distribution which is the amount of vehicle gross weight supported by the vehicle's rear wheels compared to that supported by the front wheels—with the vehicle at rest. By moving components around it is possible to effect the polar moment without changing either gross weight or static weight distribution. Figure (14) illustrates. It is now accepted practice to place the majority of the vehicle's static weight (60 - 65%) on the rear wheels in order to enhance the tractive capability of the rear tires and, by reducing the load on the front tires, to reduce the amount of power wasted in scrubbing them around a corner. Rearward weight bias also results in improved rear wheel braking performance. These objectives, combined with the desire to reduce the polar moment of inertia, are the motivating factors behind the steady march of radiators, oil tanks and such auxiliaries toward the center of the racing car. It is interesting to note that, before we finally learned to defeat rear end aerodynamic lift and its attendant high speed instability with spoilers and wings, most designers were convinced that high speed stability required the highest possible polar moment so that the car could resist its aerodynamic instability with high inertial resistance—a mechanical crutch for an aerodynamic problem.

DYNAMIC LOAD TRANSFER is the load transferred from one wheel to another due to moments about the vehicle's center of gravity or its roll centers as the vehicle is accelerated in one sense or another. Dynamic load transfer does not affect gross vehicle weight—only its distribution. Dynamic load transfer is algebraically additive to static load on a given wheel.

AERODYNAMIC LOAD is the load on a wheel, a pair of wheels or the total vehicle due to the vertical forces exerted by the vehicle's passage through the air. It can be either upward (lift) or downward (downforce). It is algebraically additive to the vertical load. In all cases we want our aerodynamic load to be in the downforce direction—we must avoid lift.

Let's start with the gross weight of the vehicle. First off, with the racing car, quoted weight is not always what it either claims to be or seems to be—and can be misleading. Weight is always stated without fuel and driver and, in some cases without oil and water as well. Ignoring these little items can give some pretty erroneous impressions. A Can Am Car with a quoted weight of 1400 lb and 550 BHP would seem to have a power to weight ratio of 2.55 lb per HP. However, on the grid with 180 lb of driver and driving gear and 30 gallons of fuel we see a 1760 lb vehicle with a power to weight ratio of 3.20. Attempting to determine the power to weight ratio of any given car for comparison purposes is difficult as the truth about either factor is almost impossible to find. Human nature being what it is, every constructor claims to have less weight and more power than he actually has. Even race track weighbridge figures are suspect as the scales are liable to be of dubious accuracy and the amount of fuel actually in the car is difficult to check. Besides, in those classes of competition with a minimum weight limit, dastardly things have been known to happen with removable ballast. As a point of interest it was once considered that the human limit of control would be reached at six pounds per horsepower—a figure now found in Formula Atlantic.

Speaking of weight limits, I would like to digress for a moment in order to enter a plea for sanity. If a minimum weight

Figure (14): Polar moment of inertia.

cg

HIGH POLAR MOMENT OF INERTIA

LOW POLAR MOMENT OF INERTIA

cg

must be imposed, then that weight should include the driver. Being of manly proportions myself, I fail to see why the proverbial ninety-eight pound jockey should be given an absolute performance advantage over his 190 pound rival. It may not make much difference in NASCAR, but it can easily be five percent of the power to weight ratio in a Formula Ford Race. This can be particularly galling after you have sweated blood and spent money to get a Formula Atlantic Car down to the one thousand pound minimum and then get to install your 180 pound hero to go and do battle with some 100 pound stripling.

WEIGHT THAT GOES AWAY

The static weight distribution and the vertical load on each tire starts to change the instant that we put the car in motion and continues to change until the car stops. It does so because of various factors and in accordance with certain natural laws.

The first, and simplest, case that we will consider is the fuel load. The start line weight of any race car includes a finite weight of fuel which is going to progressively decrease as the race progresses. This will be insignificant in a ten lap Formula Ford Race but can be twenty percent of the all up weight of a Formula One Car. Obviously then, we can expect a noticeable improvement in lap times as the power to weight ratio improves—right? Maybe! The trouble is that, if the fuel load is a significant percentage of gross weight, those familiar "all other things" are not liable to remain equal as it burns off.

With more than about fifteen U.S. gallons of fuel, it is difficult to arrange it symmetrically about the car's c.g. The c.g. of the fuel load inevitably ends up ahead of the c.g. of the vehicle (mid-engined). As fuel is burned off, the gross weight is reduced, which is a good thing, and the vehicle's c.g. is slightly lowered and moved back, which would also be a good thing—if we hadn't been forced to adjust the balance of the car for the original load condition. Springs being what they are, the front ride height becomes progressively greater as the fuel goes away. This deranges the geometry in the direction of understeer, reduces suspension droop travel and allows air to pack under the nose causing aerodynamic understeer. At the same time, the rearward movement of the cg increases the vertical load on the rear wheels and decreases that on the front wheels causing still more understeer. So the overall effect of the steadily reducing fuel load will be increasing understeer as the race wears on. "So what?" you ask—"It's the same for everyone." Not so! The designer or tuner who has cleverly placed his fuel load has given his team an edge. So has the team that has foreseen this eventuality and set its car up a little on the oversteer side with full tanks. So has the driver who has nursed his front tires when he was heavy with fuel. So has the team who has provided its driver with a cockpit adjustable sway bar. Mercedes Benz at one point had a driver-operated tee handle that reset the rear torsion bar level on pit command after a given amount of fuel had gone away. McLaren had hydraulically adjustable front ride height and weight jack on their original Indy car. There are many levels to this business . . .

The obvious place to put your fuel is as low and as close to the vehicle c.g. as possible—and equally disposed on either side of the centerline. It is not difficult, but the number of designers who don't even try is amazing.

So much for the changing fuel load and its effects (we'll cover surge as a part of load transfer). The next bit is just that—dynamic load transfer due to the forces generated as the vehicle brakes, accelerates and changes direction. For convenience and, we hope, clarity, we will divide this phenomenon into three separate cases, longitudinal, transverse and diagonal. It must be remembered, however, that under actual operating conditions, all three are taking place simultaneously while, at the same time, the sprung mass is moving vertically—which is one of the reasons that it is so difficult to quantify what is going on.

LONGITUDINAL LOAD TRANSFER

We'll start with the load transfer which occurs in the longitudinal plane under linear acceleration or deceleration. We have seen that all accelerative forces are, by definition, reacted through the vehicle's center of gravity. Since the c.g. is necessarily located at some distance above the track surface, any acceleration is accompanied by a longitudinal shift of load, rearward in the case of acceleration and forward in the case of braking. The total weight of the vehicle does not change; load is merely transferred from the wheels at one end of the car to the wheels at the other end. The amount of longitudinal load transfer that will take place due to a given acceleration is directly proportional to the weight of the vehicle, the height of its center of gravity and the rate of acceleration. It is inversely proportional to the length of the wheelbase. Figure (15) illustrates. The actual formula is:
Longitudinal load transfer =

$$\text{acceleration (g)} \times \frac{\text{Weight (lb)} \times \text{cg height (inches)}}{\text{Wheelbase (inches)}}$$

Not all the king's horses nor all of the anti dive or anti squat geometry in the world will significantly reduce the amount of load transferred under a given linear acceleration unless the vehicle's weight and/or c.g. height is reduced or its wheelbase is lengthened. In addition, whether we like it or not, unless the tanks are full, longitudinal acceleration is going to be accompanied by some amount of fuel surge—acting in the same direction as the load transfer and adding to it. Foam in the cells slows down the surge and keeps the fuel from rebounding, but it doesn't stop it. Baffles do a better job in that respect.

In the case of braking the effects of load transfer are several—and all bad. First off, by unloading the rear wheels, the amount of braking energy that they are capable of transmitting to the road is reduced which means that the overall braking capacity of the vehicle is limited by the traction potential of the smaller front tires. Even if they are the same size—as on some sedans—load transfer between a pair of wheels reduces the capacity of the pair. At the same time, since the load transfer increases the vertical loading on the front tires, it also compresses the front springs which cambers the tires in the negative direction (in at the top) which may help in a cornering situation but does nothing good for braking (or acceleration). These same front tires, if the suspension geometry should be less than optimum, may also be caused to scrub transversely across the track as they move into the bump position due to the compression of the springs. The generation of negative camber also gives rise to

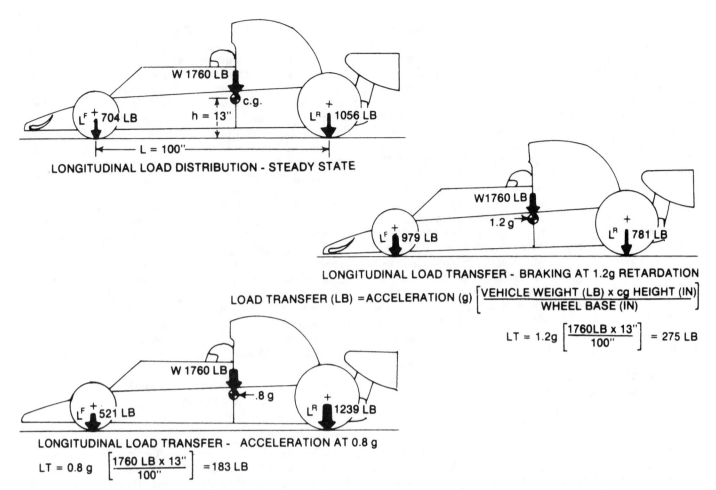

Figure (15): Logitudinal load distribution and transfer due to linear acceleration.

some surprisingly fierce gyroscopic precession on the part of the tires. Racers have pretty much forgotten about this particular unpleasantness—but only because our predecessors were only too well aware of it and went to great trouble to eliminate it by reducing compliance in suspension pivots and, most especially, by getting rid of the kingpin associated with the beam front axle. Anyone who has ever experienced precessional tramp at high speed under the brakes will go to great lengths to avoid loose ball joints.

Anyway, the compression of the front springs from the load transfer uses up some portion of the available suspension bump travel and brings the nose and/or chassis into perilous proximity to the race track. More suspension travel is about to be used up in roll as the vehicle enters the corner—still with the brakes on. This means that, if the car hits a bump under these conditions, the chassis may bottom on the track—which makes a nasty noise, grinds away the skid plates (if there are no skid plates, it will grind away rivets, or water tubes, or whatever and you will deserve whatever happens to you because you did not provide skid plates) and the wheels unload. Worse yet, the suspension may bottom which feeds fearsome loads into the spring and shock mounts and, even if nothing breaks, is most upsetting to the chassis and to the driver.

Since the increased front vertical load came from the rear wheels to start with, we find the rear springs extended (wings have helped this situation a lot) and the rear wheels extended

a bit in the droop position. If the droop geometry is not good, this position can be accompanied by some amount of positive camber which not only reduces the braking capability of the tires but is a bit of an unstable situation in itself.

As if these antics weren't enough, if we project ourselves down the track to the corner whose rapid approach caused the braking in the first place, we find ourselves entering the corner with the nose scraping the ground, the rear jacked up and the tire cambers all over the place. We'll have some words on driver technique in this situation later on—for now we'll assume the worst, since that is what is going to happen every time that Fred Herodriver goes in too deep anyway.

At some time in the corner, the driver will see his way clear to push on the throttle and start accelerating. More longitudinal transfer will now occur—but in the opposite direction. Load will now be transferred from the front wheels to the rear. This is particularly fortuitous because it is at this precise moment that we need all of the rear tire thrust potential that we can get in order to deal with the combination of cornering power that the rear tires have been developing and the accelerative thrust that we have just called upon them to deliver—remember the traction circle. The rearward load transfer will supply this extra tire capability in the form of increased vertical load. Naturally, we don't get something for nothing. The cost, in this case is that the rearward load transfer now compresses the rear springs, uses up suspension

33

travel, and cambers the rear tires in the negative sense. While a bit of negative camber is, as we have seen, a good thing, the probability is that we will get too much—especially if the driver jumps on the throttle instead of "getting the car up on the tire" and squeezing the throttle like a trigger—but what the hell, we can't have everything.

By now it should be pretty obvious that the less of this waving about of wheels we have to put up with, the better off we're going to be. Fortunately, at least with Formula Cars and Sports Racing Cars, we get a lot of help in this respect from the basic design of the vehicle itself. The wheelbase is long enough and the c.g. low enough and far enough back that dive and squat do not present serious geometric problems. The magnitude of the physical change in ride height and attendant camber change is small enough that present suspension design can cope with it and the wheels will remain pretty much upright. The tire designers help us a whole bunch in dealing with the changes that do exist. So far as the magnitude of the load transfer itself is concerned, unless we change one of the limiting factors—lengthen the wheelbase, lower the c.g. height, reduce the vehicle weight or—perish the thought—reduce the rate of acceleration, we are not going to change it. The wheelbase is pretty much fixed in the basic vehicle design—although large changes in midseason are not unknown. These changes are usually aimed at either reducing load transfer or changing static load distribution rather than the more oftenquoted reasons of increasing stability or reducing the polar movement of inertia. Gross weight and c.g. height should have been minimized by the designer/constructor. If not, then any significant change is going to take a lot of time—it will be worth it. Actually, I refuse to admit that there is such a thing as an insignificant reduction in c.g. height—cost ineffective, yes—but insignificant, no. Weight and c.g. height, like drag and lap time, is the accumulation of tiny increments, and you only get the desired results by constantly working at it. Any damn fool can see the difference between mounting the battery high and forward and low and aft—or between using a big Life Guard and a Varley—but few care where the starter solonoid is mounted. It is very difficult to take meaningful or cost effective chunks of weight off an already built car—particularly a new one. In fact, the race car almost invariably gets heavier as it is campaigned. Part of this unfortunate fact is due to the inevitable beefing up that becomes necessary and part of it to the heavy fiberglass and bondo repairs and to additional coats of surprisingly heavy paint. Care and forethought can prevent most of the former and minimize the latter.

If excessive nose dive under the brakes does exist, the easiest, most obvious and, therefore, most popular method of nullifying its effects is to increase the front spring rate and/or raise the front ride height. Raising the front ride height will keep the chassis off the ground. It will not reduce the linear amount of dive nor the amount of negative camber generated by the dive. It will also decrease the rake of the chassis, put the front wheels on a different portion of their camber curve, decrease available droop travel and raise the front roll center—all of which lead in the direction of understeer. Naturally it is necessary to play with ride height at different tracks, but in very small increments. With a couple of exceptions, I don't believe that I have ever had to change ride height more than ¼ inch in order to achieve happiness—

except to lower F.I.A. cars after tech inspection. The exceptions, places like the Targa Florio and Halifax, are so bad that ride height becomes unimportant.

Increasing the front spring rate will indeed reduce the amount of dive and negative camber produced by a given load transfer. Assuming that the original spring rate was close to optimum for ride and roll control, it will also decrease the amount of time that the tire is in contact with the road and increase front roll resistance—again causing understeer, some of which can be compensated for by decreasing the front roll bar stiffness—or by raising the rear spring rate a proportionate amount.

We'll get into this in more depth in Chapter Six, but my preferred method for curing minor scrapes due to running on a track with unique irregularities is to either add silasto bump rubbers or to increase the front and rear wheel rates by proportionate amounts. This way we disturb our optimum set up by the least amount. In the initial testing phase of new car development it becomes a question of finding the springs and wheel rates which will keep the thing off the ground when it is set to optimum ride height.

Everything that we have said about nose dive under the brakes applies to acceleration squat of the rear suspension—although it is necessary to be very careful with springs and bump rubbers to avoid power on oversteer.

ANTI DIVE AND ANTI SQUAT GEOMETRY

Geometrically, the application of "anti dive" and "anti squat" suspension geometry can sometimes be beneficial. Much nonsense has been circulated about "anti" suspension. The most prevalent fallacy being that it reduces load transfer. It doesn't—not to any appreciable extent. There are two types of anti dive front suspension. The first, illustrated by Figure (16A), uses brake torque reaction through the suspension links, which are convergently inclined toward the c.g. location in side elevation, to reduce or cancel the diving tendency. If the point of convergence of the extended wishbone pivot axes intersects a line drawn from the tire contact patch to the c.g. of the sprung mass, then the torque reaction will cancel out the diving moment and we will have 100% anti dive. If, for example, we should determine that we want 50% anti dive, then the line extended from the contact patch through the wishbone axes convergence point would intersect a perpendicular dropped from the c.g. to the track surface at a point halfway between the c.g. and the ground.

The alternative method, illustrated by Figure (16C) is to maintain the wishbone pivot axes parallel to each other and to incline them both downward toward the front. What happens here is that, under braking, the inertia of the sprung mass tries to rotate the sprung mass about the front wheels. The inclined pivot axes from an inclined plane which forces the wishbones into the droop position which effectively lifts the front of the vehicle. In this case, to achieve 100% anti dive, the wishbone pivot axes must be parallel to the line drawn between the tire contact patch and the c.g. We are using the inertia of the sprung mass to jack up the front of the car.

At first glance, anti dive would seem to be the "something for nothing" that we are always looking for. Alas, a further

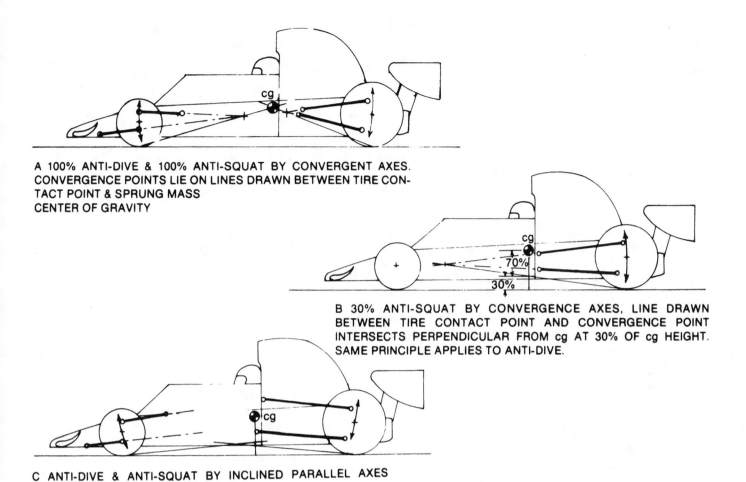

A 100% ANTI-DIVE & 100% ANTI-SQUAT BY CONVERGENT AXES. CONVERGENCE POINTS LIE ON LINES DRAWN BETWEEN TIRE CONTACT POINT & SPRUNG MASS CENTER OF GRAVITY

B 30% ANTI-SQUAT BY CONVERGENCE AXES, LINE DRAWN BETWEEN TIRE CONTACT POINT AND CONVERGENCE POINT INTERSECTS PERPENDICULAR FROM cg AT 30% OF cg HEIGHT. SAME PRINCIPLE APPLIES TO ANTI-DIVE.

C ANTI-DIVE & ANTI-SQUAT BY INCLINED PARALLEL AXES

Figure (16): Anti-dive and anti-squat suspension geometry.

look, or rather some practical experience, reveals that both methods have unfortunate side effects that pretty much cancel their effectiveness. Each method utilizes the upward force of brake torque reaction to oppose the downward force of load transfer. This opposition of forces means that the suspension becomes stiffer and less sensitive with vertical wheel travel and so is less able to absorb the shocks caused by track surface irregularities and load transfers. Under the brakes, should the front wheel(s) hit a bump at a time when the upward force opposing the load transfer is close to the downward force of the transfer, equal and opposite forces will be achieved and the suspension will effectively bind solid. Naturally this does terrible things to the tire's compliance with the road and the tires go into a very severe tramp. If the driver doesn't lose control, the best he can hope for is that the front brakes will lock as they unload. This effectively limits the amount of anti dive that can be built into any racing car to about 30%—and that only in heavy front engined cars.

In method one, the converging inclination of the pivot axes causes front wheel castor to increase with vertical wheel travel. This increases the steering effort and gives rise to a certain amount of darting due to uneven castor as the car hits bumps and/or rolls. The effect is more noticeable with the present generation of wide tires which require little static castor to begin with.

In the second method, jacking the car up by its bootstraps, the parallel but inclined axes cause the wheel to move forward as well as upwards in reaction to vertical loads. However, nature insists that, in order to absorb bumps, the tire should move rearward under impact. This opposition of forces means that the suspension becomes stiffer and less sensitive with upward wheels travel and we get into the patter thing again.

If we attempt to combine the two methods, usually by inclining the axis of the lower wishbone downward towards the front and leaving the upper parallel to the ground, we get both castor change and loss of suspension response.

How much anti-dive a given car can tolerate is a question of the height and fore and aft location of the c.g., wheelbase length, mass and the expected rate of retardation. Present practice is to use none on Formula Cars and Sports racing Cars—they don't need it and, due to their inherently sensitive natures, they can't tolerate the upsets. Large front engined Sedans, on the other hand, aren't very sensitive to begin with and need all of the help they can get and typically feature 20% to 25% anti dive.

ANTI SQUAT

At the rear, the problem with vertical load transfer under acceleration is chassis squat with its attendant negative camber. It can be resisted by anti squat suspension linkage.

35

The same two methods apply, converging the pivot axes toward the c.g. or inclining them upward toward the front. Again Figure (16) applies. Once more we are resisting the natural downward force of load transfer with a reactive upward thrust so it is possible to lose sensitivity and get into tire patter and the like if too much anti squat is employed. This will manifest itself as power on oversteer. One disadvantage found at the front does not exist at the rear—when the pivot axes are inclined upward toward the front, bump movement will force the wheel rearward—in the natural direction to absorb the energy of the bump, rather than to oppose it. The fact that the wheelbase changes slightly while all of this is happening doesn't seem to bother anything. It is, however, necessary to carefully adjust the rear suspension to avoid undesirable bump steer characteristics. This was covered in *Prepare to Win*.

Present practice, particularly with vehicles featuring a high power to weight ratio is to employ some anti-squat in order to restrict rear tire camber change and the physical raising of the front suspension under acceleration. About 20% seems to be the maximum before we get into tire compliance problems. The lower the power to weight ratio, the less is required—or can be tolerated. Fortunately, anti-squat is pretty easy to play with by providing alternate mounting points at the front of the radius rods. I should point out that anti-squat can be built into the beam axle by inclining the torque arms or the leaf springs.

LATERAL LOAD TRANSFER

Lateral load transfer is caused by forces very similar to those which cause longitudinal transfer—with the operating axis turned ninety degrees. In any cornering situation, centrifugal force, acting through the vehicle's c.g. tends to throw the car out at tangent to its intended path. This centrifugal force is resisted by the lateral forces developed by the tires. Since the vehicle's c.g. is necessarily located above the track surface, the tendency of the c.g. to fly sideways while the tires roll on their curved path gives rise to a moment of force which transfers some of the load from the inside tires to the outside tires. Lateral load transfer is a bad thing. In Chapter Two we found that any transfer of load from one tire of a pair to the other reduces the total tractive capacity of the pair.

The basic load transfer equation applies—in this case:

$$\text{Lateral load transfer (lb)} = \frac{\text{Lateral acceleration (g) x weight (lb) x c.g. height (inches)}}{\text{Track width (inches)}}$$

So that, for our Can Am Car, with total rear wheel load of 1080 lb., a c.g. height of 13 inches, a rear track width of 60 inches and cornering at 1.4 g, we would have:

$$\text{Load transfer} = \frac{(1.4) \times (1080 \text{ lb}) \times (13")}{(60")} = 328 \text{ lb.}$$

This means simply that, under this steady state condition, 328 lb. of the load on the inside rear tire would be transferred to the outside rear tire giving a resultant inside rear tire load of 212 lb. and an outside tire load of 868 lb. We have transferred 61% of the inside tire vertical load to the outside tire. Going back to Figure (5) we find that we have reduced

the cornering force of the pair of rear tires from 1512 lb. to 1400 lb. This cannot be good.

The only way to decrease the magnitude of this lateral transfer for a given lateral acceleration is to decrease the weight of the vehicle, increase the rear track width or lower the center of gravity. On our calculator, and in Figure (17) let's increase the rear track by a quick 4" and see what happens:

$$\text{Load transfer} = \frac{(1.4) \times (1080 \text{ lb}) \times (13")}{(64")} = 307 \text{ lb.}$$

Cornering Force = 1440 lb.

Next we'll remove 50 lb. of weight from the rear of the car:

$$\text{Load transfer} = \frac{(1.4) \times (1030 \text{ lb}) \times (13")}{(60")} = 312 \text{ lb. and}$$

Cornering Force = 1358 lb.

Lastly, we'll lower the vehicle's c.g. by 1":

$$\text{Load transfer} = \frac{(1.4) \times (1080 \text{ lb}) \times (12")}{(60")} = 302 \text{ lb and}$$

Cornering Force - 1445 lb.

This is all very interesting, but what can we do with it? Very little except realize that we can juggle lateral load transfer at either end of the car with track width and, above all, never lose an opportunity to lower the c.g. or remove weight.

One of the most widespread misconceptions in racing is that the amount of load transfer taking place is directly related to chassis roll. Two opposing theories are prevalent:

(1) The car that rolls a lot transfers more load and so develops more cornering force.

(2) The car that is strongly restricted from rolling doesn't transfer as much weight and so develops more cornering force.

The amount of chassis roll resulting from a given lateral acceleration is dependent on a multitude of factors: vehicle weight, c.g. height, roll center height, track width and the resistance in roll of the suspension springs and anti-roll bars. Obviously, if the vehicle has NO springs, it cannot roll—as in Go Kart. It will still transfer load in the lateral plane. Let's consider the hypothetical case of a four wheeled vehicle with solid axles, no springs and solid tires which is being accelerated in a circular path and is restrained to that path by a wire attached to its c.g. and pivoted at the center of the circular path. Without springs or pneumatic tires, the vehicle cannot roll. That lateral load transfer is indeed taking place will be demonstrated by the progressive lifting of the inside wheels as velocity and centrifugal force increase. Eventually the c.g. will be outside of the outside tire's contact patch and the vehicle will overturn. For a more practical demonstration watch a Go Kart driver counteracting lateral load transfer with his body english.

Actually, the lateral load transfer picture is a bit more complicated than I have yet indicated. It is generated in four separate ways:

(1) By the side forces generated by the tires as they resist centrifugal force. These forces are reacted on the sprung mass through the roll centers.

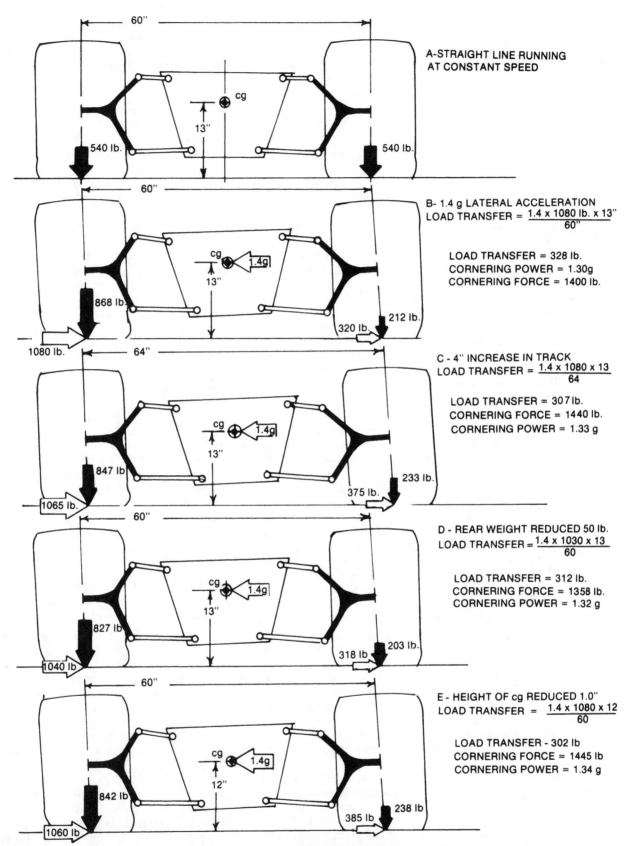

Figure (17): Simplified illustration of the relationship between track width gross weight, center of gravity height and lateral load transfer—and between lateral load transfer and cornering force (Figure 5 used to determine cornering force for given values of vertical load).

(2) By physical compression of the outboard springs due to roll and by deflection of the anti-roll bars.

(3) By the jacking tendency inherent in any independent suspension system.

(4) Lateral displacement of the c.g. due to roll has a minor effect which we will ignore.

The tire side forces, reacted through the roll centers, are instantaneous functions of lateral acceleration while the generation of roll and the attendant spring compression take place over a finite amount of time. For a given rate of lateral acceleration load transfer generated by the tire side forces and by jacking are affected by roll center height while that caused by spring compression is affected by the magnitude of the roll couple and by the roll resistance of the springs and anti-roll bars.

Looking at the vehicle as a pair of front wheels and a pair of rear wheels, let's first examine the tire side forces reacting through the roll centers. The basic relationship here is very simple: the greater the lateral acceleration the greater the centrifugal force and the greater the tire side forces we must develop in order to balance it and so more load transfer will take place. The tendency of a given vehicle to roll due to a given lateral acceleration will vary directly with the length of the vehicle's roll moment and the amount of mass involved. The tire forces are reacted through the roll center. The part of the car that is going to roll is the sprung mass. Centrifugal force, being an acceleration, will act through the c.g. of the sprung mass. The greater the vertical distance between the roll center and the c.g., the greater will be the roll couple produced by a given lateral or centrifugal acceleration. The roll couple will be resisted by the suspension springs and by the anti-roll bars. The greater the resistance of the springs, the less roll will result—but there will be no significant effect on the amount of lateral load transfer because the roll couple has not been changed and there is no physical connection between the springs on opposite sides of the car. The same cannot be said of the resistance of the anti-roll bars. In this case, because the bar is a direct physical connection between the outside wheel and the inside wheel, increasing the stiffness of the anti-roll bar will both decrease roll angle and increase lateral load transfer.

If the amount of roll generated by a given lateral acceleration has no real effect on load transfer, then why worry about it? There are two reasons:

(1) We will see in Chapter Four that roll causes unfortunate wheel cambers which strongly affect tire adhesion.

(2) The generation of chassis roll takes a finite period of time, during which load is transferring and camber angles are changing. The shorter we can make this time the more positive and stable will be the vehicle's response to changes in direction.

So we want to restrict chassis roll. We can do so either by increasing the roll resistance of the suspension springs, and/or anti-roll bars, or by reducing the roll moment by raising the roll center. We have already determined that with a typical independent suspension layout we can place the roll center virtually anywhere we want it. If we put the roll center at each end of the vehicle at the same height as the concentration of mass at that end, then there will be no roll couple and the chassis will not roll at all. There are two overriding objections:

(1) Again we will see in Chapter Four that high roll centers produce unfortunate wheel camber curves.

(2) High roll centers cause high jacking thrusts.

JACKING

So it is time to examine another of the most misunderstood phenomena in racing—the infamous "swing axle jack." We have all heard the term and we all realize that, in some mysterious fashion, the independently suspended automobile tends to "jack itself up" as it goes around a corner. The first type of independent suspension was the simple swing axle—as in Volkswagen—and they really do it, hence the term. However, any independent system with the roll center above ground level will jack to some extent. As shown in Figure (18) the effect is caused by the fact that the reaction force at the tire which balances the centrifugal force of the turn must act through the roll center. If the roll center is above the ground, then the line of action between the tire contact patch and the roll center will be inclined upward toward the vehicle centerline. This being so the side force developed by the tire will have a vertical component which will tend to lift or "jack" the unsprung mass. This lifting action, in addition to raising the c.g., will also move the suspension into droop with unfortunate results in the camber department. The higher the roll center (and the narrower the track), the steeper the inclination of the line of action and the greater the jacking force. Naturally the vertical component also detracts from the useful cornering force. The effect is at its very worst with the true swing axle with its combination of very high roll center and very steep positive camber curves in droop—follow a classic VW Bug around a corner at any reasonable rate of speed for a truly graphic demonstration—and it is the real reason why the pre-war Auto Union Grand Prix cars developed their fearsome reputation and why I just cannot consider Formula Vees to be real race cars. Jacking is to be avoided on any car and is the single major reason why today's projectiles feature very low roll centers.

LINEAR ROLL GENERATION

It is a bit difficult to visualize the relationship of the vehicle's roll centers to its c.g. when the roll centers are, by definition, located in the transverse planes of the front and rear axles and the c.g. is located somewhere in between. Not only is the visualization difficult, it is pretty useless—because it isn't valid. Since the roll axis is not going to pass through the c.g. anyway, let's compare the roll axis to the mass centroid axis instead of the c.g. If the roll axis at one end of the car is further below the mass centroid axis than it is at the other end, then that end of the car will have a greater roll moment and therefore lateral load transfer will take place more quickly at that end, and traction will suffer. It is often stated in print that the reason why the front roll center is always lower than the rear is to ensure a more rapid transfer of lateral load at the front than the rear and thus build in stable understeer. Close, but no cigar. What we really want is for the roll axis to be pretty much parallel to the mass centroid axis so that the front and rear roll couples will be about equal, and we will end up with a vehicle featuring linear front and rear roll generation and lateral load transfer. We can modify this roll couple distribution with the rates of the anti-roll bar and suspension springs, but we establish

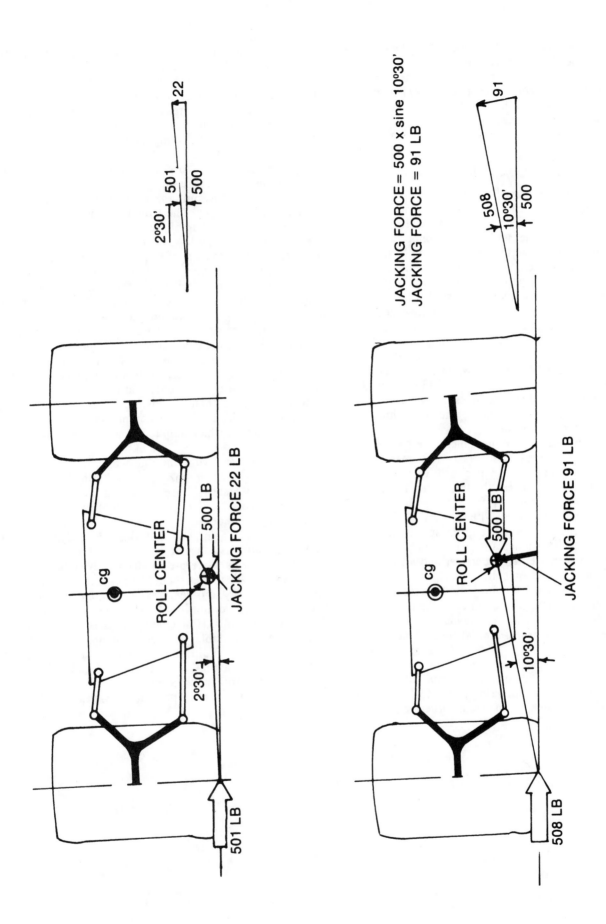

Figure (18): Effect of roll center height on generation of vertical jacking force simplified by considering effects on outside wheel only.

the linear or neutral vehicle with inclination of the roll axis so that it is parallel to the mass centroid axis—with some adjustment for the difference in mass between the front and the rear. The front roll couple must be somewhat greater than the rear so that we will have some natural understeer and so that we will have excess traction capacity at the rear for acceleration.

DIAGONAL LOAD TRANSFER

Those of us who have played at adjusting vehicle corner weights on the scales are well aware that the vehicle is not a pair of front wheels and a pair of rear wheels. It is a four-wheeled machine with the four wheels connected by a, hopefully, rigid chassis structure. When we add load to one wheel of the vehicle by jacking up its spring perch, not only do we reduce the load on the other wheel at that end of the car, but we increase the load on the wheel at the diagonally opposite end. This is due to the torsional rigidity of the chassis itself which connects the top abutments of the suspension springs. How much of the load transfers diagonally and how much transfers laterally is a function of torsional rigidity, spring location, wheelbase and track widths. It is calculable, but only just and not worth the effort. All that we need to know is that diagonal load transfer does take place. For our purposes it takes place on corner entry, when it is critical and on corner exit, when it is less so.

We have already seen that, as the vehicle enters a corner, a portion of the vertical load on the inside rear tire is transferred to the outside rear tire and that the same transference takes place between the front tires. If this were all that happened in the load transfer picture, and if the roll axis were correctly positioned with respect to the mass centroid axis and the roll resistance of the springs and sway bars were correctly apportioned, then we would have a slight amount of stable corner entry understeer and all would be well—the picture would not be upset by the normal longitudinal load transfer due to braking. However, the moment we combine turning, or lateral acceleration with braking or linear deceleration, some of the load from the inside rear tire, instead of being transferred where God meant for it to go—to the other rear tire—is shifted diagonally to the outside front, and this upsets the whole equation. What actually happens next depends on vehicle configuration, but basically we have lost rear cornering power by transferring load to the front, and we have lost front cornering power by

generating an understeer torque about the vehicle's c.g. We may have lost further front cornering power either by overloading the outside front tire or by compressing its spring to the point where we fall off the tire's camber curve. This is one more reason why it is not a particularly good idea to enter the corner with the brakes on hard and why braking is the last thing that the road racing driver learns to do really well.

Coming out of the corner the situation reverses itself which is no bad thing under the circumstances—load is transferred diagonally onto the inside rear wheel which needs all the help it can get. The trouble is that understeer can result from the unloading of the outside front. Driver technique can go a long way toward avoiding this power application understeer—don't apply the power with steering lock toward the inside of the corner and it won't happen.

So what have we decided in this Chapter? Basically, anytime that the race car experiences acceleration in any direction, load is going to be transferred—in a complex manner—between the wheels. Further, anytime we have a combination of centrifugal acceleration and linear acceleration load is going to be transferred longitudinally, laterally and diagonally. These load transfers have two effects—one by decreasing the traction potential of the tires which lose vertical load more than increasing that of the tires which gain load and the second by compressing the springs attached to the tires which gain load and thus causing camber change.

Additionally we have found that we cannot avoid chassis roll—we can't even minimize the couple which causes it by raising the roll centers. Since we fervently wish to limit roll as much as possible, we are going to have to do it with springs and sway bars.

In closing I'll point out that this whole dynamic load transfer situation is considerably more complex than it first appears. If race cars operated under steady state conditions on large skid pads then it should be possible to calculate the optimum geometry, moments, rates, etc., and decide on the best overall compromise. Fortunately, we don't operate under these conditions. (Fortunately, because it wouldn't be much fun.) The variables induced by bumps, dips, hills, corners of varying radius and camber, track frictional characteristics, available net torque and traffic are obvious—and are the reasons why controllability and response are still more important than ultimate cornering power.

CHAPTER FOUR

SUSPENSION GEOMETRY

Within a given field of study, the more variations that are possible, the more mysterious the field is liable to become. Since the variation possibilities inherent in the suspension geometry of the racing car are almost infinite, it follows that the resultant mystery and confusion should also approach infinity—and so they do. I am not at all sure that we are going to succeed to any great extent in reducing the confusion, but we are going to try.

First we'll define the field. The geometry of any wheel suspension system determines the linear and angular paths that the wheel and tire will follow when it is displaced from its static position—either by the effect of road irregularities on the unsprung mass or by movement of the sprung mass in response to the load transfers produced by accelerations in the various planes. The shape of these wheel paths will depend on the relative lengths and inclinations of the suspension links while the magnitude of the deflections will depend on the absolute length of the links, the masses involved, the amount of the displacing force and the rate and placement of the suspension springs and anti-roll bars. In this chapter we will be concerned with both the shape and the magnitude of the wheel paths but only from the geometric point of view—we will leave the springs and anti-roll bars for Chapter Six. The design of the geometry of the suspension system consists of first choosing the type of suspension to be employed and then selecting the pivot point locations, absolute and relative link lengths and inclinations and the wheelbase and track dimensions that will result in the most acceptable compromise of roll center locations and wheel paths to suit the operating conditions to be encountered. It also includes making damned sure that all of the components involved, and their attach points, have sufficient stiffness and strength to minimize compliance and to avoid disaster.

We'll start with the descriptions of the basic types of automobile suspension which are common to books of this nature. Since everyone is more or less familiar with them and probably owns at least one book which features lots of drawings, and since I am basically lazy, we will dispense with the usual illustrations.

THE SOLID OR BEAM AXLE

The beam axle was probably invented by the Assyrians. It is currently found only at the rear of those passenger cars whose designers, for whatever reason, chose not to spend the money necessary to provide independent rear suspension. It is an archaic and much maligned device. It also does a pretty damn good job—at least on vehicles designed to be driven on freeways—at very low cost. If you race a car with a beam axle you will have a serious disadvantage—unless everyone else has one, too. Overcoming, or minimizing, the inherent design faults of the beam axle deserves a section by itself. This section is included in Chapter Fourteen.

THE SWING AXLE

The swing axle is an abortion. It should never have been invented; today its use would not be considered by any automotive engineer let alone a racing car designer. It is of interest only to those fanatics involved in Formula Vee, where its use is a requirement. For reasons which totally escape me, it is also featured on most Off Road Race Cars. Its disadvantages include: a very high roll center, extreme jacking, extreme camber change and almost total lack of adjustment. It has no advantages other than ready availability from the junkyard. The Formula Vee brigade has developed its own technology aimed at making the best of a very bad thing, and I am content to end the discussion there.

THE DE DION AXLE

The De Dion Axle is basically a beam axle arranged so that the final drive unit is part of the sprung mass. This is its only real advantage over the beam axle. It is not currently in use on racing cars and has not been for twenty years. I feel safe in assuming that it will not return. Therefore we will not discuss it.

SLIDING PILLAR FRONT SUSPENSION

If you own a Morgan, there is nothing that you can do to improve your sliding pillar front suspension except to install Koni shocks and replace the pivot bushes constantly. If you do not own a Morgan, there is no reason that you should be aware of the existence of this system.

TRAILING LINK FRONT SUSPENSION

Trailing link front suspension has a minimum number of parts—all arranged so that, in order to withstand the loads involved, they must be truly massive. The wheel paths are very bad indeed. It is a fit companion to swing axle rear suspension and that is where it is found—Formula Vee, old Porsches and some Off Road Racers. No discussion.

THE MACPHERSON STRUT

The Macpherson strut is now used, with some variations, at the front of most small passenger cars—and a large number of sports and GT cars. It is therefore very common in Touring and Grand Touring Race Cars. Its popularity has come about because it is very cheap to produce and offers pretty good camber control. Unfortunately the camber control isn't that good. It is difficult to arrange sufficient component stiffness to avoid compliance—particularly when race tires are used—and it is virtually impossible to hide the strut inside a wide wheel—so that the steering offset on your production racer is going to become extreme when you bolt on the wide wheels. If low frontal area is a prime requirement, the necessary height of the strut itself rules out its use.

Years ago Colin Chapman—clever devil—adopted the Macpherson Strut principle to the rear of several early Lotus racing cars and to the road going Lotus Elite. It worked just fine with the tires available then but would not be suitable for use on a racing car today.

I have never been associated with a race car which used struts. I can see no reason why, once the compliance bushings have been removed and the strut modified to drop the ride height and to adjust the camber, they shouldn't work just fine. Naturally the modifications necessary are easier said than done. Tilton Engineering of El Segundo, California, manufactures and markets a line of really good and ingenious hardware to adapt Macpherson struts for racing use. The kits allow the car to be lowered without giving up suspension travel and you end up with adjustable camber, castor and ride height.

THE DOUBLE WISHBONE
OR FOUR BAR LINK
INDEPENDENT SUSPENSION SYSTEM

This is where eighty years of motor racing development has led us. For the past fifteen years at the rear and a lot longer than that at the front, virtually every serious racing car has employed one form or another of the four bar link independent suspension. We'll devote the rest of the chapter to this system, starting with a brief historical analysis.

A LITTLE BIT OF HISTORY

Early racing cars, like carts and carriages, were built with beam axles at each end. Surprisingly, with some notable but not very successful exceptions, this situation continued until the late 1920's or early 1930's. Very early on it became apparent that the beam axle had inherent limitations which placed very definite limits on vehicular performance. Chief among these was the simple fact that, with a pair of wheels connected to a common axle, any force that upsets one wheel must necessarily upset the other. This is not good at all, especially if the road surface should be less than perfect. The beam axle is also very heavy—all unsprung—requires a lot of space, if we are going to have provision for a reasonable amount of vertical wheel travel, calls for some heavy point loadings to be fed into the chassis and has a high roll center—which is why the early race cars didn't roll much. While is is simple, easy to locate reasonably well and will tolerate a certain amount of slop, it is difficult to keep the axle from skewing when a one wheel bump is encountered or when the sprung mass rolls. At the front the necessity to steer the front wheels made a narrow based kingpin system necessary and this led to bushing trouble, wear, gyroscopic precession of the wheels, shimmy and tramp—features that have all but disappeared from our vocabularies.

Since the problems associated with the beam axle are more noticeable at the front of the vehicle, the next move was to trailing link independent front suspension. This had the advantage of being cheap, simple and independent—one wheel upsets were not transmitted to the other wheel. It kept the wheels at a constant camber angle during vertical move-

ment and had no track change. It also had serious disadvantages: camber is equal to chassis roll (in the wrong direction) and unit loadings in the pivot areas and in the links are very high which causes early pivot wear and bending in the links unless they are really strong. It is also difficult to avoid compliance in the vertical plane—again except by massive components. None of this was totally limiting until the wide, flat profile, tire arrived upon the scene. At this point even Porsche, who had stuck with the trailing link for decades, got rid of it in a hurry.

At the rear, when they ran out of the development possibilities with the beam axle—and they had some very clever locating systems indeed—the first move was to the De Dion set up, which was a damn sight better. While the De Dion is not independent—one wheel upsets are still transmitted to the other wheel—its unsprung weight is vastly superior to the simple beam. In addition to hanging the final drive unit on the sprung mass, it allows the use of inboard brakes and rear mounted gearboxes. Because of the peculiarities of the swing axle, the De Dion stuck around right up through the late 1950's.

The swing axle was the first prominent independent rear suspension layout. It arrived with the Auto Union Grand Prix Car designed by Dr. Porsche in the mid-1930's. There were only ever three men who could drive these fearsome machines, Bernd Rosemeyer, Tazio Nuvolari and Hans Stuck. Their instability and awesome tail wagging scared racers away from independent rear suspension and mid-engined race cars for a quarter of a century. In actuality they may well have been the most advanced racing cars ever seen: They were the first mid-engined cars, had the first limited slip differentials, placed the fuel load at the c.g. and featured a host of other innovations, all of which worked—except the swing axle. Looking back, with the wisdom of twenty-five years of other people's thinking, it is very probable that swing axle jack and camber change were the only major problems the Auto Union had. Anyway, the swing axle got a new lease on life when Ulenhaut at Mercedes developed the low pivot swing axle for the post war Grand Prix and Sports Racing Cars, but even the die hards at Porsche gave up on it the late 1960's.

The wishbone or four bar link system started out at the front of the car—and pretty rudimentary it was. The wishbones were narrow based, equal in length, parallel to each other and to the ground at ride height, and were very short. They had to be short in order to achieve any stiffness at all with their narrow bases—even though they were heavy forgings. Often a transverse leaf spring formed either the top or the bottom link. These early systems left a lot to be desired in wheel location and the lack of camber change in vertical wheel travel was more than made up for by the extreme change (again in the wrong direction) in roll and by the amount of track change caused by the short links. Development was spotty. I have seen a very sophisticated independent front suspension system on a 1936 or 1937 Maserati Grand Prix Car, but the Lister Jags and the like in the late 1950's, as well as many of the all conquering Italian Grand Prix and Sports Racing Cars of the same time, were still using equal length and parallel short wishbones. At any rate, development continued and, as time passed, the lower wishbone became longer than the top one which gave rise to negative camber in bump, but the positive camber of the laden or outboard wheel in roll was considerably reduced and things started getting better. In the late 1950's the English, led by Messrs. Chapman and Broadley (Chapman is usually regarded as the father of the modern racing car, but the first sophisticated, wide based, four bar link suspension I ever saw was on Broadley's original Lola 1100 cc Sports Racing Car) got serious and the present era started. The first big move came when John and Charles Cooper stuck the engine between the driver and the transaxle. The next moves involved some very serious thoughts as to wheel location, camber change and load transfers and roll center relationships. Very quickly the present ubiquitous system of very broad based unequal and assymetric tubular links and wishbones came into being. From about 1962 the system has been all but universal, and while everyone has his own ideas about the most effective compromises, and while different types of tracks and tires demand different geometry, in principle, all systems have been the same ever since.

THE OBJECTIVE OF
THE SUSPENSION SYSTEM

So much for history. Now let's see just what we want the wheel suspension system to accomplish. First of all, we must have four-wheel independence, so that as far as possible, upsets will be confined to the wheel and tire which experiences the upset. We are certain of this much and, within reasonable limits, any independent system will give it to us. Second, although we must provide enough vertical wheel movement so that the wheels and tires can absorb road surface bumps and vertical accelerations of the sprung mass, we want there to be no change in toe-in—or at least adjustable change in toe-in—while the wheels are moving. With attention to detail, this is not a problem. Third, we want no compliance within the suspension system or its attachment to the sprung mass. This is a question of the stiffness (rather than the strength) of the links and the rigidity of the pivots, axles, hub carriers, and attachment points as well as the direction in which the loads are fed into the chassis and the base over which the loads are spread. The four bar link system lends itself admirably to this goal—more so than any other arrangement. Attention to detail design is required and many designers are deficient in this respect, but the system itself is not. All links can be arranged so that they are loaded in straight tension or compression with no bending moments imposed and link stiffness is merely a question of calculating compression loads. Feeding the loads into the chassis properly requires a bit more thought, but it is not that difficult.

Next we require minimum weight—and again the system is ideally configured to achieve it. Further, the wide base over which we can feed the loads into the chassis obviates the necessity for massive and heavy attach structure.

This much is easy. Next we want to control change of wheel camber angle and change of track dimension with wheel and/or sprung mass movement. There are two separate problems here. In order to achieve the maximum footprint area and an even pressure pattern so that we can realize maximum tire tractive effort under braking and acceleration, we wish the wheel to remain upright when the suspension is subjected to the vertical movement of the

sprung mass caused by longitudinal load transfer. We also want it to remain upright when the wheel itself is displaced vertically by a bump or a dip—although this is a more transient condition and less important in the overall scheme of things. At the same time, and for the same reasons, we want both the inboard and outboard wheels to remain vertical *to the track surface* as the sprung mass rolls due to centrifugal acceleration. We also do not want the track dimension *at the contact patch* to change under any of these conditions as that would cause the tire to be scrubbed sideways across the race track when it is already at or near its limit of adhesion and would upset things in the traction department. While all of this is going on it would be nice if the roll centers at each end of the car were to remain a constant distance away from their respective centers of mass so that we could retain our linear rate of roll generation and lateral load transfer.

Sounds simple enough—but it is just not possible to achieve. While we have infinite permutations available with combinations of link lengths and inclinations, none of the combinations will achieve all of the above.

THE NATURE OF WHEEL MOVEMENT

Let's look at what actually happens with wheel or chassis movement. There are two separate types of movement— vertical movement of either the wheels or the chassis and the movement of the chassis in roll. First we'll look at Figure (19) while I explain what we will be looking at in the suspension diagrams from now on. The right side of Figure (19) shows what the rear suspension of a typical Formula 5000 or Can Am Car might look like when viewed from the rear. The left side shows how we are going to represent the linkages of that system in our discussions. This representation has the double advantage of making the pertinent points easier to see and the drawings easier to make.

We'll consider vertical movement first. It doesn't matter, from the geometric point of view, whether the wheel moves because of a bump or a dip in the road or whether the chassis moves in response to a load transfer or to a change in aerodynamic downforce. If the wheel moves, it takes the outboard pivot points of the suspension links with it which forces the links to describe arcs about their inboard pivots. The wheel must then change its angular position relative to both the road surface and to the chassis as a function of those arcs. If the chassis moves, the inboard pivot points move with it and the same thing happens. The geometric results will be the same. Since movement of the chassis in response to load transfers is of more interest to us than transient wheel movement in response to bumps, all of the illustrations will show this case. Figure (20) shows the effect of bump and droop movement on wheel camber, spring axis length, drive shaft length and roll center location. There are no surprises here except for the fact that, due to camber angle, track change at the center of the footprint is not equal to the change in length of the half shaft.

When the sprung mass rolls, however, as in Figure (21) the whole picture changes. In this case the inboard link pivots move with the chassis which must roll about the instantaneous roll center of the suspension. This means that, on the laden side (side away from the center of the turn) of the chassis, both the upper and lower pivot points will move downward and out from the chassis centerline. The upper

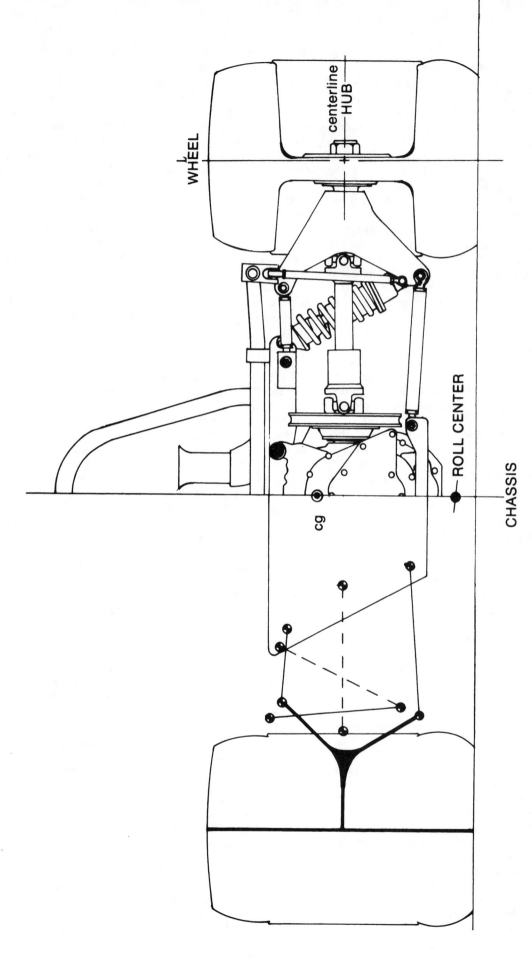

Figure (19): Explanation of diagrams to be used to illustrate suspension geometry—right side shows rear suspension in end view—left side shows links, link pivots centerlines and instantaneous centers only:

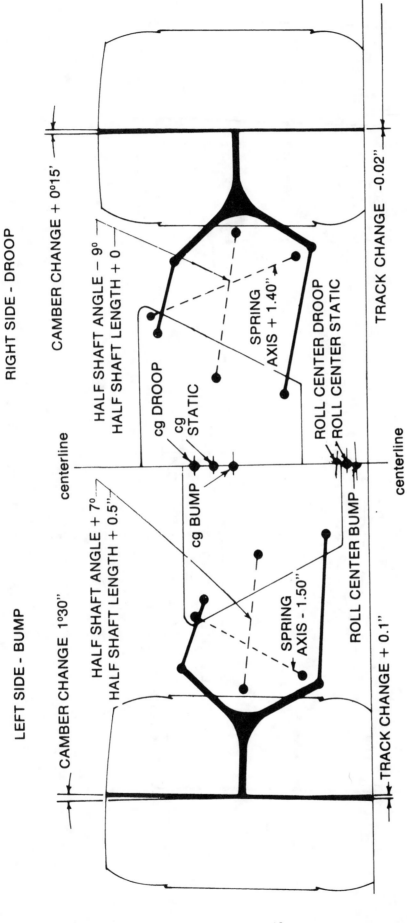

RIGHT SIDE - DROOP

CAMBER CHANGE + 0°15'

HALF SHAFT ANGLE – 9°
HALF SHAFT LENGTH + 0

SPRING
AXIS + 1.40"

cg DROOP
cg STATIC

ROLL CENTER DROOP
ROLL CENTER STATIC

TRACK CHANGE – 0.02"

centerline

LEFT SIDE - BUMP

CAMBER CHANGE 1°30"

HALF SHAFT ANGLE + 7°
HALF SHAFT LENGTH + 0.5"

cg BUMP

SPRING
AXIS – 1.50"

ROLL CENTER BUMP

TRACK CHANGE + 0.1"

centerline

Figure (20): Effect of vertical chassis movement on wheel camber, spring axis length, drive shaft length and roll center location.

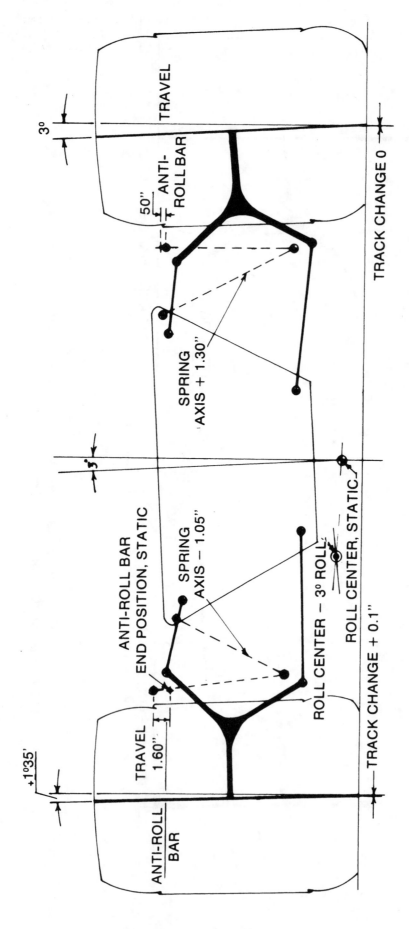

Figure (21): Effects of chassis roll.

pivot point, being on a longer radius from the roll center, will, however, move further than the lower. Since the suspension links are of fixed length, this difference in pivot point movement will force the laden wheel to assume a positive camber angle (out at the top) relative to the surface of the race track. The opposite set of conditions exist on the inboard or unladen side so that tire will be pulled to a negative camber angle. This is not what most of the books tell us for the simple reason that most of the books reference wheel camber to the chassis. Unfortunately, no one tells the tire about any camber relationship except that which exists between the tire and the road surface. We could care less about the angular relationship between the wheel and the chassis.

The next shock is what happens to the location of the roll center when the chassis rolls—it moves—not only downward but also sideways. Again most books tell us that the roll center, and therefore the roll axis, remains on the vehicle centerline. It doesn't—not when the vehicle rolls. The roll center of a vehicle in a roll condition is the intersection of the line drawn between the instantaneous center of the laden wheel and the center of its contact patch with the similar line drawn between the instantaneous center and the contact patch of the unladen wheel. It is very unlikely that this intersection will ever be located on the centerline of the chassis. This is not shown in Figure (21) because I ran out of room on the paper. It is shown in Figure (22) which illustrates the effects of a combination of chassis roll and bump travel—conditions which exist at the front of the car on corner entry and at the rear on corner exit.

PAPER DOLLS

About now, we are faced with two basic choices on how to attack the rest of the chapter. I can write and draw until I am blue in the face—and still not put a dent in the possible combinations of link lengths and angles—or we can construct a two dimensional model of the four bar link suspension system and you can play games with it. Since the choice is mine, we will construct the ¼'' scale model shown in Figure (23). Somewhere in the back of the book—if I don't forget to put it in—you will find a tear-out page on which the pieces for the model are printed. Glue them onto an old manila file, cut them out, get a cheap protractor and lay out the background shown in Figure (23A). With a box of thumbtacks, a couple of straight edges and some string, you are now equipped to spend hours at a card table driving yourself nuts—and convincing anyone who happens to wander in that you have already succeeded. By punching suitably placed holes in the chassis, suspension upright and link portions of paper doll and inserting thumbtacks for pivot points you can construct a scale model of any independent suspension system that you like. Hold the tire centerpoints against a straight edge on the ground line and move the chassis up and down to observe the effects of bump and droop movement— wheel camber and track change read directly on the background. Find the roll center by extending the link pivot axes with either a straight edge or string, stick a thumbtack through the roll center, roll the chassis one degree and watch the wheels. Find the new roll center and repeat the exercise. Then combine roll and vertical chassis movement. The comparison will not be exact because we are ignoring a few fac-

tors, but it is plenty close enough to be educational—and it is going to save me writing several thousand hard to follow words. You will learn more playing with the model.

BASIC LAYOUTS

Although there are endless possible combinations of link lengths and inclinations, we can break them down into three basic layouts, equal length and parallel links, unequal length and parallel links and unequal length, non parallel links. We will briefly examine the characteristics of each in turn.

EQUAL LENGTH AND PARALLEL LINKS

Figure (24) shows an equal length and parallel link system with short link lengths. Because the links form a parallelogram, there will be no camber change with vertical movement. There is, however, considerable change in track width—which is not good. When the chasis rolls, the wheels and tires change camber by the exact amount of chassis roll—with the outside wheel cambering in the positive direction. This is not good under any condition and, the wider the tire involved, the less good it is. Since the links remain parallel under all conditions, the location of the instantaneous center—the intersection of the extended linkage axes—is located at an infinite distance from the chassis centerline. We assume the roll center to be at ground level and to pretty much stay there.

We can reduce the amount of track change for a given amount of vertical motion by the simple expedient of lengthening the suspension links, as in Figure (25). With this change, a given amount of vertical wheel or chassis movement results in less angular displacement of the wheel and therefore in less change in the track dimension. Alas, the linkage remains a parallelogram and the roll camber situation remains basically as before, although the amount of camber change is slightly reduced because the inboard pivots are closer to the vehicle centerline and so are displaced less for a given amount of roll. Also, while we can reduce the track change by lengthening the links, we cannot eliminate it, or even get it down to reasonable dimensions—and we will not have room for infinitely long links.

UNEQUAL AND PARALLEL LINKS

If we make the upper link relatively shorter than the lower, as in Figure (26), we achieve some significant changes in the wheel paths. Now, in vertical travel, the upper link has a shorter radius than the lower which results in the wheel assuming a negative camber angle in both bump and either negative or positive camber droop. The amount of camber change is dependent upon the relative lengths of the upper and lower links—the shorter the upper link becomes, the steeper the camber change curve. The assumption of negative camber reduces the change in track dimension considerably and, with care, it can become insignificant.

When the sprung mass rolls, the wheels are still forced into camber angles in the same direction as the chassis roll, but the positive camber assumed by the all important laden wheel is considerably reduced. Unfortunately, the negative camber of the unladen wheel is increased.

Although the links are parallel to each other at ride height, the fact that they are unequal in length means that they will not remain parallel with vertical wheel movement (they

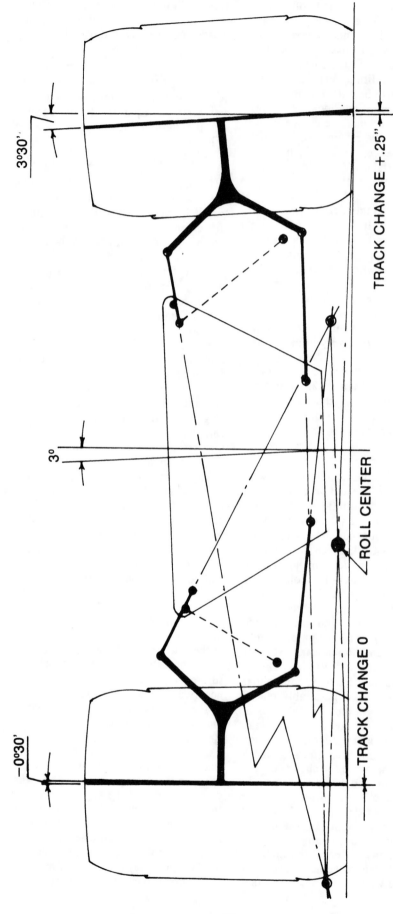

Figure (22): Effects of combination of chassis roll and bump movement.

48

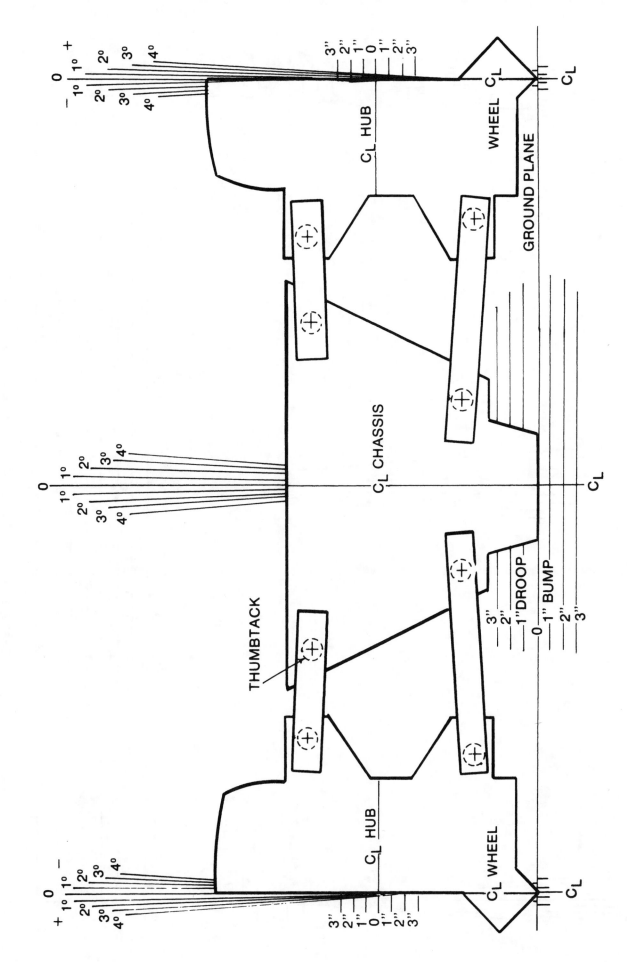

Figure (23): Scale of model of suspension linkage geometry.

49

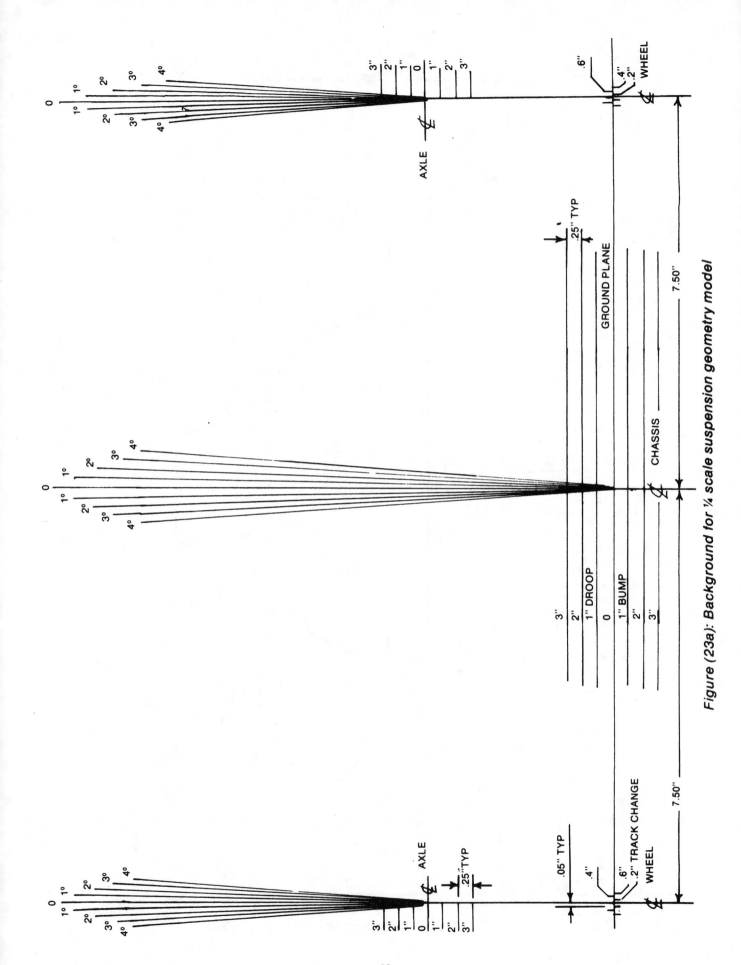

Figure (23a): Background for ¼ scale suspension geometry model

50

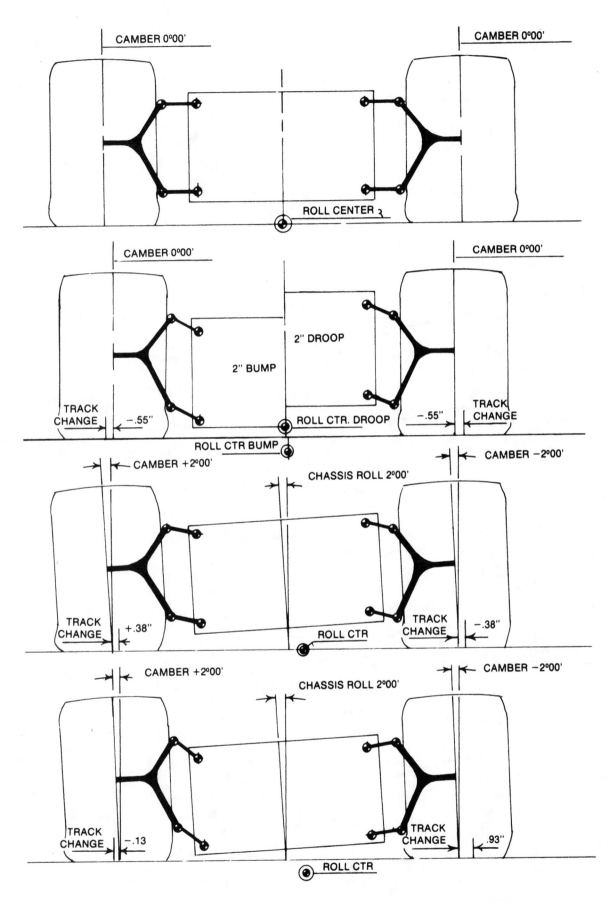

Figure (24): Equal length and parallel link system with short links.

51

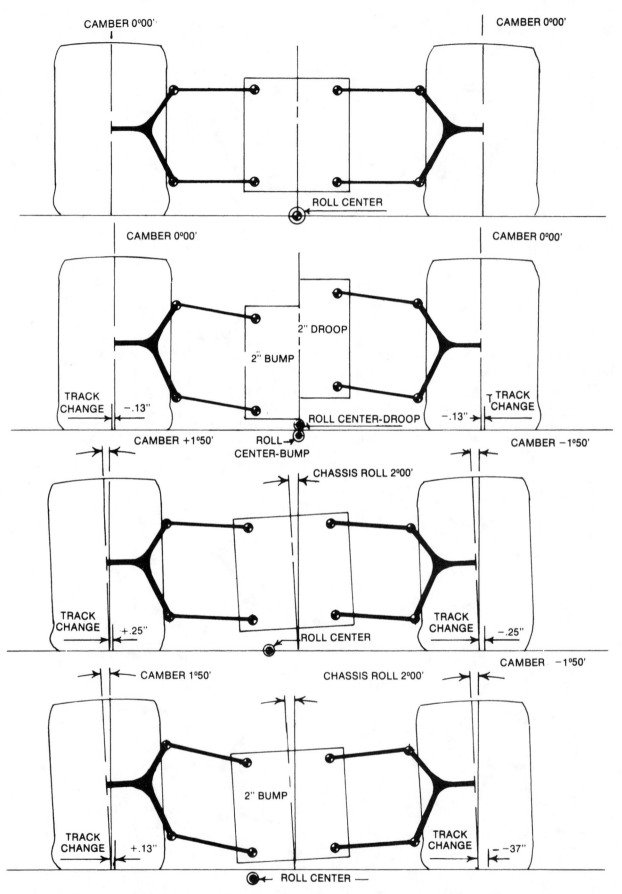

Figure (25): Equal length and parallel link system with relatively long links.

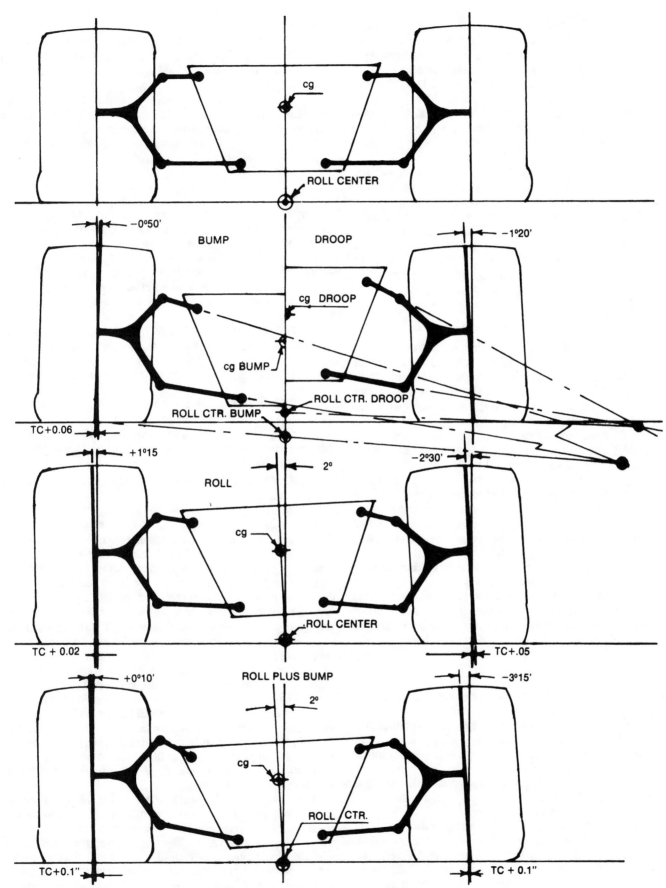

Figure (26): Unequal length parallel links.

almost do in roll) so the instantaneous swing arm length varies quite a bit. This means that, if the wheels are allowed to travel very much, the camber curves will become very steep indeed. If great gobs of wheel travel are required—as in off-road racing—it is necessary to make the links closer to each other in length—try it on the model. At any rate, the roll center with unequal but parallel links stays pretty constant in relationship to the center of mass. Therefore the roll moment remains more or less constant, which is a good thing.

Naturally, there is no law that states that unequal and parallel links must be parallel to the ground at ride height—but a little experimentation with the model will explain why they normally are. About now I should mention that static ride height may well be different from the operating ride height if wings or effective spoilers are employed to generate downforce in meaningful quantities. Further, the operating ride height will then vary with road speed. Just one more little complication that we really don't need.

UNEQUAL AND NON PARALLEL LINKS

While the unequal and parallel link set up reduces the positive camber of the laden wheel in roll, it does not reduce it enough for some tires to get really happy—and it produces really low roll centers. By inclining the link pivot axes with respect to each other we can place the roll centers wherever we please—at least in the static position—and we can further reduce the positive camber of the laden wheel in roll. Figure (27) illustrates. Admittedly things are a bit extreme in this diagram, but I wanted to illustrate what can happen when we go too far in any given direction. In this case, inclining the upper link downward toward the centerline of the vehicle has indeed notably reduced the positive camber of the laden wheel when the chassis rolls. But it has also rooted everything else. What has happened is that the inclination of the upper link is too steep, resulting in a very short instantaneous swing arm with the attendant very steep camber curves. By raising the inboard points of both the upper and the lower links we would achieve far better camber curves while maintaining the roll center in the same static location—of course then the roll center would move around more . . . As I said, I could go on forever but this is what the model is for.

BASIC TRUTHS

After you have played with the model long enough, some general truths will begin to become evident:

(1) While it is possible to control wheel camber either during vertical movement or during chassis roll, it is not possible to achieve very good camber control under the combined conditions—we have an "either—or" situation.

(2) The longer we make the suspension links, the less angular and linear wheel displacement will result from a given amount of chassis or wheel movement.

(3) In vertical movement, the roll center moves with the center of gravity, tending to keep the roll moment constant.

(4) Increasing the effective swing arm length decreases the amount of camber change due to vertical wheel movement, decreases the amount of vertical roll center movement relative to the c.g. and increases the amount of lateral roll

center movement.

(5) Except in the case of equal length and parallel links, long effective swing arms don't stay long when the wheel moves into the bump position or, for the laden wheel, when the chassis rolls.

(6) Increasing the inclination of the upper link (or shortening its relative length) results in more negative camber in bump, less positive camber on the laden wheel in roll and a decrease in the amount of wheel or chassis movement before we lose camber control.

COMPROMISE

Given the fact that we cannot achieve Utopia in the geometry department, it becomes necessary to compromise. Everyone in this business has his own ideas as to which aspects of wheel path and roll center location control are more important and so we are very liable to see, in the same class of racing cars, lots of geometric variation. Despite this variation, most racing cars work very well. This is due to three factors:

(1) The present generation of racing tires is relatively insensitive, within reasonable limits, to camber change.

(2) Load transfer characteristics are more important to tire performance and vehicle balance than camber curves are.

(3) Different design philosophies tend to even out in terms of lap time—the car whose geometry tends to limit its absolute cornering power may well put the power down better—what you gain on the straights you lose in the corners and so on.

A few basic guidelines do exist to aid us in the selection of our geometric compromises:

(1) The front camber curve should keep the laden wheel more upright in roll than the rear. As the vehicle is turned (or pitched) into the corner, the combination of load transfers is going to compress the outboard front spring a whole bunch and we will need all of the camber compensation we can stand to keep from washing out the front end. In addition, due to its lower section height, the front tire is liable to be less tolerant of camber than the rear. For the same reason the front tire will offer more directional stability than the rear in order that the vehicle's steering response will be predictable and precise. A third factor is that, since the major portion of total vehicle lateral load transfer will take place at the front, the rear will roll less anyway.

(2) The front roll center will always be lower than the rear. If it is too much lower, we will have a car that does not enter corners well and which exits corner on three wheels. The big trick here is to keep the front and rear roll center movements approximately equal to each other—and in the same direction—as the car does its various things while negotiating a corner.

(3) We can control wheel camber within narrow limits of chassis roll and rather more broad limits of vertical movement. At some point in the generation of roll or vertical movement, the geometry will go to hell and the wheel paths will start to change very rapidly. The longer that we make the suspension links, the more movement can take place before we lose camber control—and the less wheel displacement we will suffer per unit of chassis movement.

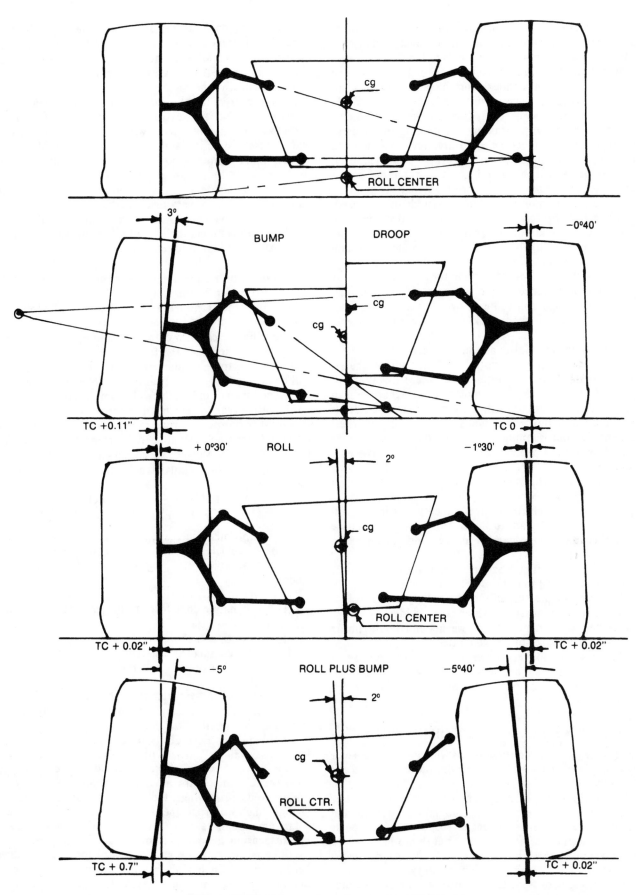

Figure (27): Unequal and non-parallel links.

My own pet ideas on suspension geometry and camber control stem from my firm belief that vehicle balance or driveability is more important in terms of lap time and winning races than ultimate cornering power. If I were a racing tire, I would resent any tendency on the part of my suspension links to abruptly change my camber, or to suddenly scrub me across the race track as I tried to smoothly change my operating mode from braking to cornering to acceleration in my efforts to follow the rim of traction circle. I would respond to such attempts by breaking traction momentarily. I would do the same if the lateral load transfer at one end of the car suddenly became a lot more than that at the other end because the roll moment at that end suddenly increased. I would bite and grip again after things had settled down—if they did—but I would momentarily lose traction due to the upset. It is not very likely that the driver would appreciate these antics.

So, I feel that we should design the geometry of our suspensions to minimize rapid changes of camber and relative front to rear roll center movement as the car goes through its transitions from braking to cornering acceleration.

The geometric possibilities are limited here and we are going to find it necessary to restrict the amount of chassis movement that takes place in response to centrifugal and to longitudinal acceleration. On most race tracks, we can strongly restrict chassis roll with only minor adverse side effects. We cannot, however, usually restrict vertical wheel movement without running into reduced tire compliance which will inevitably produce severe side effects—like slow lap times.

We have four methods available to us to restrict chassis roll—or reduce its effects:

(1) We can use high roll centers which result in low roll moments. We do not want to follow this approach because we will then have poor camber curves and high jacking forces.

(2) We can use anti-roll bars at each end of the car stiff enough to restrict roll to our desired maximum.

(3) We can use the suspension springs to restrict roll—either by making them stiffer, which is a bad idea, or by optimizing their placement so that we get maximum linear spring travel per degree of roll generated.

(4) We can use longer suspension links to reduce the amount of camber change generated per degree of roll.

We will go into these options in more depth in Chapter Six.

TRACK AND WHEELBASE DIMENSIONS

The last geometrical considerations which we will consider are the length of the wheelbase and the widths of the track dimensions.

The advantages of a relatively long wheelbase are increased straight line stability, reduced longitudinal load transfer and pitching moments, somewhat easier reduction of the polar moment of inertia and more room to put things in.

The advantages of a relatively short wheelbase are reduced overall weight and increased maneuverability.

The advantages of wide track widths are reduced lateral load transfer for a given amount of centrifugal acceleration

and room for longer suspension links. The major disadvantage is increased frontal area. When we get into aerodynamics, we will see that, at least on open wheeled cars, the importance of frontal area is overrated.

Very basically, the racing car with a long wheelbase and relatively narrow track widths will be very stable in a straight line at the expense of cornering power and maneuverability. The vehicle with a shorter wheelbase and wide tracks will be less stable, more maneuverable and will develop more cornering power. It will also be more difficult to drive to its limits. In general I favor moderately long wheelbases and wide tracks. I will point out, however, that if all of the corners are very fast, the disadvantages of narrow tracks can be overcome with aerodynamic downforce and, for USAC type racing the idea of a narrow tracked car with long suspension links and reduced frontal area is very attractive.

The situation becomes more complex when we consider the relative width of the front and rear track dimensions. I believe that the front track should be considerably wider than the rear track. More heresy! My reasons have to do with turning the car into corners and jumping on the power coming out. The wider the front track, the more resistance there is going to be to diagonal load transfer and the lesser will be the tendency for the car to "trip over itself" on corner entry and/or to push into the wall from the effect of the drive on the inside rear wheel when the power is applied. I believe that most of our present road racing cars, with roughly equal front and rear tracks, would benefit from an increase in front track width. The slower the corners to be negotiated, the more important this relative track width becomes.

DIFFERENT STROKES
FOR DIFFERENT FOLKS

The compromises in suspension geometry will vary with the type of vehicle and the nature of the race track upon which the car will do its thing. Factors to be considered include:

(1) Power to weight ratio

(2) Aerodynamic downforce to be generated and range of vehicle speeds

(3) Tire width and characteristics

(4) Track characteristics—smoothness, corner speed, degree of banking present and the amount of braking that will take place.

Let's now briefly consider the specific case of some different types of race cars and see how the operational conditions and factors affect the design of the geometry.

The ubiquitous Formula Ford features low engine power, low gross weight, narrow tires, virtually no down force generation, and crazy drivers. They do not accelerate very hard because they don't have much torque. Since they are not allowed to run wings, the operating ride height does not change much with road speed. The narrow tires will tolerate a fair amount of camber. What Formula Fords need from the suspension geometry is maximum braking power and maximum cornering power. They need the braking power, because one of the few places for a Formula Ford to get by another one is in the braking area. They need the cornering power, because they cannot afford to slow down any more

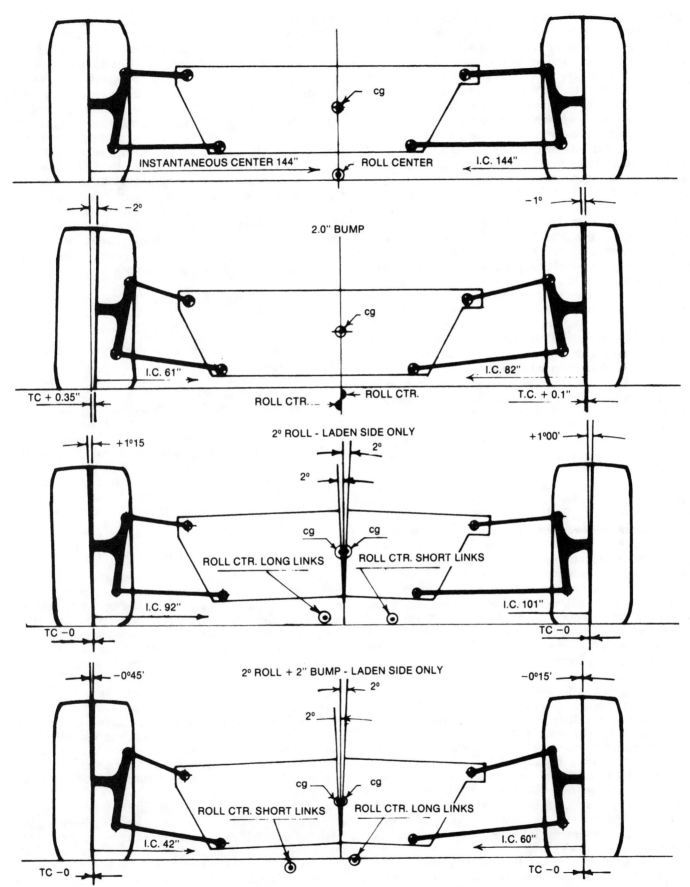

Figure (28): Long links vs short links.

than is absolutely necessary—with their low available torque, it takes forever to regain the lost speed. We get the braking power by keeping the front wheels as upright as possible in bump and not allowing the rear wheels to go into positive camber in droop. This means long links with not much inclination at the front—take a look at an ADF or an Eaglet. At the rear, we don't need to worry a lot about the effects of squat since we won't have enough torque to cause much of it. We do, however, have to worry about the camber of the laden wheel. As no limited slip diffs are allowed, we also have to avoid inside rear wheelspin which means lots of droop travel, avoidance of extreme negative camber generation on the inside wheel and minimum lateral load transfer at the rear.

Formula One, Can Am and the late lamented Formula 5000 cars offer a more complex set of operating conditions. Their road speed on a given track can vary from about forty mph to over one hundred ninety. The wings generate gobs of downforce which causes large differences in operating ride height from high speed to low speed. The tires are very wide and camber sensitive, and there is a lot of torque available to squat the chassis out of low and medium speed corners. The key to lap time in these vehicles lies in acceleration out of the corners. We have to ensure that the camber doesn't vary much with the changing ride height and that the rear camber doesn't get all upset as the chassis squats. To achieve this we sacrifice keeping the tires upright in roll and accept a somewhat lesser ultimate cornering power at the rear. This is compensated for by the simple fact that the rear tires are enormously larger than the fronts to accept the engine torque and that they will tolerate more camber than the fronts will anyway.

If we can tolerate some camber change at the rear, we cannot at the front. The low section tires just don't like it at all. The Chevy-engined brigade doesn't seem to have caught on to the advantages of very long front suspension links, but the Formula One group surely has. Figure (28) illustrates the effect of lengthening the links of a front suspension setup while maintaining the relative link lengths, track width and static roll center location the same. It gives one pause for thought.

Indy Cars on 2½ mile ovals operate in a relatively narrow, if very high speed, range—say 180 mph at corner apex to 220 at the end of the straights. While the torque available to squat the chassis is, even at those speeds, considerable—it is the same for each corner exit. Ride height change due to downforce is not super critical so long as it is realized that the operating ride height has little to do with the static ride height. When laying out the geometry and while aligning the car, the change in ride height from the shop floor to rolling into a slightly banked corner at 200 mph must be taken into account. Nose dive under the brakes is not a factor—except on the mile tracks or the road circuits—so negative camber due to forward load transfer can be pretty much ignored. Since the tracks are relatively smooth and the road speeds are very high indeed, relatively stiff springs and bars can be employed and chassis roll can be—and is—severely restricted. The compromise is weighted toward reduction of bump camber and track change.

Front engined sedans, with their high cg's and forward weight biases require that the outside front tire be kept as upright as possible—even at the cost of heavy bump camber

change which can be reduced by anti-dive suspension.

In the world of Off Road Racing a number of things that the rest of us just barely realize the existence of become critical—like pitching moments. Roll shrinks to relative unimportance, and it becomes a matter of vast amounts of suspension travel and very effective damping. The big thing would seem to be to keep the wheels—particularly the driving wheels—on the ground for traction. Track change is not likely to be critical on offroad courses, but bump and droop camber probably are. I doubt that enough centripetal force can be generated on the surfaces involved to make roll camber very important, but the release of the energy stored in the rear springs when the vehicle hits one of those mini-cliffs that they call bumps can—and does—cause some spectacular endos. Why they still use swing axles is beyond me. My own opinion, totally unsupported by any experience, is that there is a lot of performance to be gained in this field in the geometry, cg height and polar moment areas.

THE RELATIVE PLACE
OF LINKAGE GEOMETRY
IN THE OVERALL PICTURE

I believe that it is a hell of a lot more important to get the roll center locations and movements happy with each other and with the mass centroid axis than it is to get the camber curves perfect—which we can't do anyway. When we change the suspension pivot points —either inboard or outboard— and register a gain it is almost always because we have changed the roll center location rather than because we have modified the camber curve. I must also admit that we usually improve the balance of the typical English Kit Car by raising the front roll center—even at the cost of shortening the effective swing arm length. Mainly it is a question of getting the rate of generation of the front and rear lateral load transfers happy with each other.

MODIFYING THE GEOMETRY

Once we have decided that our particular race car might benefit from a modification to its suspension geometry, we are faced with some decisions about how best to accomplish the desired end. Here we have to bear several factors in mind—structural soundness, cost—in both time and dollars—ease of returning to where we started (in case it doesn't work) and the feasibility of doing a valid back to back test to find out whether it works or not.

Changing link length or track dimensions is going to require the fabrication of new suspension links which, depending on the skills, time and equipment available, may or may not be a big deal. If you decide to make the links longer, take a really good look at the structural factors involved—they will necessarily have to be stiffer, particularly at the front, due to the brake torque loads being reacted over a longer distance.

Raising or lowering pivot points, at the front, is simply a case of making spacers for the ball joints, or of reducing the height of the uprights. It is always easier to do it outboard than inboard—except on production cars. The opposite condition exists at the rear where the outboard pivots are pretty well fixed in the hub carrier design but the inboards are bolt on structures or cross members which can be pretty easily replaced or modified.

So do what you think that you have to do. Align and bump steer the car with the alternate setups, write down how many turns you have to move what to achieve alignment and bump steer after you change setups; go to the race track and find out if it works. If it does, you may pat yourself on the back and feel good—but try to figure out WHY it worked while you are congratulating yourself. If it doesn't work, do not commit suicide—most bright ideas do not work. Make sure that you have not overlooked a contributing factor—like not readjusting the wheel alignment or bumpsteer when you changed the setup—and try to reason out why it didn't work. We normally learn at least as much from our mistakes as we do from our successes. The best development driver/engineer I ever knew once told me that he reckoned that about 20% of his bright ideas worked.

CHAPTER FIVE

STEERING GEOMETRY AND SELF STEERING EFFECTS

All intentional turns are initiated and, to some extent, controlled by deliberate turning of the front wheels. Therefore, the response to the driver's steering motion must be precise, linear and consistent. Simple enough, but things are seldom that simple. Let's look at the actual geometry involved.

If we ignore slip angles and assume no skidding, in order for a four-wheeled vehicle to negotiate a corner of any given radius, the geometric center of the vehicle's path of curvature must be located on an extension of the line of the vehicle's rear axle—otherwise the rear tires must skid. Due to track width, the front wheels must follow arcs of different radii and, if the steering linkage is so arranged that the front wheels remain parallel to each other as they are steered, one front wheel must skid.

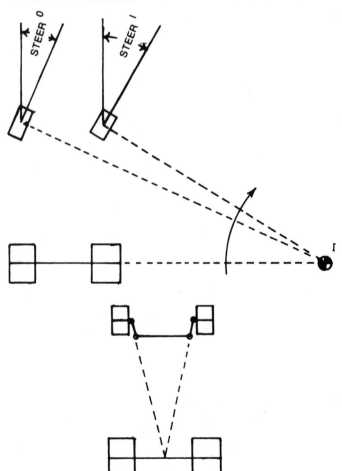

Figure (29): Ackerman steering principle.

ACKERMAN STEERING

The people who designed horse drawn buggies and carriages realized this fact and came up with the Ackerman steering principle illustrated by Figure (29). All that this means is that the extended axes of the steering arms meet at the center of the rear axle and, when the vehicle is following a curved path, the inside front wheel will be steered to greater degree than the outside front so that both can follow their individual radii without skidding. No single intersection point will result in true Ackerman steering over the whole range, but by moving the intersect point in the longitudinal plane, you can come close in the normal range of steering angles.

This is neat for a coach and four showing off in Hyde Park but the minute we put pneumatic tires on our racing car and place Fangio in the seat, the whole picture changes due to slip angles. We have already determined in Chapter Two that, in order for the vehicle to change direction, each of the four wheels must assume some slip angle and that the side force generated by any tire must act in the direction perpendicular to the rolling path of that tire. This modifies the Ackerman picture considerably as shown in Figure (30).

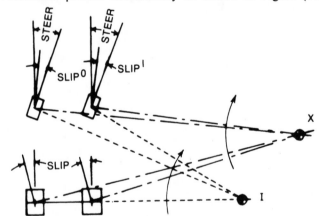

Figure (30): The Ackerman picture modified by slip angle.

Because the rear wheels have developed a slip angle, the instantaneous center of curvature has moved from position I to position X. If we want the front tire slip angles to be similar to those of the rear tires, and similar to each other, then the front wheels are going to end up more nearly parallel to each other than in the Ackerman setup. In addition, lateral force transfer during cornering assures us that the outside front tire is going to run at a higher slip angle than the inside front and will do almost all of the steering. Under these conditions, if the inside front is at a greater steering angle, it will scrub across the race track. For these reasons, racing cars do not employ as much Ackerman correction as street cars. Some designers have even employed "anti-Ackerman" steering geometry in an effort to even out the front tire slip angles.

So what does all of this mean in practical terms? I'm not at all sure. I am, however, certain of a few things:

(1) The crew spends a lot of time pushing the car around garages, pits and paddocks. If parallel steering is employed, it is damned difficult to push the car around a sharp corner. If anti-Ackerman geometry is employed, it becomes almost impossible. This cannot be right.

(2) Once the lateral load has been transferred between the front wheels, within reasonable limits, it doesn't make much difference where the inside front wheel is steered because it has virtually no load on it anyway. Banked corners are an exception to this case.

(3) Ackerman or lack of it becomes unimportant during corner exit when the whole front end is unloaded.

(4) Therefore the time when differential steering angles of the front wheels can affect the behavior of the racing car occurs during corner entry.

(5) If the racing car is properly set up and driven, steering angle will virtually never exceed eight degrees; if it does, the inside front tire will be off the ground. Total available steering angle of the front wheels is typically about eighteen degress.

(6) Practical experience indicates that, with racing cars employing modified Ackerman steering, corner entry understeer can be significantly reduced by adding either mild static toe out of the front wheels or minor amounts of front bump steer in the toe out in bump direction. Either of these modifications work in the direction of parallel steering angles or equal slip angles on the front tires. This leads me to the following conclusions, which I cannot prove:

(1) The racing car should probably be arranged so that the front wheels are effectively parallel for the first increment of steering angle and then move toward Ackerman steering.

(2) It is not very critical.

OTHER CONSIDERATIONS

There are some other requirements that the steering system must meet. It must offer sufficient precision and stiffness so that the driver can actually feel what is happening at the front contact patches without becoming confused by slop and deflection and so that component deflections do not generate wheel steering angles all by themselves—particularly under braking loads. This is a structural consideration and requires the use of high quality components, stiff links and the replacement of any compliance bushings in the system.

The steering must be "fast" enough so that the vehicle's response to steering and to steering corrections is virtually instantaneous—this normally translates to a steering ratio of about 16:1 which gives approximately two turns from lock to lock. Depending on the driver and the car, somewhat faster than this may be better, but 16:1 is about the workable minimum.

The steering must offer enough "feel" to the driver so that he can sense what is happening as he approaches the cornering limit of the front tires. It must also have some self returning action, but it cannot be so heavy as to cause fatigue or loss of sensitivity. This feel, feedback, and self returning action picture is a function of the kingpin inclination, steering offset or scrub radius, castor angle and the self aligning torque characteristics of the front tires. Kingpin inclination is included in front suspension design so that the whole mess can be packaged with the steering axis coming out somewhere near the center of the tire contact patch. If the steering offset is too great, then the feedback through the wheel and the self returning action will be excessive; if it is too small, then there will not be enough feel. Kingpin inclination is normally around six to eight degrees, and the scrub radius varies a whole bunch depending on front wheel load and tire characteristics. Increasing front track by means of wheel spacers increases the scrub radius by the thickness of the spacer and is unlikely to have any beneficial effects upon the steering.

Castor is built into the front suspension to promote straight line stability and to provide feel and self returning action. How much is ideal has to be played with.

As explained in Chapter Two, steering offset is a constant, castor angle almost is, but the pneumatic trail or self aligning torque of the tire itself varies with slip angle, and so the combined effect provides the driver with a feel for the limiting slip angle of the front tires.

There are side effects to both kingpin inclination and castor angle. As the wheel is steered, positive kingpin inclination will cause the outside suspension to be jacked up by an amount proportional to the kingpin inclination. The dynamics here are a bit confused, but I suppose that, to some extent, this jacking offsets the effect of lateral load transfer. At the steering angles we are talking about, I cannot conceive of this being a significant factor. Positive castor causes the laden wheel to camber in the negative sense when it is steered and so might offset some of the positive camber caused by chassis roll. Again, I don't see how the amounts can be significant at the steering and castor angles we are talking about, although with large front engined sedans, which naturally understeer in corner entry, a lot of castor could help—if you either have a driver strong enough to cope with the steering forces which result or if you have power steering.

SELF STEERING

That's about all that there is to the geometry of the steering system itself. In addition to the intentional and deliberate driver induced steering of the front wheels, every vehicle has some amount of self steering effect. This can be either intentional on the designer/tuner's part or not and it can be beneficial or not. There are three separate modes of self steering: aerodynamic, which we will consider when we discuss exterior vehicle aerodynamics, bump steer, which is change of toe-in with vertical wheel travel and roll steer which has to do with change in camber, vertical load, slip angle and what have you under lateral acceleration.

TOE-IN AND STABILITY

Toe-in between a pair of wheels, at either end of the vehi-

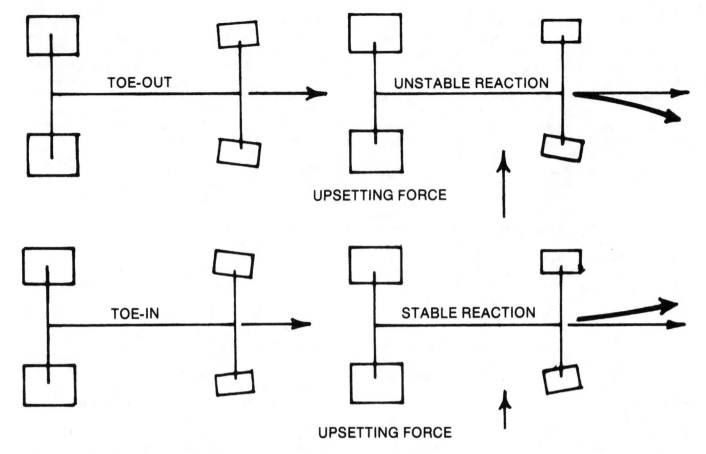

TOE-OUT

UNSTABLE REACTION

UPSETTING FORCE

TOE-IN

STABLE REACTION

UPSETTING FORCE

Figure (31): Effects of toe-in and toe-out on directional stability in response to up-sets.

cle, is a dynamically stable condition. If load is transferred laterally between a pair of wheels, by a bump or a wind gust—for instance—the load transfer will cause a relative increase in the slip angle of the more heavily laden wheel. If the wheels should be toed out when this occurs, then the deflection will cause the vehicle to steer towards the inside wheel which is pointed toward the upset to begin with and away we go. This can be most upsetting at the front of the car. At the rear, it is downright vicious—undriveable is the usual description. On the other hand, if the wheels are toed in, the vehicle still steers toward the inside wheel, but that wheel is pointed in the direction that we want the car to go and the vehicle is self correcting or dynamically stable. Figure (31) illustrates. It works about like dihedral in an aircraft wing. Too much in either direction is unstable.

TOE-IN AND BUMP STEER

I described the geometric causes of bump steer and detailed the procedures used in adjusting it in *Prepare to Win*, which means that if you don't have a copy, you will now have to buy one. At that time I basically stated that the front bump steer should be adjusted to as close to zero toe change as could be arranged but that toe-out in bump should be avoided at all costs. I further stated that a degree of roll understeer could be arranged by forcing the rear wheels to toe in in bump and out in droop, but that it probably wasn't desirable. This was a very safe statement. Although it is possible to make your car faster by playing with bump steer, it is

equally possible to make your car undriveable by doing so. In *Prepare to Win* I did not want to discuss vehicle dynamics at all—and I didn't. Now we must. The methods of adjusting bump steer are just as described in *Prepare to Win*—altering the relative heights of the inboard and outboard ends of the steering track rods at the front and altering the inclination of the hub carrier at the rear.

We can use deliberate amounts of bump steer to alter the response of the vehicle in cornering. Basically, building in a minute amount of toe-out in bump will effectively decrease the slip angle of the outside front tire at small steering angles during the corner entry phase—while load is being transferred and slip angles are building. This can, and often does, reduce corner entry understeer. If we put in too much, however, the vehicle will become dynamically unstable over bumps and under the brakes (toe-out is an unstable condition as we have just seen). Since bump steer curves are typically pretty linear in the first two inches of vertical wheel travel, I have never made more than about sixty thousandths of an inch toe-out at two inches of bump travel work and have seldom run more than about thirty thousandths. Remember that every time that you change castor by a significant amount, you will change the bump steer. The best method is to carry around front bump steer spacers predetermined and marked to give you different curves and play with it as necessary. The difference in spacer height to achieve the magnitude of curve changes that we are talking about is not going to affect static alignment.

62

At the rear we can use toe-in in bump to reduce power oversteer by allowing acceleration squat to point the rear tires toward the inside of the corner and, in straight line acceleration, to allow squat to increase rear wheel toe-in when it is needed and reduce it when you don't want it. Before playing with this feature of your toy, it will pay you to remove the deflection steer that is probably built into it by making considerably stiffer radius rods and making very sure that the forward attach points for the radius rods aren't waving about. When it comes to link stiffness, what we are looking for is maximum sectional moment of inertia, and tube diameter is going to buy you a lot more stiffness with less weight than tube wall thickness. One and one quarter inch O.D. by .049" wall tubing makes very stiff radius rods. The dangers here are getting enough toe-in in bump to either slow the car down, wear the tires or actually cause understeer. I think that you would have to go some to get enough toe-out in droop (it goes along with toe-in in bump) to make the car unstable under the brakes. Before we leave the bump steer bit I will one more time warn the reader not to believe the common misconception—encouraged in print by some people who should know better—that the popular parallel lower link system eliminates rear bump steer. It does nothing of the kind. We switched from reversed wishbones because the parallel links gave more room for inboard rear discs, were easier to manufacture, offered easy adjustment of rear toe-in and were structurally sound. Geometrically they are no different.

ROLL STEER

Roll steer is a pretty complex phenomenon. It is basically the self steering action of any automobile in response to lateral acceleration and consists of slip angle changes due to camber change, toe change and the inertias of the sprung mass. Other than reducing gross weight, cg height and polar moment of inertia to their minimums, eliminating deflection in the suspension and its attachments to the chassis, and adjusting bump steer, there isn't much we can do about it. Figure (32) shows vehicle cornering force vs average tire slip angle. The various aspects of self steering—bump steer, roll steer and deflection steer affect the slope of the lower part of the curve—in other words, the transient period when we are building cornering force. If we were going to operate at a steady state condition in the corner, once the loads were transferred, the wheels had assumed their angles and the

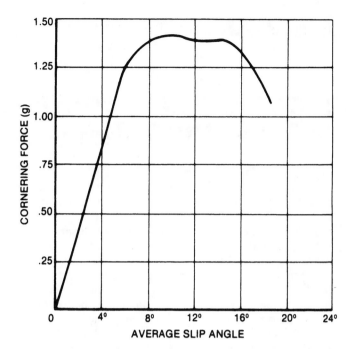

Figure (32): Vehicle cornering force vs average tire slip angle.

tires had assumed their final slip angles, none of the self steering bits would make any difference (until we hit a bump). This has been pointed out in a number of books and is perfectly true. However, the racing car is very seldom in a steady state cornering condition. In the normal racing corner sequence, the car is either decelerating or accelerating almost all of the time and so is in a constant transient state with regard to load transfer and slip angle. Transients are all important to total performance—besides, good transient response makes the car a damned sight easier and more pleasant to drive.

The steering geometry and self steering characteristics of the vehicle have a major influence on the vehicle's transient responses. While it is unlikely that, in anything other than a backyard special or a converted street car, the designer or constructor will have been out to lunch in these areas, it is almost certain that you can get some pretty real performance improvement by stiffening things up and playing around with the bump steer.

CHAPTER SIX

RATES AND RATE CONTROL — SPRINGS AND ANTI-ROLL BARS

In order to make the contact between the tires' contact patches and the track surface as continuous as possible and to avoid shaking the car and/or driver apart, racing cars must have some sort or other of springs. The springs allow the wheels to deflect in reaction to accelerations—i.e., they act as shock absorbers.

When a vehicle is sprung, longitudinal accelerations and load transfers will cause vertical movement of the sprung mass and centrifugal acceleration will cause the sprung mass to roll. Road surface irregularities will cause vertical deflection of the unsprung wheels in relation to the chassis. All of these antics cause the wheels' camber to change in relation to the road surface and, in addition, they cause large amounts of energy to be stored in the springs as they compress. If this stored energy is not damped by some form of shock absorber, the car will proceed down the road like four pogo sticks in loose formation to the immense detriment of both tire adhesion and passenger comfort. We'll worry about shock absorbers later.

The amount of vertical wheel deflection caused by a given acceleration or its resultant load transfer is determined by the wheel's ride rate resistance expressed in pounds of force necessary to cause a deflection of one inch and measured at the wheel centerline. The resistance to the chassis roll caused by a given centrifugal acceleration is determined by the vehicle's roll rate resistance, expressed in pounds of force necessary to resist one degree of roll generation. This force will come from the compression of the outboard springs in roll and from the resistance of the anti-roll bars.

Our treatment of the ride and roll rate subject is going to differ in two respects from usual practice:

(1) We are going to consider that the sprung mass moves and the wheel stays on a level road surface. This is what happens in the majority of real life situations *on the race track*. On a rough road, the passenger car designer will attempt to achieve his ideal of the sprung mass remaining steady at a constant level while the wheels jump up and down in response to bumps and dips. On most race tracks, bumps and road surface irregularities are relatively minor and are, in any case, transient conditions. We have to allow for the worst bump that the individual track has to offer, but these transients are much less significant in terms of lap time than the vehicle's response and reaction to the load transfers caused by the three major accelerations. Obviously the rougher the race track, the more important will be movement of the unsprung mass in reaction to the road surface—it is a lot more serious at Sears Point than at Ontario and becomes critical in Off Road Racing. Technically I suppose that the viewpoint really doesn't matter—but I find it easier to visualize the concepts involved if I assume that the chassis

is doing the moving.

(2) We are not going to consider the resistance rate of the springs themselves except as a factor in the determination of wheel rate and roll rate. Spring rate is just not a valid basis for comparison because the whole resistance picture is dependent upon the mechanical advantage of the wheel over the spring—or the anti-roll bar. You cannot profitably compare the front spring rate of your Ralt Formula Atlantic to that of someone else's March because the mechanical advantages of the spring installations are different. You must compare wheel rates.

THE WHEEL RATE IN RIDE

If we were able to mount the spring directly over the centerline of the tire and we were able to mount it vertically, as in Figure (33), then the wheel rate would be equal to the spring rate. We cannot achieve this due to packaging considerations. The spring must be mounted inboard of the tire centerline, usually by some considerable distance and, nor-

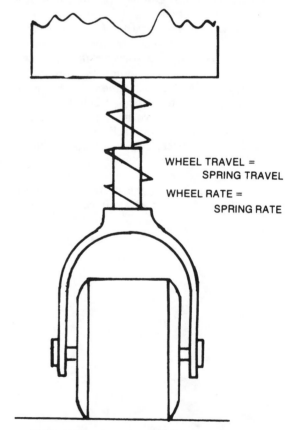

WHEEL TRAVEL = SPRING TRAVEL

WHEEL RATE = SPRING RATE

Figure (33): Wheel rate equal to spring rate.

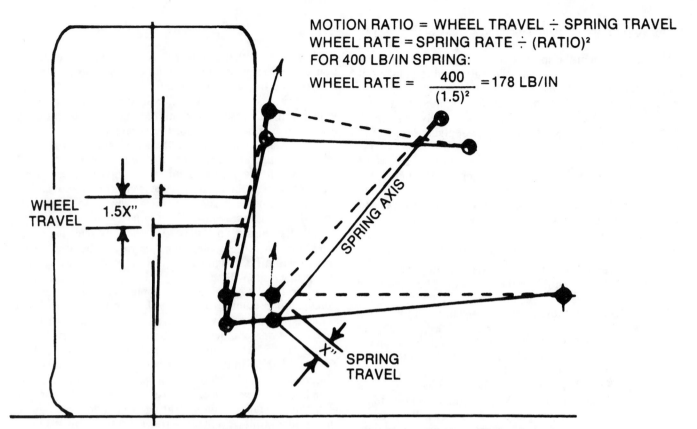

MOTION RATIO = WHEEL TRAVEL ÷ SPRING TRAVEL
WHEEL RATE = SPRING RATE ÷ (RATIO)²
FOR 400 LB/IN SPRING:

$$\text{WHEEL RATE} = \frac{400}{(1.5)^2} = 178 \text{ LB/IN}$$

Figure (34): Wheel rate vs spring rate, conventional layout.

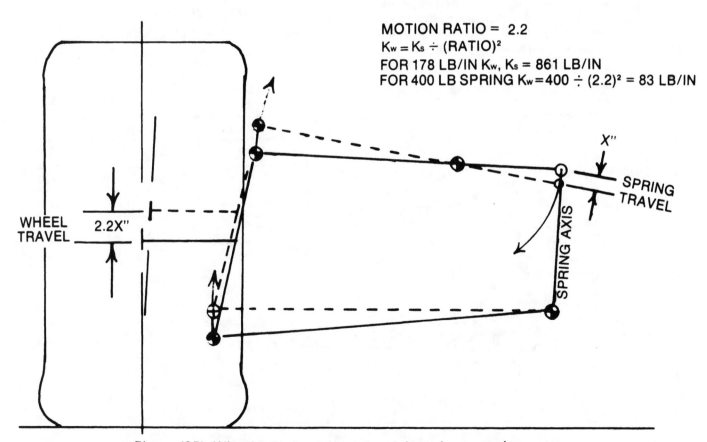

MOTION RATIO = 2.2
$K_w = K_s ÷ (\text{RATIO})^2$
FOR 178 LB/IN K_w, K_s = 861 LB/IN
FOR 400 LB SPRING $K_w = 400 ÷ (2.2)^2 = 83$ LB/IN

Figure (35): Wheel rate vs spring rate—inboard suspension.

65

mally, it must also be inclined at some angle to the vertical. We have two basic choices, illustrated by Figures (34) and (35). We can mount the spring outboard, in the conventional position, with the upper spring pivot attached to main chassis structure and the lower to either the lower wishbone or to the hub carrier or we can mount the spring inboard and actuate it by a rocker arm—which is usually the upper wishbone. In either case, since we are applying leverage to the spring, the wheel rate will be less than the rate of the spring itself and the linear distance traveled by the wheel will always be more than the compression or extension of the spring. The relationship between wheel rate and spring rate is a function of the motion ratio between wheel travel and spring axis travel. The actual formula is:

$$\text{Wheel Rate} = \frac{\text{Spring Rate}}{(\text{Motion Ratio})^2}$$

There are several alternate ways of determining the motion ratio. I measure it—either on the car or on a one half scale layout drawing. Due to the inclination of the spring axis, the motion ratio is not liable to remain constant as the spring compresses. It can be either increasing, Figure (36), or decreasing as in Figure (37). The structurally convenient method of making the top spring eye co-axial with the upper control arm pivot invariably leads to a decrease in wheel rate with increasing wheel travel. Intuitively, we can figure out that this situation is not good. We want the wheel rate to increase slightly as the spring compresses—or at least to remain linear. We achieve this by moving the upper pivot spring outboard and up—as in Figure (36). If this modification is beyond our resources on an existing vehicle, we can achieve the same result with either progressive springs or progressive bump rubbers. We'll cover both of these alternatives when we discuss rising rate suspension.

THE WHEEL RATE IN ROLL

We have seen that chassis roll is restricted by a combination of the compression of the outboard springs due to load transfer and the resistance of anti-roll bar. We need an anti-roll bar because, if the suspension springs are stiff enough to limit roll to our desired maximum, the wheel rate in ride inevitably would be too high for tire compliance.

The physical placement of the suspension springs determines how much roll resistance they will offer. Figure (38) illustrates a single spring mounted at the vehicle centerline. Quite obviously, the roll resistance is effectively zero and the sprung mass is very unstable. If, however, we replace the central spring of Figure (38) with a pair of outboard mounted springs as in Figure (39), then, by selecting spring rates, we can achieve the same ride rate as before, but the springs will offer a high degree of roll resistance as well and the sprung mass will be stable.

Naturally, it's not quite that simple. We don't get all that much spring compression in roll — especially with the amounts of roll that we are prepared to tolerate (from 1 degree to 4 degrees, depending on the type of vehicle we are talking about). At two degrees of roll we are typically talking about something in the neighborhood of 0.6 inches of spring compression—with a 400 lb/inch spring that adds up to 240 pounds of roll resistance. We also want to avoid ending up with roll resistance from the springs which decreases as the sprung mass rolls. Again, as in ride resistance, this is a question of spring axis geometry.

THE ANTI-ROLL BAR

So, even with our very low cg's and our relatively wide track dimensions, we are going to need pretty stiff anti-roll

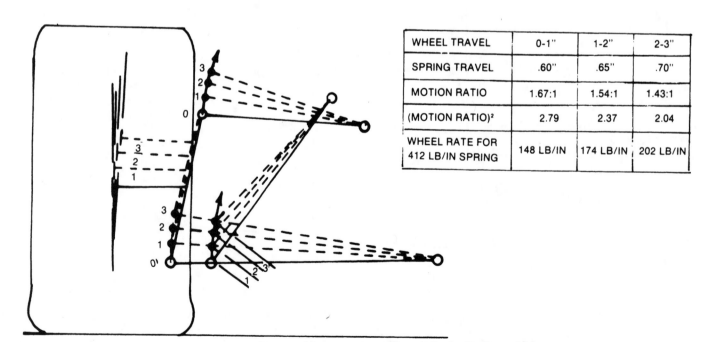

WHEEL TRAVEL	0-1"	1-2"	2-3"
SPRING TRAVEL	.60"	.65"	.70"
MOTION RATIO	1.67:1	1.54:1	1.43:1
(MOTION RATIO)²	2.79	2.37	2.04
WHEEL RATE FOR 412 LB/IN SPRING	148 LB/IN	174 LB/IN	202 LB/IN

Figure (36): Increasing wheel rate due to spring axis geometry.

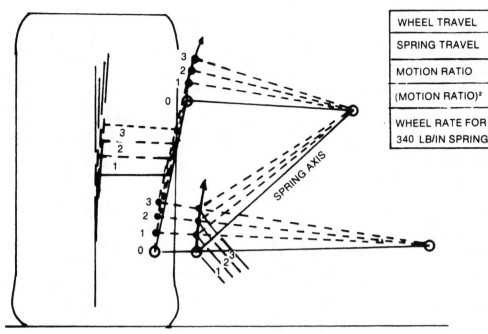

WHEEL TRAVEL	0-1"	1-2"	2-3"
SPRING TRAVEL	.65"	.60"	.55"
MOTION RATIO	1.54:1	1.66:1	1.82:1
(MOTION RATIO)²	2.37	2.78	3.31
WHEEL RATE FOR 340 LB/IN SPRING	148 LB/IN	126 LB/IN	106 LB/IN

Figure (37): Decreasing wheel rate due to spring axis geometry.

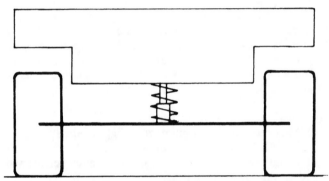

Figure (38): Zero roll resistance from suspension spring.

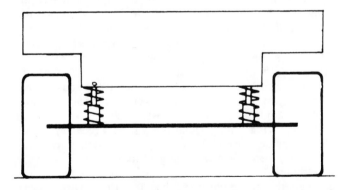

Figure (39): High roll resistance from wide spring base.

bars in order to reduce chassis roll to the limits that we can live with in terms of wheel camber control. The less work we get from the suspension springs in roll resistance, the stiffer our bars must be. Another factor that enters in here is the simple fact that we have no way to dampen the action of the sway bars—the shocks only work when the springs are compressed or extended. The more spring movement we get per degree of chassis roll, the more the rolling forces on the sprung mass will be damped by the shock absorbers. Theoretically, lack of dampening in this area can lead to a condition called "roll rock back" in which the sprung mass oscillates in roll. This would be most disconcerting if it ever happened, but I have never run into it and I have run some pretty fearsome anti-roll bars. With any sane layout, I think that the bars would have to approach the legendary "solid axle conversion kit" dimensions before we got into trouble with lack of dampening in roll.

We can, however, get into trouble with stiff anti-roll bars in other areas. The first consideration comes from the very nature of the bar itself. An anti-roll bar is nothing but a torsion bar which is fixed to the sprung mass but free to rotate in its mounts and connected through a jointed link to the unsprung mass at each side of the car. If both wheels are deflected vertically in the same direction at the same time, as in hitting a bump—or if the unsprung mass moves vertically due to load transfer, the anti-roll bar merely rotates in its mounts. When the sprung mass rolls, the bar resists the roll by an amount directly proportional to the stiffness of the bar and inversely proportional to the length of the arm through which it acts. It also transfers load laterally from the unladen wheel to the laden one—just like compressing the outboard spring does. Unfortunately, when only one wheel is deflected, as in one wheel or diagonal bump, or, perish the thought, hitting a curb, the bar goes into its resistance mode, the two wheels are no longer completely independent and load will be transferred laterally by the bar itself.

This can lead to the situation, on a very bumpy race track, where the car darts and tries to follow the bumps. Again it can be disconcerting but is unliable to happen with anything less than the solid axle conversion kit.

Long before we reach the point where lack of independence or load transfer under bumps becomes a real factor we will achieve the situation where we have too much roll resistance and the car gets very slidy due to the suspension being too stiff in roll and losing its sensitivity.

So anti-roll bars restrict the rolling tendency of the unsprung mass without increasing the ride rate of the suspension, which is good. They also detract from the independence of the suspension and laterally transfer load, both of which are bad but not terribly so. They do one other thing of great interest—they allow us to change the understeer/oversteer balance of the vehicle quickly and easily. If we make the rear anti-roll bar softer, either by lengthening its actuating arm or by decreasing its effective diameter, then relatively less load will be transferred laterally at the rear of the vehicle, the rear wheels will be able to generate more traction and we will achieve reduced oversteer. It's a hell of a lot quicker and easier than changing springs and every bit as valid.

In order to get maximum usage from the bars, we want their links to attach to the suspension as far outboard as we can arrange them. Since the bars and their mounts have a finite weight, we want them as low as we can get them. We have to be careful in two areas here, first that the bars and/or their links cannot contact any of the suspension links during suspension travel and second that we do not end up with linkage geometry that results in a decrease in effective bar resistance with increasing roll. Both of these undesirable results are remarkably easy to achieve. The first results in very sudden breakaway at the end of the car that is affected—the cause is often not as easy to trace as it would seem. The second, decreasing rate roll resistance, gives a sloppy vehicle which doesn't respond to bar changes. There are two possibilities here—either the attach point of the link to the suspension is too far inboard or outboard of the attachment on the bar itself so that the link goes over center as the chassis rolls or the suspension attach point is too far forward or behind the attachment on the bar and the link goes over center in side elevation. We have to watch this last possibility as we adjust the lever arm length of the bar. In either case, a little attention to the basic layout and the use of long links will ensure that the condition does not exist.

TUBULAR ANTI-ROLL BARS

Many years ago we figured out that the center portion of the anti-roll bar contributed nothing but weight to the performance of the vehicle. We then did a bit of stress analysis and determined that there was no structural reason why we couldn't use thin walled tubular bars. No one uses solid bars any more. Most people use either mandrel bent or sand and heat bent mild steel—which is adequate, but only just. I am a lazy coward. I have spent a little bit of time chasing anti-roll bars which yielded due to a high stress level. It was no fun at all—embarrassing because it took me all day to figure out what was happening, and costly because it took several days to make and heat treat proper bars. I now use seamless E 4130 tubing and heat treat them to Rockwell C 34 to C 38—hanging them in an atmospheric oven to minimize distortion. I will never have trouble again—and I get to correct any linkage geometry defects when I make the bars. Some people drill holes in anti-roll bars to make them softer. These people are properly termed idiots and are seldom capable of

figuring out why the bar broke. These same folk are liable to weld the stop that prevents the bar from sliding in its mounts all the way around the tube. This will also cause the tube to break; all that is required is a couple of 1/8-inch tacks—before the bar is heat treated. Like everyone else I mount my sway bars with split aluminum blocks. Since I don't enjoy making the blocks, I normally use a Thompson flanged "Nyliner" for a bearing—they are dirt cheap and don't weigh anything and keep the blocks from wearing out. Speaking of weight, 1/4-inch bore by 5/16-inch shank rod and bearings are plenty strong enough for link and bearings with any reasonable anti-roll bar.

SPRINGS, DESIGN AND MANUFACTURE OF

Springs, when used as such and not as locating devices, don't give us much trouble—their effects sometimes give us trouble, but not the springs themselves—if they are good springs. Good springs are hard to come by. Bad springs are not. Bad springs do lots of things—they yield and they sag and they do not do so evenly. They do not have even loaded heights which makes it difficult to set the corner weight on the car which doesn't matter because when they will yield and sag, the corner weight will change anyway. The car will also lose ride height and suspension travel.

Use no cheap springs. I have tried literally dozens of sources. Good springs come on Eagles, Chevrons and Marches. I now use springs from the Mechanical Spring Division of Rockwell International in Logansport, Indiana. They make perfect springs—but not cheap springs. No matter who makes your springs, you will have to supply the basic parameters and package dimensions. The spring maker needs to know:

(1) Inside diameter of the spring
(2) Maximum and minimum free length of the spring
(3) Length at which the spring will become coil bound
(4) Length of the spring at ride height (loaded height) and load on the spring at that height.
(5) Desired rate of the spring in pounds per inch of compression.

The reason for going through this exercise instead of just stating an I.D., a free length and a rate, is that if you are going to spend the money to obtain good springs, you might just as well make all of the fronts and of the rears to the same load at the same height so that you can change them at the race track without having to put the car back on the scales to re-adjust the corner weight. If the springs are so constructed, you can do just that and the corner weight will not vary more than ten pounds. To arrive at these envelope dimensions, a bit of measuring and calculation will be necessary. First, with the car at ride height, measure the distance from the lower spring perch—in the center of its adjustment—to the top retainer. This will be the loaded height of the spring. Next, jack the car up until the wheel is in the full droop position and remeasure; this dimension will be the minimum free length. Add to this dimension the distance between the present position of the lower perch and its lowest adjustment position and you have the maximum free length that you can live with. Remove the spring and the bump rubber and jack the wheel up until the shock goes metal to metal and measure the distance from spring perch to top retainer and you have the solid stack height for the spring. You can either calculate the load at loaded height, or measure it. To measure the load, simply place the spring over the center of a scale mounted on a press, compress the spring to loaded height and read the load. You probably won't have a setup to do this with but any local spring manufacturer will. A rough calculation can be made by multiplying a known (not assumed) spring rate by the difference between loaded height and free length. It is better to measure. The spring I.D. should give you about .01 to .03 clearance over the adjustable spring perch. Do not try to design the number of coils and spring wire diameter—that is for the spring maker. Note that you want closed and ground ends (if you do—and you should) and that the springs must be pre-set so that they will not sag in service. They must also be shot peened. I tend to avoid plating my springs for two reasons: I am terrified of hydrogen embrittlement—even if they are baked after plating—and it is almost impossible to keep a plated spring looking good—they are diabolical shapes to polish. I paint mine—with a good coat of zinc chromate primer and some nasty spray lacquer that comes off easily for repainting at frequent intervals.

SPRING FREQUENCY

Most of the books on vehicle dynamics tell us that we should be vitally interested in the natural frequency of our springs. I have never figured out why. I will admit that if the natural frequency of the front suspension were equal to that of the rear, the car could get into a pogo stick mode, but with the natural harmonic frequency of the unsprung masses modified by the tire hop frequency and the whole mess dampened by the adjustable shocks, it becomes a real mess to calculate, and the odds against the front and rear ending up at the same harmonic frequency are negligible. I ignore spring frequency. I also ignore the fact that, if the spring or the shock is too stiff, then the tire hop frequency will be undamped and the frequency of the spring and the tire can theoretically combine to cause trouble and the fact that the torsional frequency of the chassis itself must be well above the tire hop frequency—it always is. That's all I have to say about the various frequencies associated with rates—we don't need to know about them.

LAST WORD ON SPRINGS

My last word on springs is to damn the popular practice of letting the coil spring rattle loose when the suspension moves into the droop position. I admit that it makes spring changes easy—and spring design as well—but it allows the suspension to move from full droop to some position of compression without restraint by the spring and the spring will not force the unladen wheel into the droop position—both of which are dumb. If we must carry the weight of the springs around with us, we might as well use the damned things. If, for example, the front wheels happen to be in the droop position because the car is flying through the air, when it eventually lands, we are going to need all of the effective spring force we can get in order to keep from grounding the chassis. If the wheels have to move from full droop upwards for a couple of inches before the springs start to compress and resist the downward motion of the chassis, then either we have to run stiffer springs than we should or we have to run the ride height higher than is necessary. It's not that difficult

to juggle loaded height, free length and spring rate and it is well worth the trouble.

RAISING RATE SUSPENSION

OK, we have seen that the suspension springs exist to keep the chassis off the ground, to absorb road shocks and to restrict roll. They must be soft enough to give good tire compliance, allow both effective damping and sufficient vertical wheel movement to absorb the shocks of road surface irregularities, and they must be stiff enough to keep the chassis off the ground. If we could arrange things so that the vehicle's ride rate would remain soft for the first increment of wheel travel so that we would have good tire compliance and shock absorbing capability under normal conditions and then gradually become stiffer so that greater wheel travel would result in greater resistance and therefore less camber change and ride height change, then we might achieve the best of both worlds with minimum compromise.

A great deal of thought, energy and money has been expended in this direction in the last decade or so—with somewhat confusing results.

The first thing we realized, a very long time ago, is that the black rubber "bump stops," which had been in use forever, existed only to somewhat cushion the blow when you eventually bottomed the suspension. They were there to prevent structural failure and, under no circumstances, could we allow them to come into play while the car was on the race track—they were for off road and curb hitting excursions only. We couldn't even use them on the high banks at Daytona. When you hit the bump rubbers, the wheel rate shot towards infinity and the car went crazy. We all knew that and had known it for years—and some of us, despite advances in bump rubber construction, haven't learned better yet. Progress started with the Aeon Rubber from the Armstrong people. This was a hollow rubber bellows shaped device which fitted over the shock piston rod and had a progressive rate so that when you just kissed it, it didn't do much. But the resistance increased progressively with compression. They were too stiff to be of much use and weren't adjustable for anything but length and even the length wasn't very adjustable because you had to cut off a whole convolution in order to shorten them without destroying the progression characteristics—but they got people thinking. Unknown to most of us, there was a whole range of hardnesses, sizes and progression characteristics available from the factory. Anyway, we played with them and found that we could use them to effectively stiffen up the last 30% or so of vertical wheel travel without going so stiff that sudden oversteer or understeer resulted. However, they were stiff enough so that if you got into them hard under the brakes the car would dart like a mad thing, and you had to avoid touching them in roll. This limited their utility.

About when we got to that point, KONI, in addition to suddenly supplying a shock absorber far superior to anything we had seen before, came out with the silasto bump rubber. Also mounted on the shock piston rod, this little jewel was, and is, totally progressive due to the properties of the elastomer used. The length, and therefore the location, on the wheel travel curve where they come into play, can be varied by the use of a sharp knife or adding more silasto, and both the progression and the total resistance can be varied by

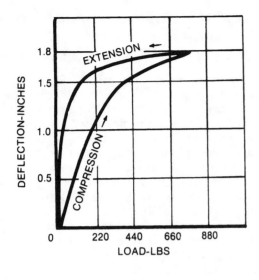

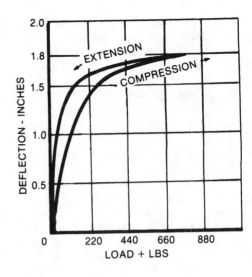

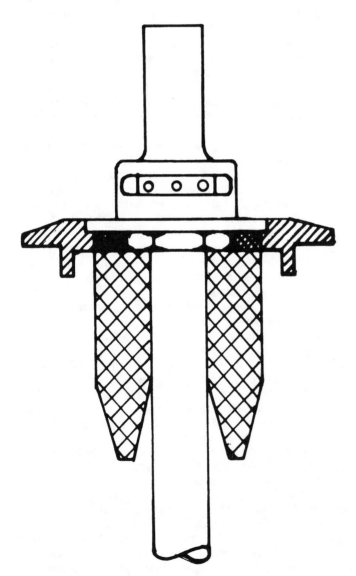

Figure (40): Stock silasto bump rubber load vs deflection curves.

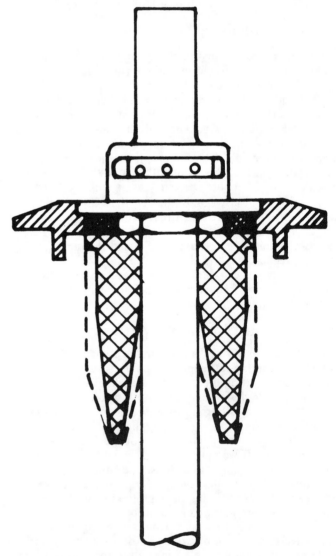

Figure (41): Modified silasto bump rubber load vs deflection curves.

WHEEL TRAVEL	0-1"	1-2"	2-3"
SPRING COMPRESSION	0.80"	0.90"	1.00"
MOTION RATIO	1.25:1	1,11:1	1:1
(MOTION RATIO)^2	1.56	1.23	1
WHEEL RATE WITH LB/IN SPRING	148 LB/IN	187 LB/IN	230 LB/IN

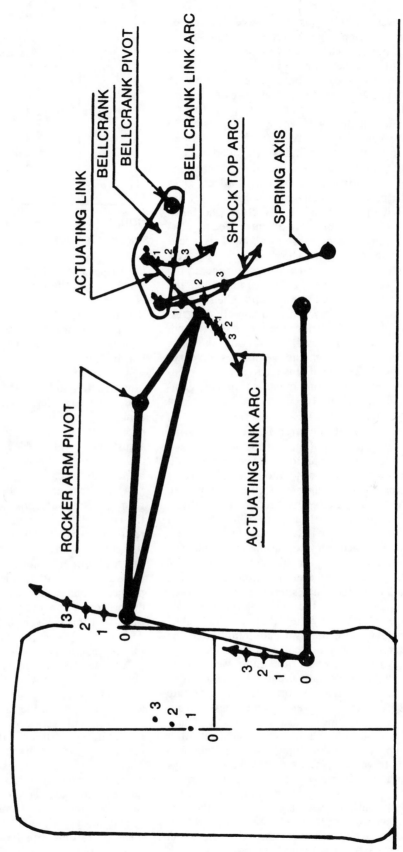

Figure (42): *Mechanical raising rate suspension linkage — inboard spring and shock.*

71

grinding—either the O.D. of the cylinder or the length and angle of the cones. Figures (40) and (41) give an indication of what can be achieved with silastos. Fun—and full of possibilities! Also very cheap. One note of caution—never remove the cone from a silasto—you will lose the progression and end up with a rubber bump stop.

Next someone took a look at motorcycle valve and/or suspension springs and discovered that resistance of the compression spring does not have to be linear. By progressively pitching the coils as the spring is wound, it is possible to create a spring in which the rate increases with compression. We all tried this in various forms and we all found out two things—first that the progression is achieved by progressively collapsing the more tightly wound coils—which gives lumpy steps in the progression curve; second, that they are diabolically difficult to design and manufacture; and third, that the good spring houses weren't really interested in making them in the quantities we were talking about. This forced us to the backyard spring makers who made lousy progressive springs which confused the issue, at least for me, to the point where it just wasn't worth it. Porsche came up with the ultimate solution—in addition to making their racing springs from titanium wire, they achieved smooth progression by taper grinding the wire before the spring was wound. The progression is thus achieved by varying the wire diameter rather than the coil pitch and the progression curve gets smooth and lovely. The method is a trifle on the expensive side, but more and more spring manufacturers are gaining the capability of making this type of spring. I am looking forward to playing with the idea.

Next Gordon Coppuck at McLaren figured out that, if you mount one end or the other of the suspension spring on a bellcrank, you can force the spring to compress further with increasing wheel travel and so can tailor the ride rate vs wheel travel progression to anything your little heart desires. Figures (42) and (43) illustrate two of the many alternatives. Figure (43) also illustrates that it *is* possible to obtain favorable amounts of spring axis travel per inch of wheel travel with inboard suspension. So raising rate linkages, front and rear, simple and complex, blossomed all over the place for a couple of years. And everybody got terribly confused. Car A would be faster than a speeding bullet at Track X. The next week, at Track Y, the car would be a stone—and, despite fiddling with everything that was fiddleable, would remain so. One more time we had complicated the vehicle beyond our capability to deal with it. Let's take a look at the basic dynamics of wheel rates and raising rate.

We are faced with two separate situations—the front of the car and the rear of the car. At the front, the ride rate problem is basically one of preventing the chassis from scraping on the race track under hard braking and of supporting the outside front wheel as the car is pitched into a corner, while keeping the ride height low, still retaining enough suspension travel to negotiate bumps, keeping things soft enough for tire compliance and stiff enough for camber control. Forward load transfer under braking naturally decreases the ride height. If it decreases it enough, then the chassis hits the ground, or, if you have, not very cleverly, installed solid shock spacers to prevent this, the suspension bottoms. In the first case, a nasty grinding noise is produced, the wheels unload, and the brakes lock. In the second case,

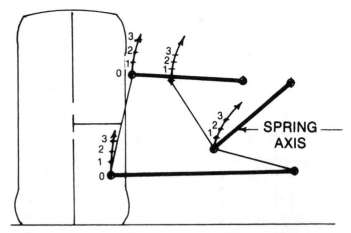

Figure (43): Alternative mechanical raising rate suspension linkage.

the suspension bottoms, the ride rates become infinite, the car darts and the wheels lock when they react into rebound. Neither is good and we would be much better off if none of the above were happening.

The three obvious solutions are: more ride height, stiffer springs or more silasto bump rubber. Only the silasto is a feasible solution.

A mild raising rate suspension linkage will achieve the same result—so long as it is mild enough that the combination of load transfers as the car enters a corner doesn't cause enough wheel rate gain to result in extreme understeer. The raising rate should be kept simple and the curve must be adjustable—preferably without upsetting the alignment of the suspension. This is best achieved by substitution of parts, rather than by changing the length of links.

At the rear an entirely different situation exists. At first glance, raising rate looks good here too. After all, the further the car rolls or the bigger bump that it hits, the more ride resistance we can use—right? Right, BUT—under acceleration, as in exiting a corner, the rearward load transfer compresses the rear springs, causing squat. If the wheel rate increases much while this is happening, we will lose tire compliance which will cause oversteer which will increase in direct proportion to the increase in rear ride rate. I don't think that this is a very brilliant concept.

The combination of raising rate at the front and raising rate at the rear produces an almost unpredictable race car—at least on road circuits. The problem here is that we are not able to determine what the optimum relationship between the front raising rate and the rear raising rate should be at any given point on the race track—let alone for a complete lap. Even with access to a computer and a good programmer, I do not believe that it is practical to attempt to optomize a four-wheel raising rate system for road racing. There are just too many simultaneous variations. If we ever do get the monster set up right, any relative deterioration in the performance of either the front or rear tires will cause the car to become the next thing to undriveable.

This does not mean that the investigation and development of raising rate has screeched to a permanent halt. Sooner or later we will see racing cars with four-wheel independent raising rate suspension, controlled by some form of sensing feedback and integrated so that individual wheel rate, ride height and camber will be kept at their instantaneous optimums. The technology exists. I sincerely hope that I am not around to see it.

For the present, however, I believe that we can best achieve whatever raising rate that we require and can tolerate with a combination of spring axis geometry, progressive springs and progressive bump rubbers without going for the complexity of linkages. The optimum system, at least for those of us who want to race, rather than to pioneer and are not overendowed—either with brilliance or with bucks—is to use a gentle (no more than 20% slope) raising rate at the front with progressive springs and a very gentle (5% slope) setup at the rear—along with a fist full of modified silastos, springs and bars. STICK TO BASICS—at least until you can afford to make large development mistakes from the viewpoints of both time and money.

DETERMINATION OF RATES

I wish that there were hard and fast rules for the determination of optimum wheel rates. To my knowledge, there are none. Optimum wheel rates vary with gross vehicle weight, power to weight ratio, aerodynamic downforce generation, tire width, track characteristics, driver preference and technique and, quite probably, the phase of the moon. My basic system is to run the softest rear springs that will keep the car off the track—and maintain some semblance of camber control—at the ride height that I want to run. I then balance the understeer/oversteer with the front springs—and equal rate front and rear bars. I try to do this in long, medium speed corners so as to simulate steady state conditions and at low enough road speeds so that aerodynamic downforce doesn't confuse the issue (say 60 mph). I would probably use a skid pad if I had access to a good one. This gives the basic front and rear ride rates. I then repeat the performance playing with anti-roll bar stiffness until we arrive at close to optimum roll stiffness. The setup is then modified for actual race track conditions by playing with shocks, silastos and bars to attain the necessary transient response. We'll go into this in more detail when we get to oversteer and understeer, but that is the basic method that works for me.

There are a few do's and don'ts:

(1) Don't change springs in tiny increments—about 10% of wheel rate is a reasonable step.

(2) Don't be afraid to play with silastos and anti-roll bars.

(3) For a rough race track, what we need is wheel travel. You will be far better off if you increase ride height and/or silasto than if you increase the ride rates. If you increase the height much, you will probably have to reset camber.

(4) Once you have established the basic front and rear wheel rates which balance the car, make your spring changes such that the front to rear wheel rate ratio remains constant.

(5) Don't be afraid to try things—that's what testing is for.

(6) Most race tracks don't vary enough to require changes in wheel rates from one to another. Trim the car with the bars and silasto rubbers.

CHAPTER SEVEN

THE SHOCK ABSORBER

THE SHOCK ABSORBER

Sometimes I think that I would have enjoyed racing more in the days of the friction shock. Since you couldn't do anything much to them or with them I would have spent a lot less time being confused.

FUNCTION

We need shock absorbers—even if they do not absorb shocks, which they do not. Springs absorb shocks by compressing in response to vertical accelerations. Shock absorbers dampen the energy which is stored in the springs as the springs compress.

Okay, we'll start over again. The springs exist to ensure that the shock loads caused by load transfers and road bumps are not transmitted to the unsprung mass. The springs perform this function by compressing and allowing the wheels to move in relation to the unsprung mass under the influence of accelerations to either the sprung or unsprung masses. When the spring is compressed, a rather large amount of kinetic energy is stored in the spring. When the force which caused the compression goes away, this stored energy is released and the spring extends with a lot of force. Enough force, in fact, to carry the attached wheel past its ride height position and push it into full droop—the spring will then oscillate at the natural frequency of the unsprung mass. If this oscillation were not dampened, then every time that one or more wheels were displaced vertically, the vehicle would proceed down the road like the previously mentioned four pogo sticks in loose formation—until the energy stored in the springs eventually dissipated itself. This would do terrible things to the tire's compliance with the road—and to the driver, both physically and mentally. The shock absorber was developed to dampen the energy that would cause this bouncing by converting it from kinetic energy, which is hard to get rid of, to thermal energy, or heat, which is relatively easily dissipated into the air stream. Normally this is accomplished by means of a hydraulic damper (only in the U.S.A. is the device referred to as a shock absorber) consisting of a piston which moves in an oil filled cylinder. The piston is attached to the sprung mass by a piston rod and the cylinder is attached to the lower suspension link or to the hub carrier. There is a pivot at each connection. When relative motion occurs between the sprung mass and the unsprung mass the piston is forced through the fluid in the cylinder and, by metering the fluid through suitable orifices, the kinetic energy stored in the spring can be damped before it is transmitted to the sprung mass. The characteristics of the damping action can be controlled by varying the configuration and complexity of the metering orifices.

Shock absorbers are inherently velocity sensitive. The faster the piston moves (or the more vertical acceleration that takes place) the more damping will result. This is due to one of the laws of fluid dynamics which states that a fluid's resistance to flow through any given orifice will increase directly as the square function of flow velocity. The law is immutable but the effects can be varied by spring loaded valves or progressive orifice locations to obtain virtually any "characteristic" desired. The characteristic of any given shock absorber is the term used to describe the relationship between piston velocity and resultant damping force. The characteristic can have any one of three forms. It can be linear, in which case dampening will increase at the same rate as piston velocity; it can be progressive—in which case the damping will increase at a greater rate than piston velocity or, if the damping forces increase at a lesser rate than piston velocity, it can be degressive. Because the shocks are velocity sensitive, they are also load sensitive because the velocity is produced by an acceleration which is composed of force and velocity. At the time of this writing, racing shocks are not position sensitive. In order to maintain desired suspension sensitivity at low displacements, valving is arranged so that little damping takes place at low piston velocities.

TYPES

Shocks fall into two broad categories—double tube and single tube—which are never used terms. The terms in common use are hydraulic for the double tube shock and gas filled for the single tube. For racing use we are talking about KONI, Monroe, Armstrong and SPAX for hydraulic shocks and Bilstein for gas shocks. Miracles are claimed for the Bilstein shock. There are no miracles. What the Bilstein does have going for it is increased piston area which allows very sensitive damping at low displacements and piston velocities and more options for the designer when he is working out the characteristic curve. This is inherent in the design of the gas filled shock and is its only real advantage. It is an important enough advantage that the gas shock will probably replace the hydraulic unit. Gas shocks claim to be self adjusting over a wide range of conditions. This is an advertising corruption of semantics—what they mean is that the manufacturers have built in a progressive characteristic, which can also be done to the hydraulic types. Fade due to frothing of the damping fluid is also reduced (but not eliminated—they still use fluid) in the gas types but formulation of trick silicon based fluids fixes the problem in racing hydraulic shocks.

So what is the disadvantage of the gas filled shocks? There are several, but none that cannot be overcome by design and development. First of all, they are presently non adjustable—totally. Not only are you stuck with the characteristic of the shock as set by the factory but you can change neither the total damping forces nor the ratio of bump to rebound damping. I feel that to attain the same level of competitiveness that we achieve with KONIs, I would have to buy, and carry around, about six sets of Bilsteins. They are also not available, in racing form, with characteristics and damping levels to suit anything larger than Formula Atlantic, and there is no engineering backup on this side of the Atlantic.

It is interesting to note that most of the Formula One Teams use KONIs—a couple Armstrongs, and none—to my knowledge—use gas filled shocks. There must be a clue there. Part of the answer is the constant attendance at Formula One Meetings of the KONI technicians who are ready, willing and able to build shocks with whatever characteristics anyone desires—on the spot. Part of it must also be the superb quality and almost total external adjustability of the KONI.

In this country, the major advantage of using KONIs can be stated in two words—John Zuijdijk. John Z. is the resident engineer at Kensington Products, our friendly KONI importers, and knows more about shock absorbers from the racing vehicle dynamics point of view than anyone I have ever known. If you can talk his language (shock absorbers and vehicle dynamics, not Dutch) he can and will tailor your shocks to suit your requirements. Fortunately this isn't often necessary because KONI has been building racing shocks for a long time and, given vehicle parameters, they know how to valve the shocks. Only when you get to the genius driver level is custom tailoring beneficial—or possible.

All of the above may very well change in the very near future—for the same reason that we got a whole new world in tires a decade and a half ago. Mickey Thompson has come into the racing gas shock business in a big way. He has built the most comprehensive and sensitive shock dynomometer I have ever seen and is busily finding out things that no one else knows. Naturally, he is mainly into Off Road Racing but he is interested in Road and Circle Track Racing as well. His results so far have been nothing short of spectacular—among other things his gas shocks can be made position sensitive and are completely adjustable. Admittedly damping in Off Road Racing just has to be more critical than it is in any other form of racing, but there is a lot of room for improvement in racing shock absorbers as they are today.

PITFALLS

There are a couple of basic things that must be kept in mind with shocks—of any type. First, there must be provision in the length and in the mounting of the shocks for adequate suspension travel. Second, the mechanical advantage of the unit must be such that we get the maximum practical amount of shock displacement per unit of wheel travel. Third, provision must be made for enough air flow to cool the shock. I know that this sounds so basic as to be ridiculous, but the number of times that one or more of these factors gets overlooked is mind boggling. Let's look at them each in turn.

An improperly designed or installed shock can artificially limit either the bump travel or the droop travel of the suspension unit. The results are about equally bad—if somewhat different. If the shock bottoms before full designed bump travel is reached, we will probably break the shock internally. Worse, the wheel rate at that corner instantly raises to infinity and the tire breaks loose. Some fearsome loads are also fed into both the chassis and suspension attachment points. This is not as uncommon as it should be—particularly at the rear of racing cars and at the front of front engined sedans. The number of cars that have been cured of sudden front or rear tire breakaway characteristics by increasing bump travel is incredible. There are several possibilities for error. First is a basic design goof, which is rare. Second is a replacement shock which is too short—less rare. Third is an increase in tire diameter followed by an adjustment to get the ride height back to original specification. This leads to decreased bump travel and increased droop. The fourth, and probably most common, goof is the installation of solid spacers on the shock piston rod in an effort to keep the chassis off the race track. Minimum liveable front wheel travel in bump is 2½ inches, and 3 is a lot better—with more needed at the rear. If the car is scraping hard, you either raise the ride height or increase the wheel rate; you don't decrease wheel travel.

An artificial droop limit, caused by a shock with too short an extended length, means that, at some point in the lateral load transfer process, the unladen wheel is going to be pulled off the road surface by the shock. If this should happen while there is still dynamic load on the tire involved, that end of the car is going to break loose—right now. This is fairly common at the front and is particularly nasty when entering corners. It is less common at the rear where it causes sudden power on oversteer. Other than modifying or replacing the offending shocks, there isn't a lot that can be done about it. If sufficient bump travel is available, it is sometimes possible to cure the situation by substituting longer top shock eyes (KONI stocks at least three lengths). The same effect can be achieved by running with too much droop or rebound adjustment—the shock doesn't let the unladen spring extend as quickly as it should—or by running with springs that have too short a free length so that they rattle loose when the wheel moves into the droop position instead of pushing the wheel down. Three inches of effective droop travel is about right for most classes of road racing.

Since the shock damps by forcing fluid through a series of orifices, it won't work unless the piston is displaced. The more the piston is displaced for a given amount of wheel movement, the better the shock will function, and the more sensitive it will be. Normally we run into trouble in this department only with inboard or rocker arm front suspension designs and then only if the mechanical advantage is great. If the shock manufacturer knows that the shock is going to be mounted with an unfavorable motion ratio, he can compensate to some extent by using larger bore pistons and cylinders—if you have left room. But they have to know about it. It is also quite common with rocker arm suspension to just plain run out of shock travel—which is why so many of them feature shock tops that stick out of otherwise smooth bodywork and funny looking additions to the shock mount at the inboard end of the rocker. These normally become evident after some testing has taken place—mainly because no one ever thinks that race cars require as much suspension movement as they do.

COOLING

Shocks work by converting kinetic energy into thermal energy. In doing so, they get plenty hot. When they get hot, the damping fluid loses viscosity and gets gas bubbles in it and the shocks fade. The thermal energy produced by damping must be dissipated into the airstream. On open wheeled cars with outboard suspension, even with "sports car noses," it is difficult to avoid adequate shock cooling. Inboard suspension requires a cooling duct, which would be no problem except that the typical inboard mounted shock lives in a virtually closed box. It is easy enough to direct air at the shock but difficult to get it out again and achieve a flow. It won't do much good to bring air to the shock if you make no provision to take it away—it takes a lot of air flow to dissipate heat.

Closed bodywork makes things a bit more difficult—but not much. Since the wheel wells should be designed as low pressure areas for aerodynamic reasons, it will only be necessary to make sure that you get air to the shock—it will be naturally drawn out again. If the wheel well is not a low pressure area, you will have to make it one anyway and the shock cooling will follow.

HOW MUCH SHOCK?

If shocks dampen springs and race cars come with adjustable shocks, we must determine how much dampening we want. Too much leads to loss of suspension sensitivity and tire compliance while too little gives a mushy car that floats all over the place. First of all, we figure out that we need more damping force in rebound than we do in bump. This is simply because the bump stroke damps the movement of the unsprung mass which is, by definition, much less than that of the sprung mass and, in addition, doesn't vary much due to dynamic load conditions. The rebound stroke, on the other hand, damps the reaction of the sprung mass to the spring compression which took place during the bump stroke.

The manufacturers are aware of this and they provide more force in rebound than in bump. With non adjustable or single adjustable units, the ratio of bump to rebound forces set at the factory is what you get. With double adjustable shocks—which are the only hydraulic shocks that should be used on a race car—we can vary the relationship between bump and rebound forces. In either case, adjusting the shock does not change the characteristic.

We determine what we can do with the shocks and when they are right by driving the car and by guessing a lot! If the vehicle is underdamped, it will be mushy and will wallow a lot—like a Detroit car with 50,000 miles on it. If it is overdamped it will be choppy and the wheels will patter. What we are aiming for, from a pure spring damping point of view, is enough damping so that the car is quick and responsive with the wheels returning to the track with minimum oscillations and the sprung mass doing a minimum amount of hunting, but not enough damping to cause wheel patter and loss of suspension sensitivity. If that were all there is to the shock absorber story, it would be relatively simple.

THE SHOCK ABSORBER AND LOAD TRANSFER

Damping of the springs is, however, not the whole story.

The shocks also influence load transfer. Actually, they have no effect on the *amount* of load that will be transferred, in either plane, due to a given acceleration or on the *amount* of roll that will be generated by a given cornering force. They do, however, affect the rate at which load is transferred due to spring compression and the time that it takes a given load transfer to effect a change in wheel camber. They also affect wheel camber and tire slip angle by preventing oscillation of the sprung or unsprung masses and attendant camber change. Basically, relatively stiff shocks give rapid response and good transient characteristics—they help the race car to "take its set" quickly. Among the things that we don't need in the racing car is sloppy response to control movement and hunting around as load is transferred. Therefore, all racing cars are overdamped by conventional comfort standards.

PLAYING WITH THE SHOCKS

Different tracks will require different shock adjustments. The ratio of bump to rebound forces usually stays pretty much the same as does the ratio of front to rear damping, but the total amount of damping required changes with the nature of the track—as may the nature of the shock characteristic. This is why KONI attends Grands Prix Races.

While the general layouts of most racing cars are close enough to each other (at least within the two broad classifications of front engined and mid engined cars) to allow the shocks for various makes to be built with identical characteristics and valving, some cars have their own little deficiencies which can be propped up by the application of knowledge and technique with the shock absorbers.

Examples:

Race cars with solid rear axles characteristically display fierce rear axle tramp under hard breaking. For years we attributed this tendency to wind up or rotation of the axle caused by brake torque reaction and we tried all kinds of fixes—ranging from radius rods pivoted at the natural center of axle rotation to horizontally mounted shocks leading forward from the axle—and nothing that we did made much difference. So we ended up running about 80% of the braking effort on the front wheels so that we could maintain control. Finally, by a combination of figuring out that the tramp was a lot less on smooth tracks and by noticing that it was considerably reduced when we happened to be testing with some worn out shocks, we determined that the problem wasn't axle rotation at all but vertical hop caused by too much shock damping at small displacements and low piston velocities. Opening up the low speed leak in the foot valve made a great improvement—allowing us to put a lot more braking effort onto the rear wheels and also improving controllability and corner entry. Overall damping and ride control was reduced, but lap time and driver happiness improved.

The McLaren M8E Can Am Car of several years ago came with very little front wheel droop travel. It also rolled a lot. The bottom line was that, as the car was turned into a corner, the inside front wheel was lifted off the ground by the short shock while it was still laden, resulting in sudden and drastic understeer. The real fix was longer shocks and stiffer sway bars, but just taking almost all of the rebound adjustment off the front shocks made the car driveable until we got the new parts.

The March 76B, 77B & 78B Formula Atlantic Cars' front springs rattle a couple of inches at full droop. This means that there is no spring pressure forcing the inside wheel onto the track as you roll the car into a corner and the resistance of the chock lifts the tire off the ground causing corner entry understeer. Run full soft on rebound and the car will enter corners. You pay for it with a floaty front end, but it is an overall plus. Of course, the real fix would be decent front springs.

I could go on forever, but you get the idea.

TESTING

About the only valid way to learn anything about the effects of shock absorbers on vehicle dynamics is to devote a test day to playing with them. Start out by running full soft and finding out what a wet dish rag feels like—then go full hard and rattle the driver's teeth out. You will very quickly determine that neither extreme is good. Devote the rest of the day to playing with the shocks and experiencing their effect on the car's behavior—particularly with respect to the transient responses. Basically you will find out that, up to the point where the shock makes the suspension too stiff, increasing front bump reduces corner entry understeer and, until the suspension gets so soft that the laden corner falls over, reducing rear bump reduces corner exit oversteer. Too much droop at either end will cause breakaway at that end either by hanging the unladen wheel up in the air or reducing tire compliance. Too little rebound adjustment results in a floating or oscillating car.

Before you go home, run a few laps with one front shock adjusted full soft—first in bump, then in rebound and, finally, in both. Repeat the process with one rear shock. Your driver will then know—and hopefully remember—what a dead shock feels like. Someday his ability to pinpoint a failed shock is going to save a lot of time and confusion.

CHAPTER EIGHT

EXTERNAL AERODYNAMICS

EXTERNAL AERODYNAMICS

From the very beginning, racing car designers have realized the importance of aerodynamic drag to vehicle performance. For the first half century or more, that is all that they realized in the field of aerodynamics. Reducing drag consisted of reducing the cross sectional area of the vehicle to its practical minimum and "streamlining" everything that stuck out in the air to whatever extent was possible. Streamlining was achieved by intuition and eyeball. Most of the efforts at producing all enveloping streamlined body shapes failed because, while the car might be faster in a straight line than its open wheeled rival, it was invariably heavier and usually had all of the roadholding characteristics of a windshield wiper. In the 1960s we began to realize that lift was at least as important as drag and the present era of race car aerodynamics began. Since then we have progressed from spoilers through various wedge shaped bodies to wings with a too brief stop at Jim Hall's now outlawed vacuum cleaner. Today any racer who wants to win must know as much about vehicle aerodynamics as he does about all the other areas of vehicle dynamics. This doesn't mean that we have to be aerodynamicists. You don't have to be capable of designing a gearbox in order to use one intelligently—but you had better understand what it does, how it does it and what the possible performance trade-offs are. To begin with we need an uncharacteristically long list of practical definitions:

FLUID: Webster defines a fluid as "a substance tending to flow or to conform to the shape of its container." This means simply that a fluid is any substance which has little internal friction—i.e., one that will easily yield to pressure. All liquids and all gasses are fluid at any temperature or pressure that interests us. For sure air is a fluid and must inexorably obey all of the laws of fluid mechanics. Just because the internal friction between the particles which comprise the air that we breathe and through which we force our race cars is very low does not mean that there is no pressure present or that the air will behave in the way that we want it to. It will behave in accordance with the laws of fluid mechanics and in no other way. So we had best achieve a basic understanding of those laws.

STATIC PRESSURE is defined as the ambient pressure present within a certain space and is expressed in units of mass related to units of area as in pounds per square inch (psi).

DYNAMIC PRESSURE is defined as one half of the product of the mass density of a fluid times fluid velocity squared. We don't have to know that. We do have to know

that the dynamic pressure of a fluid is proportional to the difference between the undisturbed static pressure present ahead of a body moving through a fluid and the local pressure of the fluid at the point along the body where we are taking the measurement. Dynamic pressure is directly proportional to the local momentum of fluid particles.

STREAMLINE: If a small cross-sectional area of a fluid in motion is colored with something visible (colored smoke in a wind tunnel or dye in a liquid), a single line becomes visible in side elevation. This line is called a streamline and allows visual study of fluid flow. Bodies are miscalled streamlined when they are so shaped that most streamlines passing around the body will do so without crossing each other and without becoming disrupted or dissolved.

LAMINAR FLOW is that state of fluid flow in which the various fluid sheets or streams do not mix with each other. In laminar flow all of the streamlines remain essentially parallel and the relative velocities of the various sheets or streamlines remain steady—although the fluid velocity may be either increasing or decreasing. Laminar flow is what we are always trying to achieve.

TURBULENT FLOW is that state of fluid flow in which the various fluid sheets or streamlines exhibit erratic variations in velocity and do not remain parallel but mix and eddy together. Turbulent flow causes drag.

A common example of laminar and turbulent flow is the behavior of a plume of cigarette smoke in still air. At first the plume will rise smoothly and the smoke will remain in streamlines. Sooner or later the plume gets tired, becomes unstable, and turbulence becomes visible as the streamlines cross and become disrupted.

THE BOUNDARY LAYER is a comparatively thin layer of decelerated fluid adjacent to the surface of a body in motion through a fluid. Friction between the body and the fluid slows the fluid flow from its full external value to effectively zero at the surface of the body. The flow within the boundary layer can be either laminar or turbulent and the layer can be either thin or thick. At the front of a reasonably well shaped body, as the fluid starts to move out of the way, the boundary layer will normally be thin and the flow will be laminar. Internal fluid friction and the friction between the fluid and the body dissipate some of the energy in the fluid and, as the flow moves rearward over the body, the boundary layer will normally thicken and become unstable. If it becomes thick enough, or turbulent enough, or if it must flow into a region of increased pressure, the boundary layer will separate from the body. A common example of this is the flow about a circular cylinder as shown in Figure (44). At the front of the

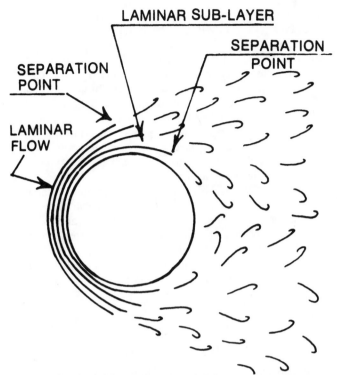

LAMINAR SUB-LAYER

SEPARATION POINT

SEPARATION POINT

LAMINAR FLOW

Figure (44): Flow characteristics within the boundary layer of a cylinder boundary layer thickness vastly exaggerated.

cylinder, the pressure is maximum. As the boundary layer flows over the front towards the top and the bottom of the cylinder, the pressure continuously drops, but past the crests of the cylinder the pressure increases very rapidly. The boundary layer cannot negotiate this "uphill struggle" and separates at or just past the crests to create a high drag separated wake. To varying degrees the same picture holds true for most bodies which are not neatly faired in at the rear.

PRESSURE DIFFERENTIAL is the local pressure at a given point along the surface of a body less the static pressure ahead of the body. Variation of the pressure differential along the surface of a body is referred to as the pressure gradient. A positive pressure gradient—one in which the pressure differential increases in the direction of flow—is termed an adverse pressure gradient and can lead to flow separation.

TOTAL PRESSURE AND THE LAW OF CONSTANT PRESSURE: Bernoulli assures us that, under steady and non viscous conditions, the sum of static pressure and dynamic pressure will remain constant. This explains the generation of pressure induced drag. Both the velocity and the pressure of fluid particles approaching a body reduce. Therefore the static pressure immediately ahead of a body in motion is increased—by the "bow wave," as it were —the fluid is getting ready to get out of the way. In the perfect or ideal condition, a corresponding exchange between static and dynamic pressure would take place at the rear of the body; equilibrium would exist and there would be no pressure induced drag. In the real world, viscous friction, boundary layer deceleration and separation do exist and so the flow pattern around a body

in motion is modified from the ideal state. The deceleration of the fluid particles upon reaching the rear of the body and the corresponding pressure recovery are not complete. The resultant of the increased static pressure ahead of the body and decreased pressure behind it is pressure induced drag.

FLOW SEPARATION originates within the boundary layer and results in a bulk separation of the flow. In simple terms the fluid flow is not able to follow the shape of the body. Boundary layer separation takes place when the frictional shearing forces between the sheets of the boundary layer become too great for the layer to remain attached. This occurs when there is too steep an adverse pressure gradient, too much turbulence within the layer, a rapid change in body shape or when the boundary layer "trips" over a skin joint or a protuberance. It is possible for a boundary layer that has separated to become reattached at some point downstream of the separation point.

Examples of bulk flow separation are wing stall and the large turbulent wake at the rear of blunt bodies. Whenever the flow separates, a notable increase in drag is instantly realized. In the case of wings, stall also produces a dramatic decrease in lift force.

ATTACHED FLOW is the opposite condition to detached flow and is much to be preferred. It is possible for fluid flow to be turbulent but to remain attached. In fact, a laminar boundary layer may separate sooner in an adverse pressure gradient than will a turbulent boundary layer.

DRAG is the retarding force which acts on any body in motion through a fluid. Its action is always parallel to and in the opposite direction from the direction of motion. Drag is due to the transfer of momentum between the body and the fluid and is caused by displacement of the fluid by the body and by friction between the fluid and the body.

PRESSURE DRAG, or PROFILE DRAG is that drag force caused by the displacement of a fluid by a body in motion through that fluid. Fluid arriving at the leading edge of a body causes a positive pressure at the leading edge which resists the motion of the body. As the fluid flow progresses past the leading edge, the pressure rapidly decreases, may become negative for a time, and then slowly increases until flow separation occurs. The pressure in a region of separated flow will be negative and will pull against the forward motion of the body just as the high pressure at the leading edge pushes against it. The sum of these two retarding forces is pressure induced drag and is the major component of total drag for unstreamlined or semi-streamlined bodies—which happen to be the sort of bodies that we will be discussing (with the exception of our wings, which we hope will be more efficient shapes). With streamlined bodies, skin friction drag is normally greater than pressure drag. Even with streamlined bodies, we cannot entirely eliminate pressure drag.

INDUCED DRAG: Induced drag is the drag force produced by a lifting surface as a result of the lift. A wing, in order to produce lift, will necessarily impart momentum to the fluid. This momentum is not recovered and appears as drag. The lift doesn't come free and the greater the lift, the greater the induced drag. We can only hope to induce the minimum amount of drag per unit of lift generated by appropriate design of the lifting surface. The most effective way of minimizing the induced drag of a wing is to increase its span. Nature understands this and has given all of her efficient soaring birds wings of great span. Our sanctioning bodies must also understand since they have decreed that racing car wings be small in span. As a result, the induced drag of racing car wings is their major drag component.

PARASITE DRAG is the drag produced by the friction and pressure caused by the various protuberances on the body such as fasteners, heat exchangers, mirrors, air scoops and the like. Most studies treat skin friction drag as a portion of parasite drag. We will consider it to be separate.

SKIN FRICTION DRAG is the drag force caused by friction between the surface of a body and the fluid through which it moves. Its magnitude is a function of surface finish and of surface area. Strangely enough, skin friction drag is not terribly important in the case of the racing car—but it is really easy to do something about it.

MOMENTUM, defined as mass times velocity, is an indication of the amount of energy that a body in motion can release if it is stopped. Momentum is constantly transferred from a body in motion to the fluid through which it moves—by displacement of fluid in order for the body to pass and by the heat of friction between the body and the fluid. Momentum transferred per unit time is equal to drag. In order for a body to continue moving through a fluid at a constant speed, the lost momentum must be constantly replenished by a power source. In order for the body to accelerate, the power source must produce more thrust than is lost by the transfer of momentum. Otherwise a vehicle will decelerate or an aircraft will lose either velocity or altitude. Momentum is transferred from a body to a fluid by:

(1) The displacement of a certain volume of fluid in the direction of motion and of more fluid in a direction perpendicular to the direction of motion.

(2) The placement of a certain volume of fluid into turbulent or irregular motion.

(3) The containment of a certain volume of fluid in a system of regular vortices.

(4) The generation of heat by friction between the fluid and the body and between fluid sheets moving at differing relative velocities.

VISCOSITY is the molecular resistance which fluid particles exhibit against displacement in relation to each other and with respect to the surface of a body. Most directly this type of resistance presents itself in the form of frictional drag—as a tangental force when fluid moves past the surface of a body. This tangental force is skin friction drag and increases with viscosity. The viscosity of air is, for our purposes, independent of pressure and although it decreases with rising temperature, we shall consider it to be constant.

COMPRESSIBILITY is the quality of a gaseous fluid of reducing in volume as static pressure is increased. In practical terms, liquids are not compressible and gasses are—which is why bubbles in the braking system cause a spongy brake pedal. At vehicle speeds we do not approach

incompressible airflow, so we will not worry about it.

REYNOLDS NUMBER is a dimensionless quantity which varies directly with air speed and size of the body in motion and inversely as fluid density and viscosity. Its chief value lies in enabling fluid mechanicists to predict full scale results from model tests. It has limited practical application within the scope of this chapter.

THE COEFFICIENT OF DRAG is a dimensionless quantity used to compare the drag caused bodies of different shapes It is abbreviated to CD and is obtained by measuring the drag force and dividing it by the dynamic pressure and the reference area.

THE COEFFICIENT OF LIFT is another dimensionless quantity which compares the lift generated by different shapes. It is normally abbreviated Cl and is obtained by measuring the lift force and dividing it by the dynamic pressure and the reference area.

For our purposes we will divide the study of exterior vehicle aerodynamics into three separate but inter-related areas:
Aerodynamic drag
Aerodynamic downforce
Aerodynamic stability

AERODYNAMIC DRAG

At road speed over 100 miles per hour, aerodynamic drag is the most important limiting factor in straight line performance. It is obvious that a reduction in drag will result in the attainment of a higher top speed for the same amount of engine power. Not so obvious, but more important, is the fact that a reduction in aerodynamic drag will also make available a greater power surplus at any speed below the top speed of the vehicle. The greater the power surplus, the greater the rate of acceleration and the lower the all important elapsed time. The basic formula for automotive drag is:

$$\text{Drag (lbs)} = \frac{\text{Drag coeff. x (surface area in feet}^2) \text{ x (Velocity in mph)}^2}{391}$$

To put some real numbers in the formula, let's assume that we are talking about a Formula 5000 car near the end of the back straight at Riverside. The drag coefficient is .65; frontal area is 17 square feet and the car is traveling at 180 mph:

$$\text{Drag} = \frac{(.65) \text{ x } (17 \text{ ft}^2) \text{ x } (180 \text{ mph})^2}{391} = 915 \text{ lb}$$

Unfortunately 915 pounds of drag doesn't mean much to us. We are going to have to translate pounds of drag into the horsepower required to overcome it before the figure becomes meaningful. The formula for drag horsepower is:

$$\text{Drag HP} = \frac{\text{Cd x Frontal area x (Velocity)}^3}{146,600,}$$

Using the same numbers, we now have:

$$\text{Drag HP} = \frac{(.65) \text{ x } (17 \text{ ft})^2 \text{ x } (180 \text{ mph})^3}{146600} = 439 \text{ HP}$$

At first glance it appears that if the engine puts out 560 horsepower, we have 121 horsepower available for acceleration at 180 mph. However, remembering Chapter Three, we have to account for transmission frictional losses, the losses due to the rotating inertia of the engine, drive line and wheels

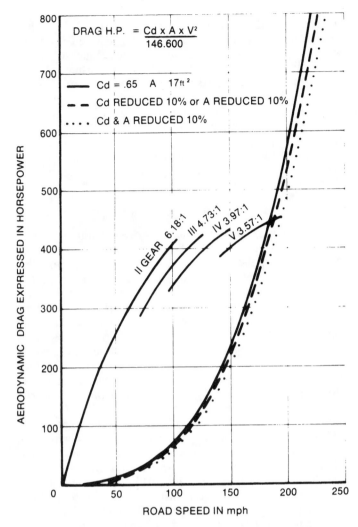

$$\text{DRAG H.P.} = \frac{Cd \times A \times V^2}{146.600}$$

—— Cd = .65 A 17 ft²

– – Cd REDUCED 10% or A REDUCED 10%

···· Cd & A REDUCED 10%

II GEAR 6.18:1 III 4.73:1 IV 3.97:1 V 3.57:1

AERODYNAMIC DRAG EXPRESSED IN HORSEPOWER

ROAD SPEED IN mph

Figure (45): Drag horsepower vs road speed.

and the rolling resistance of the tires. If we assume 5% transmission loss, 6% total rotating inertia loss at this very high roadspeed and correspondingly low rate of acceleration and 60 HP worth of tire rolling resistance, we find that we have available at the rear wheels 439 HP and we have reached the theoretical top speed of the vehicle.

If we plot the road speed of our vehicle vs drag HP at road speed, we will end up with the very steeply rising curve of Figure (45)—the solid line. To illustrate what we are up against, if we were to succeed in reducing either the frontal area of the vehicle or the Cd by 10%—either of which would be very difficult—we would end up with the dashed line in the illustration and if we were able to combine the reductions we would end up with the dotted line. Neither represents an enormous quantitative improvement. This is simply due to the fact that drag horsepower increases with the first power of both Cd and frontal area but as the third power of road speed. In order to gain an increase in top speed of, say, 5%, we will therefore have to decrease frontal area by 5%, improve the Cd by 5% or increase engine power by about 15%. It is most unlikely that anything that you or I can legally do is going to increase a race engine's output by 15%.

If we go one step further and add the net horsepower

available at the rear wheels in each gear to our graph, then the area between the two curves is an indication of the net power available to overcome aerodynamic drag at any road speed. In this case we are conveniently ignoring the fact that the mass of the vehicle itself will resist acceleration—but that's okay—we ignored aerodynamic drag in Chapter Three. It will all come together down the line—I hope. Anyway, looking at the illustrations, it becomes all too apparent that, with any race car, after we pass about eighty miles per hour, the big wall of air that we are trying to push gets a lot bigger—in a hurry—and that anything we can do to reduce the size of the wall is going to pay dividends in lap time from increased accelerative capacity. It also becomes evident just why the ability to come off the fast corners at a greater road speed than the opposition is so critical—at high road speeds we just don't have the reserve thrust available to accelerate hard enough to hide our deficiencies. Let's examine the vehicle drag picture with the objective of trying to improve our lot in life.

FRONTAL AREA

Frontal area is pretty much fixed when the vehicle is designed. Even the designer doesn't have a lot of scope in this region. The package dimensions of wheels and tires, driver, fuel load and engine size pretty much limit what can be done. About the only way that the designer has of further reducing frontal area in the present generation of racing cars is to reduce the track width—and we have seen that there are overwhelming reasons why he should not do that, having to do with cornering power and vehicle balance, except maybe at Indy. We will assume that we are stuck with what we have and, from now on, we will ignore frontal area.

COEFFICIENT OF DRAG

By necessity, most of our efforts at reducing aerodynamic drag must be directed at improving the coefficient of drag. Here, ignoring the internal aerodynamics of the vehicle, which we will consider separately, we have two basic choices—we can improve the basic shape of the vehicle in order to reduce profile drag and/or we can clean up the detail aerodynamics and reduce parasitic drag.

SHAPE

The body shape of the racing car is designed around three separate and conflicting functions. First the body must enclose the various vehicle components, including the driver, to whatever extent the pertinent regulations allow, and it must do so in a practical manner. The panels must be readily detachable for maintenance, they must be light in weight but strong enough to withstand air loads and require a minimum of supporting structure, and the resulting package must be of practical dimensions with minimal overhangs. Second, the final shape must generate as little aerodynamic drag as we can arrange. Third—and perhaps most important, the shape must not generate aerodynamic lift. Indeed, it would be nice if we could arrange for the body itself to generate downforce.

The first thing that we have to realize when considering the basic shape of the racing car is that hypersonic aerodynamics and high speed shapes, with their knife-edged leading edges, are not for us. Those guys are dealing with' compressible flow which is of no interest to us. We need large radiuses and gentle transitions. I am reminded of the first real aerodynamicist I ever worked with—a hypersonic man from an aerospace concern with an indirect interest in a road racing program. After witnessing his first vehicle test, the man said, "We deal in Mach Two and above. You need the man who designed the DC3." He then went away.

The second thing that we must bear in mind is that the racing car—and particularly the mid-engined racing car—does not lend itself to low drag shapes. At the air velocities we are talking about minimum drag requires the familiar "teardrop" shape with a far forward location of the maximum cross section and a very large radius on the leading edge followed by a tapering tail. This would make things difficult for the driver and would leave no room for such auxiliaries as the engine, exhaust system, etc. This is less than tragic as everyone is in the same boat, and really low drag shapes on four-wheeled ground vehicles tend to generate a lot of aerodynamic lift anyway. Any lift generated by the basic body shape will have to be overcome by drag producing downforce generators before we can get down to the job of building traction by downforce.

In order to minimize the generation of lift, we have to accomplish two things. First, we must not allow a high pressure area to form beneath the vehicle and, second, we must prevent the formation of a low pressure area on the top surface. Ideally, we would not allow any of the airflow to pass beneath the vehicle, which would give us a low pressure area on the underside and we would minimize the flow of accelerated air over the top. This would require us to direct as much of the air, which must be displaced somewhere, in order to allow the passage of the vehicle, around the sides as we can. This is pretty easy to achieve with motorcycles and narrow tracked vehicles such as drag cars and land speed record cars. It is not at all easy with cars which are called upon to go around corners and so require wide track widths. We can but try. There are some priorities involved:

The most important thing is to prevent as much of the air flow as possible from passing under the car. This is why we run front air dams on production based cars and why we use skirts on formula cars. We'll get into this subject a little later. Second, since our efforts to minimize the flow over the top of the vehicle are not going to work too well, we must keep that flow attached to the body surface to the maximum extent practical. Separated flow means low pressure, and low pressure on the upper surface means lift as well as drag. Basically this means smooth shapes with minimum obstructions/protuberances and with gentle changes in shape. At the rear we have to face the fact that the flow is going to separate—streamlined tails are just too bulky to be practical.

THE PENETRATION MYTH

For several years now we have heard and seen the term "aerodynamic penetration" applied to the "chisel nosed" configuration which is now almost universal in Formula One and USAC. Penetration may be a valid concept in hypersonic aerodynamics, ballistics and some indoor sports—but not in race car aerodynamics. The chisel nose is effective for several reasons—none of them having to do with penetration. The configuration allows the use of front wings of max-

imum aspect ratio (span divided by chord) and area which means that the wings can generate their required downforce at low angles of attack which reduces the amount of induced drag and makes the downforce more consistent. It also forces the maximum possible percentage of the flow down the sides of the body and offers an increasing surface area to that portion of the flow which does pass over the top—tending to keep the flow attached. Thirdly, it is a very practical, light and elegant shape. Last, it encourages us to place our water and oil heat exchangers in the optimum position for both weight distribution and ducting efficiency. The shape has nothing to do with penetration.

OPEN WHEELS

When looking at a real racing car (one without fenders) the first thing that strikes the eye is those big fat wheels sticking out in the airstream. Instinctively we realize that those things just have to produce an enormous amount of drag and turbulence—particularly since they are rotating. For once, intuition is right—exposed wheels are a big drag. As a point of interest, they also produce a measurable amount of lift. Both USAC and the FIA are absolutely determined (and rightly so) that all Formula Cars shall be open wheeled. Not only do they specifically require that the wheels shall not be enclosed by the "coachwork," but they also specify that any body work ahead of the front wheels shall not extend above the rim of the wheel and can be no more than 59.05 inches in width. Between the front wheels and the rear wheels, body width is restricted to a maximum of 51.18 inches. These wise restrictions make fairing the rear wheels impossible and make effective fairing of the front wheels virtually so. If the vehicle is designed with a front track width of sufficient dimension to achieve competitive cornering power, then a minimum of five inches of each front tire is going to stick out beyond any legal fairing.

For some years, many of the Formula One Teams tried all kinds of partial front wheel fairings while Ferrari, McLaren and Lotus stuck with variations of the chisel nose and front wing set-up. The only "Sports Car Nosed" Formula One Car to achieve any notable success was the Tyrell (four-wheeled version) — which, in the hands of Mssrs. Stewart and Cevert, and under the direction of Ken Tyrell, was enormously successful. Thus encouraged, Tyrell very courageously came up with the six-wheeled car featuring four very small and almost completely faired front wheels. Everyone expected the car to be impossible to drive and to be faster than a speeding bullet in a straight line. It was never fast in a straight line—in fact it was slow. What it did do well, after the front tracks had been somewhat increased, was to turn into slow corners—which is more than most Formula One cars of its day would do. Although it won some races, it was never a super competitive car and has been abandoned. As a matter of fact, in Formula One, the whole narrow track/sports car nose configuration has been abandoned and the entire crop of 1978 cars sport narrow chisel noses, high aspect ratio front wings and relatively wide front tracks.

There are several reasons for this trend—both in Formula One and in USAC racing. First, the front wing generates more consistent (and adjustable) down force than the sports car nose. Second, it encourages a much larger percentage of the displaced air flow to pass down the sides of the vehicle. Third, the designers have found that by extending the chassis/body width to the maximum permissible dimension between the front and rear wheels, not only do they get to place the fuel load and radiators in their optimum positions, but they are able to at least partially reattach the turbulent wake of the front wheels to the side of the body and, to some extent, clean up that area. Fourth, if the bottom of the tub is kept clean and as much air as possible is prevented from flowing under the car, a low pressure area is created beneath the car which can generate considerable downforce at minimum cost in drag—in fact drag may be significantly reduced. The larger the area of the undersurface, the more downforce can be produced—ergo the present generation of wide tubs. It is sort of like Jim Hall's vacuum cleaner without the auxiliary engine—and, of course, with a small fraction of the downforce. If there is a low pressure area under the tub, then the relatively high energy air flowing down the sides will attempt to migrate to the underside. The flexible skirts affixed to the sides of the tubs discourage this migration and maintain the low pressure area. The side skirts are usually complemented by a pair of chevron shaped skirts where the tub widens. These block air from entering the underside of the body.

If Formula One has standardized on the chisel nose, the smaller Formulas—Formula Two, Formula Atlantic and Formula Three—have gone the other way and the narrow track/sports car nose is almost universal. The rationale seems to be that, with their limited horsepower, they need all the help that they can get in the drag department. I disagree and I think that the trend is due to the fact that most of these cars are produced by March—who originated the sports car nose concept and persevered with it long after everyone else in Formula One had given up. The rest of the Small Formula Car Manufacturers seem to copy March. If I were designing a Formula Atlantic Car (and I would love to), it would feature wide tracks, a wide and shallow tub, skirts, a narrow chisel nose, long suspension links—the lot. It would, in fact, be a Mini Formula One Car.

Anyway, there seems to be a general agreement as to what constitutes effective race car aerodynamics in the two major fields of open wheeled racing—Formula One and USAC. The reason that I hold these two groups up as shining examples is that the two formulas have been static for several years and these two areas are where the most money and the best minds are found—so any consensus of opinion is liable to be valid and to point the way for the rest of us. In this business the man who is too proud to copy is doomed to early failure—as is the man who copies something without understanding how whatever he is copying is supposed to work. USAC seems to be about split down the middle on the nose configuration question, with Foyt and Bignotti running low profile sports car noses (Bignotti presently with a wing on top of it) and McLaren, Gurney and Vel's-Parnelli sticking with the chisel nose and wings. There doesn't seem to be anything in it—and if there is any form of racing where drag is super critical, it just has to be USAC Champ Cars.

The general agreement on what works extends to the closed wheel cars as well—the CAN AM cars all look alike and the GT cars all look like Porsches. In GT, the "spook" front air dam is universal where it is allowed (and where a rear wing is allowed to balance the downforce).

I am not going to show a bunch of pictures of various cars to point out the trends. For one thing, unnecessary pictures in books cost money, and I am having quite enough trouble keeping the price of this effort within limits as it is. For another, I hate taking pictures and don't own a camera and, lastly, anyone who buys this book is flat guaranteed to have no shortage of books and magazines with lots of race car pictures. Instead we will describe the points that the designers seem to be in agreement on. They are all discouraging any flow of air under the car. They have all figured out that separation of the boundary layer is going to cause drag—even if it becomes reattached later on. To this end they have gone to some trouble to get rid of bumps and protrusions everywhere on the surface of the car. They have also realized that increasing the total surface area (or wetted area) only increases skin friction drag which is of minor importance when compared with direction of flow and maintenance of laminar flow and so have enclosed the engines and roll over bars, faired in the mirrors and placed vestigal fairings ahead of the rear wheels shaped to start the air moving in the direction that it must go before it gets there, cleaned up the wing mounts and in general done everything that they can to maintain some semblance of laminar flow over the entire vehicle. The days when aerodynamics ended at the roll over bar are gone. The tubs are wide, but they are very low, with a high narrow cockpit sticking out of the middle to house the driver (it is getting to be more and more of an act to get into the things). They are even making sure that the join between the plexiglass windscreen and the fiberglass cowl has no gaps. It all counts.

PARASITE DRAG

It has taken racers almost as long as it took the lightplane industry to get around to worrying about the small increments of drag caused by bumps, protrusions, joints, surface roughness, etc. Here we have a situation analogous to the importance of tiny increments of lap time—or of weight. In all probability we will not be able to measure the difference in performance gained by detail improvements to parasitic drag—it's like saving ounces of weight—but the effect is there, and it is positive. I'm going to harp on this one— everyone is entitled to his hang-ups, and this is one of mine.

The drag produced by, for instance, an exposed bolt head on the nose of your racer is two-fold. There is first the miniscule drag produced by the object itself. Second, and more important, is the fact that the flow will separate at the object and that the turbulent wake produced will propagate at the standard 20 degree included angle of all wakes until the flow reattaches—if it does. This sort of thing can, by lack of thought rather than lack of effort, make very significant differences to the overall drag picture. While the drag coefficient is a valid tool for comparison purposes, it is important for the sake of sanity to think in terms of total drag rather than in terms of coefficient which tends to be pretty meaningless. Figures (46) and (47) give Cd for various types of fasteners and skin joints while Figure (48) tabulates the Cd of a pre World War Two fighter aircraft wing surface in various states of surface finish. If we do a very rough calculation based on the wetted area of a typical small Formula Car at 120 mph we come up with a difference of about 4 drag

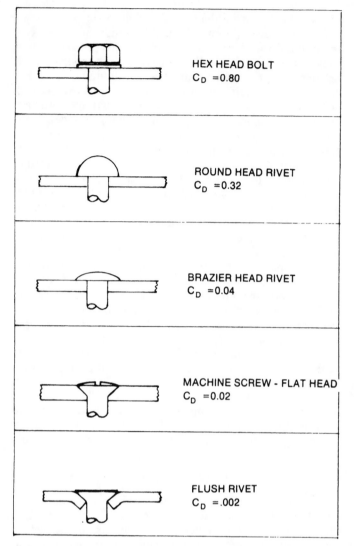

Figure (46): Independent drag coefficients of bolt and rivet heads exposed to airstream

cars with drag coefficients in the 0.35 range. I have never seen one, not even a LeMans car. The reason is simple—if it were that clean it probably wouldn't cool and for sure it wouldn't develop enough downforce to go fast around a corner—and if it won't cool and it won't go around corners, it will not win races. Period.

Formula One and Formula 5000 cars typically have Cds in the .55 to .65 range and they go around race tracks faster than anything the world has ever seen except maybe Mark Donahue's Turbo Panzer. On the other hand, the Porsche 917 (short tailed version) had about 630 horsepower on tap, weighed 2100 pounds with about 14.5 square feet of frontal area and a Cd of 0.45. Yet it was not as fast in terms of lap times on the same circuits as the Formula One cars of its day which had almost 200 horsepower less, about the same surface area and Cds in the 0.6 to 0.7 range. We can assume that the state of vehicle development was almost, if not quite, equal. The level of driver skill was comparable. The power to weight ratios were very similar. So what the hell? The basic answer is that the Formula One Car is a pure projectile—about the only part that does not directly contribute to performance is the fire extinguisher—even the deformable

horsepower between the best condition and the worst condition. In practice it wouldn't be that much—but it would be significant—and wax and elbow grease are cheap.

The most critical areas for attention to detail drag are the forward one third of the body itself plus the forward 30% and all of the underside of the wing. The trick is to delay flow separation to a point as far aft as possible—and one way to do it is to avoid tripping the boundary layer over the joints, rivets, gouges, etc. It doesn't make a lot of sense to spend heavy bucks for an efficient wing, spend more to get a good flow of air to it and then lose a notable percentage of its efficiency by not paying attention to the details of mounts and access holes. Figure (49) applies.

NUMBERS

A flat plate dragged crosswise through the air has a drag coefficient of 1.5. At the same Reynolds number a round tube has a Cd of about 0.60, while aircraft structural teardrop tubing has a Cd of about 0.06! Figure (50) illustrates.

There has always been a lot of talk about "clean" race

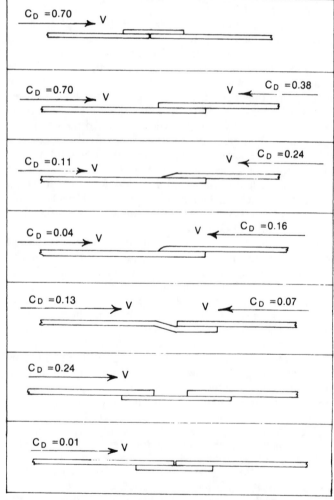

Figure (47): Independent drag coefficient of various sheet metal joints. Sheet thickness is constant.

A. ALL JOINTS FILLED; SURFACE POLISHED
$C_D = 0.0064$

B. SERVICE CONDITION: STANDARD RIVETS & JOINTS, STANDARD CAMOUFLAGE PAINT $C_D = .0083$

C. SERVICE CONDITION AS ABOVE WITH MUD SPLATTERS FROM UNPAVED AIRFIELD (SINGLE TAKEOFF) $C_D = .0122$

Figure (48): Drag coefficients for sub-sonic military aircraft wing at various conditions of smoothness.

structures add to structural rigidity and are aerodynamically effective. On the other hand, the long distance car carries a lot of non-productive auxiliary equipment, either by necessity, as in the lighting and refueling systems, or merely required as in the spare tire and passenger's seat.

Some pretty obvious drag areas are consistently ignored in your typical kit car—the roll over bar for instance. Here we often have a sizable chunk of round tube stuck directly into the airstream 2" above the driver's helmet. Round tube is a very good shape from the point of view of structural strength, but, from a drag view, it produces almost ten times the drag of a faired tube. As a point of interest, the ideal fairing at the air speeds we experience has a thickness to length ratio of 2.781 and is shaped like Figure (50). Why no-one puts fairing discs on the rear wheels (assuming inboard rear brake) is beyond me.

The numbers that we are talking about, assuming that the original designer wasn't terrible, are pretty damned small. So it will not be cost effective to expend great gobs of time and money in this area. On the other hand, if your racer's bodywork ends at the roll over bar, or if it features a lot of blunt objects sticking into the airstream, you can quite probably get some pretty real performance improvement by cleaning things up.

From the drag point of view, the usually neglected underside of the car is almost as important as the part that you can see. It should be smooth and flat—as in belly pan—and the undertray should extend just as far rearward as you can get

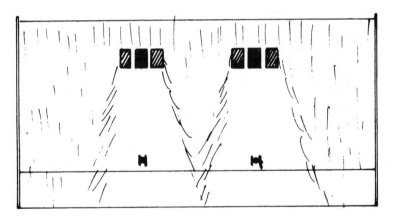

ACCESS HOLES OPEN—APPROX. 20% OF WING AREA INEFFECTIVE

ACCESS HOLES COVERED

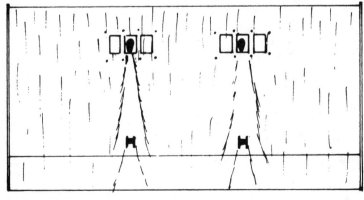

Figure (49): Effect of open and covered access holes on flow pattern evidenced by oil and dirt tracks on underside of wing.

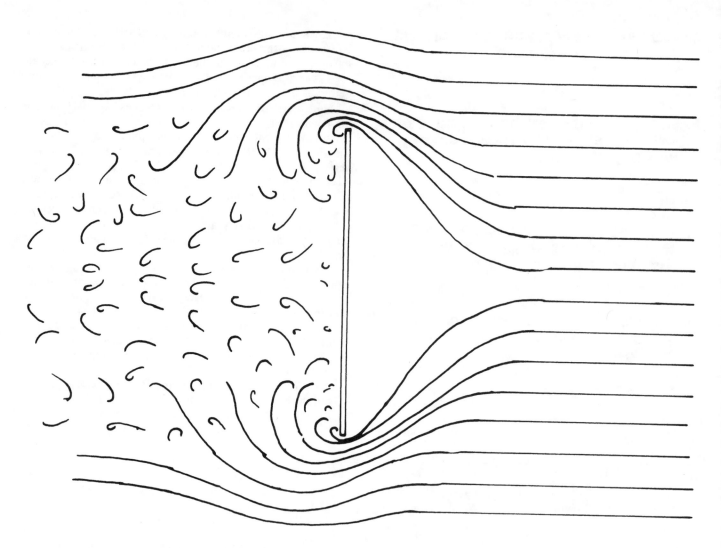

Figure (50a): Flow around a flat plate normal to airstream. Cd-1.5.

Figure (50b): Flow around round tube $C_D = 0.60$

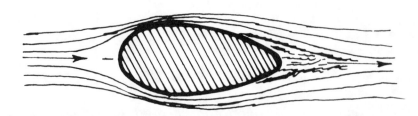

Figure (50c): Flow around streamline tube $C_D = 0.06$

it. One has to be a bit careful when enclosing the engine bay not to end up cooking things. A fearsome amount of heat is radiated from the surface of the engine and the exhaust system. This heat must be dissipated into the airstream. Otherwise vapor lock, melted lines, wires, etc. may plague you. Usually leaving the engine compartment open at the rear and ducting a little air in at the front will eliminate this possibility.

AERODYNAMIC DOWNFORCE

From the time that racing cars first began to travel at speeds in excess of 140 mph or so, the racers realized that the faster the car went, the less stable it became—in a straight line, let alone in corners. Drivers were particularly aware of this state of affairs and, while they didn't like it much, they accepted it as a part of the natural order of things. Designers were aware of the situation as well and compensated for it by building in giant amounts of stable understeer and deliberately designing cars with high polar moments of inertia. This, of course, meant that the cars were reluctant to change direction at all and had to be horsed around by very strong men. It also meant that diabolical understeer was common on slow corners so that the car could be driven at all at high speeds. With the wisdom of hindsight, we now realize that this state of affairs was due to the aerodynamic lifting tendency of the typical automobile body shape—especially if it has been intuitively streamlined. What happens is that, at some value of road speed, the air flowing over the top of the body separates and goes into turbulent flow. This creates a low pressure area over the rear of the car—which then lifts, forcing the rear suspension into droop—it can even come off the ground in exaggerated cases. This naturally unloads the rear tires and we have drastically reduced rear tire cornering potential so that any disturbance to the contact patch will result in instant oversteer which is a dynamically unstable condition. This reduction in rear tire vertical load combines with the adverse effects of aerodynamic drag. At high speed, more thrust is required from the driving tire contact patch which leaves less traction available for cornering. The same situation can occur at the front if air packs under the nose and lifts the front end of the car. It is that simple. The faster the car goes, the more lift a given body shape will generate, and the more unstable the car becomes.

We finally realized that this directional instability was aerodynamic in origin in the late 1950's, and tail fins sprouted all over the place. These worked like the feathers on an arrow and, if they were large enough, improved straight line stability by moving the aerodynamic center of pressure rearward. They did nothing to combat lift, but, to an extent, made the instability less severe. Naturally the condition was more noticeable in Sports racing and GT cars with their enclosed bodies. The open wheeled cars did not generate as much lift simply because they were such dirty shapes to begin with and their body surface areas were considerably less. Finally, in the 1960's, it dawned on us that the problem was one of lift, not of center of pressure and we began to kill the lift with the addition of spoilers. At the front of the car we started with chin spoilers designed to direct the air outwards down the sides of the body rather than allowing it to pack under the nose. At the rear, the spoiler created a high pressure area on the front side and a turbulent low pressure area on the back side with a resultant downforce which combated the natural lift of the body shape. The technique was to stick enough front spoiler on the car to keep the nose on the ground—or at least near enough—and then to balance the car by adjusting the vertical height of the rear spoiler. To our surprise and delight we found that we could run a fair old amount of spoiler without doing a thing to top speed—in fact, it often increased. We also found that, after we had raised the rear spoiler to some given height, it suddenly became critical in terms of top speed—that a very small further upward adjustment could take a couple of hundred rpm off the top end. Next we noticed that, despite the decrease in top speed, very often more spoiler resulted in decreased lap time. About that time the penny dropped and we began to figure out that there was another side to the aerodynamic lift situation. If we could achieve aerodynamic downforce, then we could increase the vertical loads on the tires and so increase both tractive effort and cornering force without adding inertia producing weight to the car. Of course, the generation of downforce does add to both drag and rolling resistance, but the increase in traction and cornering force is worth the penalty.

The first thing that happened was that the spoilers got bigger. Then Jim Hall showed up with a wing on the Chapparal and the present era of winged racing cars began. Naturally it took the rest of us a while to (1) understand what the wing was about and (2) get brave enough to try it—especially when one of Jim's early wings came off in full view of everybody.

Since there were no wing regulations, we attached the wings to the logical place—straight onto the suspension uprights so that the downforce was fed directly onto the tires and did not compress the suspension springs. We also stuck them up as high as our courage allowed us to so that they could operate in clean air. The result, not surprisingly, was a rash of structural failures which were immediately followed by total loss of control and some truly horrendous crashes. The fault, of course, was not in the placement of the wings, but in the detail design of the wings and supporting structures. The F.I.A., realizing that it was not practical to attempt to enforce good structural design, almost followed the usual procedure with anything new and outlawed the wing entirely. Some fancy footwork by the constructors resulted in the present regulations which limit the span and the height of wings and make it mandatory that they be mounted to the sprung mass of the vehicle. Since we can no longer make the wings more effective simply by making them bigger and sticking them higher up into the free air stream, we have been forced to become more clever with wing design.

I suppose that I should mention that there was a period during which quite a few designers were convinced that they could achieve enough aerodynamic downforce by body shape alone without the complication, weight and inherent drag of wings. They found that this was not possible and gave up. This was the era of the wedge shaped body—all of which sprouted wings just as soon as they were proven to be uncompetitive—which was usually the first time that they were raced.

HOW THE WING WORKS

·The racing car wing functions just as the aircraft wing does—with a couple of important differences:

(1) It is mounted upside down so that it produces downforce instead of lift.

(2) By definition it must operate both close to the ground and in air that is, to some extent or other, disturbed by the vehicle's passage through the air and by its closeness to the ground.

(3) We are prevented by regulations from changing the angle of attack while the vehicle is in motion.

Some more definitions are now necessary:

THE ANGLE OF ATTACK of a wing is simply the angle between the plane of the wing and its direction of motion. With the race car wing, if we drop the front of the wing, we will increase its angle of attack and, up until the point at which the wing stalls, we will increase its downforce. Figure (51) illustrates.

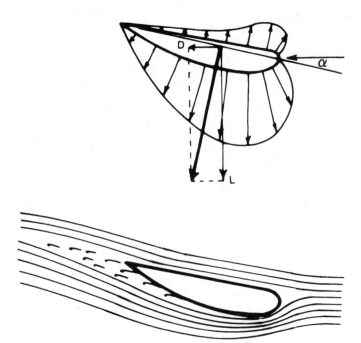

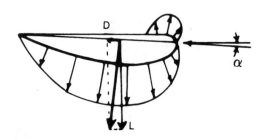

Figure (51a): Pressure vectors, resultant lift and drag vectors and streamlines at low angles of attack.

Figure (51b): Vectors, lift and drag at moderate angles of attack.

STALL: If we continue to increase the angle of attack, at some value, the flow around the wing will separate. When this flow separation becomes critical, we will cease generating more lift but will generate lots more drag. Our aircraft will fall out of the sky and our racing car will drastically slow down or fall off the road. We do not wish to stall our wing. For any given wing, the stall point is a function of both angle of attack and the condition of airflow ahead of the wing.

ASPECT RATIO: The aspect ratio of a wing is defined as the ratio of its span to its chord (span/chord). The higher the aspect ratio, the more efficient the wing will be—as in seagull or soaring aircraft.

LIFT TO DRAG RATIO is the ratio of the lift (or downforce) that a given wing generates at some given airspeed and angle of attack to the total drag produced by the wing under the same conditions. It will not be the ratio of the C_l to the C_d tabulated in any of the NACA airfoil charts because these coefficients are dimensionless indications and the actual performance of a given airfoil is dependent upon the planform and aspect ratio of the actual wing as well as the flow conditions in which it lives.

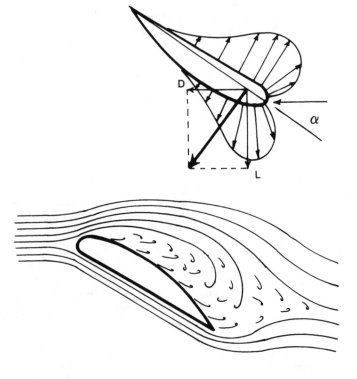

Figure (51c): Pressure vectors, lift/drag and streamlines at high angle of attack—wing stalled.

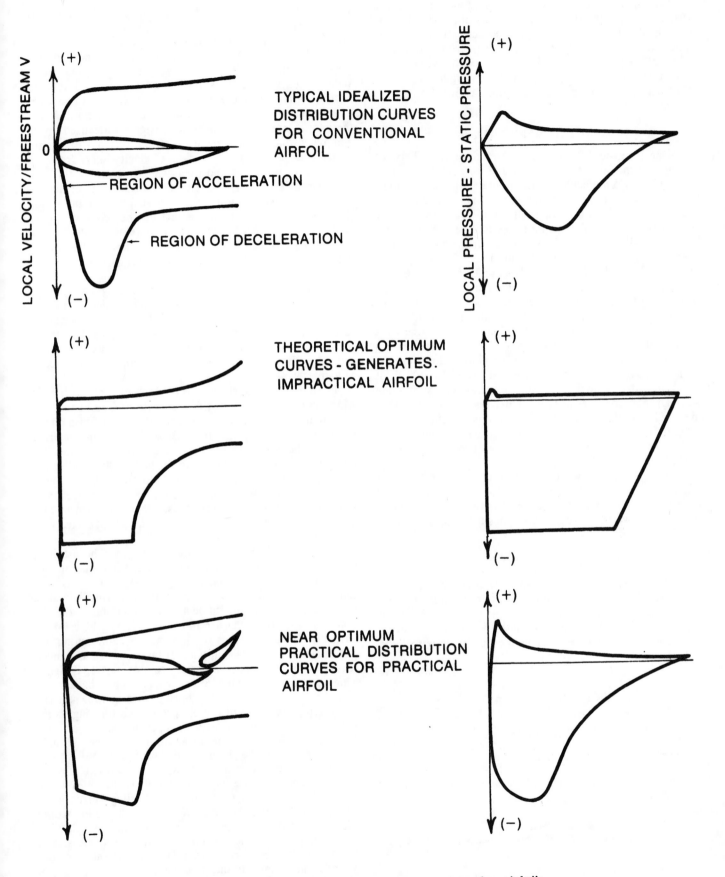

Figure (52): Air velocity and pressure curves for airfoils.

THE CENTER OF LIFT is the point on the chord of a wing, analogous to the center of gravity of a body, through which all of the lift or downforce acts. It is normally located about 1/3 of the distance back from the leading edge of the wing (further aft if a flap is employed). It is of practical interest to us only in that the wing mount should be near to the center of lift to avoid a chordwise rotating moment.

LIFT GENERATION

A wing generates lift due to a pressure differential between the top and the bottom surfaces of the wing. Going back to Figure (50), two molecules of air approaching the wing must arrive at the trailing edge at the same time (nature abhors a vacuum). In order for both particles to reach the trailing edge at the same time, if we arrange for the particle which will pass under the automotive wing (over the aircraft wing) to travel further, whether by shaping the airfoil or by angle of attack, then Mr. Bernoulli tells us that, since the velocity of flow on the undersurface of our wing must be greater than that on the top surface, the pressure under the wing will be less than that over the wing and we will end up with a net downforce. Since Lift = Surface Area x Cl x air density x V^2, the lift generated by a given wing will increase as the square of velocity —i.e., if you have 100 lb of downforce at 80 mph, doubling your road speed will result in 400 lb of downforce at 160 mph. Unfortunately, drag works the same way (Drag = Cdx surf area x air density x V^2). This is an idealized situation, since the flow condition ahead of the automotive wing and/or along its surface is not liable to remain constant over any great range of air speeds, but you get the idea.

Figure (51) also shows idealized differential pressure vectors at high and low angles of attack for a very conventional wing section. You will note that lift acts vertical to the direction of air flow and that drag acts opposite to the direction of air flow.

AIRFOIL DESIGN

A kitchen table section at an angle of attack will generate downforce. It will also generate a lot of drag. An intelligently designed and constructed wing will generate the same amount of lift and a lot less drag. In the beginning, the racers went off in several directions in the actual design of the

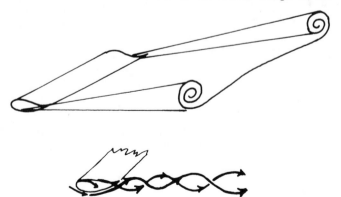

Figure (53): Wing tip vortices.

wings—ranging from very thin section symmetrical airfoils which were originally designed for high subsonic aircraft to airfoils from soaring aircraft, which were a lot closer to what we needed. When Messrs. Robert Liebeck and Bernard Pershing came into the race car wing business, wing design suddenly got very complex indeed and it is now a total waste of time for any of us to attempt to design a competitive wing. These gentlemen start by looking at the flow field in which the wing is expected to function, design an idealized upper and lower wing surface pressure distribution curve to operate under these conditions, generate a velocity curve from the desired pressure curve and then generate a practical airfoil shape from that. Pershing carries things a lot further by designing the wing planform and twist for optimum operation under race car conditions. Just for the hell of it, Figure (52) shows idealized pressure and velocity distribution curves. None of us (or very few) are capable of this type of design so the best that we can hope for is that our wing design is a good one (most of the "Banana" wings are, although they are often deficient in leading edge radius design—one of the objects here being to convince as much of the airflow as possible to go over the top, and another being to generate an optimum pressure curve slope) and then try to make it work as efficiently as possible. In increasing order of difficulty, the ways available to us to increase the efficiency of a given wing are:

(1) Improve the surface finish. Much of the idea behind wing design is to prevent flow separation. One of the best ways to do this is to put a really smooth surface finish on the wing—especially on the front 30% of the wing. Mirror polishing the skin looks neat when the wing is brand new, but doesn't last very long. The best bet is a really good epoxy paint job, truly rubbed out and followed by frequent smoothing with #600 wet or dry paper as the wing becomes sandblasted. Dents, as from rocks, should be filled in with bondo as they occur and the wing should be kept waxed with hard wax.

(2) Get rid of surface protrusions and holes. The last thing to use in wing construction is dome headed rivets because of local flow separation. Considering the skin thickness, you can't cut countersinks, so aluminum skinned wings would be dimpled, flush rivets should be used and they should then be sanded flush. Worse yet are the typical gaping holes found on the underside of wings to allow access to mounting/adjusting bolts. Figure (49) applies. It just doesn't make much sense to spend the money necessary to obtain a well designed wing and then wipe out 15% of its efficiency by careless mounting. The same is true of fairing the mounting stut(s).

(3) Tip plates. One of the big problems with wings is the simple fact that, since the wing operates in a real three dimensional world, the air, in addition to flowing straight chordwise across the wing as we want it to, also flows spanwise—three dimensional flow, with the lower pressure air on the under surface trying to migrate to the top. When it flows off the wing tips, it forms a whirling vortex as illustrated by Figure (53). These vortices produce a lot of drag and some lift. The greater the span of the wing, the relatively less significant will be the effect of the tip vortices. Our wingspans are fixed by regulation. However, the addition of a well designed wing tip and plate can, by reducing the flow around the wing tip from the low pressure to the high pres-

sure areas, significantly increase the effective span of the wing and so improve the actual Cl and decrease the drag as illustrated by Figure (54). Most tip plates, however, are not particularly well designed. The portion above the top surface of the wing is not particularly critical—so long as there is some. The portion that extends below the wing is, however, critical and should extend a minimum of three times the chord thickness below the lower surface. Its effect becomes more important as we move further back so that it is perfectly acceptable to taper it in side elevation as was shown in Figures (15) & (16). Again, since the leading edge of the tip plate is forward facing, it should be generously radiused in plan view. Pershing has done some interesting work in which complex shaping of three dimensional tip plates has been shown to significantly reduce the induced drag of the wing and, by straightening out the flow over the wing surface, increase lift.

(4) Improving the air flow to the wing itself. The smoother or less disturbed the flow field ahead of and surrounding the wing, the more efficient the wing will be. In the case of the rear wing, the whole damned car has a shot at disturbing the air before it reaches the wing. Anything that we can do to improve this flow is going to help—often significantly. Items often at fault here include poorly designed or non-existent engine covers, or air boxes as in Figure (55), exposed rollover bars and the driver's head.

(5) The wing mount itself. There are only two acceptable methods of attaching the wing to the sprung mass—the central blade, which must be carefully shaped and faired into the lower surface of the wing and the extended tip plates. On a full bodied racing car, there is no real choice—we just about have to use the tip plates to mount the thing although structural considerations usually dictate the use of one or more central streamlined tubes to transfer most of the download directly into chassis structure rather than making the bodywork heavy enough to withstand the loads. On open wheeled cars, the auxiliary structure necessary to mount the wing by tip plates is heavy enough to cause second thoughts, although the method is fast becoming more popular. Structurally, tip plate mounts are easier to design and fabricate, but I believe that the central blade is lighter. In either case, angle of attack adjustment should pivot the wing about its trailing edge so that it remains at legal maximum height as it is adjusted.

THE FLAP AS A LIFT PRODUCING DEVICE

In aircraft, flaps and leading edge slots are used to allow the generation of very high lift forces at high angles of attack and low airspeed—as in landing and taking off—and to increase wing area under those critical conditions. Most of the present generation of race cars' wings are two-element wings which use a flap for somewhat different reasons. In this case the flap allows us to generate more lift at a lower main plane angle of attack and consequently less drag than would be necessary with a single element wing and also to generate more lift at low airspeeds than a single plane wing. As usual, it's not that simple and a great deal of attention must be paid to the geometry of the slot between the main plane and the flap. Most of what we see consists of two airfoils as in Figure (56a) which may not be as efficient at different flap settings as the set-up of Figure (56b). The former is, of course, much

easier to fabricate and that accounts for its popularity. Contrary to popular opinion, a well designed flap, with good slot geometry, will generate less drag for a given amount of downforce than a single element wing—simply because the main plane can be run at a much reduced angle of attack and, with a well designed gap, can reduce flow separation at the trailing edge of the flap.

INDY ANGLE IRON

Some years ago, all of the race car wings suddenly sprouted pieces of extruded aluminum angle at the trailing edge. It was a case of monkey see, monkey do. The works Eagles started it, and they were very fast indeed, so everyone copied and the cars went faster. Basically what happens here, Figure (57), is that the angle creates a low pressure behind itself which serves to accelerate the air from the under surface of the wing and so delay separation and increase the pressure differential. So long as the height of the angle is kept very low (1/4" is about maximum—regardless of what you may see on some cars) there is no significant increase in drag. Of course, the more inefficient the wing design, the higher the piece of angle that can be used. It is of some importance that the angle not form a ledge on the underside of the wing surface as this will obviate the desired result.

CANTILEVERED WINGS

Our grasp of first principles is not always what it should be. Until 1973 our rear wings sat directly over the rear wheels. Then Colin Chapman figured out that, if he cantilevered the wing well behind the rear wheels it would operate through a lever arm, would push down harder on the tires, would be operating in much cleaner air, and would have a vastly greater amount of clear space beneath the all important lower surface. This means that we can produce more downforce at lower angles of attack and so significantly reduce drag. Naturally, as illustrated in Figure (58) there is a penalty. Like a seesaw, a lifting force is applied to the front wheels. However, this is quite simply cancelled by increasing the downforce generated by the front of the vehicle. The significant improvement here is probably gained not so much from the increased downforce from cantilevering but from placing the wing in a much more favorable environment and reducing drag by reducing angle of attack. Wings just don't work terribly well unless there is good airflow underneath them which is difficult to arrange when they are directly over and necessarily close to the main body of the car.

PROBLEMS ASSOCIATED WITH AERODYNAMIC DOWNFORCE

It is perfectly true that the downforce generated by the modern racing car is probably the most significant single factor in the enormous decrease in lap times evident in the last decade. We have seen that the downforce is somewhat of a mixed blessing because of the increased drag produced by the generation of downforce. Naturally, a great deal of the designer/developer's time must be and is spent in trying to achieve minimum drag for maximum downforce. A lot of his time is also spent trying to figure out how much is optimum in the downforce department. We have come a long way.

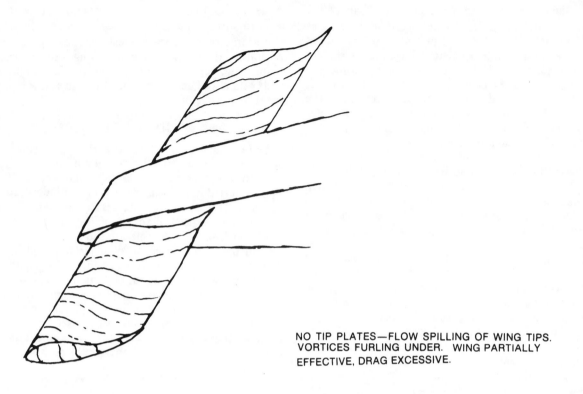

NO TIP PLATES—FLOW SPILLING OF WING TIPS.
VORTICES FURLING UNDER. WING PARTIALLY
EFFECTIVE, DRAG EXCESSIVE.

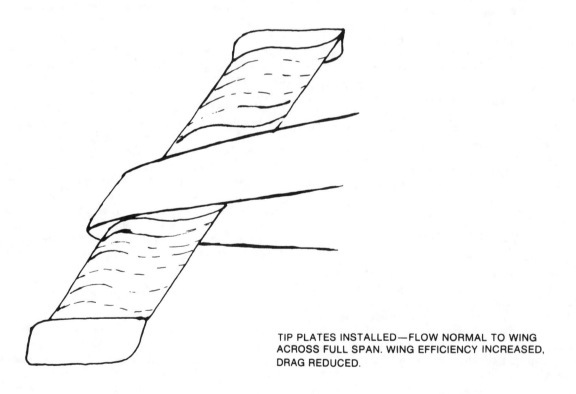

TIP PLATES INSTALLED—FLOW NORMAL TO WING
ACROSS FULL SPAN. WING EFFICIENCY INCREASED,
DRAG REDUCED.

Figure (54): Effect of tip plates on flow pattern of front wing—evidenced by oil and dirt tracks.

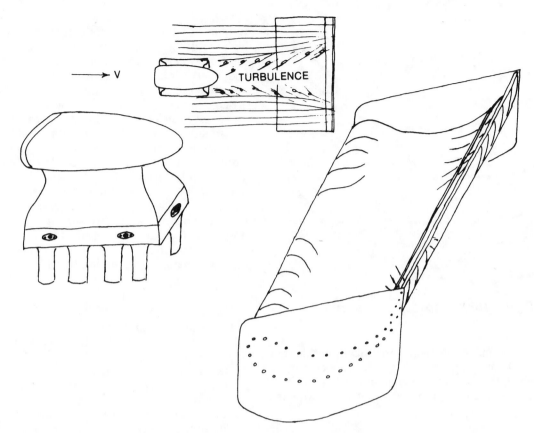

Figure (54): Airflow pattern of rear wing due to poor streamlining of engine.

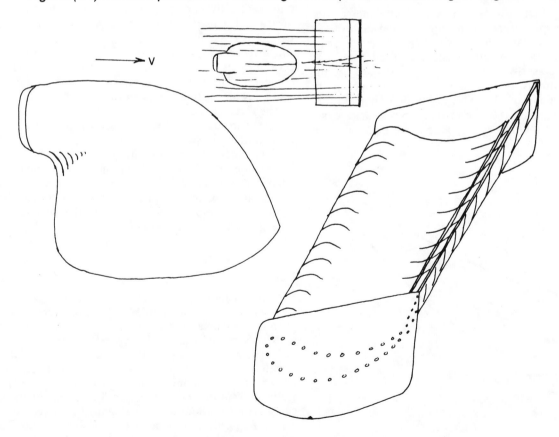

Figure (55): Airflow pattern of rear wing with well streamlined engine cover.

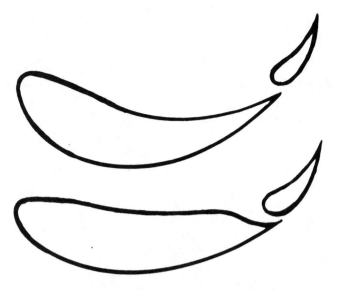

Figure (56): Flap slot geometry.

However, optimum aerodynamic efficiency is not the end of the downforce question. Two other factors are even more crucial—keeping the downforce balanced between the front and the rear wheels and figuring out what to do with the downforce.

DOWNFORCE BALANCE

We have seen that downforce increases with the square power of vehicle speed. Since both wing area and angle of attack are fixed, it would seem that the ratio of front to rear downforce would then remain constant as road speed increases. Not necessarily! The front wings, or nose lip, or whatever, will always, in the absence of traffic, operate in clean or unturbulent air. The flow separation point on the race car body will, however, invariably move forward as speed increases so the rear wing will be operating in a more

Figure (57): Indy angle iron.

turbulent environment than the front at high speeds. Also at high speeds the download will reduce the ground clearance of the front wings which may further increase their download and create aerodynamic oversteer. High speed oversteer is a condition which we fervently wish to avoid, so we must arrange things so that the rear downforce increases with increasing vehicle speed at a slightly greater rate than that of the front downforce. The nature of the airflow works against us and the greater relative rear wing area and cantilever works for us. Depending on vehicle configuration, we can also make the low pressure area beneath the car work for us in this area. Since the front of the chisel nosed car is narrow and the rear is wide, we get more rear downforce, assuming that we maintain the low pressure area, than we do front. If it works well enough, we can significantly reduce the angle of attack or the area of the rear wing. This is about the only case of something for nothing that I know of in motor racing.

GROUND EFFECT

The term "ground effects" is usually used to point out the differences in the aerodynamic behavior between bodies operating in close proximity to the ground and those operating in clear air. There are many factors and differences. We really don't have to worry about most of them because we never operate in clear air. Two possibilities do, however, bear some thinking about. The first is the possibility of the race car doing a gainer and flipping over on its back as it crests the brow of a hill. This is a real possibility only with fully bodied cars on which the underside of the nose area is closed—which isn't a good idea anyway. In this case, it is possible for enough air to pack under the nose to flip the car with no warning whatsoever. It has happened several times in Can Am Racing and nothing good has ever come of it. The underside of the nose must be open!—it gives more downforce that way, anyway.

The second possibility, with some configurations of "sports car noses" and with wings which are mounted very close to the ground, is that at high road speeds and low ride heights, the front can "grab the ground" and virtually lock in the down position. I really don't know what to do about that. I have never run into it, but other people have, and about all that I can think of for a quick fix is less front downforce and more front bump rubber. Obviously the only real fix is a redesign of the offending item.

AERODYNAMIC STABILITY AND
THE CENTER OF PRESSURE

A few pages ago we briefly mentioned straight line stability and the aerodynamic center of pressure. I should explain in more detail and since the question is vaguely related to downforce balance, this is as good a place to do so as any. The center of pressure of the vehicle is that point in side elevation at which the side gust reactions will act—it is sort of like an aerodynamic cg. In order to achieve aerodynamic yaw stability, this point must be located aft of the vehicle cg—it is a situation much analogous to the feathers on an arrow. Regardless of the idiot Detroit/Nader ad of a decade ago—for straight line stability it doesn't matter a damn whether an arrowhead is made of stone or of light alloy—

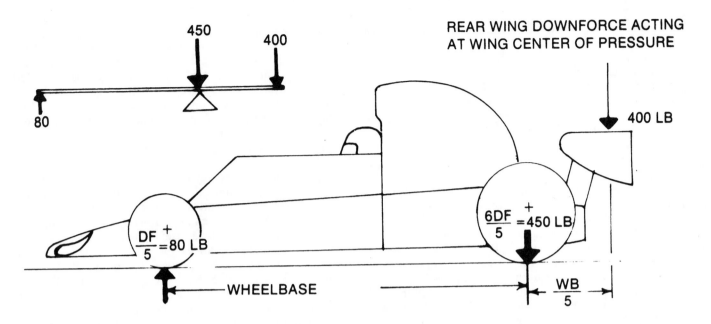

450   400

80

$\frac{DF}{5}+=80\ LB$

$\frac{6DF}{5}+=450\ LB$

400 LB

WHEELBASE

$\frac{WB}{5}$

Figure (58): Cantilevered rear wing producing rear tire aerodynamic load in excess of actual wing downforce with attendant front tire upward load.

and it doesn't matter where the engine in the car is located— so long as the feathers on the arrow and the center of pressure on the vehicle are located aft of the cg. When a side wind gust hits the car, or when the car gets sideways and starts to operate at a yaw angle to the airstream, we really want its action to be self correcting. A rear located center of pressure does this all by itself. Yes—the wing side plates do count as area in this case and, along with the airbox, virtually guarantees that the center of pressure location will be favorable in the modern mid-engined race car. And, no, the late and unlamented tail fins on U.S. passenger cars weren't, even at their worst, big enough to make any real difference. However, the tail fins on D type Jags and the LeMans Bristols were functional. This is another of those things that are calculable but not worth calculating. We must remember that aerodynamic stability is only a part of the overall stability picture. The tires still do most of the work and that is why a balanced front to rear downforce ratio is so critical to the handling of the vehicle.

DOWNFORCE AND SPRING COMPRESSION

The major problem with downforce stems from the relationship between downforce and vehicle speed. Most road racing corners are in the 50 to 100 mph speed range with very few corners over 140 mph—and they are getting fewer with each passing year. We can very easily generate more downforce than we can use—in two ways. Obviously, since downforce costs drag, we must somewhere on the downforce generation curve reach a point where any further increase in downforce will be more than cancelled out by the resultant increase in drag and our lap times will be slower. Finding out where this point is, for any given track, is a question of keeping records from past races and testing and of playing with it during practice. Not so obvious is the fact that we can stick our car so hard to the race track with the wings that it loses its agility—it won't dance—becomes un-

responsive and sluggish. With state of the art wings, we can achieve this condition long before the wings stall. The trouble is that a car in this condition is liable to feel really secure to the driver and so he may not recognize the condition. Another reason for playing with downforce.

However, the main problem with downforce is that downforce compresses the suspension springs. This does two things—both bad. It reduces available suspension travel and suspension sensitivity, and it changes tire camber. Now this is no great problem at Ontario Motor Speedway where the maximum straightaway speed is probably around 220 mph and the minimum turn speed is about 185.—and the track is smooth as the proverbial baby's bum. We just figure out where the ride height is going to be in the corners and design the suspension around that ride height. The downforce at the end of the straight will be about 1/2 again that in the corners but it really isn't going to affect anything much so long as we put enough ride height into the car so that it doesn't scrape, allow enough suspension movement and design the camber curves to suit. It would be better if the downforce and the drag could remain constant—but it can't because we are not allowed to trim the angle of attack of the wing while the car is in motion and that is that—all we have to do is to figure out, by experimentation, what the optimum amount of downforce for lap times is and balance the car at that figure. Of course the front end gets all buffety and funny in traffic, but the driver has to cope with that.

On your typical road racing circuit, however, we have a different situation. If we were to spring our Can Am Car as softly as we would like to, the resultant change in ride height between 60 mph and 180 mph could be as much as two inches—this would mean a dangerous lack of available bump travel at high speed and either too much positive camber at low speed or too much negative at high speed. Accordingly, we have gone to stiffer springs than we would really like (more wing, more spring) and we have loaded the vehicle camber curves to keep the tires upright in vertical travel direction. This is why we can't just stick a wing onto a car that was designed to work without one and expect good results—the camber curves will be wrong and we will have to go to ridiculous springs to compensate.

What we really need, of course, is wings, or other downforce generators which work better at relatively low speeds than they do at high speed—without increasing the Cd as they start working less well. We have known that for a long time and we are working towards it. Without being able to trim the angle of attack, it's a bit difficult, but we are making some progress. Since we caught on to using the low pressure air under the car to generate some of the downforce, we have been able to reduce the wing size and get rid of some induced drag—the low pressure area under the car doesn't seem to produce much drag and it may, in fact, reduce it. The super sophisticated wing shapes produce more downforce at low speed than the old ones did and so, again, we are able to reduce either wing area or angle of attack and keep the same total downforce. We have all thought of terribly clever ways to cheat on the fixed angle of attack bit, but, to my knowledge, no one has yet come up with an effective method that is not going to get him instantly caught.

WING CONSTRUCTION

Actual wing unit loadings are not excessively high—no more than 0.8 lb/square inch. If the wing and its mount are strong and rigid enough that the vehicle can be pushed by the corner of the rear wing, then it is strong enough. This means that you can make the wing really light—and you had damned well better, because it is just about the highest point of the car and is cantilevered out the back like a trailer. If you should happen to decide to build your own wings, and should luck into someone capable of designing a sophisticated wing, you are very quickly going to discover that the tolerances in some areas, like the leading edge radius, the transition from the radius to the roof and to the floor and the flap gap geometry get very critical for sheet metal work—especially on a one off basis. Bernie Pershing's wings work like gangbusters, but they are diabolical to build—in aluminum. But there is another way—lighter, more accurate, cheaper and infinitely messier.

The men who build experimental private aircraft are very clever indeed—some of them. Probably the most clever of them is a guy named Burt Rutan who has designed and built two very advanced aircraft called the Vari-Viggen and Vari-Eze. The whole thing is made from cores (both solid and hollow) of closed cell rigid polyurethane foam in 2 lb/cubic foot density and covered with unidirectional fiberglass cloth (2 layers layed up at 45 degrees from the long axis of the part and saturated with special epoxy resins. This forms a true monocoque structure of unbelievable strength, rigidity and, particularly if the core is hollow, lightness. The foam core can be very readily shaped with great accuracy by using a hot wire between rigid templates and achieving twist in a wing is no problem. The glass layup is by hand and messy and the desired surface finish is achieved by the use of microballoons and resin which is also messy. There have been some articles in AIR PROGRESS, the EAA probably has some literature available, and there is a useful, but not very detailed pamphlet entitled "Foam, Fabric and Plastic in Aircraft Construction" by Lou Sauve, available for about $2.50 from *Aircraft Spruce and Specialty Company*, P.O. Box 424, Fullerton, California. They also stock the foam, unidirectional cloth and epoxy resins—all specially formulated by Rutan to do the job. If and when I have to start making wings again, that's the road I'm going to take—it just takes too long and costs too much to make alloy experimental wings.

We've spent a lot of time in this investigation of vehicle aerodynamics and, hopefully, we've learned a bit. The trouble is that aerodynamic knowledge is difficult to apply unless you happen to be a major racing team. The design of a sophisticated wing is beyond almost all of us and just its construction is a major effort. Very few readers are ever going to make a new body for their racer. However, belly pans, side skirts, wing end plates and various fairings are within virtually anyone's abilities and resources. The use of foam and shurform files to make fiberglass moulds has opened up whole new worlds. For testing there is nothing like foam fairings and non-structural shapes covered with model airplane heat shrink skin. You can find out a lot about detail aerodynamics by testing without spending money—kerosene and lampblack or kerosene and whatever color water color powder will show up against your bodywork will tell a whole bunch and any drag strip or big parking lot will let you do it.

The basics are deceptively simple—keep the airflow from going under the car, deflect as much as possible around the sides, keep the flow laminar and attached for as long as possible, use big radius on forward facing edges, and don't let anything stick out that doesn't have to. Good luck!

CHAPTER NINE

COOLING AND INTERNAL AERODYNAMICS

COOLING AND INTERNAL AERODYNAMICS

The very first priority in the design of any racing car should be the provision of adequate engine cooling. If the car won't cool it cannot be driven long enough to find out if it is capable of doing anything else. Further, the entire budget will soon be consumed in the rebuilding of cooked engines. We run into two problems here—one having to do with human nature and the other with geography and the seasons. The first is that cooling provisions, for reasons which escape me, tend to be both afterthoughts and underestimates. The second is that most of our racing cars are designed to be run in England which is a relatively cool Island and are tested in the early spring when it is just downright cold. This last bit is also true of U.S. made racers. The car whose oil and water temperatures stabilize at 85° C. at Snetterton in March is very likely to be pronounced satisfactory and released for production. Doubtless this is due to the euphoria which often clouds early testing—on both sides of the Atlantic. Since engine temperatures enjoy virtually a one-for-one relationship with the ambient temperature, this optimism is going to be of very little comfort to the customer on a nice hot day at Riverside. Touring and GT car cooling packages are usually designed around far less horsepower than the race car puts out.

The internal combustion engine is thermally inefficient. Woefully so. Depending on engine design, between 15% and 30% of the total heat of combustion must be dissipated to the airstream via the oil and the water (or air). This is one hell of a lot of heat. By the way, don't assume that the engines are 70-85% thermally efficient—most of the rest of the heat goes out the exhaust or is radiated. Getting rid of it involves the use of heavy, bulky and expensive heat exchanges and plumbing lines. The heat exchangers are very liable to be vulnerable, and they are going to cost us a significant amount of aerodynamic drag. Both the weight and the drag penalties can be minimized by efficient design.

HEAT EXCHANGER CHARACTERISTICS

Every transfer of heat between two fluids—and what we are trying to do is to transfer a percentage of the heat of combustion from the two cooling fluids to the airstream—is directly proportional to the mean temperature difference between the two fluids, to the area of interface between the two fluids and to the volume of the cooling fluid flow. In other words, in order to increase cooling we must increase the surface area of one or both sides of the heat exchanger or we must increase the volume of the airflow per unit time through the core. Maximum area of the cooling interface is a question of heat exchanger design, and we'll briefly look at that aspect first.

Obviously what we want here is the maximum cooling area within the minimum physical dimensions. By concentrating liquid tubes and air fins we can achieve a surface area of well over 100 times the frontal area of the heat exchanger and still maintain efficient air flow. It's not quite that simple (it never is). Efficient design means narrow air fin passages and lots of them plus excellent thermal transfer between the liquid tubes and the air fins. The designer must have a pretty good idea of the viscosities of the two fluids involved and their flow rates, as well as the expected temperature differential between the fluids and the amount

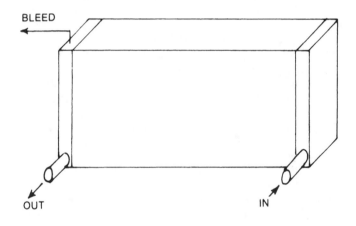

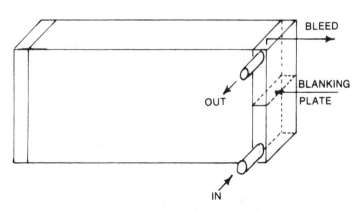

Figure (59): Conversion of single pass water radiator to double pass.

of temperature drop that the heat exchanger must achieve. This means that the design of heat exchangers is a job for specialists. It also means that efficient heat exchangers are designed for specific applications—or at least specific types of applications. This is the reason, for example, why large automatic transmission coolers, no matter how cheap they may be, do a poor job of cooling engine oil in a race car. As a matter of fact, they also do a poor job of cooling automatic transmission fluid.

We don't need to know how to design heat exchangers. We do need to know which of the available ones are suitable for our purposes—and why.

We are concerned with two separate types of liquid to air heat exchangers—water and oil—let's right now stop using the term, "radiator." Radiators used to be used to heat houses. Heat exchangers are used to cool race cars. Efficient water units will feature flat water tubes, usually about 3/32" high by 3/8" wide, they will not be in line with each other and the unit will feature a vast number of air fins. It will not be painted—although, if it is aluminum, it should be anodized or have a very thin coat of baked-on trick heat exchanger paint.

English cars come through with either Serck Speed or Marston water coolers. They are both excellent units—although they tend to be a bit thin in the core thickness department for our conditions. Replacement cost is ferocious. The USAC racers virtually all use G & O cores which are outstanding. Your best bet when you need a radiator is to find a good local shop that stocks G & O cores and have them make your radiator. It costs very little more to go up in core thickness and the extra cooling capacity will be more than worth the additional weight and drag—the only "Kit Cars" that I know of which had adequate cooling for U.S. racing were the '76 and '77 Marches. Minimum efficient core thickness is two inches with four inches being an absolute maximum.

There are conflicting opinions as to the desirability of aluminum water coolers. My own opinion is that they are just very nearly as thermally efficient as the more popular copper and brass units and a damn sight lighter. I run them when I can. They are also more expensive, more difficult to modify and to repair. The very best aluminum units are made by Standard Thompson, and no one can afford them. The Harrison parts which are made in a variety of thicknesses and sizes for Corvettes are excellent. Modine also makes some. All of these units can be sectioned across the tanks on a band saw to change their heights—of course you then get to weld on new tank plates, but you will have to weld in your own inlet and outlet tubes anyway. Unfortunately, there is nothing you can do to change the width of any of the proprietary coolers. The VW Rabbit comes with a very efficient and very light aluminum unit. If the dimensions are suitable for your installation, it could be ideal. Due to the elastomoric join between the tubes and the tank it cannot be modified and its pressure capacity is limited. Use the stock VW pressure caps.

If you are having a minor water temperature problem, converting your heat exchanger from the normal single pass configuration to double pass is usually worth about 5° C. Figure (59) shows the layout and it is not necessary to achieve a perfect seal between the blanking plate and the in-side of the tank. You will have to re-route one water line or the other. Given a choice, come in at the bottom and out at the top. All that happens here is that each individual drop of water is forced to pass through twice the tube length of a normal single pass radiator.

OIL COOLERS

The best oil coolers that I have found are the English Serck Speed units distributed in this country by Earl's Supply. They are relatively inexpensive, come in one width, one core thickness and several heights. They are also available with male AN ports which makes plumbing more pleasant and neater. They offer better heat rejection per unit weight and volume, less oil pressure drop and less aerodynamic cooler drag per unit of heat rejection than any other cooler which I have had tested. Southwind Division of the Bendix Corporation, Air Research, and Harrison make very good coolers for aircraft. They are very expensive and were designed for higher airstream velocities than we reach, which makes them a bit less efficient than the Serck Speed units for race car use. Modine makes a very good range of automotive oil coolers but they are expensive, bulky and hard to find. Mesa makes a cooler which, at first glance, looks similar to the Serck Speed. It is not similar and it is not efficient. The aftermarket auto transmission coolers—all of them—are useless for our purposes. As a matter of fact, you will greatly increase the reliability of your tow vehicle, camper or whatever if you throw away the transmission cooler that is on it and install the appropriate Serck. Sometimes you can get lucky and find good oil coolers in the surplus houses—but you have to be careful. Many of the surplus units were designed for stationary applications and don't work efficiently at our airspeeds.

Before we get away from the heat exchanger side, here are a few tips:

(1) Do not paint your heat exchangers. Black radiator paint, beloved of all radiator shops, instead of promoting heat transfer, actually acts as a thermal barrier and reduces efficiency.

(2) Keep the air fins straight so as not to block the flow through the core. A plywood or aluminum cover, taped in place while the radiator is out of the car, saves a lot of tedious fin straightening.

(3) When using multiple heat exchangers remember that the greater the difference in temperature between the liquid to be cooled and the air that is doing the cooling, the greater will be the temperature drop across the cooler. This has two ramifications of interest to us. First, plumb multiple coolers in parallel rather than in series. Second, do not mount your oil coolers directly ahead of or behind your water radiator. The air coming out of the water matrix is just about at water temperature and won't do much of a job of cooling the oil and vice-versa. I am perfectly aware that many good race cars have been getting away with one or the other (or both) of these sins since time immemorial—but that doesn't make it right—or efficient.

(4) A heat exchanger doesn't work very well if the liquid side is full of air. This means that oil coolers should never be mounted with both inlet and outlet ports on the bottom, that every effort should be made to de-aerate the

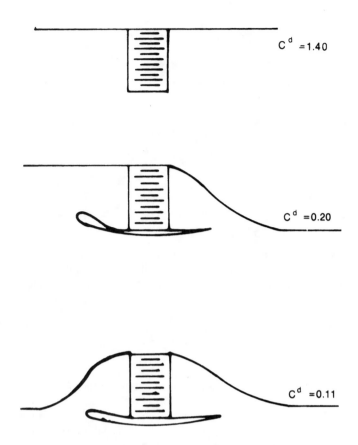

Figure (60): Drag coefficients for various cooler installations.

$C^d = 1.40$

$C^d = 0.20$

$C^d = 0.11$

tunately, a lot of this information is not directly transferable to race cars because the birdmen were concerned with relatively narrow speed ranges. They were not at all concerned with what might happen when the aircraft assumed a yaw angle relative to the airstream. Neither are a lot of race car designers. They should be.

Very little of current aircraft expertise is valid for our purposes. The aircraft are too fast—they are into compressible flow which changes the whole picture. As with wings, what works for them will not work for us.

For a given heat exchanger, the rate of heat dissipation varies directly with the mean temperature difference between the cooling surface and the air stream, approximately the .6 power of airstream velocity and the .8 power of air volume through the core. Both thermal efficiency and internal drag are reduced by slowing down the air velocity in the core. This means that we need high energy (i.e., laminar and high velocity) air coming into the duct and that we want to slow the air down before it gets to the core. In order to provide an extractor effect and to ensure that the exiting air is travelling at or near free stream velocity when it rejoins the freestream, we also want to accelerate the air after it has passed through the cooler and before it rejoins the freestream. To achieve all of this, we need a duct.

A properly designed duct is made up of five parts as shown in Figure (61). First we have an *inlet* which allows the entrance of the right amount of air. The inlet is followed by an expanding section called the *diffuser* in which the incom-

oil before it gets to the cooler and that all water coolers must have a small diameter bleed from the top (outlet side) back to the header tank.

Inadequate engine cooling can be caused by bad heat exchanger design, inadequate heat exchanger size or by insufficient cooling air flow with the latter being more common. On the water side, we can also get into trouble by pumping the water through the cooler too fast—but that is almost always due to running a stock water pump too fast and is, at any rate, beyond the scope of this book.

AIR FLOW AND DUCTS

If we want a flow of air to cool something, we have three choices: We can ignore the problem and hope that it will either take care of itself or go away. We can hang the item to be cooled out in the open airstream. Or we can build a duct for it. In the case of liquid to air heat exchangers, we normally have some choice in both dimensions and design of the cooler. In the case of ducts we have virtually unlimited choice—which can be confusing. If you want maximum cooling for minimum size, weight and drag you are going to have to build a duct. Hanging the thing out in the open is hopelessly inefficient. Figure (60) which shows the result of some pre World War II experiments with the drag of ducted and unducted heat exchangers should make a believer out of almost anyone.

Fortunately for the racer the aircraft industry did a lot of subsonic ducting research in the 1920 s and 30 s. Unfor-

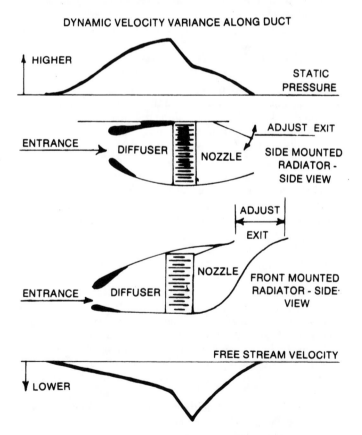

DYNAMIC VELOCITY VARIANCE ALONG DUCT

HIGHER

STATIC PRESSURE

ENTRANCE — DIFFUSER — NOZZLE — ADJUST EXIT — SIDE MOUNTED RADIATOR - SIDE VIEW

ADJUST EXIT

ENTRANCE — DIFFUSER — NOZZLE — FRONT MOUNTED RADIATOR - SIDE VIEW

FREE STREAM VELOCITY

LOWER

Figure (61): Typical ram type heat exchanger ducts.

ing air follows Mr. Bernoulli's theorem and trades some of its velocity for pressure. The diffuser will also direct the incoming air through whatever (hopefully minimal) directional changes are necessary before it reaches the *obstruction* (heat exchanger in this case) in which it is heated (and therefore expanded). Leaving the obstruction the air flows through a contracting chamber termed the *nozzle* which is very often mistakenly left off of race cars. The purpose of the nozzle is simply to reaccelerate the air up to free stream velocity so that when it rejoins the freestream at the duct *exit* it will do so in the most orderly fashion possible. Velocity differences and/or direction changes at the exit point invariably lead to drag producing turbulence, which we don't need. As a point of interest, during World War II clever people on all sides of the conflict were able to use the combination of the adiabatic heating and expansion of the air in the core plus near optimum nozzle and exit design to produce a net thrust at cruising speed instead of a drag. To achieve this they always used a variable area exit and sometimes a variable area entrance, because the areas which were most efficient at cruising speed were inadequate at take off and landing speeds. We cannot achieve this laudable aim for that very reason. We are not allowed to create moveable aerodynamic surfaces and even if we were, the small gain in total drag would not be worth the trouble. In fact, all of our ducts will end up being slightly inefficient at top speed—otherwise the entrance would be too small to provide cooling at the medium speeds where we spend most of our track time.

Let's attack the duct section by section. The critical factors for the inlet are location, area and edge radius. The inlet must be located in a region of high pressure and laminar air flow. If your chosen area is not such, then you will have to make it such or your duct will not work. It also helps a lot to get the inlet up off the track surface in order to pick up cool air. There can easily be a 20° F. difference between the air temperature at the surface of the track and ten inches above the track surface. This is one of the reasons why the attempts to pick up cooling air under the nose have always been unsuccessful. If the inlet is in the nose of the car, or raised artificially into the airstream, then we don't have to worry, being in a high pressure region of laminar flow unless it is behind a downforce ledge. Virtually anywhere else on the car, we do. Remember that the boundary layer exists everywhere and it gets thicker as we move toward the rear. By definition the boundary layer has very little energy. We must keep it out of our ducts or our air flow volume is going to be much lower than we think it is—or than it could be. The solution as shown by Figure (62) is simple enough. Either move the duct inlet far enough away from the body surface so that the boundary layer can't get in or install a splitter in the duct to direct the boundary layer around the end of the heat exchanger. This last method requires a gap between the heat exchanger and the bodywork. To find out how thick the layer is you can either use yarn tufts on a safety wire matrix or a simple water manometer—or you can guess.

If there is a way to calculate the optimum inlet area for a given race car duct I don't know about it and I wish that I did. Our road speed variance gets to all of the formulas. In the aircraft industry accepted practice ranges from 1/8 to 1/4 of the heat exchanger cross-sectional area. For us 1/4 is

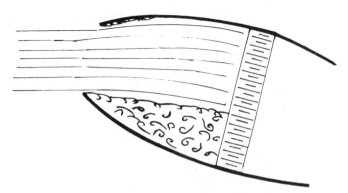

Figure (62a): Flow in duct with "knife edged" entrance at 15° yaw angle.

about minimum and we may have to use 60% for a poorly located duct—as in side mounted radiators. It is not an exact business and I highly recommend testing with rough ducts which allow both entrance and exit areas to be varied with aluminum and tape.

Many race cars are equipped with duct edges that approach knife edges. These work on hypersonic aircraft and they are easy to make. They do not work on race cars—particularly when the race car is sideways—even at relatively moderate yaw angles. If we are sideways to the road we are also sideways to the airstream. If we are sideways to the airstream a knife edge is going to develop a turbulent wake—quite a wide one. If this turbulence enters a duct, the duct, by definition, becomes inefficient for so long as the car is in a yaw state. Figure (62) illustrates. We deliberately spend a lot of our track time in yaw attitudes so we must radius the edges of all duct intakes—generously. A radius of 1/4" is the minimum—1/2" is a lot better.

The diffusor is not very critical. About all we have to do is blend smoothly from the area of the inlet to the area of the heat exchanger, keeping the wall angles in the eight to fifteen degree area—the smaller the angle the better. If we must exceed this angle because sufficient duct length is not available, then we may have to use internal vanes or splitters to direct the air and keep from effectively blanking part of the core due to detached flow on the duct walls.

At the heat exchanger face all we have to worry about is getting as good a seal as we can without being ridiculous. Given any kind of a chance, air will follow the path of least resistance and gaps between the duct walls and the heat exchanger are definitely the path of least resistance. Since we do not want the skin of the duct to rub on the heat exchanger, weatherstrip is the answer.

As with the diffuser, the internal design of the nozzle is very much a case of close enough is good enough. The one thing that must be avoided, however, is the all too common practice of asking the air to exhaust against a surface virtually normal to its direction of flow. This is often done in the case of front mounted heat exchangers and plays hell with the air flow.

The exit must be in a region of lower pressure than the inlet. It will only flow downhill. If a natural low pressure region is not available, or needs help, a small kicker plate just upstream of the exit will produce one. For development testing, the exit area should be made adjustable to allow playing until you get it right.

BREAKING THE DUCT RULES

Changing the direction of airflow as it passes through a heat exchanger core is rightfully considered an unnatural act. So are a lot of other things. Quite often mounting the core at an angle to the natural airstream is a very convenient way to increase the cooling area—as in Lola T 332's and many varieties of USAC and Formula One Cars. We get away with this, at some cost in drag, by breaking the rules of ducting. In this case a converging or decreasing area duct will work better than expanding diffuser. What happens here, as illustrated by Figure (63b) is that the pressure across the face of the core is kept pretty constant by allowing the air velocity to remain constant in the duct. In this way we get more or less equal air flow through all areas of the core. What is lost in efficiency is gained back in heat exchanger volume. In this case three inches is probably the maximum core thickness before drag gets out of hand.

The once common practice of hanging the oil coolers out in the open at the rear of the gearbox is indefensible on several grounds. It is aesthetically objectionable, renders the coolers vulnerable to minor crash damage (for which reason the FIA has outlawed the custom, and other sanctioning bodies should follow suit), makes long oil lines necessary and creates a lot of unneeded work when gear ratio change time comes along. The coolers are also very liable to mess up the flow on the underside of the wing.

For a while we saw a trend toward mounting the water coolers vertically alongside the engine and parallel to the longitudinal axis of the car. Mr. Postlewaithe originated the idea on the Hesketh ne Williams and, at the time of writing, the Williams still features this configuration. The idea here is to suck the air through the core from the relatively high pressure area outside to the relatively low pressure area inside. Some cleverness is necessary to make sure that the low pressure is of sufficient magnitude to ensure an air flow. Even if it is, the cooler size has to be very large indeed—although the core thickness is necessarily small. The advantage lies in reduced cooler drag. The disadvantages include increased weight and rearward placement of that weight (the extreme rearward static weight distribution of a few years ago turned out to be a not so good idea from the low speed understeer point of view).

A half way measure that enjoyed a great vogue for a time was the less than clever practice of hanging the water coolers just outboard of the rear suspension radius rods, also without a duct.

At the moment, most of the Formula One Brigade mount their coolers amidships. There is no general agreement on the type of ducts, but I think that the Lotus is the most clever of all—in addition to optimum placement from the weight distribution point of view, they have very efficient looking ducts which probably generate a measurable amount of downforce.

We have been talking about ram ducts. There is another type, more subtle, more difficult to make work and considerably more efficient. These are variously called flush ducts, submerged ducts and NACA (National Advisory Council for Aeronautics) ducts and, at one time and another, have been extensively used on racing cars. Figure (64) shows a typical installation. The principal advantage here is that since they do not involve a hole in the nose or an addition to frontal area they do not measurably add to profile or parasitic drag except for the drag of the cooler itself. There is also liable to be less downstream disturbance of the air flow.

The disadvantages are that, in order to work they must be constructed very closely to the design laid out in Figure (65); they must be located in a region of laminar flow with a shallow boundary layer; they must be aligned parallel to the *local* air flow and they tend to take up a lot of room. If the designer deviates very much from any of the above, then the

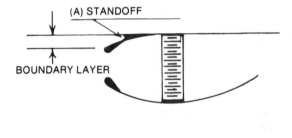

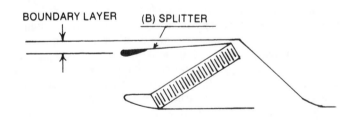

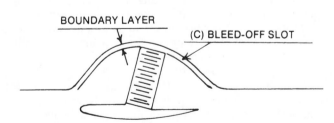

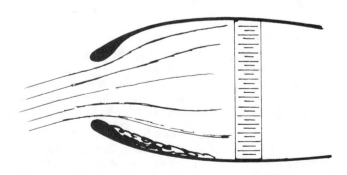

Figure (62b): Flow in radiused entrance duct at 15° yaw angle.

Figure (63): Alternate of preventing entrance of boundary layer into duct.

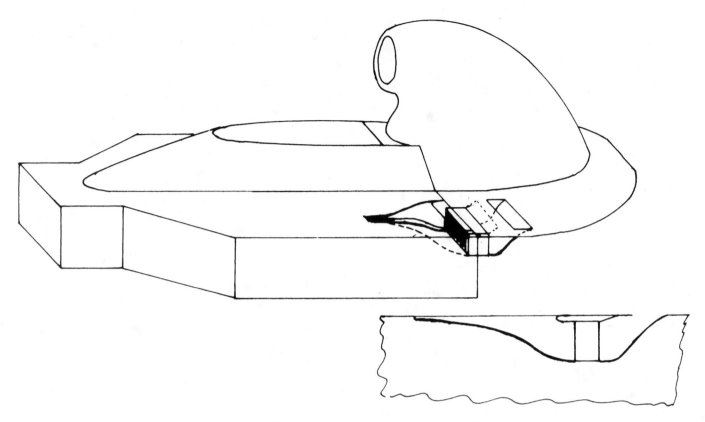

Figure (64): Installation of oil cooler in NACA duct.

flow into the duct is dramatically reduced, the hoped for cooling doesn't happen and NACA ducts are one more time pronounced unsuitable for racing cars. There are obvious areas where NACA ducts will work very well. Properly aligned to the airstream, they will work on any forward facing part of the bodywork with a positive pressure gradient— i.e.—an upslope or a region of increasing cross-sectional area. Since the thickness of the boundary layer generally increases as we move aft from the nose of the vehicle, the further forward the duct is located, the more efficient it will be. They make excellent front brake and shock cooling ducts. They make lousy rear brake ducts because the flow is almost always at least partially separated by the time you get that far back (although they work well on the vertical surface of well designed Formula Car engine covers/air boxes. They also work quite well on the horizontal surfaces of the bodywork outboard of the cockpit on both Formula and Sports Racing cars and less well of the vertical sides of the body in the same area (much more turbulence and a thicker boundary layer). I don't favor their use for water radiators because it is not possible to arrange the duct dimensions required. I do favor their use for the much smaller oil coolers, brake ducts cockpit cooling, etc.—particularly on Sports racing cars with their acres of bodywork.

The important aspects of the design of the NACA duct itself (as opposed to its location) are that the angle of the ramp floor should be kept at a maximum of ten degrees; the ratio of duct depth to duct width should be as high as practical (deep ducts); there must be a radiused lip at the rear of the skin opening and the duct corners must be kept square. With NACA ducts as with any others, the exit region is at least as important as the entrance—the air must have somewhere to go and just hoping that it will happen isn't good enough. The duct must also be sealed and smooth. Very often we have to make wide and shallow ducts which will also be much shorter than optimum design. We can get away with all of this so long as the duct is properly located and we pay sufficient attention to the other parameters. It is also possible to get depth by the sides of the duct above the surface of the bodywork but this tends to be expensive and probably isn't worth doing.

ENGINE AIR BOXES

Current practice in Formula One and Formula Two should convince us that engine ram air boxes must contribute significantly to overall vehicle performance. I am an air box addict and have been for a long time. A properly designed air box can do several things:

Increase engine power by increasing the flow of air through the engine and by providing the coolest available air to the engine.

Even out the distribution of air to the intake stacks.

Smooth out the flow of air to the rear wing, thus reducing the amount of drag induced for a given downforce.

However, it isn't easy to arrange all of these admirable features—or even part of them. The development period was both long and confusing. For several seasons we saw most of the Formula One Teams trying the air box of the week—and often throwing them away in practice and running the race with naked intakes. Finally, as so often happens, everyone figured out the way to do it and we had a couple of seasons

X/X$_{max}$	Y/Y$_{max}$
0	0.042
0.1	0.070
0.2	0.102
0.3	0.138
0.4	0.178
0.5	0.227
0.6	0.295
0.7	0.377
0.8	0.460
0.9	0.496
1.0	0.500

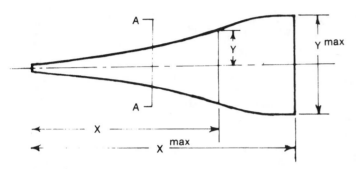

MAKE CORNERS OF DUCT AS SHARP AS POSSIBLE

SECT. A-A

Figure (65a): NACA duct co-ordinates—plan view.

with every team running virtually identical air boxes. These all had very large intakes, complete with generous radii. The intakes invariably lived well up in the breeze—just behind and over the driver's head. The inlets fed large diffusors which also served as plenums, and the bases of the diffusors were sealed to the intake stacks. The outside shape was carefully sculpted both to reduce drag and to provide a smooth flow of air to the rear wing. Not only did they work, they looked good and they moved the aerodynamic center of pressure aft for increased aerodynamic yaw stability.

For 1976 the C.S.I. decreed high air boxes illegal and development started all over again. The air box of the week returned and was frequently discarded. This time, however, previous experience had convinced all the Teams of the advantages of a working air box and they are starting to look alike much sooner than before. The exceptions are Ferrari and Brabham/Alpha whose flat twelve engines with low intake stacks allow the use of a really elegant system—they take the air in through two large NACA ducts located on either side of the vertical cockpit surround and feed it into a low plenum neat!

The V-8 brigade has pretty much settled on a pair of inlet horns extending into the airstream on either side of the driver's head and feeding a central plenum. The shape of the intake has not yet been standardized.

So what is actually required to make an air box work—and why do so many of them not work?

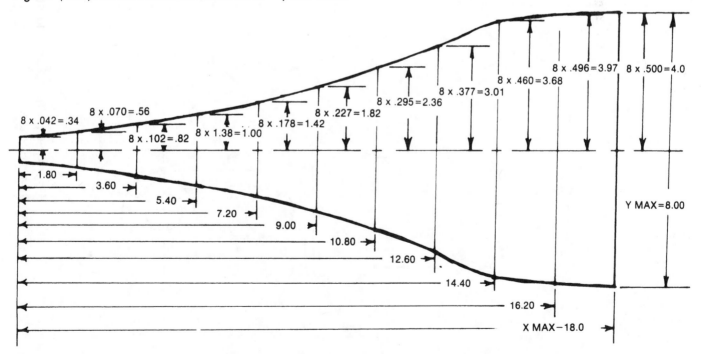

Figure (65b): Layout of NACA duct—plan view.

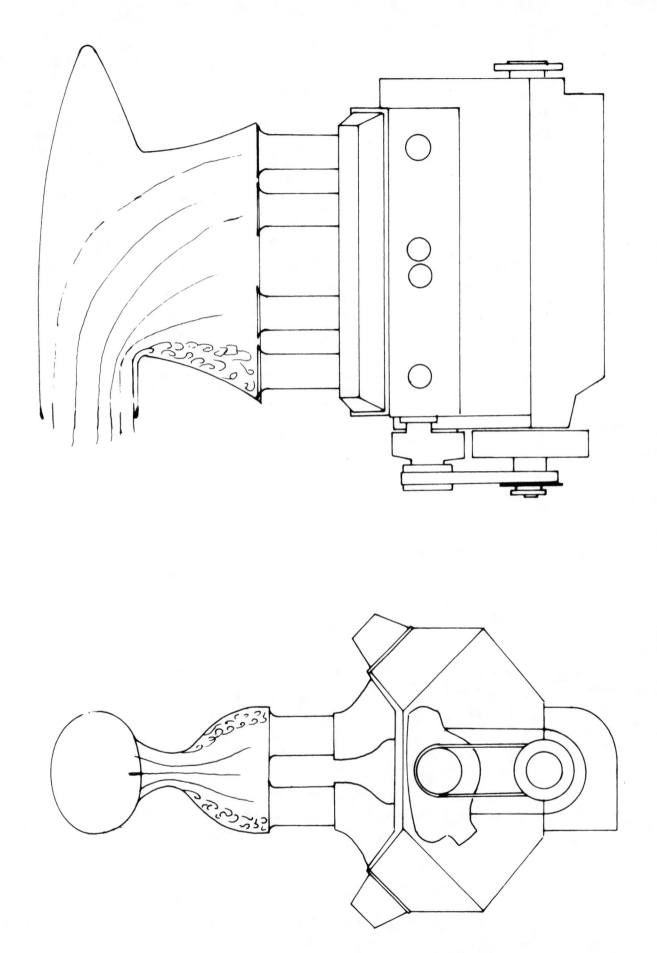

Figure (66a): Inefficient engine inlet cold airbox with poor diffuser design showing flow separation from walls.

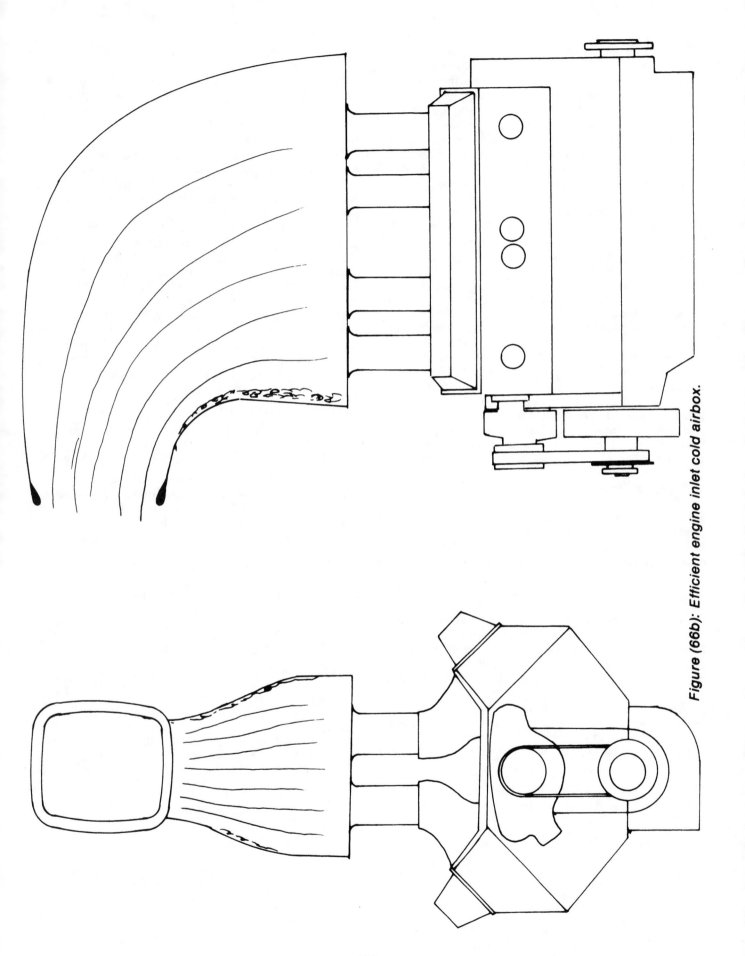

Figure (66b): Efficient engine inlet cold airbox.

First, the intake must have enough area to get a sufficient volume of air to the engine at low road speed when the ram doesn't work. Remember that airflow into the box varies with road speed while air required by the engine varies with rpm. We're not trying to ram at low speeds—we are merely trying to avoid choking the engine. A large enough inlet for low speeds probably means that we will over ram at high speed. The most common method of dealing with this situation is to depend upon leakage between the plenum base and the intake stacks or on small bleed holes in the plenum. I personally think that a spring loaded pressure relief would be tricky and I keep meaning to try it but never have. Along these lines, it is absolutely necessary, if you are using carbs, to make sure that the float chambers are seeing the plenum pressure. Otherwise your mixture strength is going to be so far off that the whole exercise will be hopeless. If the air box is really working it will also be necessary to supply more fuel to the engine or you will run lean—maybe even lean enough to burn a piston.

Next the edges of the intake opening must be well radiused to avoid partially stalling the inlet at high yaw angles. The intake must be so located that it cannot be blanked out by some part of the vehicle at high yaw angles. It must also be served by high energy air which means out in the free airstream for a ram duct or in a laminar flow area with a strong positive pressure gradient for a NACA duct. Be very sure that your intake is not picking up the heated air exhausting from a heat exchanger duct—you want the coolest air you can find—which means that you want the intake as high as you can get it.

If the inlet bit is straight forward, the diffusor/plenum isn't. The purpose here is to persuade the airflow to turn ninety degrees as smoothly as possible and to provide an expanding chamber in which the velocity component of the airstream energy will be converted to pressure which will be equal at each intake stack. We also have to avoid turbulence at any of the intakes.

We don't have a lot of room in which to accomplish this—particularly with large V-8 engines. Figure (66a) shows how bad things can get and Figure (66b) shows how to do it right. Theoretically the plenum should clear all of the intake stacks by at least 1/2 stack diameter and a full diameter would be better. This is sometimes a bit difficult to achieve. It is probably more important to get the shape right and to keep the last six to eight inches of the vertical walls vertical. The plenum base must be sealed to the intake stacks and this is usually done by the simple expedient of setting the base on top of the stacks and sealing with foam or rubber grommets. There is a theory that the stacks should extend into the plenum chamber to minimize turbulence but it doesn't seem to make any practical difference.

Speaking of the inlet stacks, any basic air conditioning book informs us that for maximum undisturbed flow the lip of an inlet stack should have a full radius. For some reason only Cosworth, Ferrari and Porsche seem to have caught onto this simple fact.

The outside shape of the airbox/engine cover is a question of minimizing drag and interference with the rear wing. With a high box we can actually improve the airflow to the wing. Again there is pretty general agreement about what shape will do the job and looking at current photos will get you up to date with the state of the art. With a high air box—as on a Can Am car, it is possible to bleed off some of the air to cool the magneto or the rear brakes. Some sort of rock screen should also be employed and you should make very certain that the whole thing is securely enough attached that there is no possibility at all of its coming off.

In keeping with my self-imposed practice of assigning some basic numbers to the features under discussion, let's see just what the ram aspect of the air box adds up to:

Intake Ram (psi) =

$$\frac{\text{Air Density (lb/ft}^3) \times (\text{Air Velocity in fps})^2}{288g}$$

At 80 mph—Intake Ram = $\dfrac{0.076 \times (118)^2}{288 \times 32.2}$ = 0.11 lb/in^2

At 160 mph—Intake Ram = $\dfrac{0.076 \times (235)^2}{288 \times 32.2}$ = .45 lb/in^2

In both cases we have assumed a 100% efficient duct, which is not possible—75% efficient would be a good one. So the figures become 0.083 p.s.i. and 0.34 p.s.i. respectively. They don't sound like much—and they aren't—in the quantitative sense. But a gain of 0.34 p.s.i. inlet pressure is a percentage gain of 2.3% over standard atmospheric pressure—which is worth talking about.

If we can manage to grab cooler air for the inlet system through our box than it would otherwise receive, then we will gain 1% in air density for every 3° F. that we cool the air—yes, that is why turbos and superchargers use intercoolers on the inlet side.

The largest gain in engine performance, however, will come from the even distribution of inlet air to the individual intake stacks that is provided by a well designed and efficient plenum.

My last word on airboxes is that they work. They work on any type of race car and they work with either carburetors or fuel injection. They only work if they are correctly designed. It is worth taking the time and trouble to make a good one.

CHAPTER TEN

THE BRAKES

THE BRAKES

Don't expect miracles from tuning on the brakes—improvement, yes—but no miracles. There are two reasons for this. First, the racing disc brake system has been developed to a very high state indeed so that there just isn't a lot left in the line of practical improvement and, second, we just don't spend very much time under the brakes. On the average road racing circuit, something less than ten percent of the time required to complete a lap is spent braking. Therefore, a five percent improvement in braking performance (not brake efficiency) would net a theoretical improvement in lap time of one half of one percent—or about one half second in a 90 second lap. In actuality, the improvement would be somewhat less because human and practical limitations always prevent us from realizing the full potential benefit from any performance improvement.

The big payoff of a well sorted out braking system comes, not from any increase in braking power itself, but in the confidence, consistency and controlability that it provides to the driver. This is particularly true when it comes to corner entry—entry speed, placement, precision and repeatability are all directly dependent upon braking performance and consistency.

I would be astonished to learn of a modern road racing car which was delivered with inadequate brakes. Badly arranged or badly set up I'm willing to believe, but inadequate—NO. This statement is valid only so long as we do not change tire size, power output and/or gross weight all out of proportion to the original design. It is definitely not true in those classes of production based touring car and G.T. Car racing where the sanctioning body, through sheer ignorance and/or bloody mindedness prohibits changes to the braking system.

BRAKING POWER: WHERE DOES IT COME FROM?

It takes an astonishing amount of energy to decelerate a moving vehicle—in fact it takes the same amount of energy to decelerate from one speed to another as it would to accelerate between the two speeds—except that we can decelerate faster because most of the inertial forces are working for us rather than against us. The actual energy required to decelerate our racer is given by the equation:

Energy (lb/ft) =

.0335 x [(mph max)² (mph min)²] x gross weight (lb).

For a 1760 lb car braking from 150 mph to 60 mph we are talking about .0335 x [(150)² – (60)²] x 1760 =1,114,344 lb/ft. No matter what terminology we use, this is a hell of a lot of energy absorbed in a very short period of time. Somebody once converted the braking energy put out by a GT 40 over

the twelve hours of Sebring and came to the conclusion that the same amount of energy could supply the electrical requirements of a fair sized city for a goodly period of time. So where does the energy come from—what actually stops the car?

Some comes from the rolling resistance of the tires—not much, but some. A notable amount, at least at high road speeds, comes from the vehicle's aerodynamic drag. A little bit comes from the friction generated between the moving parts of the entire mechanism. Most of it, however, must come from the vehicle's braking system which converts the kinetic energy of vehicle inertia into thermal energy which must then be dissipated into the airstream—because we have yet to figure out a practical method to collect it, store it, and use it for propulsive thrust. We really aren't very efficient. This chapter is devoted to investigating the braking system itself. We shall conveniently ignore the other factors which

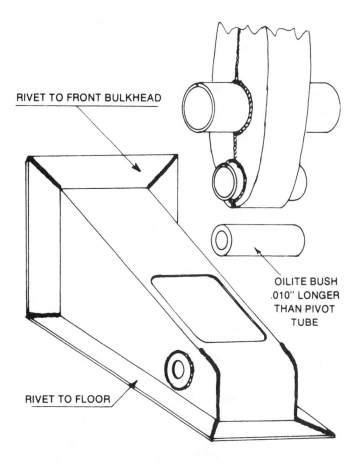

Figure (67a): Boxed brake pedal mount

slow the car because what we really want to do with them is minimize them to increase the acceleration of the vehicle.

WHAT WE CAN EXPECT FROM THE BRAKES

What exactly are we looking for in braking system performance? First of all we need a braking system which is capable of developing enough braking force to exceed the deceleration capacity of the tires—at any speed that the vehicle can reach—time after time, for the duration of the race. All racing cars, and many modified production cars, have such a system—provided that it is properly installed, adjusted and maintained. The braking effort produced must be directly and linearly proportional to the pedal pressure exerted by the driver. Further, the driver effort required must be reasonable, pedal pressures must be neither so great that Godzilla is required to stop the car nor so light that it will be easy to lock the tires. The pedal position must be correctly matched to the geometry of the driver's foot and ankle, must remain at a constant height and should be really firm and have minimum travel. The system must deliver optimum balance of braking force between the front and rear tires so that the driver can maintain steering control under very heavy braking and yet use all of the decelerative capacity of all four tires. Lastly, the system must offer complete reliability. If the driver is braking as deep and as hard as he should be, any brake system failure will inevitably result in the car leaving the circuit. What happens after that is up to the man upstairs. Brake failure in a racing car at the limit has to be experienced to be understood. This is why even the most heroic drivers are liable to give the brake pedal a reassuring tap before they arrive at their braking marker.

We need a vehicle suspension system capable of dealing with the loads and forces generated by heavy braking without wheel hop, suspension bottoming, compliance, adverse camber effects, pull or darting. Most of all we need a driver sensitive and skillful enough to balance the car on the edge of the traction circle under braking and under the combination of braking and cornering. If we do not provide the driver with all of the system parameters listed above, he can not provide us with the skill and daring necessary to ride the edge of the traction circle.

EVALUATION AND DRIVER TECHNIQUE

We'll start out with what is probably the most difficult part of the whole braking scene—evaluation of what you have. Measuring the braking performance of your particular projectile against that of the competition is no easier than comparing any other aspect of vehicle performance—and for the same reasons—too many variables and too much ego involved. This is where instrumentation is invaluable. The biggest variable is, of course, the driver. The very last thing that a really good racing driver learns to do truly well is to use the brakes. Most people take too long to get them on hard, leave them hard on too long and brake too heavily too deep into the corner. Almost invariably the lap times generated by the King of The Late Brakers are slow. His adrenalin level is liable to be abnormally high and he has a tendency to fall off the road. There are several reasons for these characteristics. When you leave your braking too late you are very liable to arrive at the point on the race track where you really want to start your turn only to find that the

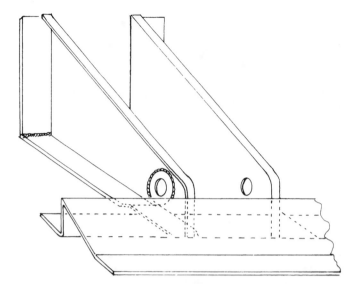

Figure (67b): Flanged brake pedal mount.

car will not turn. It will not do so because, in your efforts to save your life, you have the binders on so hard that all of the front tires' available traction is being used in deceleration and there is none left to allow the generation of the side force necessary to turn the car—or, should you somehow succeed in initiating a turn, to keep it in a balanced cornering state. In addition, the front tires are liable to be very nearly on fire and dangerously close to the compound temperature limit. Thirdly, if you are still hard on the brakes when the turn is initiated, forward load transfer has unbalanced the car, the front suspension travel is about used up, the front tires are steeply cambered and, if the thing turns at all, things are going to happen a bit quickly.

If you persist in braking too late, the spectators will "ooh" and "ahh" and be impressed no end and the announcer will mention your name frequently—noting that you are really trying out there. You will complain pitifully about corner entry understeer followed by an incredibly rapid transition to power on oversteer. The other drivers will pour by you—either while you are exploring the grey areas of the track in your frantic scrabble for traction or on the way out of the corner when they have both higher exit speed and a better bite. You will do a lot of exploring as your self induced understeer forces you into unintentional late corner entries. Your team manager will eventually catch on, wander out on the course and observe your antics. If the ensuing frank discussion of technique does not inspire you to mend your ways, he will seriously consider either another driver (if you don't own the car) or another job (if you do).

So any time that you are going in noticeably deeper than the competent opposition (assuming similar cars) but your lap times are not reflecting the degree of heroism that you feel they should—and the car is entering corners badly—have a good think about the wisdom of your braking points. Slow in and fast out will beat fast in and slow out every time. Of course fast in and fast out beats either of the above—and that's what we are trying to achieve—but you won't come out fast if you go in with the car unbalanced and the front tires on fire. This is not to say that a super late brake application followed by a deliberate early corner entry and a bit

108

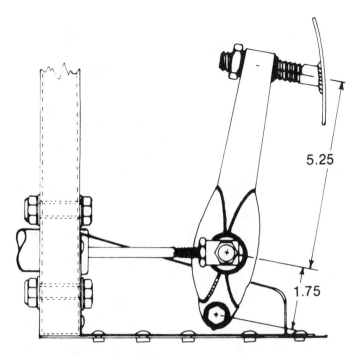

5.25

1.75

Figure (68): Typical brake pedal showing 3:1 mechanical advantage.

of slithering around which uses up a portion of the track that might otherwise be useful to someone else is not a valid desperation maneuver. It is, and it will continue to be—but it isn't very often fast and it is even less often repeatedly fast.

THE BRAKE PEDAL

Having disposed of the system actuator, it is time to discuss hardware. We will begin with the brake pedal since it is the closest part to the driver. The brake pedal should be very strong—and so should its attachment to the chassis. This may sound very basic and a bit ridiculous—and so it should. Any fool should be able to figure out that if the brake pedal, or any of the associated bits, fractures, bends or tears out of its mountings, big trouble is about to happen. And yet it happens—not very frequently—but it does happen. It has even happened to very good operations. Don't let it happen to you. Take a long hard look at the pedal/master cylinder setup and, if anything even looks like being questionable, redesign and/or reinforce as seems necessary. Remember that the typical brake pedal has a mechanical advantage of at least 3:1 and it may be as much as 8:1. The pedal arm must be plenty stout and it must be generously gusseted at the intersection of the bias bearing tube. If the pedal bracket is a chunk of 20 gauge aluminum pop riveted to the floor, it won't be good enough. If it doesn't eventually tear out, it will distort and it is difficult enough to modulate brake pressure without the pedal waving about. The pedal pivot support should be at least 18 gauge steel, it should be either boxed or flanged and it should tie into a corner of major structure. Figure (67) applies. You are going to lean on the pedal very frequently and plenty hard. If the master cylinders are mounted to either sheet metal or to slightly stiffened sheet metal, you will end up with a soft or vague pedal. This particular design sin is nowhere near so rare as it should be—

especially in those vehicles which do not employ a front bulkhead (a major sin in itself). I'll be damned if I know why this is ever allowed, but it is easily detected and remedied. Also look at the master cylinder push rods. It is very desirable that they should not bend. In normal lengths, the stock Girling bits will do just fine. Trouble starts at about six inches. We can also get into trouble with really thin wall tubular extensions and with butt welds.

PEDAL GEOMETRY AND ADJUSTMENT

Take some time and adjust the fore and aft position of the brake (and clutch) pedal to suit the driver's geometry and preference. To do this right may not be as simple as it sounds. The easiest method is that practiced by Lolas, who screw the foot pad into the pedal shaft with a long bolt which is welded to the pad. This gives lots of adjustment without deranging the pedal geometry and offers the added advantage of allowing you to install the pad at an angle should your driver prefer. Figure (68) illustrates the arrangement.

It is vital that the swing of the pedal be properly positioned on its arc. If the pedal is allowed to go over center as it is pushed, we will have an unfortunate situation where, the harder we push on the pedal, the less braking effort we get—and confusion is a certain result. Once the (minimal) free play has been taken up, we are not going to push the pedal very far, just hard, so that it is a relatively simple matter to adjust the actuating rod length and the position of the pedal pivot so that increased pressure results in increased, or at least linear mechanical advantage. Do so. All of this may involve new brackets, actuating rods, or even a new pedal. It really is important, so do it.

We no longer row our way down through the gears to decelerate the car—pity, one more glorious sound gone away. The present racing disc brake system is plenty powerful enough to exceed the tire capacity without help from engine friction. Downshifting while braking merely upsets the balance of the car, involves unnecessary foot movements and makes it more difficult to precisely modulate braking effort. However, we still do downshift. So long as racing drivers must downshift, the traditional heel and toe exercise with the brake and the throttle is a necessity. Otherwise, we will snatch the rear wheels when the clutch engages and instantaneous oversteer will be achieved. As the downshift always occurs either during corner entry or immediately prior to it, oversteer—even transient oversteer—is not to be desired. Whilst downshifting, we are, by definition, braking and, more than likely, braking hard. It would be best if the driver could still modulate the brakes while jabbing at the accelerator. The common deficiency in this department is for the driver to unintentionally decrease brake pedal pressure while stabbing the throttle. Watch the braking area before a slow corner at any race—you can actually see the noses of the slow cars come up during downshifts. Next watch the aces and note the difference. You will also notice that the nose of the ace's car comes up before the car is locked over into the corner. At any rate, if the driver is not going to upset the pedal pressure while downshifting, the relative positions of the brake and throttle pedals must be perfect—for the individual driver.

There are two workable methods of "heel and toeing"— that I know of. The first involves rocking the right foot sideways and catching the throttle with the side of the foot. This is probably the more popular method, but it is difficult to control brake pressure while rocking the foot. The second way is to so arrange things that the heel of the right foot is carried further outboard than the ball and to jab the throttle by extending the heel. It is very much a case of personal preference and ankle geometry. In either case, the throttle pedal, or some part thereof had better be ready to foot when the time comes—we do not want to either hunt for it or stretch for it. Contrariwise, it must be impossible for the driver to inadvertently hit the throttle when he goes for the brakes or to get his foot tangled between the pedals—don't laugh. The necessary fiddling about and moving of things can be greatly facilitated by a bit of forethought. The pedal system most compatible with human geometry and lie down cars is to pivot the brake (and clutch) pedals on the floor and hang the accelerator from the ceiling. It helps a lot if the throttle setup incorporates a left and right hand threaded connector at the pedal end. It is unlikely that your first efforts at getting it right will be successful—drivers have trouble making up their minds and what feels right sitting on the jack stands may not be worth a damn on the race track—especially if the driver was wearing street shoes when you set it up. You may get to do a lot of this sort of thing for a while (sometimes I regret telling drivers that the pedals can be adjusted) so you may as well make it easy on yourself. This may well include making a larger access hole in the top of the tub for your hands. Remember that after each adjustment to the throttle pedal you get to reset the full throttle stop and that, if you change master cylinder sizes, you get to do it all over again. Playing with the shape of the throttle pedal and its arch often pays unexpected dividends.

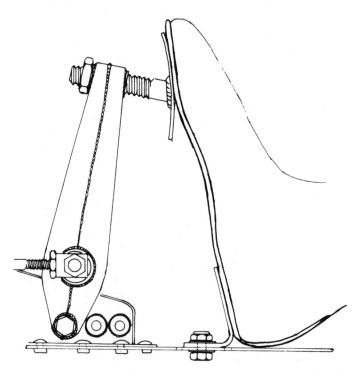

Figure (69): Adjustable heel support.

Most drivers insist on some sort of heel locating plate or brace running transversely across the cockpit floor. If the driver does not insist on one, you should—he needs it. Figure (69) shows an easy and lightweight method which also offers adjustment. It is as well to locate the plate and determine the angle with the driver in the car.

The last pedal is the left footrest. There should be one. It provides a place for the driver to brace himself and does away with the worrisome possibility that he might unintentionally rest his left foot on the clutch to the detriment of the clutch plates. Its height should be the same as the clutch pedal and it should be located slightly behind the clutch so that the left foot can simply be slid sideways when required. It should be as wide as practical—making sure that the clutch can be depressed without getting the foot trapped between the two. There usually isn't a lot of excess room in the foot well so the clutch pedal may have to be made more narrow in order to create room for the dead pedal. The footrest should be well attached to the chassis because it will take a lot of pressure, and it is bad if it comes undone.

BIG FEET IN SMALL COCKPITS

All English racing drivers must have size six feet! If your hero features size twelve, his fancy footwork in the average kit car is going to suffer some impairment due to interference between his toes and the bodywork, the tub, the anti-roll bar or the steering rack. This is one of the major reasons why the cockpit extends so far forward on the present Formula One Cars. Extensions and/or blisters are sometimes a necessity. Occasionally you will run into foot interference of a more serious nature—worst possible case being the steering rack—the anti-roll bar is a less serious case because it is easier to move. A situation of this nature calls for moving either the offending member or the driver—or maybe finding a driver with smaller feet. Minor interference can be cured by shoe surgery. If you move the driver you will also have to move the pedals. If you move the rack, you will have to re-do the geometry. It is easier not to buy a car with this type of built-in problem. Finding out about this sort of thing on your first test can ruin your whole day—so find out early—particularly if your driver, or his feet, are oversized.

DISC BELLS OR TOP HATS

We have now arrived at a point where the pedals fit the driver and nothing is going to bend or fall off—so what can we do to help the actual retarding mechanism? *Prepare to Win* covered the plumbing, installation and maintenance ends of things and all of this has to be done—step by step. It did not, however, cover the now popular method of attaching the brake discs to the top hats or bells by six bolts in single shear. It did not cover it for the excellent reason that I had not dreamed that anyone would do such a thing. Wrong again! I had reckoned without Lola and March. Not only do these otherwise fine firms cheerfully commit this crime against nature, but they do not allow sufficient bolt hole edge distance or flange thickness to stabilize the bolts and they have been known to use less than optimum grades of aluminum for the bells. They also use fully threaded Allen bolts. Talk about looking for trouble! Chevron also use the same basic system, but their flange thickness is sufficient to get away with it.

The layout is a lot less bad and critical on Formula Atlantic cars simply because both vehicle speed and vehicle mass are considerably less than, say Can Am Cars, and so the brake torque is less. Still I have seen the rear bells shear on an Atlantic car. Nothing good has ever been reported about this sort of thing. If you happen to have lots of money, the obvious solution is to get rid of the whole mess and install dog drive discs and bells. This is probably not practical as the dog drive top hats are very expensive to make. So let's explore the alternatives.

Step one is to scrap the stock bolts. They are not the prime offenders, but getting rid of them is both cheap and easy. You will have to use either a twelve point or an internal wrenching NAS bolt. If you cannot obtain them, use an "Unbrako" Allen bolt with the correct grip length and cut off the unneeded thread. If you can get the NAS bolts, you may have to turn down the heads to make them fit. In some installations, it is just not possible to use a washer under the bolt head—even a turned down washer. In this case, the bolt hole must be countersunk to clear the radius under the head of the NAS bolts. Do not use stainless or titanium bolts in this application, and use all metal lock nuts.

Unfortunately, the prime offender is the top hat itself. It may have several shortcomings. Normally there is both insufficient flange thickness to stabilize the bolt and insufficient edge distance to prevent the bolt from tearing out. The material may also be soft, allowing the bolt head to work into the aluminum which results in a loose assembly and eventual self destruction. The alloy may also be unstable under the heat involved which will cause disc runout. If you check the stupid things as frequently as you should, you will detect the symptoms before a disaster occurs—unless, of course, you are running on a really severe course where you get airborne under the brakes—like Long Beach or Elkhart Lake. In this case the disaster may happen before you notice the symptoms and your driver will go through the experience of shearing the discs off the bells. He will not enjoy the experience, and you will not enjoy rebuilding the resultant wreck.

For about 50% of the cost of a stock disc bell, any decent machine shop can make units from high quality forged alloy stock. Probably the best alloy to use is 2024-T4 with 7075-T651 and 2017-T451 being acceptable. 6061 is not a good alloy for this application. If space permits, increase both the edge distance and the flange thickness. Save yourself some money by drilling twelve bolt holes instead of the required six and indexing the disc when the holes show elongation or cracking. In addition to lasting a lot longer, the bells will remain more true—especially if you set them up in a lathe and take a truing cut off them every so often. Tilton Engineering makes good top hats and a very clever steel plate to convert bolt on discs to dog drive.

SYSTEM FORCE RATIO

If the brakes are either so sensitive that it is easy to inadvertently lock one or more wheels (as in early Detroit power brakes) or if they require all of the strength that the driver can muster in his right leg to slow the car, efficient braking will be difficult indeed. Therefore we must choose the optimum mechanical and hydraulic force ratios for a given vehicle.

The system's mechanical advantage is determined by the mechanical advantage of the brake pedal itself and by the mean diameter of the discs. It is normally not possible to increase the diameter of the front discs since they are inside the wheels. If it is possible, do so—there is no disadvantage. Rear disc diameter is usually limited by the proximity of suspension members and is also a relative function of front disc diameter. The mechanical advantage of the pedal—at least on racing cars—is somewhat limited by package dimensions and by the fact that pedal travel gets excessive as the mechanical advantage is increased. It is normally from 3:1 to 5:1 as in Figure (68) and there isn't very much that we can do with it.

The hydraulic force ratio is determined by the relative area of the master cylinder bore and the total piston area of the calipers operated by that master cylinder.

There is a definite relationship between the amount of hydraulic pressure required to decelerate a vehicle at a given rate and the brake pad compound. The softer the compound, the higher its coefficient of friction and the less force required—and, things being what they are, the lower the temperature at which brake fade will occur. Among the compounds presently in use, Hardie Ferodo 1103 is the hardest, followed closely by Raybestos M19. These pads are for use on large, fast and heavy cars only—they require lots of pedal effort and chew the hell out of discs. Mintex M17FF is the softest material in present use and the ubiquitous Ferodo DS11 is about in the middle. If you were to change from Mintex to Raybestos—say to avoid pad changes in a long distance race—you might well find that your driver could not push on the pedal hard enough to stop the car at its maximum deceleration rate. This, in itself, would improve pad wear—but it is probably not the way to go. Changing in the opposite direction can result in locking wheels all over the place and in brake fade. Normally we don't have to worry about this feature unless we find that our normal compound will fade at a track that is particularly severe on the brakes. We adjust the hydraulic force ratio by varying either the size of the caliper pistons or the bore of the master cylinders. Normally I tend to consider the calipers to be fixed items for financial reasons—master cylinders are cheap.

What happens here is that the area of the bore of any given master cylinder is fixed and so, therefore, is the amount of fluid displacement per unit of linear piston travel. Since brake fluid is not compressible (so long as no bubbles are present), the amount of hydraulic pressure developed by a given pedal pressure will be inversely proportional to the bore of the master cylinder. The amount of fluid displacement is, of course, directly proportional to the bore. Therefore a larger cylinder (or pair of cylinders) will require more foot pressure per unit of hydraulic pressure generated but will require less pedal travel to exert the same amount of force. My own preference, and that of virtually every driver that I have ever worked with, is for a brake pedal with minimum travel and a firmness approaching that of a brick wall. Not only does this lend itself to better brake modulation, but it has a salutary effect on the driver's level of confidence. There is something about a mushy brake pedal when

FORCE VARIATIONS VS MASTER CYLINDER BORE DIAMETER				
MASTER CYLINDER BORE	MASTER CYL PISTON AREA	LINE PRESS WITH 150 LB FORCE ON PISTON	PEDAL TRAVEL TO MOVE PADS .010" [.4 POT CALIPER 1.50" PISTONS]	FORCE APPLIED TO INDIVIDUAL DISC [4 POT CALIPER 1.50" PISTONS]
.625"	.307 in²	486 psi	1.38	3435 lb
.700"	.385 in²	390 psi	1.10	2757 lb
.750"	.442 in²	339 psi	.96	2396 lb
.875"	.601 in²	250 psi	.71	1767 lb

FORCE VARIATION VS CALIPER PISTON BORE						
4 PISTON CALIPER BORE	PISTON AREA PER PAD	PISTON AREA PER DISC	FORCE ON DISC 486 psi line press	FORCE ON DISC 390 psi line press	FORCE ON DISC 339 psi	FORCE ON DISC 235 psi
1.375"	2.970 in²	5.940 in²	2886 lb	2316 lb	2014 lb	1396 lb
1.500"	3.534 in²	7.068 in²	3435 lb	2757 lb	2396 lb	1767 lb
1.625"	4.148 in²	8.296 in²	4032 lb	3235 lb	2812 lb	1950 lb

Figure (70): Force variations vs master cylinder bore diameter.

approaching a solid obstruction at speed that leaves one feeling just the slightest bit uneasy. I tend to use the largest master cylinders which will allow the driver to develop the necessary braking force without undo leg pressure. This usually works out to be about one size up from what the car was supplied with. A useful by-product is that we end up, not only with a harder pedal, but with reduced free play and reduced total pedal travel—both good things. It is not possible to generalize about what size is best, but Figure (70) shows in tabular form some of the possible permutations.

THE DYNAMICS OF FRONT TO REAR BRAKING FORCE BALANCE

If we were to develop equal braking power on all four tires, then, even under straight line braking on a smooth road, under hard braking, the rear wheels would lock due to forward load transfer. This would rob the rear tires of their cornering power and any deviation from straight line running (side gust, road irregularity, uneven load transfer or whatever) would result in a very unstable vehicle due to total oversteer—unless the driver eased off the pedal, the car would spin. The rear tires simply would not have any cornering force available to deal with side loads. This is exactly what happens when you put the brakes on too hard with a Detroit car that is lightly loaded—even with the popular in line proportioning valve.

This nastiness is a product of forward load transfer under braking as discussed in Chapter Three. The harder the vehicle is braked, the more load is transferred from the rear tires to the fronts and, since the tires' tractive capability is a direct function of vertical load, the less braking torque the rear tires can accept without locking. If the rear tires lock while the fronts are still rolling, we must reduce the rate of deceleration or spin. This business of getting all sideways and funny in the braking area is no fun at all and should be avoided.

On the other hand, if the fronts lock first, we will merely slide onward in the direction of original travel (unfortunately this will be at a tangent to any curved path which we may have been attempting to follow) until the driver eases off the pedal enough to unlock the tires and regain steering control. In an open wheeled car the driver can see the tires stop and the smoke start, which may be of some help in figuring out what is happening. While it is not to be recommended, this uncontrolled understeer mode is preferable to oversteer under the circumstances. If things are not carried to extremes, the tires won't even be flat spotted.

Quite obviously, if the front to rear brake balance is not adjusted pretty close to optimum, we run the risk of locking one set of tires or the others which will achieve no good results. Further, we will not be able to use all of the braking ability of the vehicle because total braking capacity will be limited by premature locking of one set of tires while the other set is operating at below its maximum and is, to some extent, along for the ride. Equally obvious is the fact that the braking effort must be biased toward the front of the vehicle.

The optimum available adjustment, at the present state of the art, is to arrange things so that the front tires will lock just before the rears under heavy straight line braking. In this way, steering and directional control will be maintained when we do apply too much pedal pressure (or hit oil, etc.) while we are getting as much decelerative torque from each tire as is practically available. How much braking is proportioned to the front is a reasonably complex function of cg height, wheelbase, front and rear tire footprint area, aerodynamic downforce, tire compound and track surface conditions. It is easier to determine and to adjust than it is to describe. Most drivers run far too much front brake bias.

FRONT TO REAR BRAKE FORCE ADJUSTMENT

The basic front to rear brake effort proportioning is determined by the ratio of the area of the front master cylinder bore to the total front caliper piston area compared to the same factors at the rear. This is a design function and, properly done, we will end up with the correct force ratio and

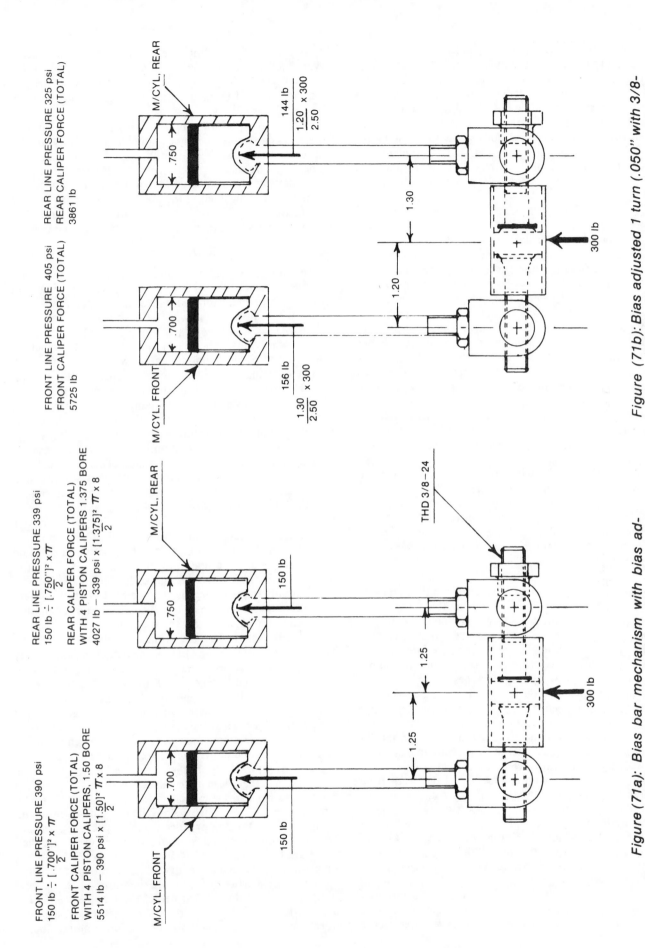

FRONT LINE PRESSURE 390 psi
$150 \text{ lb} \div [\frac{.700''}{2}]^2 \times \pi$

FRONT CALIPER FORCE (TOTAL)
WITH 4 PISTON CALIPERS, 1.50 BORE
$5514 \text{ lb} - 390 \text{ psi} \times [\frac{1.50}{2}]^2 \pi \times 8$

M/CYL, FRONT

.700

150 lb

1.25

1.25

300 lb

THD 3/8-24

M/CYL, REAR

.750

150 lb

REAR LINE PRESSURE 339 psi
$150 \text{ lb} \div [\frac{.750''}{2}]^2 \times \pi$

REAR CALIPER FORCE (TOTAL)
WITH 4 PISTON CALIPERS 1.375 BORE
$4027 \text{ lb} - 339 \text{ psi} \times [\frac{1.375}{2}]^2 \pi \times 8$

Figure (71a): Bias bar mechanism with bias adjustment in center. Front to rear force ratio 57.8:42.2.

FRONT LINE PRESSURE 405 psi
FRONT CALIPER FORCE (TOTAL)
5725 lb

M/CYL, FRONT

.700

156 lb
$\frac{1.30}{2.50} \times 300$

1.20

1.30

300 lb

REAR LINE PRESSURE 325 psi
REAR CALIPER FORCE (TOTAL)
3861 lb

M/CYL, REAR

.750

144 lb
$\frac{1.20}{2.50} \times 300$

Figure (71b): Bias adjusted 1 turn (.050" with 3/8-24 thread) toward front brakes front to rear force ratio 59.7:40.3.

113

equal or very close to equal master cylinder bores so that the linear travel of the front master cylinder will be equal to that of the rear and the bias bar will not tend to cock. To provide more relative braking force at the front we can increase the front disc diameter, pad area and/or caliper piston area or we can decrease the front master cylinder bore diameter. Practically, this almost always boils down to changing the master cylinder or reducing pad area. Most designers do a pretty damned good job in this area and all that we usually have to worry about is fine tuning the system with the bias bar.

THE BIAS BAR

We fine tune the brake balance with the bias bar. This allows us to make rapid adjustments to suit varying track conditions, tire compounds or driver preference. The device, illustrated in Figure (71) works by moving the pivot point of the bar towards whichever master cylinder we want to put out more pressure. This changes the mechanical advantage of the bar and proportions more of the driver's foot pressure to the cylinder closest to the pivot and less to the cylinder which is further away. To put more effort on the front brakes you move the pivot toward the front master cylinder. This sounds both simple and obvious. The frequency with which the brake bias gets adjusted backwards is amazing. This leads to confusion, hard feelings and harsh words and wastes valuable practice time. Use a label maker or a set of stamps and mark on the chassis which way to turn the bar in order to increase front braking effort.

The optimum brake bias will vary from track to track and from driver to driver. Usually, the better the driver, the more rear brakes he can stand. It also pays to remember that, if the ratio is right for braking on a level surface, the fronts will lock when going downhill and the rears when going uphill. We roughly adjust the bias on the jack stands and fine tune it on the track. Both methods were described in *Prepare to Win*.

Having done all of this, if we have a truly skilled and sensitive driver, we will now find that, during the corner entry phase, while flirting at the edge of the traction circle, we will occasionally lock the inside front tire. As a matter of fact, the really fast drivers, when in a real hurry, are forever emitting little puffs of smoke from the inside front. In the old days of Coopers and trailing arm Porsches, it used to stop—entirely and visibly. Of course, it was six inches off the ground when this happened. The puffs of smoke are visible evidence of very precise brake modulation and driver sensitivity. I, for one, have some difficulty in believing that this degree of feedback can be achieved by the human being with any consistency—but that is what genius is all about.

Anyway, we get away with this locking of the inside front while braking and turning because, at this point, almost all of the load has been transferred to the outside tire and the inside is along for the ride. So long as it is not upsetting the car, just take it as an indication of increasing driver skill and be happy. If it is upsetting the car and the brake ratio is correct, try loading the inside wheel a few pounds with the anti-roll bar.

The other thing that you may find out is that the optimum brake ratio may change depending on the fuel load. For sure it will change if it rains (less forward load transfer means

that you can stand a lot more rear brake). Rally cars feature driver adjustable brake bias by means of a flex cable to the fiddle bar. Depending on how far you trust your driver's good judgement, I think that this would be a good thing on road racing cars.

The front to rear brake bias is further complicated by a few more items—the front tire diameter is probably smaller than the rear and so is its footprint area. The tread compound and carcass construction may well be different, the front wheels are being steered and, if wings are installed, we will have more download at the rear. We should be aware of these factors, but since we can't do anything about them we need not worry about them. We merely tune around them.

BRAKE PADS

The pads (or shoes) have three requirements: they must stop the car controllably and without fade; they must last long enough to do the job and it helps the budget if they don't chew up the discs. What works best on a Corvette or an IMSA Monza won't work at all on a Formula Atlantic car because the pads won't get hot enough to function. Conversely, DS 11 would last about two laps on a Corvette before the lining fell off the backing plates as little mites of dust. The coefficient of friction between the pad material and the disc is a function of operating temperature. Normally the coefficient rises pretty steeply until the threshold of the design operating temperature range is reached. It then stays pretty constant (at about 0.3) until the limiting temperature is reached whereupon the pad fades. This characteristic curve will not cause trouble unless the brakes at one end of the car are operating at a vastly different temperature than the other. If this should occur in a long braking area (very high speed to very low speed), or in a section of the course where there are several hard brake applications with little cool off time, it is possible that the brake balance could change due to one end operating at a different coefficient of friction from the other—or one end could actually fade. What usually happens here is that we cool the front brakes and ignore the rears—what the hell, they're not doing that much anyway. This works okay most of the time. Then we get to Elkhart Lake and find ourselves in trouble. Temperature paint on the O.D. of the discs is as good a way as any to figure out the relative operating temperature—if there is a marked difference, you will have to get better cooling to the hot end, or increase the disc mass (heat sink). In this day and age, there is no way that you are going to get away with solid discs at the rear of a Formula Atlantic Car.

If you are operating a heavy car with brake temperatures in the 1200° F. and above range, then you are going to have to use Raybestos M 19 pads—or Hardie Ferodo 1103. The only problems that these materials cause is that they chew up the discs rather badly—especially the M-19—and they take forever to bed. If they have been well cooled down by a long straight (as in Daytona or Pocono) they will take a certain amount of time to get back up to a temperature where they will start to work—AFTER you put the brakes on. This simply means that you are not going to get much retardation for the first portion of the braking area after a long straight—or into the first corner of the race. Warming the pads with the left foot before you reach the braking area works well and doesn't slow you down worth talking about.

114

In most classes of racing, the majority of the competitors are using Ferodo DS11—which has been around almost as long as I have and works just fine. So long as brake temperatures don't get over 1100° F., it has no surprises, is easy to bed, easy on the discs and works very well indeed. However, I don't think that it is the hot tip.

Mintex M17FF is a relative newcomer to the scene, at least in this county. It is softer than DS11 but apparently has a broader operating temperature range. This is an apparent contradiction in terms which I will attribute to magic. It offers more initial bite than DS11, is easier to bed and requires less pedal pressure. It is also easier for the driver to modulate—probably because of a flatter and wider temperature vs coefficient curve. Naturally these advantages do not come free. Wear rate is rapid (they probably wouldn't last 200 miles which is, no doubt, why the Formula One contingent doesn't use them and they are hell on discs mainly because the compound has a heavy concentration of iron particles. Sometimes it appears that disc wear is almost equal to pad wear. Do not be mislead by the quick bedding feature—they still do require bedding and you will not get away with starting the race on new pads.

The real hot ticket, now that Tilton Engineering is importing the Australian Hardie Ferodo line of brake pads, is probably Hardie Ferodo "premium." These pads seem to have about the same performance characteristics as Mintex, but, because they utilize brass or copper instead of iron, they don't chew up the discs.

PAD AND DISC MODIFICATIONS

Most of the racing brake caliper manufacturers have figured out that the steel backing plates on the pads will, given half a chance, dig into the alloy caliper bodies and bind. This results in erratic braking and tapered pad wear. Girling provides a little steel box in which the backing plates are housed and against which they slide. Lockheed lets the pads slide against hardened steel stiffening plates. Hurst Airheart, at the time of writing, expects the pads to slide directly on aluminum, which they don't do very well. This is really the only fault in an otherwise serviceable caliper (they helped their seal problem some time ago). If you want your Airheart brakes to work truly well you will have to machine either the pads or the calipers and inset steel plates for the pads to slide on—a real pain. The backing plates should have slightly rounded edges and should be about .015" to .030" loose in the calipers. They should also be at least .125" thick—which is another Airheart shortcoming.

All new pads arrive with at least one radial slot moulded into the lining. The slot exists to give the lining dust some place to go other than between the pad and the disc. In many cases the slot instantly fills up with fused lining dust. This is trying to tell us something. If your slots are filling up, mill another slot at right angles to the stock one at the same depth. This helps quite a lot. If the slot is not filling up, don't waste your time and money.

Most racing discs now come with some number of .060" tangental slots milled into the operating surface. Their function is to wipe the boundary layer of incandescent dust from the rotating disc as it comes into contact with the leading edge of the pad—"wipe the fire band" is the terminology used by the technical boffins. If the slots fill up, they do no

good. In this case, double the number of slots. They are best formed with a slitting cutter on a mill, but a ball end mill will do it. They can also be cut, carefully, with a coarse hack saw blade. Do not extend the slots across the mounting flange of the disc. Slotted discs are right and left handed. They should be installed so that the slots become parallel to the leading edge of the pad as the disc is rotated. In an emergency, don't worry about it. Dynamically balancing the discs takes little time and can make things a lot smoother—especially if there has been a minor core shift in the casting of a ventilated disc. Speaking of ventilated discs, they are also right and left handed and are meant to be mounted so that the curved vanes function as an air pump. You will also notice that the outboard disc cheek is always thicker than the inboard—they are designed that way. Inspect all ventilated discs to be sure that the cheeks are of constant thickness, however. Core shifts can and do cause thickness variations which don't help the heat sink characteristics and throw the discs totally out of balance.

DRILLED DISCS

Drilled discs—a la Porsche—do the same thing as slotted discs, except that they do it better and they remove considerable mass from the disc itself. They also decrease pad taper by a notable amount at the expense of increased pad wear. They are also prone to cracking around the drilled holes. They are a bitch to drill—and it must be done correctly. There are two theories here, the Porsche pattern runs through the ventilated disc webs and the Automotive Products pattern does not. Supposedly the AP method cuts down on disc cracking. I have never been able to tell any functional difference. I believe in drilled discs—even at the expense of premature cracking. I use the Porsche pattern for curved vane discs and the AP pattern for straight vanes—but only when I cannot obtain curved vane discs.

PAD WEAR

There is a prevalent theory that, after pads are about 40% worn, they are no good. The theory is only half true. It is true that braking performance deteriorates as the pads wear. Pedal height decreases and becomes less consistent, free travel increases and the driver becomes unhappy. Substitution of freshly bedded pads returns everything to original and the driver is all happy again. So it becomes Gospel Truth that worn pads are no good.

The fact of the matter is that the deterioration in braking performance is due to taper wear of the pads rather than to any decrease in frictional characteristics. There are two types of taper wear—with distinctly different causes. Transverse taper is caused by skewed mounting of the caliper with respect to the plane of rotation of the disc or by spreading of the caliper itself due to the hydraulic loads involved. The fact that the O.D. of the disc runs hotter than the I.D. due to its greater linear speed may also have an effect. With the latest generation of racing calipers and any kind of rational brake line pressure, caliper flex should not be a significant problem and any significant transverse wear is almost invariably caused by either improper mounting or insufficient mounting stiffness.

Longitudinal taper wear is caused by either bad caliper

alignment or by the inescapable fact that the trailing edge of the pad runs hotter than the leading edge and so wears faster.

What happens with taper wear is that, once the pads are tapered to any noticeable extent, either we are no longer getting full pad contact, or in the racing car, we are distorting things to get it. With tapered pads we must either bend the backing plates or cock the caliper pistons in their bores to get full contact. This increases pedal effort, used up pedal travel, distorts seals, scours pistons and bores and causes the friction lining to separate from the backing plate—None of this does any good for any part of the system or for the driver's feel of things.

To reduce longitudinal taper wear, once we have shimmed the calipers true, stiffened the mounts as much as we can and drilled the discs, we are going to have to operate on the pad itself. The operation consists of milling away the area of the cooler running leading edge of the pads enough so that the taper wear goes away. I don't know of any method to calculate the amount of reduction—you just have to cut and try. Figure (72) shows a typical pad, modified to reduce taper wear on a heavy sedan with drilled discs. It worked well and had no measurable effect on pad wear.

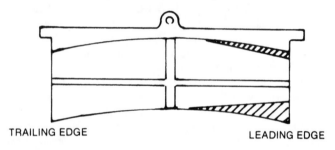

TRAILING EDGE   LEADING EDGE

Figure (72): Pad modified to reduce longitudinal taper wear.

THE EFFECTS OF SUSPENSION ADJUSTMENT ON BRAKING PERFORMANCE

It is not as widely appreciated as it should be that suspension system design and adjustment—or lack of it—can foul up a perfectly good braking system. Since braking force must be transmitted to the road surface through the tires, anything that tends to interrupt the smooth progression of wheel movement, load transfer or which puts the tire at an unfortunate camber angle, is going to detract from braking performance. For example, we often hear of a car that pulls to one side or the other under hard braking. Almost always this turns out to be due to a suspension malfunction rather than to a fault within the braking system. Pulling under the brakes is usually caused by uneven front castor settings, uneven camber, unequal corner weight or uneven spring or shock absorber forces. Darting—as opposed to pulling—can be caused by insufficient bump travel, uneven front bump stop heights, too much front bump stop, excessive front toe-in (or toe-out). Weaving, as opposed to either pulling or darting, can be caused by front bump steer or too much rear brake bias. It goes on and on. Table (73) is an attempt to categorize the probable causes and cures for the more common brake system problems. We also often hear statements such as "The Ralt outbrakes the March—therefore it must

have better brakes." Nonsense, the Ralt has a more favorable front tire camber curve and so is able to utilize more of the tires' braking capacity. The brakes themselves are identical.

OIL ON THE DISCS

We very seldom get any oil on the front discs and pads. If the rear main oil seal starts to leak, we are very *liable to* get oil on the rears. The brakes will not function very well with oil on them. The discs can be cleaned if they have been oiled, but the pads will be ruined forever. Therefore, it behooves us, if our engine is prone to leak oil onto the brakes, to build some sort of a rudimentary shield to deflect any leaking oil elsewhere.

That's about it. As I said in the beginning, once you have the braking system properly set up and sorted out, there really aren't that many meaningful improvements to be made—it's basically a question of getting everything right and keeping it that way. About all that you should have to change from track to track is a slight amount of brake bias and, maybe, the pad compound. However, knowing how to set the system up and how to optimize braking performance is one of those situations where, although all systems are created equal, they don't necessarily stay that way. If for no other reason than driver confidence, a consistent and controllable braking system is one of the differences between winning races and finishing third.

THE FUTURE

I firmly believe that the four wheel independent anti-lock braking system will make its appearance in motor racing in the very near future. The fact that I have been saying this for some years now and nothing has happened does not change my opinion. The Department of Transport will eventually demand it on street cars and—once the basic hardware is in mass production—modified, more sensitive, fail safe systems will appear in the racing car. As soon as someone gets such a system to work, we will all adapt them. However, that is in the future and has no place in a practical book of this nature.

Figure (73): Brake system problems and probable causes.

PROBLEM (SYMPTOM)

Low pedal—will pump up

> PROBABLE CAUSES
>
> Air in brake system due to:
> improper bleeding
> sub standard fluid
> loose fitting
> improperly assembled fitting
> worn or damaged master cylinder seals
> worn or over age caliper seals
> excessive pickup on caliper pistons

Low pedal—will not pump up

> Worn or over age caliper seals
> Badly tapered pads

Pad knock back (disc out of true)
Master cylinders too small
Bias bar too far off center
Caliper pistons returning too far, caused by:
    bad seal design
    wrong seals fitted
    excessive pickup on caliper pistons

Inconsistent brake pedal height

Spindle flex
Loose wheel bearing
Caliper pistons returning too far (see above)
Bias bar clevises too tight on tube
Bias bar bearing circlip not in place
Bias bar too far off center

Consistent mushy pedal

Master cylinder or brake pedal mounts flexing

Brake pedal does not return

Master cylinder reservoirs not vented
Actuating rod lacks clearance on either bias bar or
    master cylinder piston
Pedal pivot bolt too tight (bushing too short)

Front wheels locking (both)

Too much front bias

Rear wheels locking (both)

Too much rear bias

Front or rear wheel locking (one)

Frozen caliper piston on side not locking
Oil on disc/pad on side not locking
· Cross weight in chassis

All four wheels lock too easily

Master cylinders too small

Driver cannot lock wheels

Master cylinders too large
Pad compound too hard
Disc diameter too small

Excessive pedal travel

Master cylinders too small
Bad caliper seal design
Tapered pads

Pedal high and hard, car won't stop

Pad fade
Pad compound too hard
Master cylinders too large
Vacuum reservoir too small

Brakes stick on

Cone washer retaining master cylinder actuating rod
    in bore installed backward.
Ball end of actuating rod does not match master
    cylinder piston
Master cylinders not vented

Brake ratio erratic
or Car does not respond to brake ratio adjustment

Bias bar loose on shaft
Bias bar clevises binding on tube
Excessive clearance between bias bar clevises and
    tube

Pedal thumps driver's foot

Incredible run out
Cracked brake disc

Car weaves under brakes in a stable mode

Too much front brake bias
Front bump steer

Car darts under brakes

Uneven front bump rubbers
Too much front bump rubber
Excessive front toe in
Excessive front toe out
Uneven shocks

Car pulls to one side under brakes

Uneven front castor
Wildly uneven front camber
Oil on disc
Unequal corner weight
Preloaded sway bar
Uneven shock forces

Car judders (vibrates) under brakes

Loose suspension attach point
Cracked disc

Car is unstable under brakes—wants to come around

Too much rear bias

Pads are glazed and surface flaking

Brakes too hot

Master cylinder doesn't function

Front seal gone

Brakes smoke and/or smell in pit

Driver brought car in with brakes still very hot—
    chastise driver

CHAPTER ELEVEN

UNDERSTEER, OVERSTEER, STABILITY AND RESPONSE

UNDERSTEER, OVERSTEER, STABILITY AND RESPONSE

Thousands of words and reams of paper have been expended over the years in efforts to explain vehicle understeer and oversteer. The man who has done it best is Denis Jenkinson in THE RACING DRIVER. Jenks knows more about motor racing than anyone. The book was first published in 1958—in the days of skinny tires and no wings. Nothing basic has changed since then except that the traction circle has grown larger and the line between. "I've got it" and "It's got me" has become finer. Read the book.

I feel that the basic problem in understanding the subject lies not in trying to figure out what understeer is or what oversteer is—that's pretty simple—but in realizing that the same vehicle, with nothing physically changed in its set up, can—and will—understeer in some corners and oversteer in others. Further, in the same corner—on the same lap—it is not only possible for the vehicle to understeer in one portion of the corner and oversteer in another but, if the car is going to be really fast, it is mandatory for it to do so. Most of the printed explanations of the twin phenomena of vehicle balance ignore this fact and concentrate on steady state conditions which, while easier to explore, are of limited and academic interest to the racer. We are going to try for the big picture—one step at a time.

Understeer and oversteer can be explained in terms of relative front and rear tire slip angles, in terms of tire thrusts about the vehicle's center of gravity and/or in terms of tire force vectors with respect to turn centers. We'll attempt all three. We must, however, never lose sight of the fact that from the viewpoint of the sensing and controlling mechanism of the racing car—the driver—it becomes a very simple question of whether the front tires reach the limit of cornering traction before or after the rear tires do. If the fronts break loose first, the car heads—nose first—toward the outside wall. The driver then has to slow the car in order to regain steering control and, should he succeed in doing so before he hits something, will come in and complain about excessive understeer or "push." On the other hand, if the rears break loose first, the car tries to spin and the driver applies opposite steering lock and either backs off the throttle or adds power depending on circumstances and driver characteristics. He then bitches about oversteer or says that the car is too "loose." In either case it is up to the Man In Charge of the operation, be he driver, team manager, mechanic or engineer, to interpret the driver's frank commentary, ask the necessary leading questions, try to figure out what the car is really doing—where, under what conditions and why it is doing it—and then decide what to do about it. The only way that any rational decisions are going to be made is for everyone concerned to understand what the driver is talking about and for at least one of the people involved to have a basic understanding of the dynamics of understeer/oversteer vehicle balance and the physical forces that govern and modify that balance.

Before we go any further into this particular jungle we had better pause and define just what we really want to achieve in the line of vehicle balance. There are those who consider that the ideal racing car would exhibit slight understeering tendencies under any and all conditions. I do not agree. No one believes that the car should oversteer under all conditions. I shall state what I consider to be the ideal balance conditions and basically why. We'll go more deeply into the why and how of things as we go along.

Understeer, as we will see, is basically a stable condition. The understeering vehicle will follow a curved path of greater radius than the steering angle of the front wheels indicates. If the understeer is unintentional on the driver's part, this actual radius will be greater than what he had in mind. If he has planned on the understeer, or if he has induced it, he will have compensated by adjusting his corner entry speed and steering angle and the car will be headed where he intended for it to go—regardless of where the front wheels are pointing. In either case the car is not trying to spin and, assuming that the driver has room to play in, the turn radius can be reduced and the car brought back into line by slowing to the point where reduced vehicle speed with respect to the radius of curvature brings the front tire slip angles back into the traction range. Oversteer, on the other hand, is an unstable condition. The car is trying to spin and the spin must be stopped before we can worry about regaining directional control.

During straight line running then, we want the car to understeer lightly in response to any side forces that may be encountered—from bumps, wind gusts, road camber changes or aerodynamic disturbances from other cars—or from load transfers caused by acceleration or braking. We do not want the driver to be forever correcting a tendency for the car to proceed down the track backwards. Besides, if the car is not stable, we will not be able to brake really hard.

During the corner entry phase, whatever the road speed, we again want a light understeer condition. This will provide the driver with the stability that he needs while he is easing off the brakes and building up cornering force in order to use all of the tire—as in the traction circle explained in Chapter Two. He can adjust the car's actual path of motion by a combination of anticipation, corner entry speed, braking effort and steering angle.

In the mid-phase of the corner—when we have finished braking but have not yet started to accelerate, although the power will be on either to stabilize the car or to provide enough thrust at the driven wheels to maintain cornering speed—we need a very light understeer. The length of this mid-phase of the corner will vary with corner speed and with individual driver technique. In a slow corner it is about as long as it takes the driver to move his foot from one pedal to the other. In a really fast corner, it can last for several seconds.

In the corner exit phase of things, which begins when the driver first applies enough power to begin accelerating out of the corner, we want the car to gently change over to slight power oversteer so that the driver can control the path of the vehicle without having to decrease power. Actually, what we are really looking for here is probably natural neutral steer or very slight understeer which the driver converts to the desired amount of power oversteer by throttle application.

At all times we must avoid excessive understeer which, as we will see, creates front tire drag which in turn both reduces the cornering power of the front tires and requires extra thrust from the rear tires in order to maintain road speed. Just enough understeer to provide stability is what we are looking for. At the same time, too much oversteer on corner exit will require the driver to either back off the power or create lots of wheelspin in order to maintain or to regain directional control. Either way, acceleration will suffer. We need just enough power oversteer to get the tail out enough to give the driver directional control with the throttle. It is all a question of balance and, like a tightrope act, it ain't easy—it just looks easy when it is done right.

At this point it is important that we differentiate between natural power oversteer and that oversteer which is exhibited by the racing car with a high power to weight ratio when the driver slams the throttle to the floor coming out of a slow corner. Any powerful car can be made to oversteer by abuse of the throttle. The results are always spectacular and sometimes useful in regaining control—but they are never fast. One of the problems faced by young drivers when they first get their hands—and feet—on a real racing car, with real power, lies in bringing themselves to realize that they can no longer slam on the power coming out of slow corners like they did in Formula Ford or whatever. Due to the nature of the traction circle the driver must learn throttle control—it's a bit like learning to squeeze the trigger of a gun. This statement should by no means be taken as an endorsement of the pussyfoot style of driving beloved of a legion of drivers who just don't have the balls to use the throttle and who talk a lot about the importance of being really smooth. I am just saying that you shouldn't give the car more throttle than it can take lest you provoke too much oversteer and find it necessary to slow the car. If it takes a giant burst of throttle to get the car pointed make a chassis adjustment. The days when race drivers had to learn to live with and to compensate for unnatural behavior or acts on the part of their chariots are, hopefully, past.

Fortunately, the basic layout of the modern racing car has purposely evolved in such a way as to promote this gentle progression from light load understeer to power oversteer as we wend our way through the corner. In straight line running, the relative sizes of the front and rear tires and wings combine with the static and dynamic loads on the tires to ensure that response to transient upsets will be in the direction of understeer. On corner entry forward load transfer and the fact that the front tires do relatively more braking work than the rears plus the lesser section depth of the front tires all tend toward understeer. In fact, the big problem on corner entry is usually the prevention of excessive understeer. As we ease off the brakes more front tire traction is available for cornering force but we still have more rear tire in relation to vertical load than we do front so we will still be in a natural understeer condition—with some excess rear tire capacity which will allow us to begin hard acceleration while still cornering at the limit of the front tire cornering force. Once we have started to accelerate, longitudinal load transfer will increase the load on the rear tires which, in turn, will allow us to accelerate harder while still maintaining vehicle balance—so long as we don't overdo things.

THE DYNAMICS OF VEHICLE BALANCE

Now that we have defined what we want, it is time to take a look at how we get it. This is going to require a lot of illustrations and a fair bit of re-reading. Sorry about that! In order to keep the illustrations to reasonable size, all angles have been exaggerated. Looking at Figure (74) we see our racer cornering to its right with no braking or accelerating thrusts applied to the tires. Centrifugal force is represented by a large arrow or vector acting at the vehicle's center of gravity and acting away from the center of the turn. The amount of centrifugal force present will, of course, depend on gross vehicle weight, corner radius and vehicle velocity. We will assume that the vehicle is operating at its limit of tire traction. The centrifugal force is opposed by the cornering forces generated by the four tires. For simplicity's sake the cornering force of the pair of front tires is represented by a single vector at the more heavily laden outside front tire and the cornering force of the pair of rear tires by a single vector at the outside rear. To achieve a steady state condition, the sum of the cornering forces generated by the front and rear tires must equal centrifugal force. Front and rear tire slip angles are represented by αF and αR respectively. In case (A) front and rear slip angles and cornering forces are balanced and the vehicle is in a neutral steer condition. In case (B) the front slip angle has exceeded the rear and the vehicle is in an unbalanced understeer state. In case (C) the rear slip angle has exceeded the front and the vehicle is in an unbalanced oversteer state.

Assuming vehicle speed to remain constant, the understeering car will widen its turn radius until the increased radius reduces the centrifugal force to a level that can be matched by the front tire cornering force. At that point the car will enter a steady state turn to the right at the same road speed but with an increased turn radius and therefore at a decreased level of cornering force. The total cornering force, or lateral g-capacity of the vehicle is limited by the lateral capacity of the front tires.

In case (C) the vehicle will proceed at a reduced cornering radius which will automatically increase the rear slip angle and decrease the rear tire cornering force and, if the driver doesn't do something about it, the car will spin. Which is why oversteer is a basically unstable condition.

TURN CENTERS

Proceeding to Figure (75) we find our racer still turning to

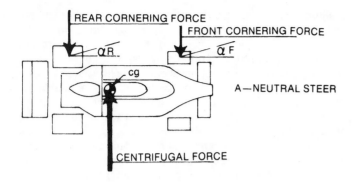

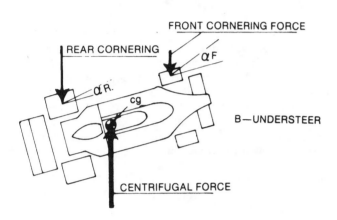

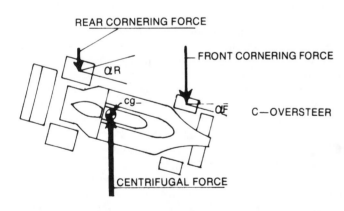

Figure (74): Balance of forces between front and rear tire cornering forces resulting in neutral steer, understeer and oversteer.

its right and still without braking or acceleration thrust. This time the front wheels are steered to some finite angle. In the absence of tire slip angles, and assuming Akerman steering, the center of the circle that will be described by the car at a constant road speed will be the Akerman or geometric turn center defined by the intersection of a line extending the rear axle and a line extending the front steering arms. We will assume that vehicle speed is such that the cornering power of the tires can deal with the centrifugal force generated by the

turn. This is a common illustration in books of this nature. Unfortunately it has little relation to the real world. First of all, in order for the vehicle to turn at all, we found in Chapter Two that both front and rear tires must develop finite slip angles. Second, in order for the vehicle to maintain a constant speed, a driving thrust must be applied to the driven tires of sufficient magnitude to balance the inertia and drag that is trying to slow the car. This changes the *whole turn center picture.*

TURN CENTERS MODIFIED BY TIRE SLIP ANGLE

The instant that a tire develops a slip angle—and, in order to develop cornering force, any tire must develop a slip angle, the tire must also develop a cornering drag force proportional to that slip angle. This cornering drag may be considered as separate from and additive to the rolling resistance of the tire. It is the actual drag produced by scrubbing the tire across the road surface at an angle to the direction in which the wheel is rotating—which is, of course, the definition of a slip angle. Returning to the traction circle concept, we see in Figure (76a) that the vector representing the total tractive capacity that the tire is capable of generating under any given conditions of load, angle and coefficient of friction can be broken down into two separate vectors. One of these will be proportional to the amount of cornering force being developed and will act in a direction

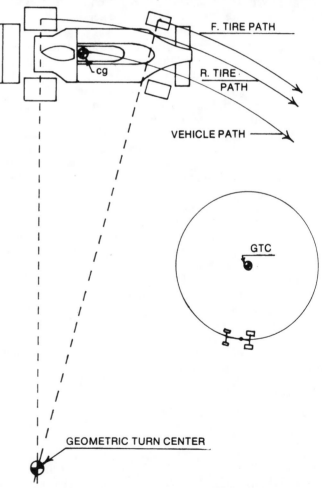

Figure (75): Geometric or Akerman turn center.

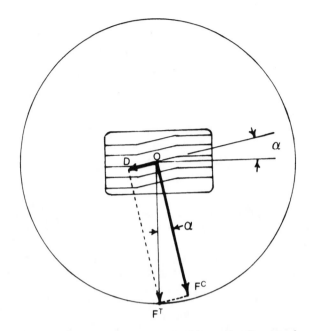

Figure (76a): Front tire operating at slip angle α with no braking thrust. Total tire tractive effort of tire, O-F_T is resolved into vectors O-F^C representing cornering force and O-D representing cornering drag.

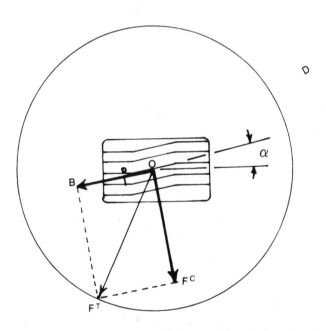

Figure (76b): Braking thrust D-B applied to tire. D-B is cumulative with cornering drag O-D. The resultant, O-B represents net braking thrust which swings the total tire traction vector, O-F^T rearwards. O-F^T is now resolved into vectors O-B, representing decelerative thrust and O-F^C representing cornering force—of lesser value than in figure A.

perpendicular to the actual rolling path of the tire. The other will represent either accelerative thrust, acting in the direction of the tire path, or it will represent drag, acting in the direction opposite to the path of tire motion. The drag component can be either drag due to braking thrust or drag due to slip angle—or it can be a combination of both—as illustrated by Figure (76b). In the case of a driven tire under an accelerative thrust while cornering there will be both an accelerative thrust and a drag component due to the slip angle. In this case, the two vectors are added algebraically and the result can be either a net thrust in either direction or a mutual canceling out. In any case, if the vertical load on a tire and its coefficient of friction remain constant, the application of either an accelerative or drag thrust will result in reduced cornering force—and vice versa. Figure (77) applies.

Figure (78) shows our racer still turning to the right with the same steering angle applied but with the slip angles necessary to establish the turn added in. At the front we have a certain amount of cornering drag and the direction of the cornering force being generated is no longer perpendicular to the plane of wheel rotation but has swung forward and is now perpendicular to the actual tire path. At the rear we have both cornering drag and enough propulsive thrust to maintain the vehicle at a constant velocity. Again, due to the slip angle, the direction of the cornering force vector has swung forward so that is is perpendicular to the path of tire motion. Since the actual location of the vehicle's instantaneous turn center is defined as the intersection of the cornering force vectors of the front and rear tires, the instantaneous turn center has moved forward with respect to the vehicle and the car is no longer describing a circle about the geometric center but a circle of the same radius about its instantaneous center. We have purposely kept the front and rear slip angles the same so the vehicle is still in a neutral steer condition. If we were to increase both front and rear slip angles by like amounts, the instantaneous turn center would move forward along the neutral steer axis while if we were to decrease them, it would move aft.

In the case of understeer, as represented by Figure (79), the front slip angle, for whatever reason, has been increased beyond the point of maximum cornering force. This has swung the front cornering force vector still further forward and moved the instantaneous center further away from the vehicle cg. The vehicle will now follow a circle of greater radius—unless it either slows or hits something.

With the oversteering car, shown in Figure (80), the opposite conditions occur. The rear slip angle now exceeds the front and the line of rear cornering force has swung forward which moves the instantaneous turn center toward the vehicle cg, forcing a shorter turn radius which, if velocity is maintained, will increase the magnitude of the centrifugal force. Since the rear tires were already operating at their limit of cornering force, they break away and the car spins.

DRIVER APPLIED CORRECTIONS

So that's what is happening from the turn center location point of view as the car shifts from neutral steer to understeer or oversteer. The question remains, what does the driver do about it. We won't worry about the effects or driver corrections on a neutral steering car. First of all,

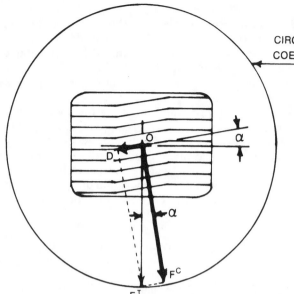

$F^C = F^T$ COSINE α = CORNERING FORCE
$O-D = F^T$ SINE α = CORNERING DRAG
IF α = 10° AND VERTICAL LOAD ON TIRE = 750 LB
F^C = (750 LB x 1.4) COSINE 10° = 1034 LB
$O-D$ = (750 LB x 1.4) SINE 10° = 182 LB

Figure (77a): Rear tire operating at slip angle α with no braking or driving thrust applied. O-F^T represents total tractive effort of tire. O-F^C represents cornering force of tire acting towards instantaneous center of turn. Vector O-D represents cornering drag due to slip angle α.

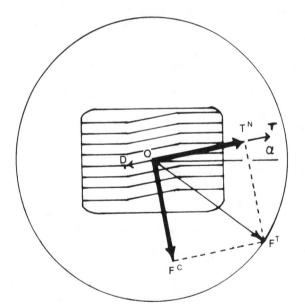

Figure (77b): Accelerative thrust O-T applied to tire. α remains 10° so O-D remains at same value and must be subtracted from O-T to arrive at O-T^N—net accelerative thrust. O-D = T-T^N. Presence of the thrust swings the total tire traction vector F^T forward so that it is no longer perpendicular to plane of tire rotation. O-F^T is now resolved into vectors O-T^N representing net thrust and O-F^C representing cornering force—which must have a lesser value than it had in figure A.

neutral steer is a rare and transient condition and, secondly, almost anything that a driver might do will convert neutral steer to either oversteer or understeer very quickly indeed. I am willing to admit that perfection would be full power neutral steer out of fast corners but even if we could achieve it, it would leave the driver no room for error because, with the hammer all the way down, if understeer should develop, he would have to come off the throttle.

Anyway, Figure (81) depicts the choices open to the driver who finds himself at the understeer limit of adhesion. Section (A) shows the front tire force vectors at the understeer limit. When the front end breaks loose and heads for the wall, the driver has three response choices. He can increase the steering lock, as shown in section (B). This will have the immediate effect of increasing the slip angle αF and the drag component O-D. Since the front slip angle threshold has already been exceeded—or else we would not be at the understeer limit—the increase in slip angle is not going to generate more cornering force, in fact it is going to cause a decrease in cornering force. The increase in tire drag O-D is going to swing the total tire force vector to the rear which will likewise result in a decrease in front tire force. So the initial result of winding on more lock when the understeer limit has been exceeded is to decrease front cornering force—which will increase the understeer still further. Not a good thing to do! There is, however, a secondary saving effect—by increasing the tire drag, we are going to effectively slow the vehicle's velocity by scrubbing off speed. If we scrub off enough speed before we hit something, the cornering force required to balance the reduced centrifugal force will be reduced to the point where the tires can deal with it and steering control will be regained so that the vehicle can proceed—at a reduced value of cornering force, but still mobile.

The driver can also apply the brakes, which is what the freeway driver does when he gets in trouble. Section (C) shows this effect. The drag is increased, the cornering force is decreased and, not shown because I can't figure out how to draw it, the tire will probably lock which will wreck the coefficient of friction. The car will understeer terminally until it either stops or hits something—unless the driver gets off the brake and performs heroics. The only time that you want to get on the brakes in an understeering car is either on a skid pad to see what happens or when you have given up all hope of regaining control and are concerned with hitting whatever you are going to hit at the minimum possible velocity. It is also true that, if the corner is slow enough and there is enough rearward brake bias, by locking or almost locking

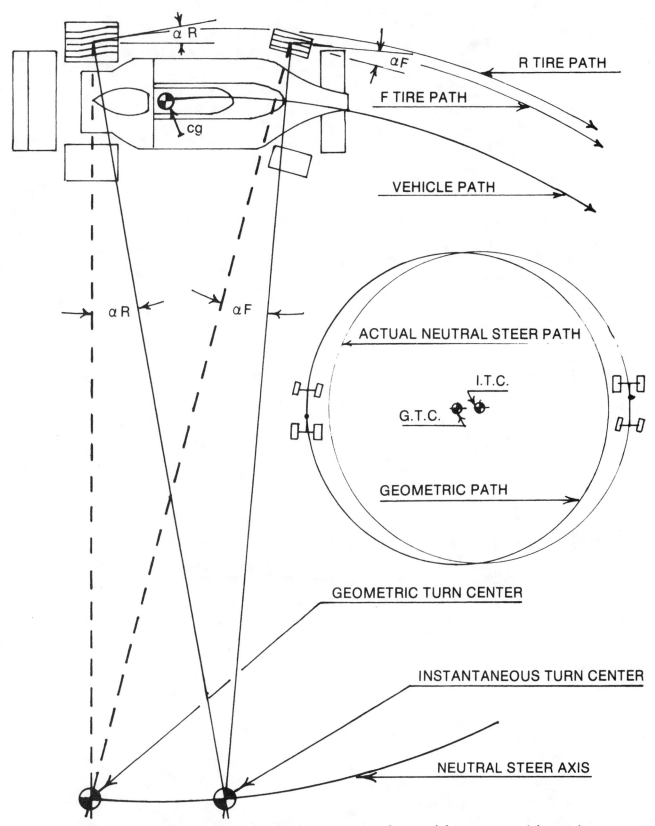

Figure (78): Displacement of actual turn center forward from geometric center due to finite slip angles necessary in order for vehicle to turn. Since in this case tire sup angle, α F = rear tire slip angle, α R, vehicle is in steady state turn at neutral steer balance. Intersections of front and rear cornering force vectors perpendicular to direction of rolling paths of tires define instantaneous turn centers. Locus of instantaneous centers for different but equal values of α F and α R defines neutral steer axis.

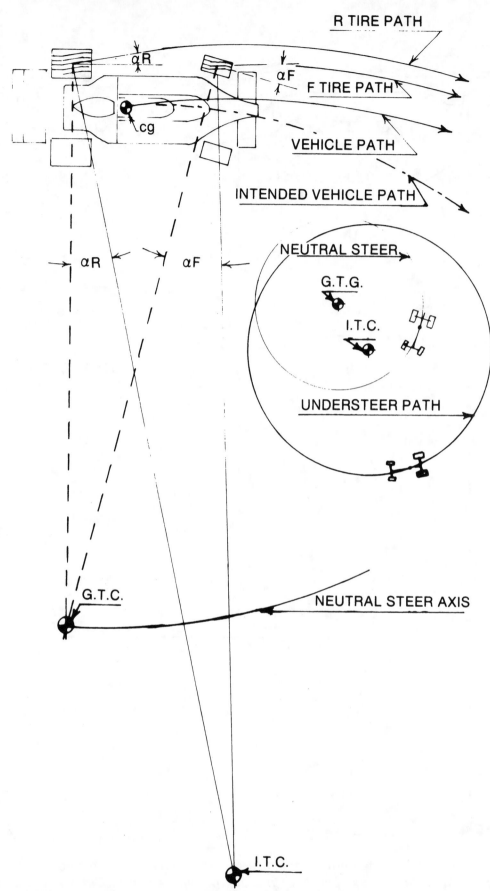

Figure (79): Front tire slip angle greater than rear instantaneous turn center displaced farther away from cg turn radius increase. Vehicle in steady state understeer turn.

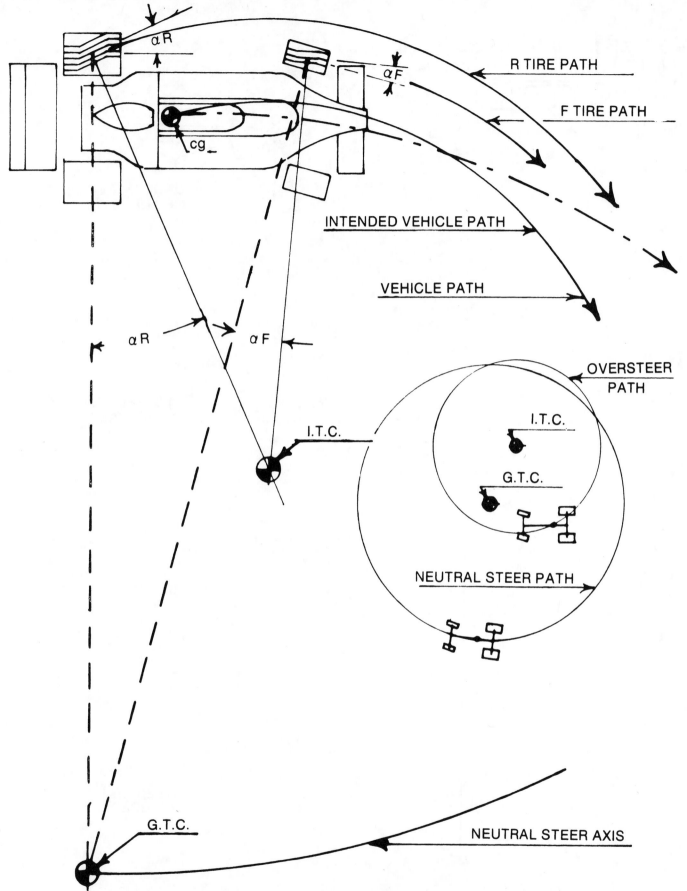

Figure (80): Rear tire slip angle greater than front. Instantaneous turn center displaced toward cg. Turn radius decreased. Vehicle in unstable oversteer condition.

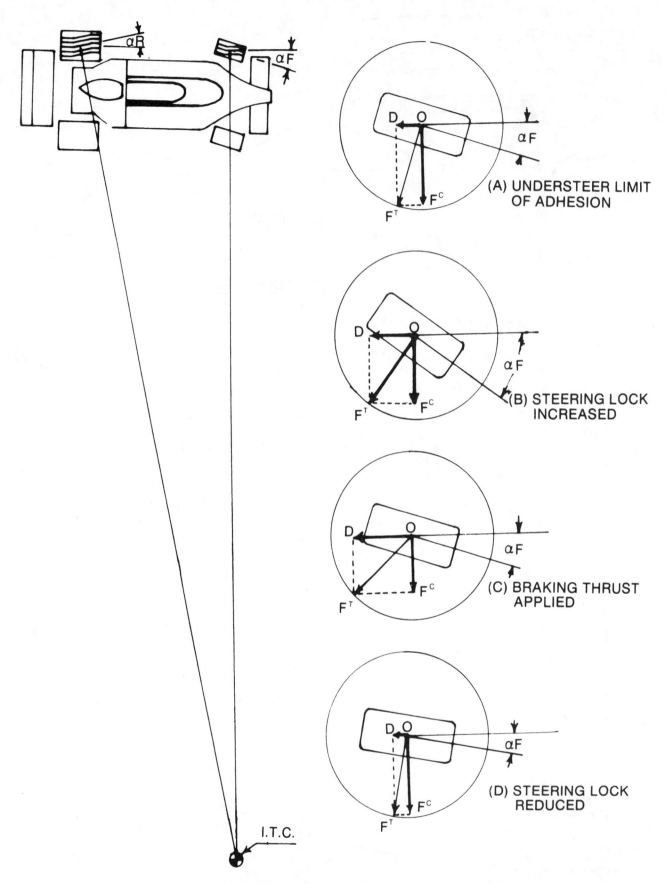

Figure (81): Vectorial representation of effects of various driver induced control corrections when understeer limit of adhesion has been exceeded.

the rear wheels, you can get the car sideways and slow enough to power your way clear. This falls under the heading of desperate maneuvers and should only have to be used as a follow-up to an error in judgment.

The third alternative as shown in (D) is to reduce the amount of steering lock. This will reduce the slip angle and increase the cornering power by a small amount. Of course it will also increase the radius of curvature but so will anything else that the driver does, other than breaking the back tires loose. With the power off, little excursions over the understeer limit are best corrected by winding the lock off until the car slows enough for the front tires to bite and then forcing it back onto the intended path at the resultant reduced velocity.

There is a fourth alternative—jerking the rear wheels loose either by massive amounts of steering lock or, theoretically, by sudden power application. The only direct effect that slamming the power on this will have on the front tires is to increase vehicle speed and reduce the front tire loading due to load transfer. Either or both effects will decrease the front cornering power. Again, if the understeer happens on the way out of a corner and the throttle response were fast enough, you might succeed in decreasing the cornering power of the rear tires enough to get the tail out and power your way out of trouble—but it is unlikely. What normally happens when we try this is that the differential takes over and the inside rear tire drives us into the wall, unless, of course, the whole sequence of events was foreseen and planned. Jerking the back loose with the steering wheel or the brakes is a better choice of desperate moves.

The oversteering car also offers the driver a series of choices as depicted in Figure (82). The normal reaction when the back end starts to slip out is to back off the throttle as in (B). This will remove the thrust component of tire force and thus add to cornering force while, at the same time, speed will be reduced and things will come back into line. If accompanied by a bit of opposite lock the whole effect will be a gentle moving over of the car out from the turn center until rear tire grip is regained and we can continue onward. Of course, we are not accelerating while all this is going on.

Hitting the brakes is not a very good idea at all. (C) shows what happens here—basically we both slow down and lose cornering force. It is quite likely that we will also turn around.

The alternative to backing off the throttle when we overstep the oversteer limit is, strangely enough, to add power as in (D). In this case, while we will inevitably reduce the magnitude of the cornering force vector, we will also swing the whole tire effort forward and, since the car is in a tail out attitude anyway, the tractive effort vector comes more into line with the turn center and we are using forward thrust as well as side force to combat the dreaded centrifugal force. This is shown in Figure (83). This leads us, more or less conveniently, to a discussion of vehicle yaw angles.

YAW ANGLE

We will define the yaw angle of our race car as the angle that the centerline of the vehicle makes with the vehicle's actual direction of motion. We can develop yaw in two directions—nose out or tail out. It has been pointed out that, in normal cornering attitudes, a vehicle is always in a tail out

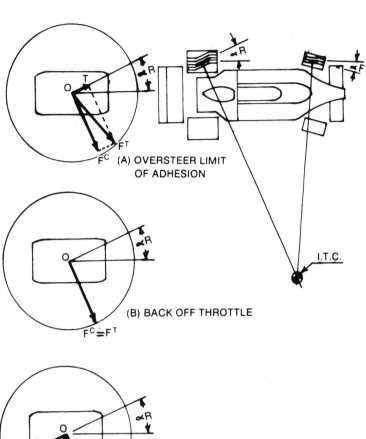

(A) OVERSTEER LIMIT OF ADHESION

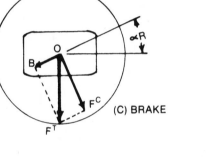

(B) BACK OFF THROTTLE

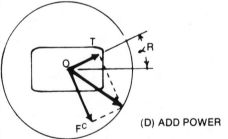

(C) BRAKE

(D) ADD POWER

Figure (82): *Representation of effects of driver induced corrections when oversteer limit of adhesion has been exceeded.*

situation—and, outside of parking lots, this is more or less true—until the understeer limit has been reached and exceeded. Up to that limit, both the understeering and the oversteering car are in a tail out attitude—although the oversteering car is more so. Only if the front end is totally wiped out will the understeering car adopt a nose out attitude—and by that time, we have stopped worrying about getting around the corner at speed and are concentrating on just getting around without hitting anything.

Large slip angles produce large yaw angles. Except on dirt we no longer see the extreme yaw angles which were com-

127

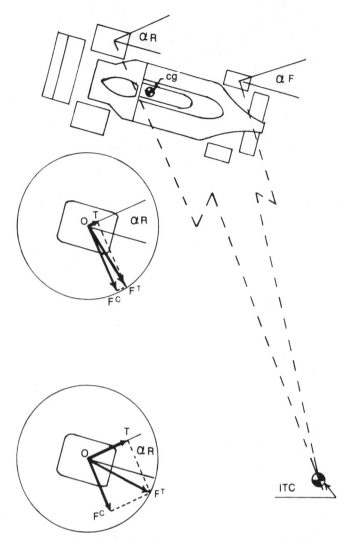

Figure (83): Application of power to oversteering vehicle stabilizes oversteer by swinging total tire force vector O-F^T toward instantaneous turn center and utilizing forward thrust to oppose centrifugal force.

mon twenty years ago. The present generation of racing tires are not efficient at large slip angles for the reasons that we pointed out in Chapter Two so the grand old days of sideways motoring are gone—except when the driver makes a mistake. Racing cars still operate at finite yaw angles and the angle is both intentional and driver controlled—it is just less obvious to the onlooker. Corner entry yaw angle is a function of entry speed versus corner radius while exit yaw is controlled by throttle application. In each case the driver is adjusting and modifying the location of the instantaneous turn center by varying the amount of vehicle yaw.

TORQUES ABOUT THE VEHICLE CENTER OF GRAVITY

While the variation of vehicle yaw angle is conscious and intentional on the driver's part, the turn center bit is not. No racing driver visualizes what is happening to the location of the instantaneous turn center as he stabs and steers his way through a given corner. Nor is he sensing anything to do with it. What the driver feels through the seat of his nomex is the effects of changes in the magnitude and direction of the various tire forces as they are reacted through the vehicle's center of gravity. Figure (84) shows a plan view of the car in a right turn situation. The circular area surrounding each tire represents that tire's traction circle and the area of each circle is proportional to the total vertical load on the tire at that moment. The vectors represent drag (D), cornering force (F^C), and total tire tractive effort (F^T). The resultant force on each tire will necessarily be reacted as a torque or turning moment about the vehicle's center of gravity. With the vehicle turning to its right, if the torque produced is counterclockwise it will tend to produce understeer. If the torque is clockwise, it will lead toward oversteer. If the total of the understeer producing torques is greater than that of the oversteer torques, the vehicle will understeer and vice versa. Anything that tends to increase front tire cornering force—or to decrease rear tire cornering force—will decrease understeer (or increase oversteer). Basically it is that simple. Unfortunately there is virtually an infinite number of factors that contribute to these tire forces and torques and isolating who is doing what with which to whom is not simple at all. The problem gets more complex when we start to consider the best and most efficient way to change the behavior or response of the vehicle. We'll start by listing the major variable factors which contribute to torques in each direction.

Understeer torque:
Lateral load transfer between the front wheels (by decreasing the total cornering power of the pair)
Longitudinal load transfer to the rear wheels
Cornering drag (understeer drag) on the front tires
Increased rear or decreased front aerodynamic downforce
Unfavorable front tire camber angles
Bottoming of the front suspension
Pulling the inside front tire off the road while it is in a partially laden condition (due to insufficient droop travel or to insufficient spring pressure in the droop position)
Increasing the relative front braking ratio
Locking the front brakes

Oversteer Torque:
Lateral load transfer between the rear wheels
Excessive accelerative thrust on the rear tires
Unfavorable rear tire camber angles
Decreased rear or increased front aerodynamic downforce
Longitudinal load transfer to the front tires
Bottoming the rear suspension
Pulling the inside rear tire off the road in droop
Increase in rear braking effort
Locking the rear brakes

We have discussed each of these factors, in some detail, elsewhere in the book. Rather than covering them again, a list of the causes and effects of various chassis deficiencies will be found at the end of this chapter.

To illustrate the way things work, however, if we return to Figure (84), we see that section (A) depicts a vehicle with too much low speed understeer. The quick way to tune it out is to

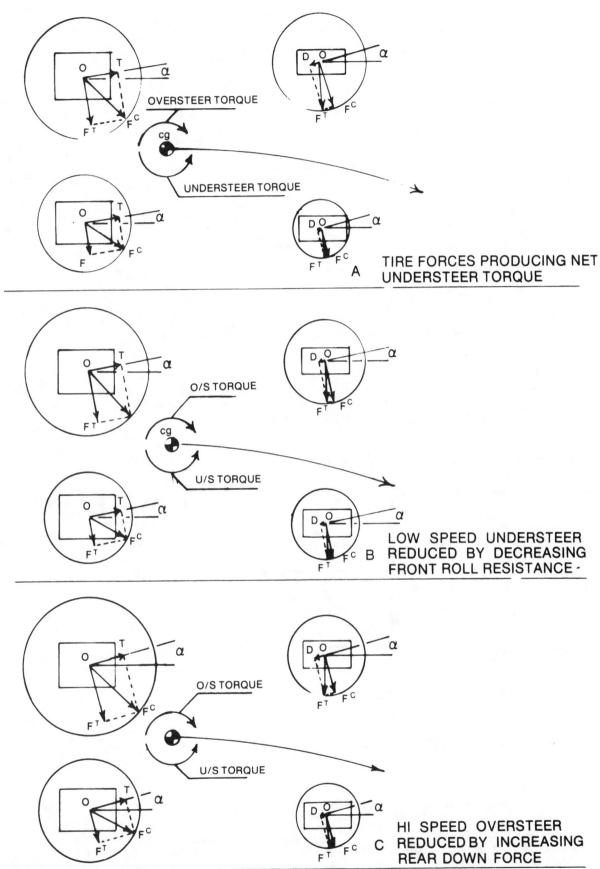

OVERSTEER TORQUE

UNDERSTEER TORQUE

A TIRE FORCES PRODUCING NET UNDERSTEER TORQUE

O/S TORQUE

U/S TORQUE

B LOW SPEED UNDERSTEER REDUCED BY DECREASING FRONT ROLL RESISTANCE -

O/S TORQUE

U/S TORQUE

C HI SPEED OVERSTEER REDUCED BY INCREASING REAR DOWN FORCE

Figure (84): Tire forces producing understeer and oversteer torques about vehicle's center of gravity.

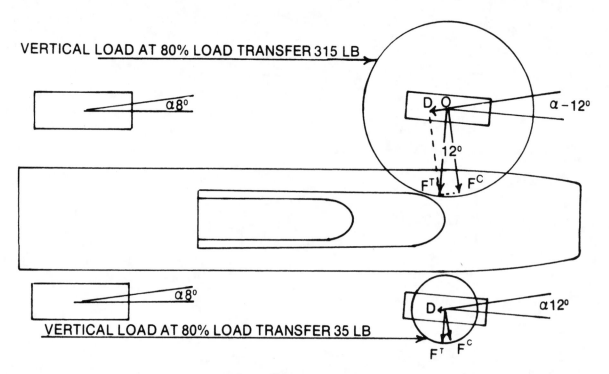

VERTICAL LOAD AT 80% LOAD TRANSFER 315 LB

VERTICAL LOAD AT 80% LOAD TRANSFER 35 LB

A - FORMULA FORD ILLUSTRATING UNDERSTEER TIRE DRAG IN FAST CORNER. STATIC FRONT WHEEL LOAD 175 lb
OUTSIDE TIRE: F^T = 315 x 1.3 COEFF OF FRICTION = 410 lb. F^C = 410 (COS 12°) = 401 lb. DRAG, O-D = 410 (SINE 12°) = 85 lb
INSIDE TIRE: F^T = 35 x 1.3 COEFF OF FRICTION = 46 lb. F^C = 46 (COS 12°) = 45 lb. DRAG, O-D = 46 (SINE 12°) = 10 lb
TOTAL FRONT TIRE FORCES ARE, CORNERING FORCE 446 lb AND DRAG 95 lb

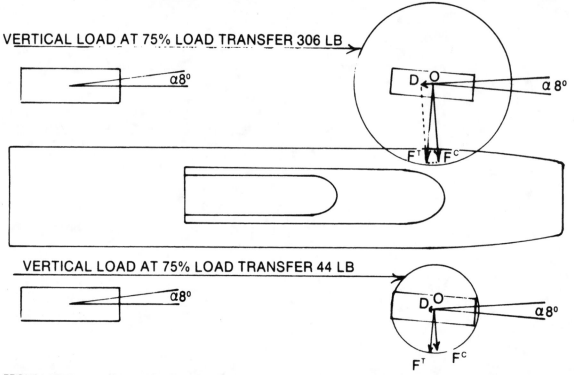

VERTICAL LOAD AT 75% LOAD TRANSFER 306 LB

VERTICAL LOAD AT 75% LOAD TRANSFER 44 LB

B - FRONT LATERAL LOAD TRANSFER REDUCED FROM 80% TO 75% FRONT SLIP ANGLE REDUCED FROM 12° TO 8°
OUTSIDE TIRE: F^T = 306 x 1.3 COEFFICIENT 398 lb. F^C = 398 (COS 8°) = 394 lb DRAG, O.D. = 398 (SINE 8°) = 55 lb
INSIDE TIRE: F^T = 44 x 1.3 COEFFICIENT 57 lb. F^C = 57 (COS 8°) = 56 lb DRAG, O.D. = 57 (SINE 8°) = 8 lb
TOTAL FRONT TIRE FORCES ARE: CORNERING FORCE 450 lb DRAG 63 lb
NET CHANGE FROM SITUATION [A] IS A GAIN OF 4 lb OF FRONT CORNERING FORCE AND A REDUCTION OF 32 lb IN
UNDERSTEER TIRE DRAG.

Figure (85): The effects of understeer drag and its reduction by restoration of understeer/oversteer balance.

reduce the lateral load transfer between the front wheels, by reducing the effective stiffness of the front anti-roll bar. Section (B) shows the effect of such a change in terms of torques about the cg. To kill two birds with one drawing, we not only reduced the front bar stiffness, we also increased the rear—which, in the relative sense, we do every time that we soften the front, or vice versa. Reducing the front placed less dynamic load on the outside front and more on the inside, which increased the cornering power of the front pair of wheels. Since the vehicle cornering power was front tire limited, this would result in an improvement in overall cornering power as well as an improvement in the vehicle's balance. On the other hand, increasing the stiffness of the rear bar, by increasing the lateral load transfer at the rear, downgraded the rear cornering power. It also balanced the car, but it did so by bringing the rear cornering power down to match that of the front rather than by bringing the front up to match that of the rear. One has to be careful . . .

Section (C) shows what happens when we increase the downforce at the rear of the car to balance out a high speed oversteer condition. In this case we have increased the vertical loading on both rear wheels and brought the rear cornering power up to that of the fronts. Of course, because the wing is cantilevered behind the rear axle, the teeter-totter effect has also slightly reduced the loading on the front tires. In this case, we must be careful that, in the process of balancing the car aerodynamically we do not end up with more downforce than we can use. I could go on drawing diagrams of this nature forever, but I don't think that it would be productive.

UNDERSTEER DRAG

I briefly mentioned tire drag due to cornering force a few pages back. Because it is very easy to tune ourselves into a condition where cornering tire drag can have a measurable adverse effect on lap time, we will now go into the subject more deeply. Our object in setting up the racing car is to get all four tires operating at their maximum potential at all times. Basically this means that we want to operate in the threshold range of the slip angle curve. The higher the value of tire slip angle that we develop, the more cornering drag is going to be produced. This is inescapable. There are three things to remember about tire cornering drag: It produces no useful work, it downgrades the cornering capability of the tire, and it requires thrust from the driving wheels to overcome. We get into trouble in this department when we dial in too much understeer—particularly in fast corners. The understeering car, at the limit of traction, can produce some significant tire drag numbers. In addition, the front tires can overheat themselves and cause the understeer to become self-increasing. Further, the drag produced by the understeering front tires must be overcome by thrust from the rear tires, and this extra thrust is then not available as either net accelerative force or as rear tire side force. So we lose both cornering power and acceleration ability. Finally, the drag component on the front tires also subtracts from front tire cornering force. The loss of acceleration potential is not a problem on slow corners where we have excess engine power, but in fast bends, particularly with relatively low powered cars, it can and does become significant. Just to put some frightening numbers on it, let's consider a hypothetical Formula Ford in a long fast corner. We'll consider that the vehicle weight is 1000 pounds with a 65/35 distribution and that we have an 80% lateral load transfer at the front. We further assume that the slip angle threshold range is from 8 degrees to 12 degrees. Figure (85) applies. If the car is in an understeer condition, with a front slip angle of 12° and a rear slip angle of 8°, then the outside front tire will be generating 401 pounds of cornering force at 1.3g and 85 pounds of cornering drag. The inside tire, virtually unladen, would be generating 46 lb of cornering force and 10 lb of cornering drag. If we balanced the car to a neutral steer condition, by reducing the front lateral load transfer to 75% and the front slip angle to 8°, then the outside front tire would generate 394 lb of cornering force and 55 lb of drag while the inside figures would be 56 lb and 8 lb respectively. The net result of balancing the car would be a gain of 4 lb of cornering force and a loss of 32 lb of front tire drag. That 32 lb of drag represents about 8% of the total drag of the vehicle at that speed and God knows that Formula Ford engines have enough trouble pushing the cars through the air at all at 120 mph without adding 8% to the load. We are talking about some significant numbers, which can be translated into even more significant amounts of lap time.

The problem here lies in the fact that an understeering car is a stable, comfortable and secure device to drive and a neutral or oversteering car is twitchy in fast bends. Naturally most drivers, left to their own devices, will opt for a certain amount of understeer and security. It may be comfortable, and it may be secure, but it will not be fast. With everything else being equal, the driver who has set up for less understeer, while he will not be measurably faster in the corner, will accelerate appreciably quicker out of it because he does not have to overcome that extra 30 lb of drag. He will also have to work harder. The thing to remember from all of this is that the closer your racer is set up to mid-phase corner neutral steer, the faster (and twitchier) it is going to be. Obviously we want to stay on the understeer side of absolute neutral steer—and by enough so that power application is not going to cause excessive oversteer. As I said, it's all a question of balance, and the faster you go, the more delicate the balance becomes.

STABILITY AND RESPONSE

There was a time, not so very long ago, when racing cars left a lot to be desired in the field of directional stability. On certain examples, the drivers worked harder while proceeding down the straights than they did in the corners. Thankfully, that time has now passed and there is no longer any conceivable excuse for having to put up with an unstable vehicle. Today, straight line instability will always be due to a lack of rear downforce, a mechanical malfunction or bad wheel alignment. Period. However, if we go overboard on this straight line—or steady state—stability bit, we will end up with a car that has too much steady state stability and so will exhibit slow response characteristics—and that's not what we want. The racing car must be nimble, it must provide instant response to control movements—it must dance. You wouldn't want to race a Cadillac! Many of the design features necessary to achieve other goals contribute to the inherent quick response characteristics of the modern racing car. The low center of gravity minimizes both lag time and pitching moments. The strong restriction of chassis roll and the relatively stiff damping, as well as the lack of compliance in suspension links and pivots all add up to improved response time. The low polar moment of inertia which is an inherent feature of the mid engined car does the same. With the exceptions of front engined sedans, the modern racing car's response time is very short indeed—in fact, it is the major reason that they are so sensitive to drive—and why they must be driven so precisely. The sloppy sedan, even when being driven at its limit, gives the driver lots of time to make corrections to compensate for his errors in judgment. The Formula One car, driven at its limit, does not. This is, of course, why the star Grand Prix and Indy drivers often don't do very well at IROC—and why we used to see Jimmy Clark sometimes lose touring car races to drivers who couldn't have come within ten seconds of his lap times in a Formula One car. It is also the reason why there have been so many drivers who were brilliant in Touring and Grand Touring cars, but couldn't get it done in real race cars.

I digress. The racing car has progressed to the point where its stability should not present any problems. The same is true of response. Basically, if you want to quicken the response of your racer, increase the roll resistance and damping. If you want to make it more forgiving, decrease them. Steering ratio has long been optimized in just about every class of racing so you are unlikely to gain anything there. It is possible to confuse lots of understeer with slow or unstable response. The car with strong understeer is quite unwilling to change direction and, once it has been horsed into a steady state turn, its transition to power oversteer is very liable to be sudden enough to feel like unstable response. Evaluation of the racing car's handling is not the easiest of exercises.

THE ACTUALITIES OF CORNERING

By now you will have gathered that the question of understeer/oversteer vehicle balance at various points on the race track is a bit more complex than it is in the steady state condition which is normally used to illustrate handling characteristics. Figure (80) is a composite of typical handling characteristics or vehicle balance curves showing understeer and oversteer response as cornering force is increased. The vehicles are following a curve of constant radius and the cornering force is increased by increasing vehicle speed very slowly so that the driving thrust at the rear wheels does not upset the picture. This is a typical skid pad technique and the curves are valid—as far as they go. We have all driven the old swing axle Volkswagens—or Corvairs—so we know what final oversteer at relatively low force levels is like—not good at all. This does not mean that such cars are, in themselves, dangerous. It merely means that the driver had best be aware of their proclivities and plan ahead. Detroit is fully aware that the average buyer is neither aware nor capable of planning ahead while he is driving a motorcar. To keep the paying public alive—and to avoid manufacturer's liability suits—they build cars with ever-increasing understeer. Again, we all know that the understeer can and does reach prodigious levels if you happen to enter a corner way too fast in a big Detroit product. I don't like it and, I hope, you don't like it. Even the magazine editors don't like it. But Detroit is right. Understeer is stable and, given the level of skill and awareness of the typical street driver, it is the only way to go. When Uncle Fred or Aunt Mary frighten themselves in a corner—which happens very seldom indeed because they don't go fast enough in corners to frighten themselves—they are going to jam on the brakes and wind on the steering lock—and that is all that they are going to

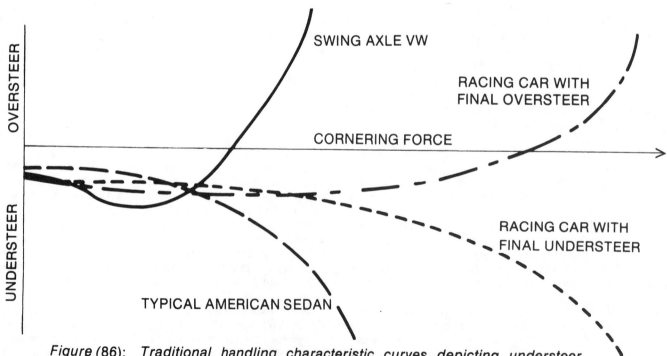

Figure (86): Traditional handling characteristic curves depicting understeer and/or oversteer balance as a function of cornering force at steady state.

132

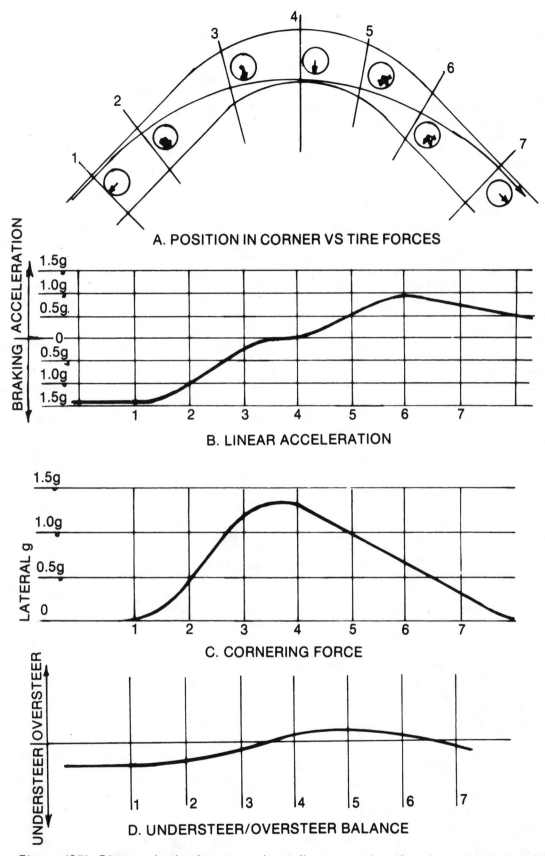

A. POSITION IN CORNER VS TIRE FORCES

B. LINEAR ACCELERATION

C. CORNERING FORCE

D. UNDERSTEER/OVERSTEER BALANCE

Figure (87): Change in tire force resultant, linear acceleration, lateral acceleration and understeer/oversteer balance as race car progresses through slow to medium speed corner.

do. If the car is a strong understeerer they stand a pretty good chance of surviving the next few seconds. If it oversteers, they are going to lose it completely. The situation is eased more than somewhat by the simple fact that the force level that causes normal or civilian driver fright reactions is, in actuality, well below the understeer limit of the tires and so putting on the brakes and winding on steering lock will, in most cases, save the situation despite the driver's efforts. The same is true in the typical freeway accident—I live in L.A. and I get to see a lot of them. What happens here is that Fred perceives, far too late, that the traffic is slowing ahead of him. He then panics and jams on his power brakes. With enough built-in understeer, a high enough polar moment and, nowadays, a reasonable front to rear brake ratio, he then proceeds to either stop or to plow into the car ahead of him—but at least he stays in his own lane, which he would not do if the car swapped ends. Anyway, those two curves are in there just for the hell of it and to give me the opportunity to say something nice about the Engineers in Detroit—some of whom are really clued-in people. The race car curves are also classic. The curve showing final understeer is often used to illustrate the English school of thought while that showing final oversteer is sometimes used to describe the Continental school. Rubbish! Final oversteer at steady state may have been a feature of German racing cars in the days of swing axles, but it wasn't intentional. If the car has final oversteer at high force levels in the steady state condition, there will be no reserve rear tire traction available for acceleration and any but the most gentle application of the throttle will result in the car's and the driver's exit from the race track. What we really need to illustrate the point in question is something like Figure (57) which relates understeer and oversteer to the car's position in the corner and to the amount of longitudinal acceleration being developed.

Although this is definitely not a book about the driving of racing cars, it is now time to make a couple of points about the line that the driver chooses through corners. It is not reasonable to expect a car to run through the mid-phase of any given corner at the limit of tire adhesion and to then accelerate out of the corner at the same level of lateral force. The traction circle tells us that it cannot be done. If we are going to produce forward bite, we must reduce side bite to some extent—longitudinal load transfer will help, but not that much. This simply means that, as he puts the power down, the driver has to allow the corner radius to open up so that he will not smite the wall—he must release the car. The actual path that the vehicle should follow through any given corner in order to get the most out of the tires is a question of corner radius, available torque, banking, balance of the car and driver preference. The more excess engine power that is available for acceleration, the more the exit radius must be opened. All of the race driving books point this fact out, and all good drivers realize it instinctively. Now we know why.

That's about the end of our discussion of the physical factors involved. Now it is time to get practical. I stated earlier that the basic layout of the racing car has been evolved over the years in order to promote just the handling characteristics that we want. This statement is true, but the basic design just sort of puts the car into the ballpark. To make it work, we have to tune on it. We'll break the subject of making the chassis work into two categories—track testing for the major stuff and race track tuning for the weekend. We have a lot more scope while testing simply because there is more time available. Saturday afternoon at the race track is no time to be playing with roll center heights or track widths. We'll cover actual test procedures in the final chapter. For now we'll content ourselves with a few generalities.

We have seen that the basic factors governing the speed at which any car can be driven through a given corner, or series of corners, are the coefficient of friction of the tires and the vertical loading on the tires. Without changing tires, the major factors affecting the coefficient of friction will be lateral and diagonal load transfer and dynamic camber angle. Lateral load transfer is governed by track width, cg height, roll center height and roll stiffness. Dynamic camber is a question of suspension linkage geometry, roll center height, load transfer and suspension movement. The understeer/oversteer balance of the car, on the other hand, is a question of relative front to rear lateral load transfers and the direction of the tire forces. There is a popular fallacy that roll steer and bump steer only affect the top 5% of the cornering force picture and so are for fine tuning only. This is true enough from the viewpoint of pure cornering power. However, since those factors exert a profound influence on the transient response and behavior of the racing car, in actuality they are critical at all times.

Of these factors, all can be modified or changed, some easily and some with great difficulty. Anyone can change the roll stiffness with the anti-roll bars and anyone can change the amount of downforce generated by adjusting wings or spoilers. On the other hand, if you want to change track width or wheelbase, you will have to have equipment, skill and knowledge. By the same token, adding a spoiler or a lip to an existing wing or body is no big thing—making a new rear wing is. As usual, what can be done comes down to a question of available resources. This should not be cause for despair among the unsponsored and impecunious. What we are talking about in tuning the chassis is balancing the car. If we can arrive at a setup that lets the driver get cleanly into the corners and still be able to accelerate out of them hard and early and if we can arrive at the optimum amount of downforce for a given race track, then we are going to have a competitive car. Balance, or driveability, and the ability to accelerate while cornering are more important than maximum cornering power—every time. Until you reach the top levels of professional motor racing you will achieve more results by optimizing the package that you have than by redesigning it.

Fortunately, when we are discussing balance, we are basically discussing the relative amounts of lateral load transfer that take place at each end of the vehicle and the relative amounts of front and rear downforce generation. This can be done without spending any real money—anti-roll bars are cheap to make.

There are three basic rules to follow when attempting to sort out any chassis. Human nature being what it is, they are often ignored or broken. They should not be. They are:

(1) Don't even leave the shop until the car is as good as you can make it. Going testing with a car that has not been aligned, or with dead shocks, or with springs which rattle

two inches at full rebound, or with a worn-out locker is dumb. You don't learn anything, you won't improve the car, you will spend money and everyone will become discouraged.

(2) Get the damned thing balanced so that you can work with it—before you do anything else. Testing all day with a car which plows into every corner like a big Buick will do nothing but wear out tires.

(3) Always work with the end of the car that is giving trouble. In other words, try to stick the end of the car that is breaking loose rather than taking the easy way out and unsticking the end that is working. Unsticking one end to balance the car is for desperate time only. Since we are absolutely certain that desperate time will eventually arrive, save your unsticking act until it does.

Since virtually every race car now has downforce generators at both ends—although, admittedly, some of them are vestigal and not terribly effective, we have to separate the vehicle balance picture into three acts—low speed where downforce is relatively ineffective and the suspension is dominant, medium speed where both downforce and the chassis play a major part in the car's behavior and high speed where downforce is dominant. Changing the front roll resistance is not liable to produce results if you are understeering in Turn Two at Riverside, although it could give some interesting reactions when you arrive at Turn Six. On the other hand, cranking up the rear wing is unlikely to cure your oversteer in Turn Nine at Laguna but very likely to give you a whole handful of understeer in Turn Two. You must learn to define the problem before you attempt to cure it.

Since lateral load transfer is governed by track width, roll center and cg heights, which are difficult to change, and by the resistance of the springs and anti-roll bars, which are easy to change, we work with the springs and the bars. Remember that nothing that you do to camber, castor, toe-in, bump steer, etc. is going to change the lateral load transfer. If you go stiffer with the bars and/or the springs at both ends, you will get more lateral load transfer for a given amount of cornering force and vice versa. If you go softer at one end only, you will not measurably affect the total load transfer at a given cornering force, but less of that total will take place at the end that you softened. Of course, if you unbalance the car, you will not be able to reach the previous level of cornering force. Present tendency is to run the cars pretty soft in ride—or in the vertical plane—with wheel ride rates just stiff enough to keep the chassis off the ground under the influence of downforce, bumps and longitudinal load transfer, and to run pretty stiff in the roll resistance department or in the horizontal plane. Any increase in springs over the basic is pretty much guaranteed to result in lessened tire capacity due to reduced compliance, so we are pretty much stuck with the bars as a method of determining both optimum roll resistance and the front to rear proportioning thereof. This is just as well as they are both easier to change and cheaper than springs. There are lots of people who believe in calculating optimum roll resistance. I do not—too many variables. Instead, I make up a whole bunch of bars, establish the basic roll resistance ratio required to balance the car and then vary the total roll resistance, both up and down, while keeping the same proportioning until we have

established the optimum for the race track in question. I do the same thing with the springs, but to a much lesser extent (more wing requires more spring). In my efforts to arrive at linear load transfer and roll generation, I also play with roll center heights and roll axis inclination by employing ball joint and link plate spacers at one end or the other—but I try to get the balance right first.

Along these lines, the requirements from track to track vary more than most racers realize. The typical Southern California error is to do all of the testing at Willow Springs because it is convenient, cheap and a good place to play with dirt bikes (which it is). It also happens to be a race track which, particularly for two-litre cars and below, demands a lot of roll resistance. If you set your car up for Willow you will find (or you may not find—and will be slow) that it is far too stiff in the bar department for Laguna. At every race track it is mandatory that, once the car has been balanced, both the roll stiffness and the downforce be varied, in both directions, until the optimum has been found. To a lesser extent, the same is true of shock absorber forces.

It now seems that we have established such a Godawful number of things to try at each race meeting (which will include a whole host of items which we have not even mentioned in this chapter—gearing, ride height, mixture strength, brake ratio, tire pressure, camber, toe settings), we are probably not going to have time to socialize, drink beer or watch ladies, let alone chase them. Unfortunately, this assumption is correct. The price of winning is always the reduction, if not the elimination, of play time. However, since racing is basically playing any way you want to look at it (real people make their livings by doing something that they hate), we can't bitch too much.

Figure (88): Table of Handling Characteristic Causes and Effects

SECTION ONE — EFFECT LISTED FIRST

A — INSTABILITY

EFFECT ON VEHICLE

Straight line instability—general

POSSIBLE CAUSES

Rear wheel toe-out, either static due to incorrect setting or dynamic due to bump steer

Vast lack of rear downforce or overwhelming amount of front downforce

Broken chassis or suspension member or mounting point

Wild amount of front toe-in or toe-out

Straight line instability under hard acceleration

Limited slip differential worn out or malfunctioning

Insufficient rear wheel toe-in

Straight line instability—car darts over bumps

Too much front toe-in or toe-out

Uneven front castor setting

Uneven front shock forces or bump rubbers

Front anti-roll bar miles too stiff

Instability under the brakes—front end darts or wanders

Too much front brake bias

Instability under the brakes—car wants to spin

Too much rear brake bias or too much positive camber on rear tires

B — RESPONSE

Car feels generally heavy and unresponsive

Too much aerodynamic downforce

Car feels sloppy, is slow to take a set in corners, rolls a lot

Too little shock absorber damping
Insufficient roll resistance or ride rate

Car responds too quickly—has little feel—slides at slightest provocation

Too little downforce
Too stiff in either ride or roll resistance
Too much shock
Too much tire pressure

C — UNDERSTEER

Corner entry understeer—won't point in and gets progressively worse

Common complaint. Can be caused by:
Insufficient front track width
Front roll stiffness too high
Front roll center too low
Insufficient front shock absorber
  bump resistance
Insufficient front downforce
Excessive dynamic positive camber on outside
  front tire
Braking too hard and too late
Too little front roll resistance—falling
  over on outside front due to track width ratio or
  diagonal load transfer. Can often be reduced by
  increasing front roll resistance even though do-
  ing so will increase lateral load transfer.

Corner entry understeer—car initially points in and then washes out

Too much front toe-in
Insufficient front download
Insufficient front roll camber compensation
Non linear load transfer due to roll axis inclination
Insufficient front wheel travel in droop
Too little front shock bump resistance

Corner entry understeer—car points in and then darts

Insufficient front wheel travel in either bump or
  rebound
Too much front bump rubber
Nose being sucked down due to ground effect

Corner exit understeer—slow corners

Big trouble. Often a function of excessive corner
  entry and mid-phase understeer followed by throttle application with understeer steering lock which
  causes the driving thrust on the inside rear wheel to
  accentuate the understeer.
First step must be to reduce the corner entry understeer. If the condition persists, increase the rear
  anti-squat and reduce the front shock rebound
  forces. Educate the driver and improve throttle
  response.

D — OVERSTEER

Corner entry oversteer

I've heard of this one, but have not run into it—
  unless something was broken. Possible causes include:
Diabolical lock of rear downforce
Broken or non-functioning outside rear shock—
  or front anti-roll bar
Severely limited rear suspension travel
  caused by interference
Ridiculous rear spring or anti-roll bar
A slight feeling of rear tippy-toe type
  hunting on corner entry can be due to excessive
  rear toe-in or to excessive rear rebound forces

Corner exit oversteer—gets progressively worse from the time that power is applied

Worn out limited slip
Insufficient rear spring, shock or bar allowing car to
  fall over on outside rear
Too much rear roll stiffness
Too much rear camber
Too little rear downforce
Too little rear toe-in

Corner exit oversteer—sudden—car takes its set and then breaks loose

Insufficient rear suspension travel
Dead rear shock
Too much rear bump rubber
Too much throttle applied after driver's confidence
  level has been increased by car taking a set
Sudden change in outside rear tire camber

SECTION TWO — CAUSE LISTED FIRST

A — RIDE AND ROLL RATES

CAUSE

Too much spring—overall

EFFECT ON VEHICLE
Harsh and choppy ride. Car will not put power down
on corner exit, excessive wheelspin. Much un-
provoked sliding.

Too much spring—front

Initial understeer—although car may point into corners well. Front end breaks loose over bumps in corners. Front tires lock over bumps.

Too much spring—rear

Oversteer immediately upon power application coming out of corners. Excessive wheelspin.

Too little spring—overall

Car contacts race track a lot
Floating ride with excessive vertical chassis movement
Sloppy response
Car is slow to take its set—may take more than one

Too little spring—front

Chassis grounds under brakes
Excessive roll on corner entry
Initial understeer—won't point in

Too little spring—rear

Excessive acceleration squat and accompanying rear negative camber
Car falls over on outside rear tire as power is applied causing power oversteer

Too much anti-roll bar—overall

Car will be very sudden in turning response and will have little feel
Will tend to slide or skate rather than taking a set
May dart over one wheel or diagonal bumps.

Too much anti-roll bar—front

Initial corner entry understeer which usually becomes progressively worse as the driver tries to tighten the corner radius

Too much anti-roll bar—rear

Corner exit oversteer. Car won't put power down but goes directly to oversteer, with or without wheelspin
Excessive sliding coming out of corners

B — SHOCK ABSORBER FORCES

Too much shock—overall

Very sudden car with harsh ride, much sliding and wheel patter
Car doesn't absorb road surface irregularities but crashes over them

Too much rebound adjustment

Wheels do not return quickly to road surface after displacement. Inside wheel in a corner may be pulled off the road by the shock
Car may be jacked down in long corners

Too much bump adjustment

Initial bump reaction very harsh
Initial chassis roll slow to develop
Car may jack up in long corners

Too little shock—overall

Car floats a lot in ride and oscillates after bumps
Response is slow and sloppy
Chassis roll develops very quickly and, in extreme cases, the chassis may even roll back after the initial roll has taken place

Too little redound adjustment

Oscillates after bumps
Does not put power down well

Too little bump adjustment

Initial bump reaction soft
Car dives or squats a lot
Car rolls quickly and may tend to fall over on the outside front during corner entry and the outside rear during corner exit

Dead shock on one corner

Surprisingly difficult for the driver to identify and/or to isolate. At the rear will cause power oversteer in one direction only and at the front will cause initial understeer in one direction only.

C — WHEEL ALIGNMENT

Front toe-in—too much

Car darts over bumps, under the brakes and during corner entry
Car won't point into corners, or, if extreme, may point in very quickly and then wash out

Front toe-out—too much

Car wanders under the brakes and may be somewhat unstable in a straight line, especially in response to one wheel or diagonal bumps and wind gusts
May point into corners and then refuse to take a set

Rear toe-in—too much

Rear feels light and unstable on corner entry

Rear toe-in—too little

Power on oversteer—during corner exit

Rear toe-out—any

Power oversteer during corner exit or in a straight line
Straight line instability

Front wheel castor—too much

Excessive physical steering effort accompanied by too much self return action and transmittal of road shocks to driver's hands

137

Front wheel castor, too little

Car too sensitive to steering
Too little steering feel, self return and feedback

Front wheel castor, uneven

Steering effort harder in one direction than in the other.

Car swerves in one direction (toward the side with the high castor setting) in a straight line

Camber, too much negative

Inside of tire excessively hot or wearing too rapidly. At the front this will show up as reduced braking capability and at the rear as reduced acceleration capability. Depending on the race track and the geographic location of the tire measuring point inside tire temperature should be 10°F to 25°F hotter than outside

Camber, too much positive

Outside of tire will be hot and wearing. This should never be and is almost always caused at the rear by running too much static positive camber in an effort to prevent excessive negative under the influence of the wing at high speed. Will cause corner exit oversteer and reduced tractive capacity. If extreme, may cause corner entrance instability.

At the front it is usually caused by excessive chassis roll or by insufficient roll camber compensation in the suspension linkage and will cause understeer after the car has pointed into the corner

Bump steer, front—too much toe-in in bump

Car darts over bumps and understeers on corner entry

Bump steer, front—too much toe-out in bump

Wanders under the brakes and may dart over one wheel bumps or in response to wind gusts. Understeer after initial point in on corner entry

Bump steer, rear—too much toe-in in bump

Roll understeer on corner entry
Tippy-toe rear wheel instability on corner entry
Darting on application of power on corner exit

Bump steer, rear—toe-out in bump—any

Same as static toe-out but lesser effect—oversteer on power application

D — SUSPENSION GEOMETRY

Rear roll center too low—or front too high

Roll axis too far out of parallel with mass centroid axis leading to non-linear generation of chassis roll and lateral load transfer. In this case the tendency will be toward too much load transfer at the rear

which will cause oversteer.

Front roll center too low—or rear too high

Same as above, but in opposite direction, tending toward corner entry understeer and three wheeled motoring on corner exit.

Front track width too narrow in relation to rear

Car tends to trip over its front feet during slow and medium speed corner entry evidenced by lots of understeer. Quite common in present generation of English kit cars. Crutch is to increase front ride and roll resistance and to raise front roll center. Fix would be to increase front track width.

E — TIRES

Too much tire pressure

Harsh ride—excessive wheel patter, sliding and wheelspin. High temperature reading at center of tire.

Too little tire pressure

Soft and mushy response, high tire temperatures, with dip at center of tread. Reduced footprint area and traction.

Front tires "going off"

Gradually increasing understeer. During the race, the only thing that the driver can do about this is to change his lines and driving technique to nurse the front tires. If we know that it is liable to happen during the course of a race, we can set the car up closer to oversteer balance than would be optimum to compensate for it.

Rear tires "going off"

Same as above but in the oversteer direction. Driver adjustable anti-roll bars come in handy here.

Inside rear tire larger in diameter than outside (reverse stagger)

Reduces corner entry understeer by dragging inside rear. Increases corner exit oversteer.

F — OTHER FACTORS

Limited slip differential wearing out

In the initial phases of wearing out the symptoms are decreased power on understeer or gradually increasing power on oversteer and inside wheel spin. The car may actually be easier and quite pleasant to drive—but it will be SLOW. When the wear becomes extreme, stability under hard acceleration will diminish and become negative and things will not be pleasant at all.

For certain I never drove a car that I felt was perfect in the understeer/oversteer balance department — at least after I had learned enough to be able to sense what was going on. In the years that I have been running racing teams I can only remember one time that a driver pronounced a car to be "perfect"—and meant it. We can get them to the point where they are very good indeed, but perfection always eludes us. Further, even given enough time and resources, I don't think that it is possible to come up with the ideal setup for any given race—the optimum compromise, yes, but the perfect setup, no. There are just too many variables.

This statement does not mean that I feel that we should not aim for perfection or that the driver should accept a substandard race car. He cannot and we should not. I am merely trying to emphasize the complexity of the overall picture and the importance of intelligent compromise and realistic evaluation. It is all too easy and far too common to waste a lot of time and effort in an attempt to make a car comfortable and balanced on a section of the race track that really doesn't matter instead of trying to improve performance in the critical areas. It is even more common to tune the car using only the driver's subjective opinions as inputs and end up with a stable and comfortable car that is a pleasure to drive—but slow. The opposite extreme, paying no attention to the driver's piteous complaints, is even worse. Every time, balance and the ability to put the power down early will beat pure cornering ability—we must learn to distinguish between side bite and forward traction. And every time, the really fast racing car—driven at its limit—is going to be twitchy and difficult to drive. Drivers, except at the top levels among the pros, tend to be a lazy and subjective lot. Tuners should bear that in mind. They should also bear in mind the simple fact that the driver who is doing his level best (we are not discussing any other type) has every right to expect more from his crew than they can deliver.

CHAPTER TWELVE

TUNING THE ENGINE

TUNING THE ENGINE

In the chronological order of writing this book, this is the last chapter to be done—because it is going to be the easiest—and the shortest. There are two reasons. First, I firmly believe that building the engine is the engine builder's job and that, with the exception of adjusting mixture strength and playing with the throttle response, track tuning of the engine is a waste of time. Second is the simple fact that there are already in print some really good books on engine building. They are: *Racing Engine Preparation* by Waddell Wilson and Steve Smith, published by Steve Smith Autosports, P.O. Box 11631, Santa Ana, California 92711. Also published by Steve Smith is *Racing the Small Block Chevy* by John Thawley. Mr. Thawley has written two other Chevy books, *Hotrodding the Small Block Chevy* and *Hotrodding the Big Block Chevy* for the ubiquitous H. P. Books. The best of the bunch is *The Chevrolet Racing Engine* by Bill (Grumpy) Jenkins, published by S-A Design Company, 11801 E. Slausen, Santa Fe Springs, California 90670. Every racer should own at least the first and the last of the above. Even if you do not and never will race stock block V-8s, the general information is applicable to any internal combustion engine and it is priceless.

So far as the building of the racing engine goes, there are two basic choices—a top end engine which will produce a whole bunch of horsepower at high rpm at the expense of the width of the torque band and mid-range power, or a torquey engine which sacrifices some of the top end to gain mid-range power and a broad usable rpm range. Admittedly the horsepower and torque curve characteristics required will vary somewhat with the nature of the race track, but the basic rule remains, "Horsepower sells motorcars and torque wins motor races."

Our basic job with the racing engine is to make sure that we don't lose any of the power that the builder put into it when we bolt the thing into the chassis. All that this requires is making sure that the engine is supplied with enough of the coolest available inlet air and the requisite amount of fuel, that we are running the exhaust and inlet systems that the engine builder had in mind, that we are not either abusing the engine or robbing ourselves of power with an inefficient cooling or lubrication system and that the ignition system works. I covered most of those areas rather thoroughly in *Prepare to Win*.

If you believe that you, personally, are going to tune on your engine and blow off the opposition, you are wrong! This does not mean that you cannot build and/or maintain your own engine and be fully competitive—you can. But it is highly unlikely that you are going to get an edge by out-engineering or out-tuning Cosworth, Hart, McLaren, Falconer, Weiss, Stimola, et al. Any edge that you do achieve—and you very well may achieve one—will be due to more meticulous assembly than a commercial shop can afford, not to demon tweaks. As a case in point, a couple of years ago I did a Formula Atlantic season with Bobby Brown. We had three Cosworth BDAs, one Brian Hart, one Swindon and one assembled from a standard Cosworth kit. The assembly and all of our rebuilds were done by Tony Cicale in his garage at home (the garage is only slightly cleaner than the average hospital operating room). All machine work was farmed out. Once we caught on to a couple of things that we were doing wrong (that March was the only race car in history with excessive cooling capacity and the BDA wants to run at 90°C to 100°C—and the Lucas Opus ignition is NFG and tricky besides) we had no engine trouble and we had no power disadvantage—to anyone. We wound our engines as tight as anyone in their right mind and had absolute 900 to 1000 mile reliability—which was a lot more than many people could say. This was a case of a truly meticulous craftsman building engines strictly by the book and getting results as good as anyone's.

Racing engine preparation consists of buying the best components and assembling them meticulously. Let somebody else play with hydraulic/pneumatic valve actuation, short stroke or long rod engines, trick oils and the like. There are lots of people out there who prefer tinkering to winning—it gives them a good excuse.

With your Cosworth DFV Formula One engine you get three fuel metering unit cams—standard, Kyalami and Mexico. You also get a seven-page instruction sheet, a twenty-page parts list and ten pages of engineering drawings that cover everything from the basic engine shape and dimensions to the recommended oil, water and fuel systems, and the exhaust system layout (they supply the intake system). They go so far as to tell you, in detail, how to start and warm up the engine. They also supply a maintenance and running log which stays with the engine and is filled in in the field by the race team and in the workshop by Cosworth. You are informed, again in detail, how to time the engine, install a new metering unit and distributor and they tell you to do none of the above except in cases of extreme emergency. Would that other engine suppliers would do the same.

There are, however, areas where we can gain real performance by tuning. These areas include the inlet system, the cooling system, the lubrication system, the ignition system and the exhaust system. We will not discuss the lubrication system because I said all that I have to say in that area in *Prepare to Win*. For now, I will say only that we can lose a lot of power by running the water and/or oil too cold—we typically want about 90°C on each. We covered the mechanics of cooling in Chapter Nine. We also covered the air end of the inlet system in Chapter Nine.

CARBURETION (OR INJECTION)

There is an old saying in racing that, "you've got to be lean to be mean." It is true. Most racers run their engines far too rich—to the obvious detriment of power and fuel consumption and, more important, to the less obvious detriment of the all-important throttle response.

There is a simple and very valid reason for this practice—if you run a little too rich you lose some power and use a little more fuel. If you run a little too lean, you burn a piston, are out of the race and get to do an expensive rebuild. Spark plugs and exhaust tubes have two purposes—one to ignite the mixture and to conduct the exhaust gases, and one to tell you how your mixture is. The trouble is, you've got to be able to read the damned things and no books or series of photos can tell you—you've got to learn from someone who knows. The tail pipe, however, requires very little experience to read—it just takes a lot of faith to believe. I firmly believe that if the tail pipe is black (assuming a plug cut, or even a normal pit entrance) you are too rich. If it is snowy white, you are too lean. It should be somewhere between light grey and white. Unlike plugs, the tail pipe doesn't tell all—but only a part of the story—and you wouldn't want to use it exclusively—but if it's black you are wasting power. Once you learn how to read plugs, there is little sense in making a ritual of it. Do plug cuts until you get the mixture right and then stop playing with it.

The power end is only part of the mixture question. The other part is throttle response. I'm not going to attempt to write a carburetion or injection manual but I cannot overemphasize the importance of throttle response—and it comes from the idle and progression circuits plus float level on carburetors and the idle end of the fuel control cam with injectors and NOBODY worries about any of the above—except the guys who do all the winning. How many times have you heard, "No, I don't bother getting the butterflies synched or the intakes balanced at idle, because full throttle is all that matters."? The driver who waits for the engine to clean itself out when he gets on the power is the driver who loses. He is also the driver who isn't going to have a lot of success at steering the car with the throttle. The amount of fuel that an engine needs at idle is just enough to keep the fire from going out and NO MORE. Probably the major cause of bad throttle response on corner exit is too rich an idle mixture, which loads up the whole system during the overrun. When the time comes to apply the power, the engine has to cough out the raw fuel that has accumulated before things can get going again. This is the familiar cough stutter syndrome, which can also be caused by too high a float level. How lean you can go at idle is demonstrated by listening to the Formula One brigade on the overrun. All you hear is crack, snap and pop due to leanness. There is next to no load, so you can get away with it. With injection, you merely lean down the idle—although you may find that you need a different fuel control cam. With carburetors it is a question of the leanest idle jets that will run and playing with fuel pump jets and cams, emulsion tubes, progression holes and float levels. Don't forget that all carburetors, including Webers, were designed in the days when 0.8 g was a hell of a lot of cornering power. The recommended float level settings are invariably too high. When you drop the float levels, if you drop them much, you are going to have to increase the volume of fuel that passes through the float valves when they are open—either by going to bigger float jets or to higher fuel pressure—or both. With Holleys and the like you also get to play with the progression on the secondary butterfly opening. Holleys will not run on a race car without slosh tubes—on both ends. I dislike stock carburetors. In fact, I dislike carburetors, period. Injection is so simple and so efficient . . .

IGNITION

Next comes ignition. If there is a good racing ignition, I haven't found it—but I'm still looking. My favorite—the Vertex Magneto, reworked by Cirello or Cotton offers two notable advantages—only one wire is required and it is easy to trouble shoot—either it works or it doesn't. Like all the rest it is prone to sudden and inexplicable failure. Some wondrous failure modes have been experienced—doesn't work on the track and checks out fine in the shop, for instance. A lot of trouble can be avoided by making sure that the stupid thing doesn't overheat—which means yet another cooling duct.

If the rpm limit will permit it (7500 max), you probably can't do better than a standard Mallory racing or Delco coil and contact breaker system.

All Cosworth and Cosworth-derived engines come with the Lucas electronic Opus ignition system and its justifiably dreaded black box. The black box is supplied with a quick release mount which is telling us something immediately. Again, if the box is cooled sufficiently—and shock mounted—reliability is increased to the just barely acceptable level. Actually a good part of the trouble with the Opus comes from the cheap nasty distributor, not the electronics as such. There is a super trick Formula Two distributor, but it is not available to the likes of you and me. About a century ago, when I was running the Coventry Climax Fire Pump Engine in "G Modified," I got tired of having the distributor fall apart—so I made one—hogged the case from a billet, made a shaft, from some standard thing or other, used the Climax gear, a US cap, rotor and cam, locked the advance and used real bearings. It took forever and solved the problem—also forever. If I were running a Cosworth, I think that I would take the time to make up my own distributor and would run it off the exhaust cam rather than the jackshaft—at least that way I'd be able to see the damned thing—even take the cap off if I were so inclined.

Speaking of distributor advance, I haven't yet figured out why we run any in most of our engines. The advance is all in by 3500 or 4000 rpm so it doesn't affect the operating range and it's one more thing to go wrong. The usual reason given is that we have to retard the engine for starting but I have run everything from Turbo Fords, 510 Chevys, small block Chevys and Cosworth BDAs locked out and they all started fine.

Racers don't pay as much attention to high tension wires as they should. Again, I made most of my recommendations in *Prepare to Win* and nothing has changed—except that people have started to run all of the plug leads in a bundle. You can't get away with that—no matter how good the HT

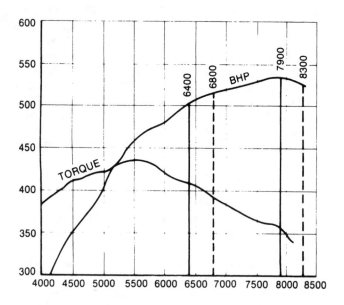

Figure (89a):Typical 5 litre BHP and torque curves.

wire that you are using may be. To avoid the danger of induction firing between cylinders which are next to each other in firing order, the HT leads must be separated—even if it means running one lead down the intake valley.

One of the race track activities that confuses me a lot is the constant checking of the ignition timing. I've had the timing slip on me exactly once and, as you would suspect, the clamp bolt was loose. Timing should be set on the dyno, checked when the engine is installed (like with a buzzer)—so that you know where it is in case the distributor has to be replaced—and then left alone. If you don't trust your engine builder to time your engine, you need another engine builder.

THE EXHAUST SYSTEM

Developing an efficient exhaust system is a real pain—it is also a job for an engine builder with access to a dyno. Both Jenkins and Wilson get into exhaust systems in depth. Unfortunately there is real power lurking in the exhaust system of the racing engine and a bad one can choke your engine to an amazing extent. So consult your engine builder—or copy the hot dogs—and build what you need. Although *Prepare to Win* outlined the easy way, it will still be no fun at all.

GEARING

I do not understand the agonies that racers go through over gearing their cars to the race track—it just isn't that difficult.

The only good explanation of optimum gear ratio theory I have seen in print is in Chapter Nine of Paul Van Valkenburgh's *Race Car Engineering and Mechanics*. If you don't have the book, you should, so I am not going to duplicate Paul's efforts.

The whole purpose of multi-speed gearboxes is to provide variations in torque multiplication so that the engine can be kept within its range of efficient rpm as road speed increases—the idea is to select the ratios that will provide the most acceleration over the speed range of a given vehicle

on a given race track. There are two theories—gear for the corners and gear for efficient acceleration. Neither is totally correct.

In order to gear the car intelligently and quickly we need a few simple things. First of all we need a driver who can and will read the tachometer and remember what he saw long enough to tell the Man in Charge. Next we need some sort of reasonable course map to ensure that the driver and the Man in Charge are talking about the same part of the race track. We will also require a set of engine torque and BHP curves like the ones in Figure (89) and a gear ratio vs rpm and mph chart like Figure (90). Usually you will have to make your own gear chart because the commercially available ones are for the wrong tire diameters. We do not need a computer.

Looking at the engine power curves with a view toward gearing, a couple of things become immediately evident. First is the fact that, on any given race track, we want our maximum rpm in top gear to coincide with the maximum BHP of the engine—as installed. If we don't reach that rpm because we are geared too short, we will give horsepower away and will lose both top speed and lap time. If we exceed the rpm by much, we will sacrifice horsepower again with the same result. In road racing I don't much worry about the effect of a possible "tow" in top gear as the engines are always safe for several hundred rpm above max power, tows are a sometime thing, and if you are getting a tow, you don't need the horsepower and so can afford to over-rev a bit.

We do not, however, wish to shift at the maximum power rpm. Again looking at the BHP curve of Figure (89a), suppose that we will drop 1500 rpm when we shift. If we shift at the power peak, or 7900 rpm, then the engine will drop back to 6400. Draw a vertical line down the chart at those two rpm points. The area enclosed under the BHP curve between

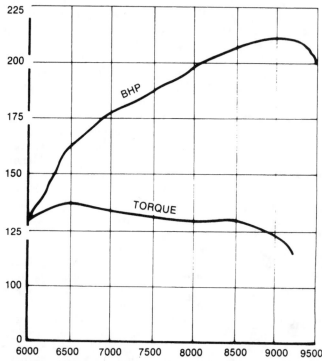

Figure (89b): Typical 1.6 litre BHP and torque curves.

142

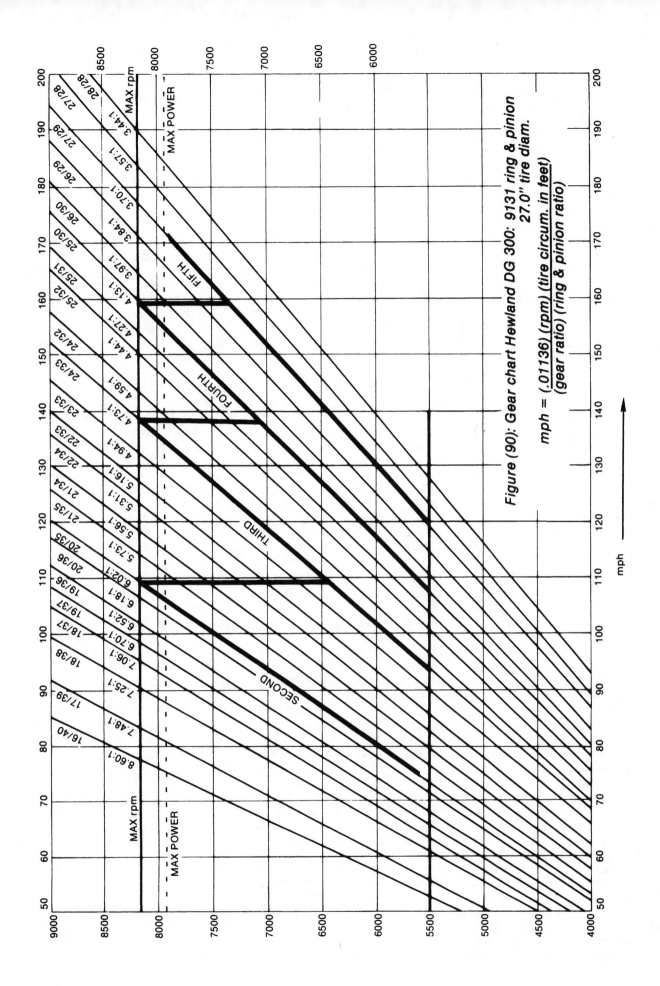

Figure (90): Gear chart Hewland DG 300: 9131 ring & pinion 27.0" tire diam.

$$mph = \frac{(.01136)\ (rpm)\ (tire\ circum.\ in\ feet)}{(gear\ ratio)\ (ring\ \&\ pinion\ ratio)}$$

mph ⟶

143

the two lines is porportional to the total power that we will have available to accelerate us from 6400 rpm to 7900 rpm in the gear that we have just shifted into. If, on the other hand, we do not shift until 8300 rpm (assuming that the engine is safe to 8300), the rpm will drop to 6800. Although the horsepower has dropped off on the top end from 7900 to 8300, there is more area under the portion of the curve from 6800 to 8300 than there is under the portion from 6400 to 7900 and we have gained acceleration. So we have to select our shift rpm for maximum area under the BHP curve. The actual shift point will vary with the nature of the curve, the step between the adjacent gears and the safe limit of engine operation. It can be found with a calculator or by eyeballing the curves and gearchart. It is of some importance to make sure that your tach is accurate—most are not.

The next thing that we have to worry about is the selection of the optimum ratio for the shortest (slowest or numerically highest) gear that we are going to use on the race track in question. If we are going to be traction limited (i.e., if the corner is slow enough that wheelspin will be a problem) then we select the longest gear that will (a) keep us just at the wheelspin limit, and (b) keep the rpm at the slowest point in the corner high enough that the engine will pick up the throttle cleanly and accelerate smoothly. Don't worry about rpm in relation to the peak of the torque curve at the slow point in the corner—we want the torque peak to coincide with the rpm at which the driver can bury his foot—not the point at which he picks up the throttle. It makes no sense at all to install so short a gear that the driver will be faced with an embarrassment of riches in the torque department. We want the car to be traction limited when he nails it—but only just. Remember, the taller that we can make bottom gear without sacrificing acceleration, the closer we are going to be able to space the remaining intermediate gears and the greater will be our overall acceleration potential. At the same time remember that he is also going to have to pull out of that same corner with a full load of fuel. If we are not traction limited, select a low gear that will allow the driver to apply full power at or very close to the engine's torque peak rpm.

Now we have to select the intermediate gears. Many racers choose intermediate gears in even steps from bottom through top. They are wrong. For maximum acceleration we want the steps between gears to get smaller as road speed increases. The reason is simply the big wall of air that we are pushing at high speed. A quick return to Figure (45) will illustrate what we are talking about. We can stand a big jump from first to second because the total resistance to acceleration at that road speed is low. By the time we are ready to shift from fourth to fifth, we need all of the area under the curve we can get and so the step from fourth to fifth has to be small so that we will have maximum power available after the shift. Again the selection can be made with a calculator—or you can draw a bunch of graphs similar to those in Figure (45). You will come just about as close by eyeball. Supposing, for instance that we are gearing a Formula 5000 car for the short course at Riverside (Figure 91). We know from previous experience that we can pull a 27/29 top gear and that a 20/35 second is just about right for turns six and seven. If we did not know, we would have to guess from experience at other tracks and a course map. Our peak torque is at 5500 rpm, peak horsepower is at 7900 and we are

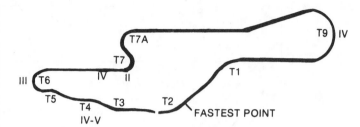

Figure (91): Riverside—2.54 mile short course.

going to shift at 8200. We look at the gearchart for reasonable steps and, on a decreasing step basis, select a 24/33 third gear and a 25/30 fourth. Shifting from second to third will drop the rpm to 6400 at 109 mph, third to fourth will drop to 7100 at 138 mph and fourth to fifth will drop to 7300 at 159 mph. On the course map these look reasonable. For a perfect progression we might have chosen a 26/30 fourth gear, but that looks as though it might be a bit tall to get a good shot out of Turn Nine, so we opt for the 25/30 for openers.

This selection can be labelled "guess one." While they will give us pretty close to ideal acceleration, we may have to modify the gears to suit the race track rather than the drag strip. For instance, we have selected our low gear (second in this case, since first is a "never-to-be-used gear" in Formula 5000) on the basis of the slowest corner on the track. However, there may be several other second gear corners which are faster than the slowest one. In this case, we may have to use a taller second for the greater good. Or we may find that third is too short for one of the lesser straights—necessitating a momentary shift into fourth just before we get on the brakes for a second or third gear corner. In this case we install a taller third. And so on—unless you are running something like the old 510 C.I.D. Can Am Cars with so much torque that, except for low and top it didn't much matter what gear you were in, the selection of optimum ratios is going to take a bit of fiddling. The peakier your engine is, the more critical the gearing will be. Do not, however, expect great gobs of lap time to result from changing gear ratios—it will not. What will happen is that the car will become more pleasant to drive.

The two most common mistakes that racers make with respect to gearing is running too short a low gear and twisting the engine too tight. In both cases the driver is probably confusing noise with power and wheelspin with forward bite. Another common failing on the driver's part is not gearing the car so that it is well within the peak torque range coming out of critical corners in the intermediate gears. A dead giveaway to this one is the answer, "Oh, it's pulling OK," when asked about his rpm coming off from turn whatever. It will pay dividends to sit down with the driver and the charts and have a ten minute chat about gear ratios.

MATERIALS

At the moment the racer has very little, if any, choice with respect to the materials from which the components of his engine will be made. About the biggest decision that we get to make is whether to use aluminum or magnesium for the water pump housing—and that only on stock blocks. Very soon this situation will change. The technology of composite materials is about to catch up with motor racing. The composites of which I speak are man grown thin filaments of either pure carbon or pure boron. The filaments are then combined or woven into various forms, saturated with very tricky epoxy resins and formed into sheets or shapes under both temperature and pressure. The resuling parts boast strength to weight and stiffness to weight ratios well beyond anything that we know about. They are temperature stable and can be made machinable. The costs of both materials and tooling are very high but are declining slowly as composites come into more general use.

While composites are eminently suited for such applications as brake discs, hub carriers and wheels, it seems probable that their first use in racing will be in engine components—connecting rods, rocker arms, valve spring retainers, pushrods and pistons come to mind. Except for the cost aspect there is no reason why blocks and cylinder heads cannot be made from composites. I foresee a golden age of very strong, rigid and light race car parts—which will be a comparative advantage to those brave enough to use them first.

I also foresee a short period of ignorance, hype and general chicanery during which a lot of substandard parts which may or may not be made from the right composites will appear on the market. Until the manufacturers and the racers figure out the technology involved, there are going to be some broken parts. I haven't exactly figured out what I am going to do when composites become available—probably buy some parts, have them analyzed and destruction tested—so I am in no position to offer advice. I will suggest, however, that the initial advertising claims be treated with the usual grain of salt.

Believe it or not, that's all that I have to say on the subject of tuning on the engine.

If all this sounds like I don't believe in tuning the engine at the track—it should. The poor little devil has to be constantly checked and the mixture may have to be adjusted for the day and the altitude, but that's it. Oh, yes, one other thing: Bounding around on the trailer is very liable to upset the float level, so that has to be checked as well. You are not going to find another 20% power by dickering with the engine at the race track—in fact you won't find any and you are very liable to lose some. So concentrate your time and energy on the chassis and aerodynamic balance. As Jim Travers used to say, "Tune your chassis and gain 100 horsepower."

145

CHAPTER THIRTEEN

THE DRIVE LINE

THE DRIVE LINE

In my mind, the drive line of the racing car includes the flywheel, clutch, drive shaft, gearbox, differential and axle shafts along with the necessary universal joints. Thanks to Borg and Beck, Mike Hewland and Pete Weismann, the clutches and transaxles that we use have enjoyed a state of development and reliability for the past ten years or so that can only excite envy on the part of those responsible for the design of the rest of the vehicle. The same cannot be said of the differentials or the axle shafts.

THE FLYWHEEL AND THE CLUTCH

The first link in the drive line is the flywheel. We saw in Chapter Three that the problem is one of mass and rotational inertia—we want to minimize each. Assuming that the regulations permit, or that you think that you can get away with bending the regs, you run the minimum diameter flywheel that you can hook a starter system to. You also design the thing so that it has the minimum possible mass at its periphery and you use aluminum. You do not use cast aluminum unless you like explosions. The friction surface cannot be aluminum which requires the use of a steel insert plate. The starter setup with a small diameter flywheel may require the exercise of some ingenuity, but it will be worth it. We no longer have to make our flywheels ourselves because Mac Tilton is making really good ones.

Everything that I have said about the flywheel is also true of the clutch—except that Borg and Beck have solved most of the problems for us. Regulations permitting, there is no logical choice but to run a Borg and Beck racing clutch for the simple reason that it is the lightest unit available and has the lowest possible moment of inertia. They make one that will hold *anything* that you can put in a race car other than a drag car. Properly installed (see *Prepare to Win*), maintained and inspected, they will last forever. They are no more expensive than any other racing clutch.

THE BELLHOUSING AND THE INPUT SHAFT

The clutch and the flywheel live inside the bellhousing. No one pays any attention to the bellhousing except to weld up the cracks that occur from time to time. Everyone should devote some time to the bellhousing. If the front and rear faces of the bellhousing are not both true and parallel and/or if the pilot diameter at the rear of the bellhousing into which the gearbox or transaxle spigots is not concentric with the crankshaft, we can get into big trouble. In the case of the gearbox, the input shaft is normally a rigid extension of top gear on the mainshaft. If the bellhousing alignment is

not perfect, a notable bending load is put into the input shaft to the detriment of the bearings involved and of the gear itself. The heat generated by a relatively small amount of bellhousing mis-alignment is awe inspiring. In the case of the transaxle, the situation is less critical because the input shaft is longer and normally splined into the constant motion shaft so that some misalignment can be tolerated. However, mis-alignment is never good—at best it will cost power through friction and can ruin the bearing where the input shaft passes through the differential casing. This will result in a lost oil seal, oil on the clutch and, when the bearing balls get between the mesh of the pinion and the crown wheel, a lost transaxle. As a point of interest, this bearing should be a really good one. The difference in price between the best bearing available for this application and junk is about $1.50 and the cheapies tend to shed their balls under the best of conditions.

You can depend, sort of, on the machining of the block face but you had better check that it is normal to the crank. You can depend on the machining of the gearbox or transaxle. For reasons which escape me, you cannot depend on the machining of the bellhousing—they must be checked for both parallelism and concentricity. Errors in parallelism are corrected by taking a skim cut on a milling machine. Errors in concentricity are detected by indicating the spigot diameter off of the crankshaft boss and corrected by repositioning the dowels in the block, the dowel holes in the bellhousing or by the use of eccentric locating dowels. This is no big trick, but making provisions for all of your bellhousings to match all of your blocks (you do not want to go through the indicator bit every time that you change engines) is a bit more difficult.

Input shafts seldom give trouble—unless someone convinces you to make a trick one from maraging steel. Maraging steel does not like stress reversals—which severely limits its usefulness on the racing car. On the early Can Am and Formula 5000 cars, when we thought that we wanted the shortest possible bellhousings, we used to break them because their torsion bar length was short. Once we caught onto spacing the engine forward in the chassis the problem went away. Still, they are a very highly stressed item, must be frequently magnafluxed and inspected for nicks and suchlike stress raisers and, on Formula 5000 and above, should be replaced every 2000 miles or so.

THE DRIVE SHAFT

There isn't much that you can do with the drive shaft of the front engined car except to realize that the stock unit is unlikely to be ready for doubled power and racing tires. Any of the specialty shops will make good ones—make sure that the welds are good and the yokes are installed true. Check the shafts for straightness and have them dynamically balanced. Use no cheap Universal Joints—the kind without grease nipples are to be preferred. A lot of drive shaft problems are actually caused by ignoring the installed angle between the pinion nose at the differential and the tailshaft of the gearbox. When the production car is lowered for racing, or the rear tire diameter is changed, this angle can be changed, which often results in the universal joints being asked to exceed their angular capability during wheel travel. The universal joints will not cooperate in this matter. They will bind, which makes torque transmission less than smooth and causes the joints to break. The fix is to adjust the pinion nose angle back to where it ought to be—with angled shims between leaf springs and the axle pad or by adjusting the locating arms with the coil sprung beam axle. The mid-engined car does not employ a driveshaft which is a positive advantage.

THE AXLES

Axles have always been a problem. They still are. Most classes of professional racing insist on the use of safety hubs because of the frequency with which the stock axles break—and when a stocker breaks, the wheel comes off. On production cars, up to but not including Trans Am, stock axles are probably OK for racing use, but they should be shot peened and must be thrown away on a schedule. About the only good thing about production car racing is that there is a good history available of component life. For TransAm, IMSA and the like, you are going to have to either have your axles made or obtain them from one of the specialty manufacturers. Three things are important here—material, heat treat and mechanical design.

The material end of things is pretty simple—if somewhat heretical. Use 4340 steel—it has better through heat treating properties than the ever popular 4130. Maraging steels are not suitable because, while they are very strong and have excellent heat treating properties, they just do not like stress reversals. An axle is nothing but a torsion bar and stress reversals are the name of the game. The only thing to avoid in the design of an axle is the stress raiser. Stress raisers are normally caused by rapid section changes and by sharp corners. Natural places for these are at the end of splines. The spline I.D. and the I.D. of any snap grooves must be greater than the actual shaft O.D. and all radii must be as gentle as possible. You will gain no strength at all by going to a shaft O.D. that is greater than the minor dimension of the spline—indeed you will set up a stress raiser and the axle will break at the end of the spline—every time. It is best if you can arrange for the retaining ring groove to be located at the outboard end of the axle. Heat treat should be in the neighborhood of Rockwell C Scale 52/56.

HALF SHAFTS

The same holds true for the half shafts used for independent rear suspension (or inboard front brakes). With the exception of Formula 5000 cars and Can Am cars, most racing cars are delivered with adequate half shafts. None of the big cars are.

The problems here are several. In addition to the obvious necessity for the half shaft to be articulated, they must have some provision to accommodate the axial plunge associated with the four bar link independent suspension system. If there is any notable resistance to this axial plunge, or change in half shaft length, the effect will be the same as a bind in the suspension and power application will be accompanied by a jerky and unpredictable oversteer. Neither the driver or the lap time is going to enjoy the sensation. The classic solution was to use a male/female splined two piece half shaft and let the splines accommodate the plunge. Naturally the splines always bound up to some extent under torque loadings and this didn't work out very well. Then Lotus came out with the fixed length half shaft which was also the upper link of the suspension system. This arrangement has been perpetuated in the Corvette and the E Type Jaguar but the geometry is limited for race car use and the half shaft feeds some unnecessary loads into the final drive unit. Next came the rubber doughnut—which worked just fine so long as it was properly located and piloted but was limited in its ability to transmit torque. In its ultimate form (Brabham, Formula One) the drive shaft had two standard universals and a rubber doughnut and was getting pretty bulky. Rubber doughnuts went away when inboard rear brakes arrived. Next came the roller spline which was simply a male/female two piece shaft made into a low friction unit by the presence of either ball bearings or roller bearings between the sliding splines. These worked pretty damned well and, properly made from the right materials, (which they haven't been since McLarens stopped making Can Am Cars), they don't give many problems. Trouble is that, since the grooves for the bearings are deep (and, in the case of roller bearings, sharp cornered) they form natural stress raisers. The shafts are necessarily short and the only way to achieve reliability is with mass of material. These units are very heavy. Hewland made a very limited number of Ferrari-type ball bearing splined shafts in the early 1970 s and they were glorious. They were also so expensive that there was no market and the project was abandoned.

The present solution to the half shaft dilemma lies in the almost universal use of the Rzeppa type constant velocity joint which has been around forever but was virtually unused in racing until the 1970 s. The reason it was not used had nothing to do with the racer's ignorance of its existence or appreciation of its virtues, but was due to its cost of manufacture and general unavailability. For example, the specially built units for the Ford powered Indy Cars and the GT 40—Mk IIs cost about twelve hundred 1966 type U.S. dollars—each. The rising demand for non swing axle independent rear suspension in passenger cars and the increased popularity of front wheel drive finally made excellent Rzeppa joints available from Porsche, BMW, Volkswagen and Fiat—and terrible ones from British Leyland. Due to the economics of mass production, we can buy two joints and a shaft that will handle a Can Am Car for very reasonable money. Of course, the shafts are either too long or too short and the joints won't bolt on to either the hubs or the transaxle output shafts so we get to make our own shafts and adopt the joints to the car. In the smaller classes, most designers simply design the car around an existing proprietary shaft so that they can use the stock unit in toto. Other (and smarter) designers, like Robin Herd at March, use stock joints but make their own shafts, for two reasons—the stock shafts are typically nowhere near as good as the stock joints and by making your own shaft you don't have to compromise such things as rear track width. For the big cars, Pete Weismann at Traction Products makes the hot setup which is his shaft—in your length—and Porsche joints with the necessary adapters.

The advantages of the Rzeppa Constant Velocity Jointed half shaft are:

(1) Maximum torsion bar length
(2) Minimum weight and moment of inertia
(3) Minimum package dimensions—which leaves more room for such things as exhaust systems and suspension links
(4) Virtually frictionless axial plunge
(5) Increased angular capacity and true constant velocity
(6) Simplicity, reliability and cost

The only problem associated with the use of the Rzeppa joint is that the joints themselves are lubrication critical and the rubber or plastic boots have a nasty tendency to either slit or melt, in which case the grease will be slung out to the detriment of the joint and the brake on which the grease lands. The solution to the grease problem is the use of Duchams QJ 3204 C.V. joint grease which was developed to solve the problem in Formula One. It has to be imported from England, but it works. The next best is Lubri-plate moly. You still have to repack the joints every Saturday night and it is a truly messy job—no fun at all. I don't know what the solution to the boot problem is—other than making special ones. I have found that one of the common causes of boot failure is lack of clearance between the boot and the adjacent exhaust pipe. It usually looks like there is plenty of clearance, even at full droop. However, the boots are bellows or accordian affairs and they grow in diameter—a lot—at high rotational speeds. This growth can be dramatically reduced by the installation of ty-wraps or "O" rings in the boot convolutions. It also helps if you don't seal the minor diameter of the boot on the shaft so that it can breathe. I still replace the boots every race. Do not attempt to use your friendly Auto Parts Store's moly grease in a C.V. joint. The moly is probably OK but the grease is junk and will quickly turn to clay which will necessitate the purchase of new joints. It is essential that *all* of the old grease be removed when cleaning and repacking C.V. joints as the deteriorated old grease will contaminate the new.

THE GEARBOX

The gearbox is one of those areas that, while often ignored, offers us some opportunity to exercise our ingenuity for the benefit of the driver. Missed shifts are embarrassing and expensive while a box that is hard to shift, slow to shift or vague in its shifting makes for both lack of speed and missed shifts. With a U.S. production box, the first step is to throw away the stock shift linkage and install a Hurst racing shifter. The next step gets expensive. If you are going to put a lot of power through the box, it probably isn't up for the job. Gears, shafts and bearings are usually good enough but the gears have to be bushed onto the shaft and the mainshaft will probably have to be grooved to get enough oil to the bearings. Also the end float on the gears and the gear stack

tolerances get critical. This is a job for a specialist, and the drag shops are good at it. You may also find it necessary to run an oil cooler on the box. To my total surprise the 12 Volt Jabsco Water Puppy electric pump (as long as it has the optional nitrile rubber impellor) will do the job—although it is a bitch to prime. The pump does not like to pump cold oil so I install a cockpit switch and turn on the pump when the box is warmed up. The only oil cooler worth using on a gearbox or a diff is the Earl's Supply/Serck Speed unit distributed in this country by Earl's Supply. The OEM and aftermarket units are JUNK. You have to be a little careful routing the cooler lines so that you can change an engine without dismantling the whole mess and so that they do not get torn off when you leave the road. You also have to remember, when filling the trans, that the lines and the cooler carry a lot of oil. The setup will also work on the differential.

To my mind, synchromesh in a racing transmission is an abomination. It slows down the shift, creates heat, makes maintenance a nightmare and makes shifting without the clutch difficult. In addition, synchromesh gives us a whole bunch of parts which weigh something and can fail. If the driver is so inept as to require the assistance of synchros in order to shift gears, he doesn't belong in a racing car. That's neat, but what do we do if the car that we happen to be racing (any production based car) comes equipped with a synchromesh box? If it's a Porsche type baulk ring box (Porsche, BMW, Alfa Romeo, Ferrari and doubtless others) we don't do anything except maybe improve the shift linkage and count our blessings. It takes a very fast hand indeed to beat a properly set up baulk ring synchro and, to my knowledge, there is nothing that can be done to improve them. Baulk rings wear out pretty quickly and a worn out setup is very slow to shift so we get to replace a lot of parts.

The normal U.S. and English cone type synchro, on the other hand, is pretty slow and can be beaten by even a moderately fast hand. Tumbling the synchros helps some and a lot of people remove every other tooth off the cones; I do not. I have very little experience with synchros, except on street cars, and I hope to keep it that way. Again, the drag racers know how to trick the boxes.

With the ubiquitous Hewland boxes, there are a few things that can be done to make things more pleasant. I have said atl that I have to say about shift linkages in *Prepare to Win*. Nothing has changed and the linkage is just as critical as it ever was—and, on the majority of racing cars, it is still every bit as screwed up. I also covered the basic adjustment of the Hewlands and again nothing has changed. The only thing that I have learned since then about maintenance has to do with the giant nuts on the back of the pinion shaft and the constant motion shaft. The biggest pain in Hewland Land is the removal and replacement of the cotter pins that ensure that these nuts don't come off. There is a way out—buy a pair of extra nuts and reduce the thickness of all four in a lathe until a pair of nuts will fit onto the shaft. This will remove the castellations, but we are not going to need them anymore. What we now have is a pair of jam nuts for each shaft. Torque up the first one and then torque up the second one behind it. One less pain and a couple of minutes saved on each gear change. It is now also impossible to forget to install the cotter pins and, although it is possible to forget the jam nut, they will be in the tray when you finish and are too

148

big to overlook.

There are a couple of little things that can be done to speed up the shifting of the Hewland—and to make it more positive. The modifications cost nothing to do, which is a pleasant change, and make life a little more pleasant for the driver. For reasons which escape me, Hewlands have a lot of lateral shift lever travel which they don't need. It takes time and subtracts precision. You can't alter the travel at the gate (there is no gate) but you can do it at the shift finger. Figure (92) illustrates the procedure. Two methods are available. The first is to weld onto the blade of the shift finger so that it will stop earlier against the side of the case in the fourth/fifth position and against the reverse hold-out plunger in the second/third position. This gets the job done but it is not adjustable, you have to do a certain amount of grinding and filing to get it right and it makes removal of the finger very time consuming. Additionally you will have to do the same thing to replacement fingers—which is OK if you do it in the shop. If, however, you have to buy a replacement shift finger at the race track, you are going to have an unhappy driver. Once a driver has driven a narrow gate Hewland, he is not going to like the stock setup ever again.

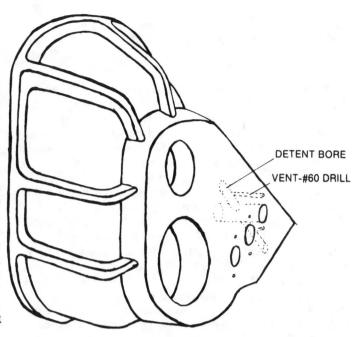

Figure (93): *Location of vents for shift rail detents.*

1/16 inch clear of the neutral position when it is against the stop. It also helps to radius the operating faces of the shift finger.

Shifting a Hewland displaces the shift detents in their housings. Since the detent bores are full of oil, a certain minor resistance occurs. If the detent bores are vented by a #60 hole drilled from the back of the case as shown by Figure (93), this resistance goes away and the shift is rendered more pleasant. It is necessary to make sure that the vent holes are not masked by either the selector housing or its gasket.

I gently radius the detent grooves on the shift rails, but I'm pretty sure that this does not accomplish anything worthwhile—force of habit, I guess. I still don't grind the top surface of every other dog on the gears and dog rings—it's a pain—my drivers know how to shift.

If I'm not going to use first gear at a given circuit, I don't run it—moment of inertia again. Since a spacer is necessary to make up the gear stack, I just take any old ruined gear and have its diameter ground down until the wall thickness is about 1/4". If I'm not going to use first, I also increase the reverse lockout detent pressure to give a more positive gate for second and third. No big thing, but every little bit counts. Don't make it too positive or Fred will twist something trying to get into reverse after he has spun.

If you are going to use first on a Hewland five speed box, you will discover that it was designed as a starting gear only—neither the fork nor the rail are meant for downshifting while in motion. All that this means, in practice, is that you get to replace the fork pretty often. This is not a big deal and you can tell by looking at it when the time has come. When the wear groove at the end of the fork gets to be about .030" deep, it's time.

I should point out that none of the above, in itself, is going to gain a measurable increment of lap time—we just don't spend that much time shifting and the car doesn't stop during the few tenths of a second that it takes to shift gears. For a couple of hours work on the box we will pick up maybe two

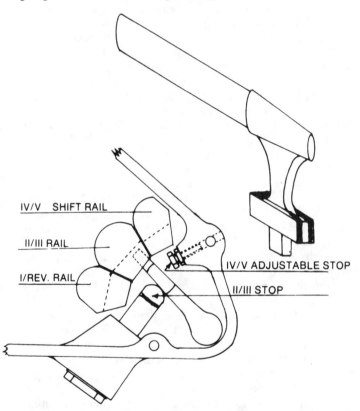

Figure (92): *Alternate methods of reducing lateral travel of shift lever.*

The second method is to drill and tap the case to accept a #10-32 screw and jam nut which will serve as an adjustable fourth/fifth stop. The reverse plunger can then be extended by welding—but remember to redrill the vent hole. Or it can also be drilled and tapped to form an adjustable stop (which must then be vented). Whichever method is decided upon, the stops should be adjusted so that the finger is from 1/32 to

seconds—in the duration of a one hundred mile race—but the driver will like it a lot.

THE CROWN WHEEL AND PINION

Other than taking the time to set it up properly and to break it in correctly, there is nothing that I know of that can be done to trick the ring and pinion. We covered all of that in *Prepare to Win*. Once, when I was working for a team with lots of money, I used the Micro-Seal process on the whole transaxle—gears, shafts and bearings. We couldn't do a back-to-back comparison so I don't know what the performance benefit was. I was, however, able to measure a difference in transaxle temperature and it was in the order of 15 degrees Centigrade. This convinced me that Micro-Seal did indeed reduce friction losses and so increased the net power. It is the only process that I have ever tried that did anything. If I ever have the money again, in Los Angeles, I will repeat the experiment. One thing that we did discover was that we had to dump the trans oil about every twenty miles until it stopped looking black, and then clean out the Weismann locker really well. With any other type of locker, it wouldn't matter.

THE DIFFERENTIAL

There are six types of differentials being used in racing; the open diff, the cam and pawl or ZF type, the clutch locker, the Detroit Locker, the Weismann and the spool.

The only reason to run an open diff is if the regulations require one. Locking the open diff is very simple—you weld the spyders solid. You will get caught, eventually. I have not personally run an open diff since the days when I didn't know that there was anything else and I do not expect to ever run one again. Therefore, I know nothing about the techniques used to trick them so that they will partially lock. I do know, however, that this has been done in SCCA production racing. I neither know nor care how it is done. The reader who is interested should be able to find out without too much trouble. So much for the open differential.

Street cars need differentials between the driven wheels because the outside wheel in any cornering situation must travel on an arc of greater radius than the inside wheel, and so will have to revolve more times in negotiating any given corner. If the two driving wheels are locked together, the unladen inside wheel will be forced to rotate at the same speed as the inside one and will therefore hop along like a rabbit. This makes a funny squeaking noise and upsets the handling of the vehicle. Street cars typically operate at low force levels so the open differential does not normally present a problem—and it is maintenance free. However, there are times—like trying to get up a steep hill in winter when one wheel happens to be on glare ice—when the limitations of the open diff become very apparent. With the open diff, the torque from the engine takes the easy way out and if, for whatever reason, one of the driving tires has exceeded its thrust capacity, all of the torque will be delivered to that wheel and it will spin—while the other tire does nothing and the vehicle goes nowhere.

This condition occurs on the race track all of the time—while we seldom end up with one tire on a good surface and the other on a slippery one, lateral load transfer ac-complishes the same end by unloading the inside tire. Since no one tells the open differential about this state of affairs, as we try to accelerate out of a corner, the diff keeps transmitting drive torque to the unloaded tire until the torque becomes more than the tire can bear and it starts to spin. About then the diff sends all of the torque to the spinning tire and none to the laden tire and we go nowhere. The problem becomes more acute as the power to weight ratio raises, but even Formula Fords get inside wheelspin out of slow corner. Wings, by keeping the unladen tire partially loaded with aerodynamic downforce, make the problem less acute. However, all racing cars, in order to realize their potential, require some sort of limited slip or locked differential—and always have. What we need here is a differential that will be open—or will differentiate—on a trailing throttle, so that the rear wheels can rotate at the required radius speed during corner entry, but will start to lock as the driver comes back on the power to stabilize the car, thus providing a degree of built-in understeer by driving the inside rear wheel, and which will gradually lock all of the way as the power is increased so that there will be no inside wheelspin. At the time of writing, no one has quite achieved this goal.

There are five types of differentials in use in racing cars today—the locked diff, the cam and pawl or ZF type, the clutch pack or Salisbury type, the Weismann locker and the Detroit Locker. With one exception, each has advantages and disadvantages. We'll start with the exception.

To my knowledge, the Detroit Locker has no advantage over any other type of differential except the open diff. It is an abortion. Its functioning can be compared to that of the ratchet on a chain fall. As load is transferred it is forever locking and unlocking, causing great lurches and changes from understeer to oversteer. The best thing to do with a Detroit Locker is to remove the center cam and run it locked. Period. End of discussion.

We all know that the Indy cars, the dirt cars, Nascar and Porsche use a totally locked diff—and they go like stink. Most of the IMSA type large sedans also use it. Why then, is the spool not used in sophisticated road racing machinery—except by Porsche? Not because people haven't tried it! The problem has to do with corner radii, weight distribution and how much we are willing to sacrifice. The high banks and the two-and-one-half-mile ovals tolerate the spool because at the corner radii we are talking about there is virtually no difference in rear wheel rpm—and the tire stagger makes up for most of that—when we only need to worry about one corner radius, we can, by making the outside rear tire larger in diameter than the inside (stagger), arrive at an equal tire rpm situation and therefore neutralize the drag moments about the center of gravity on a trailing throttle corner entry situation. So long as the driver picks up the throttle smoothly and progressively, we can then tune out the full throttle understeer caused by the drive on the inside rear wheel. It is also very important that the driver not apply sudden power during a time when he has understeer lock (toward the corner center) on the front wheels or he will understeer immediately into the wall—thump. When, as in road racing, the radii of the various corners vary considerably and the amount of the braking and turning combination taking place also varies with the nature of the corner, it is no longer possible to achieve equal rear wheel rpm in most of the corners and the resultant dragging of the unladen wheel causes corner entry understeer which limits the lap time simply because the locked diff cannot differentiate on trailing throttle. The sedans get away with it because they are pretty crude to start with. I personally believe that they would be faster with a Weismann diff—which is about the only thing available for them that will both work and live, other than the spool. I don't know how in hell Porsche gets away with it, but I suspect that it has to do with their basic power advantage. In the days of the Turbo Panzer Can Am Cars, I was interested enough to take segment times vs. the Team McLaren cars and found, to my interest, that Donahue was notably slow in the entry phase of virtually every corner when compared to Revson and Hulme. It didn't matter at all because the Porsche had such a power advantage that what happened coming out of the corners more than overshadowed what had happened going in.

Numerically, the most popular differential in road racing is the cam and pawl type, usually referred to as the ZF. This unit is fitted stock to the ubiquitous Hewland Transaxles and to most Continental High Performance GT cars. When they are working correctly, they work pretty damned well. They do not fully lock under power, but they almost do. By varying cam angles, number of lobes and such' the percentages of lockup can be varied—while the unit is being designed—and 75% to 80% seems to have been standardized. On the overrun, they function as open diffs. Two problems are inherent. First, by their very nature, they are a self destructing unit due to high rates of internal wear from friction. We never had any trouble with them until the tires got to be both big and good. Now we have nothing but trouble with them and must replace the guts every 400 to 600 miles, which is both time consuming and expensive. Further, since wear starts immediately and continues at a more or less linear rate until the things are shot, the differential characteristics do not remain constant and the car tends more and more strongly towards power oversteer as the diff wears. This makes testing and evaluation difficult and can make driving less pleasant than it should be. The second problem is that, since they do not, even when in perfect condition, lock fully under power, if we drive hard enough, we can still achieve inside rear wheelspin on the exit of slow and medium speed corners, which is wasteful and slow. They do, however, still drive the outside wheel when the inside is spinning. Problem number three arises from the limited mental capacity of the unit once inside wheelspin starts. They get all confused and start to ratchet—especially in the wet. When the limited slip gets confused, so does the chassis—followed closely by the driver. Best bet is to boot it and steer a lot.

Next in terms of population is the clutch pack locker about which I also don't know very much except that they have never been very reliable in racing. If they were to be made reliable, it would seem that they could be very good indeed in that the percentage of lock can be adjusted by shimming the clutch stack, and they lock very smoothly—unlike the cam and pawl which tends to engage with a bit of an upsetting jerk. It is rumored that Hewland is working on a new clutch pack locker, but my efforts to obtain one have been unsuccessful—"not ready yet" which probably means "not yet reliable enough to sell." They have been used very successfully in Formula Two and by one driver in Formula 5000.

Now, the reason that I don't know very much about most types of differentials is that Pete and Michelle Weismann make the Weismann Locker which I have used whenever I could ever since I discovered it. Like everyone else, I have done a fair number of back-to-back tests—against cam and pawl units and against spools. The results, at least by my interpretations and by those of the drivers and stopwatches involved, have been remarkably consistent. I use the Weismann virtually everywhere—when I have a driver who is willing and able to learn the technique involved. I am willing to admit that on long and slow corners, it is a disadvantage. There are only a few such corners in racing and, on the courses where they exist, I feel that the overall advantages of the Weismann make up for the disadvantages encountered on one corner.

So what happens inside Pete's magic unit? Not a lot. The unit consists basically of two Sprague clutches keyed together by a giant "C" spring which connects the roller cages to each other. The inner cams are individual cylinders or drums splined to the individual output shafts. If an inner cam rotates, so does the output shaft to which it is splined and vice versa. The rollers are located on each inner cam by roller cages and the cages are loaded against their inner cams by Sprague or drag springs which nest inside the inboard face of each cage. The cages for each inner cam and output shaft are keyed together by the "C" spring which engages a tang on each cage. The outer cam is common to both inners and is integral with the differential case and, therefore, with the ring gear. The outer cam is a true cam with hills and valleys. At the outboard end of each inner cam is a paper clutch disc located in the carrier and serving as a thrust bearing so that the inner cam can rotate with respect to the carrier without galling parts. The two inner cams are preloaded by means of a stack of Belleville spring washers which allows us to vary the preload.

What happens is that, under trailing throttle overrun conditions, there is not enough torque to force the rollers up into the outer cam; they sort of roll on the inner (cylindrical) drums and the unit differentiates on corner entry. When engine torque is applied, the rollers are forced hard into the outer cam ramps, which wedge them like crazy against the inner cams and the unit is locked—100%—no slip at all. So the unit is open under trailing throttle and a spool under power, giving the best of both worlds. In the days before wings, the Weismann was a virtual necessity (wings, by increasing the vertical load on the rear wheels put off the point of inside wheelspin). They are still an advantage, not only under normal race track conditions, but especially under abnormal conditions—like one wheel in the dirt, for instance, when the cam and pawl goes nuts and the Weissman doesn't even know about it. Since it does not ratchet (when in proper operating condition) it works very well in the wet.

Naturally, we don't get all of this for free. There are disadvantages. Most racers, when asked about the Weismann will flatly state that it causes diabolic and terminal understeer. To an extent this is true—if you substitute a Weismann for a cam and pawl and make no other changes to the car, the car will exhibit more power on understeer. But it will do so only because the driving torque on the inside rear wheel has been considerably increased. In addition to making the car come

151

off the corner faster (using more of the tire) this causes an understeer torque about the vehicle's center of gravity which must be tuned out of the chassis. The car is also liable to jump a little bit to the left when the driver comes off the power to get onto the brakes. This is minimal and completely predictable and is soon ignored by the driver.

For the driver there is one basic law of Weismann. NEVER APPLY POWER WITH UNDERSTEER LOCK ON THE FRONT WHEELS. If you do so, you will immediately be driven, understeering all of the way, into the outside wall. The same holds true, to a slightly greater extent, with a locked diff. In a slow corner the trick is to toss the car, arrive at the point where you are going to apply the power in a neutral steer or slightly oversteering attitude and then nail the power with the steering wheels pointed straight ahead or out of the corner, keep your foot down and steer. The past master of the technique was Denny Hulme. The other technique is to apply the power very smoothly as in a fast corner or as in Mark Donahue or Bruce McLaren. Unfortunately, when the corner in question is both slow and long—like the loop at Mid Ohio—this becomes almost impossible to do and the car with the locker is going to be slower, at the mid-point of the corner, than the car with a conventional limited slip. If the driver realizes and accepts this inescapable fact and drives around the problem, this will not be a disadvantage in lap time because, by being sensible, he can bring the car to the geographic point on the race track where he can apply the power with the car in the correct attitude to do so and make up what he lost by accelerating harder out of the corner. The truly unfortunate part comes about when either the driver runs out of sense and tries to horse the car around, or when he has to overtake in such a situation. You can't have everything. The driver's second law is not to come all the way off the power once he has applied it—the lock/unlock sequence can get a bit fierce and upsetting. Weismanns and spools demand smooth driving and give increased forward traction. It's that simple.

The mechanic also has a couple of laws that he must obey when working with a Weismann. The first is: NEVER USE MOLY OR GRAPHITE ANYWHERE NEAR A WEISMANN LOCKER. The locker is a static friction drive device and even a minute amount of either substance will prevent you from getting the car out of the pits—let alone around the race track. If the rollers are allowed to slip at all under power, there will be a lot of heat produced (normally one of the advantages of the Weismann is that very little power robbing heat is generated). In fact there can be enough local heat generated within the unit that the cams and the rollers become coated with a nasty phosphate varnish from the broken down oil and the unit will start to unload under power. This is called "popping" and is very nasty indeed. The effect is sudden and transient full throttle oversteer and a very confused and unhappy driver. The telltale tracks are axial marks on the inner cams. Popping can be caused by insufficient preload between the inner cams, by excessive backlash between the rollers and the cams, or by a worn out outer cam. It is self propagating—once it starts, and unless you do something about it quickly, it will only get worse as the rollers brinell into the surface of the outer cam. Other than proper assembly, the best way to avoid popping within the locker is to clean it—thoroughly and regularly—with MEK and Scotchbrite.

Weismanns are oil sensitive. Most of the commercially available gear oils are loaded with friction modifiers or anti-slip additives for the gears. These not only don't help the Weismann, they are a positive hindrance to proper operation. The chemical composition of racing gear lubes is changed too frequently for me to attempt the oils that work. If you own a Weismann, check with Pete or Michelle. The safe method is to load the locker with straight mineral oil—no additives—from your local truck stop, and seal it with silicone seal. Naturally, this procedure requires frequent cleaning, but it is required anyway.

If wheelspin becomes a problem, one or both of the drag springs in the ends of the roller cages has become distorted. The effect of a broken drag spring is similar to shifting into neutral. What happens here is that the rollers are no longer loaded against the inner drums. Drag springs should be inspected daily and replaced frequently.

CHAPTER FOURTEEN

THE PECULIAR CASE OF THE LARGE SEDAN

THE PECULIAR CASE OF THE LARGE SEDAN

The majority of the cars being raced in the United States are sedans based more or less on production street machines. In many cases the degree of removal from stock configuration is extreme, but they are still modified production cars. There are several reasons why this is so. First and most valid is the realization by NASCAR that the public is willing to pay money to watch cars race that they can identify with—so long as the racing is close. This idea doesn't seem to work so well for SCCA and IMSA, but it sure works for NASCAR. Another reason is that there are many Racing Associations that run various types of stock car shows at a lot of tracks and for a guy who wants to race, these associations are often the logical answer. A third reason is that many SCCA racers get into production sedan racing because they are led to believe (mistakenly) that it offers economical weekend racing.

I know nothing about the racing of sedans on circle tracks—nor do I wish to. Steve Smith Autosports publishes a good selection of books on the subject and I am content to leave the field to him. I hope that he will do the same for me. I do, however, have some recent and successful experience with the beasts on road courses—which removes my last excuse for not including this chapter.

THE NATURE OF THE BEAST

Production based racing cars have a number of inherent disadvantages—all having to do with the purpose for which the base vehicle was designed. This is, of course, why the Monzas and Mustang IIs get whipped by the specially built and designed for racing Porsches and BMWs. It is difficult to make an effective silk purse from a sow's ear—if you are going to enter into direct competition with real silk purses. Fortunately, except in IMSA, production based cars normally compete against other production based cars and so the design disadvantages tend to cancel out. We must, however, be aware of these design deficiencies, if for no other reason than to be able to do an effective job of minimizing them.

Production based racers are large, heavy and cumbersome. They are therefore very hard on brakes and tires. They lack torsional rigidity, feature high center of gravity locations and high polar moments. Their basic suspension is designed to provide passenger comfort on freeways and to understeer under any and all conditions. The body designs feature little if any downforce, and gobs of drag. They come with inadequate brakes and non-adjustable suspension links. They are hard to work on and are made up of hundreds of very heavy parts. They are very expensive to modify and to race. Further, in this country, since the death of the original Trans Am Series, it is extremely unlikely that anyone is going to make any money or advance his career by racing them on road courses.

None of the above really matters. Sedan racing is good racing and a lot of people, for their own reasons, prefer it to other forms. The type of vehicle involved is, after all, secondary. Racing is a contest between men, not between machines, and hard work and good engineering will produce a superior sedan just as they will produce a superior open wheeler or sports racing car.

THE RACER VERSUS THE REGULATIONS

More than in any other form of racing, sedan racing is a battle of reading, interpreting and bending regulations! You must start off by reading the pertinent basic and supplementary regulations until you truly understand them—in detail. The basic problem is that virtually nothing except the clutch pedal is good enough in stock configuration to go racing with—and the regulations, plus financial necessity, stick you with a lot of stock parts. Having digested the regulations, you must now sit down and figure out what is the most effective way to modify your car within those regulations and what you think you can get away with outside of them. Working outside the regs divides itself into two broad sub categories:

Areas where there is a sort of tacit agreement that you will be allowed to get away with it—like acid dipping and moving the engine in the old Trans Am.

Areas where it is difficult to identify the modifications—like cleverly hidden or covered suspension pivots instead of rubber bushes.

Areas that are easy enough to find, but difficult to measure—like minor shifts in suspension pivot or engine locations.

It is vital to realize that the average tech inspector is no dummy—and is very liable to resent any insults to his intelligence. He is also liable to be the first to appreciate a really clever ruse—but may report it. Since it is very difficult to write restrictive regulations in comprehensive terminology, there are always loopholes in production car rules. Unlike a direct cheat, they are unlikely to send you home for a loophole infraction—although you are very liable to be told to "get it off before the next race." Do not back yourself into a corner with illegal modifications which cannot be legalized in a hurry. Realize also that your machine will come under close scrutiny from the opposition who will scream loud and long if they think that it is a cheater.

THE BEGINNING

The starting point for any production based racer is a bare body shell. Strip it all the way—including any and all sound-deadening mastic, which is really nasty stuff to get off. Throw away everything that you are not required to run—all that it does is weigh. While you are at it, do whatever you have decided to do about lightening the body panels and decide where your suspension pivot and locating points are going to end up—as well as the locations for major items such as the fuel cell, battery, engine, transmission and driver.

The first basic step, and the one that will ultimately determine the success of the whole effort is the design and installation of the roll cage. You are required to install a roll cage of minimum specifications in the interest of driver safety. It is in your interest to extend that cage to provide structural integrity to the whole chassis structure, particularly in torsion. God knows that what the manufacturer provided won't do it. To be effective, the cage must tie in the front suspension mounting points, the rear suspension mounting points and the A and B pillars. It must bridge the door gaps and must be triangulated as fully as possible. A look at the state of the art and at Steve Smith's books will give you the idea—although we don't need the massive side intrusion bars required by NASCAR. We also don't need for the cage to weigh half a ton. For most of the members, 1-1/4" by .049" mild steel tubing is adequate. Cutting and installing the tubes after you have decided where they are going to go is a real pain for the amateur builder. The pain can be considerably eased by using PVC plumbing pipe for mock-ups and templates. While installing the cage, take the opportunity to seam weld the entire chassis structure. Beef up the transmission crossmember and mount both the engine and the transmission solidly—no rubber. If possible, make the engine lower crossmember a removable unit to facilitate engine changes and to allow the removal of the sump with the engine in the car. The front suspension towers will not be strong enough in stock form and the top of the engine bay will require triangulation between the suspension towers and the firewall area. This triangulation must, of course, be removable.

Rather than going through the stress analysis of the cage, I prefer to build a series of balsa wood 1/10 scale models and figure out what I need by twisting them—it's a hell of a lot quicker and, I suspect, probably more accurate.

Production cars have lots of ground clearance so that they can jump over curbs and travel down dirt roads. This gives them very high centers of gravity which leads to low cornering power and sloppy transient responses. Lowering the chassis on the suspension to the legal minimum ride height is easy enough—and usually brings the front suspension curves somewhere within reason but is also liable to run you right out of bump travel in the suspension department—which must be avoided. It is easy enough to find out what spindles, suspension arms, suspension pivots, idler arms, steering boxes and the like to use—and they are usually available from the better suppliers cheaper than you can make them. This is a case where it is wise to learn through other people's experiences. When it comes to shocks, there is no substitute for double adjustable Konis, but you won't need the aluminum model on a sedan.

Get all of the major weight masses as low and as far back as you can arrange them—don't worry about getting too much weight on the rear wheels—it just isn't possible.

Pay a lot of attention to cooling—use a towing package radiator or one of the Aluminum Harrisons made for Corvettes and make sure that the core is at least three inches thick. Slow the water pump down and cut the impellor down to avoid cavitation—remember that the stock water pump (along with everything else) was designed for 4000 rpm maximum. Seal the radiator inlet duct and keep the hot exhaust air from the radiator away from the carburetor inlet. Use the biggest oil cooler you can find room for and duct it well—headlight openings are logical places for oil cooler ducts if permitted. While laying out the cooling, make provisions for both transmission and differential coolers if permitted—they will be needed. If you are not allowed to use oil coolers for the diff and trans, duct cool air directly on to the cases—it will help quite a bit.

BRAKES

The basic decision with the brakes on a large sedan is whether or not to employ a booster. I don't believe in them, but a lot of people do. Anyway, if you feel that you need a booster, go ahead, but make very sure that you have a giant vacuum reserve tank to go with it. In the disc department, you will find a pretty wide choice—cheapest will always be an adaptation of a stock ventilated disc—Lincoln makes good ones, if you can figure a way to get them on. Hurst Airheart makes good discs and a wide range of top hats or bells to mount them with. Trouble is that the bells are cast aluminum, which warps with heat, and they are bolt-ons rather than dog drives, which is not a good way to go for a heavy car. Tilton Engineering sells a combination of high quality aluminum top hats with steel dog drives which are the best bet—they also stock a complete line of Automotive Products discs and calipers. Anyway, use the largest diameter disc you can fit inside the wheel and, on a big sedan, go for the thickest ventilated disc that you can find—at least for the front. This thickness you will find is 1-3/8" available from Tilton. A thickness of 1.1" is adequate for the rear.

Choices are more limited in the caliper department—Hurst, Girling and Automotive Products all make suitable units. The only real disadvantage to the Hurst units is the fact that you will have to make your own steel slider boxes for the pads. The only pads available are M-19 with a much too thin backing plate and, due to the seal design, they require a bit more pedal travel than the other calipers. First class is the Automotive Products (Lockheed) range of racing calipers. The big Girling 16/3 and 16/4 units are also excellent but they are hard to find and the only pad material is DS 11.

To adapt your rear axle to disc brakes, without which you will not be competitive, will require a fully floating axle—which is required by most association regulations anyway and is best purchased rather than built. Stock Car Products in L.A. builds good ones.

You will also need a twin master cylinder and bias bar setup which is best purchased again from Tilton. Don't fool around with proportioning valves—there are no suitable ones available—the ubiquitous Kelsey Hayes unit has too much hysteresis for racing and the rear brake line pressure doesn't release quickly enough.

SUSPENSION

Now we have the basics—the next question is, as always, how to make it work. As usual, this boils down to the suspension. We will conveniently divide sedan suspension into front and rear and we will assume that the roll cage is of sufficient structural integrity to tie the two together. At the front, we have problems—there is too much static weight on the front end, regardless of where we have moved the engine to, and second, the camber curves of a production sedan are wrong for racing. Once the car has been lowered, there probably will not be sufficient bump travel, the links are too short, there is too much compliance in the stock pivots, and the links may not be strong enough for racing. What we can do about any or all of this depends on the regulations. The first step is to poach the front track out to the maximum dimension obtainable so that diagonal load transfer will not cause the car to trip over itself going into corners. The second step is to locate the wishbone pivots to obtain a favorable camber curve, roll center location and sufficient bump travel. The front roll center must be considerably lower than the rear regardless of the roll moment—sorry about that. It will help a lot to lower the rear roll center. This is not a design book so we are not going into the design of the suspension— but you will need a pretty steeply inclined upper control arm in order to get about one degree of negative camber change per inch of bump movement. This will tend to keep the laden wheel more or less upright in roll. The popular alternative is to run a lot of static negative camber, but this hurts the braking performance severely. At the same time, build in some anti-dive; sedans can tolerate 25-30% and it helps a lot. I am assuming that we have already gotten rid of the stock compliance bushings. Next we discover that all of this moving things about has ruined whatever bump steer correction was built into the original vehicle. This requires quite a lot of work. Typically you will have to move the steering box and idler arm, bend the steering arms on the spindles and/or make a new cross link. Things will be a lot easier, and structurally more sound, if you substitute rod and bearings for the stock track rod ends.

Most sedans seem to run insane front spring rates—1400 to 1600 lb/inch are not uncommon. To my mind, this is ridiculous. Admittedly there is a lot of weight involved and Formula Car rates are going to be ridiculous, but I have never found that a front spring rate of over 1000 lb/in to be necessary—so long as the camber curves are somewhere near right. When laying out the suspension system, make sure that camber and castor will be easily adjustable — within a range of at least plus and minus two degrees. I would also build in weight jackers—again assuming that the rules allow them. You will almost certainly get to make your own anti-roll bars—of considerable stiffness. I favor straight bars with splined ends and as much adjustment as can be achieved—which means long links. Again, many people tend to go overboard on the bars—I have never been able to use a bar more than 1.06 inches on a road racing sedan and usually end up around .88.

THE BEAM AXLE

At the rear of the American Sedan we come up against the dreaded beam axle. The live axle has been universally condemned for racing use for more years than I have been around. It is not necessarily that bad.

I do not believe that the time will ever come when an intelligent designer would consider the use of a beam axle in a new design—for either a racing car or a passenger vehicle. The only advantages that can be thought of by even the most reactionary Detroit types are low cost, simplicity and zero camber change. Against these are the overwhelming negative features of high total and unsprung weight, excessive package dimensions (room must be provided for the whole enormous thing to move up and down at least 7"), lack of independence of wheel motion and reaction. From the engineering, passenger comfort, road holding and vehicle dynamics viewpoints, the beam axle ceased to exist long ago. Detroit, and many of the Detroit derivatives in Japan, England, Europe and Australia could care less about any of the above viewpoints. All decisions in these realms are based on cost and, in that respect the beam axle reigns supreme— particularly if you already happen to own the tooling to produce the things by the million.

Since most of the cars being raced in this country are based on production sedans, the simple reality is that anyone who wants to make his or her living racing is going to spend a certain amount of time working with beam axled cars. This simple fact should not cause dismay—for three reasons:

(1) If you are racing a beam axle car, most if not all of your opposition will be doing the same.

(2) As race tracks become smoother, the relative disadvantages of the beam axle become less important.

(3) He who understands, as always, can make his car work better than he who does not.

DESIGN CONSIDERATIONS

The design considerations of the beam axle are few indeed:

(1) Type of springs to employ—leaf or coil.

(2) Type of lateral location—Watts Link or Panhard rod.

(3) Type of longitudinal location—leaf spring with or without traction bars or coil springs with some arrangement of trailing arms.

(4) Weight reduction.

Given a beam axle, I don't really care whether it is sprung by leaf springs or coils—if anything, I lean a little bit toward the leaf simply because the leaf spring inherently provides some lateral and longitudinal axle location while the coil spring does not. Therefore, we need fewer locating links and pivots and the setup is more simple with leafs—besides, the leaf spring arrangement lends itself to tow hitches.

LATERAL LOCATION

Regardless of the springing medium, the sedan that is to be raced is going to require some sort of lateral axle location—leaf springs by themselves won't get it done. Production cars are not designed to operate at high lateral G forces and that is that. Assuming that the regulations allow axle locating devices, the choices are two—the Panhard Rod and the Watts Link—as illustrated by Figure (94).

The Panhard Rod is about as simple as anything ever gets.

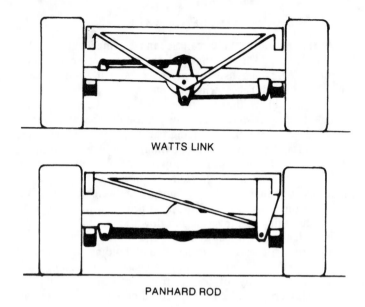

WATTS LINK

PANHARD ROD

Figure (94): Lateral locating devices for beam axles.

A tube, with a pivot at each end, is attached to the chassis at one side of the car and to the axle at the other, thus effectively constraining (although not totally eliminating) lateral axle movement. Ignoring structural deflection which should be eliminated by design, lateral movement of the axle will be restricted to the horizontal component of the arc described by the end of the Panhard Rod attached to the axle as if swings. For this reason, the Panhard Rod should be made as long as possible. For this reason also, and to keep the roll center height as constant as possible, the Panhard Rod should be parallel to the axle at ride height. The roll center of a beam axle with a Panhard Rod is located at the intersection of the Panhard Rod with the vehicle centerline. Since the Panhard Rod is asymmetrical by definition, it cannot remain horizontal with axle motion and so the roll center height changes as the vehicle rolls—and it changes differently in right hand turns than it does in left hand turns. If the Panhard Rod is connected to the chassis on the left side and to the axle on the right, then the roll center will rise during a left hand turn and vice-versa. This, in itself, will cause more load transfer to the right rear tire when exiting a left hand corner. For this reason it is normal practice to attach the Panhard Rod to the right side of the chassis for cars that normally turn left and to the left side for cars that normally turn right and thus to use the asymmetry to reduce lateral load transfer on corner exit.

Structurally the attachments to both the chassis and the axle must be plenty stiff. The chassis mount will normally be some sort of a downward tower from a frame rail or other major structure. The tower must have plenty of area where it attaches to the chassis or you will pull the whole thing out by the roots, and must have a diagonal brace to the other side of the chassis—3/4" x .049" square tubing is enough for the brace. The whole thing must mount in double shear. While we are on the subject, the Panhard Rod must also clear the axle, the diagonal brace and the fuel tank under all conditions of suspension travel. The attachment to the axle must also be gusseted to get some weld area. There are two choices for the

end pivots of a Panhard Rod—silent block type bushes or rod end bearings. Since we are trying to eliminate lateral axle movement, rubber bushes won't do much of a job—use rod ends and use a left and right hand thread on the rod ends so that you can make the rod fit. The tube itself must be strong and stiff enough to deal with the not inconsiderable loads involved—I normally use 1-1/8" x .083" 4130 with 1/2" bore 5/8" shank rod ends.

GEOMETRICAL CONSIDERATIONS

The roll center of an unconstrained beam axle is at the axle center under all conditions. Add a Panhard Rod and the roll center becomes the intersection of the Panhard Rod with the vehicle centerline. With any practical layout, this means that the addition of a Panhard Rod will lower the roll center, which is a good thing, as it is too high to begin with. In order to limit axle movement to the maximum practical extent and to keep the roll center as constant as possible, the Panhard Rod should be as long as possible and should be horizontal at ride height.

THE WATTS LINK

The Watts Link offers symmetrical lateral axle location and a fixed roll center (at the link pivot). To be effective, the pivot must be attached to the chassis, not to the axle, and the links must be parallel to each other and to the ground at ride height. I do not think that the theoretical advantages of the Watts Link over the Panhard Rod are worth the extra structure and complexity—although the cross structure necessary to mount the pivot is an ideal location for any necessary ballast. Structural considerations for the Watts Link are the same as for the Panhard Rod. Naturally, by providing alternate locations for the pivots, the roll center height can be varied, as it can with the Panhard Rod.

LONGITUDINAL LOCATION

Longitudinal axle location is by the leaf springs themselves with or without some form of trailing link with the leaf spring setup and by trailing links with the coil spring setup. We'll consider them separately.

TUNING AND PRACTICAL CONSIDERATIONS
THE LEAF SPRING

The first thing to do with a leaf spring is to get rid of the compliance inherent in the stock rubber eye bushings and shackle bushes. This compliance allows the axle to move longitudinally as the rubber is compressed under acceleration and allows the spring to twist. G-6 Nylatron or Teflon makes ideal spring bushes at very nominal cost. The stock shackles should be doubled in thickness at the same time.

Next we get into axle skewing or roll steer—yes, it does exist with the beam axle. What happens is that, as the car accelerates out of a corner due to lateral load transfer, most of the load is on the outside rear tire (in a straight line it is on the left rear tire). Therefore more compressive load is placed on the forward portion of the outboard leaf spring than on the inboard. Under any compressive loading a leaf spring will assume some sort of "S" curve and thus shorten the effective distance between the spring eye and the axle center—in addition, the eye, if it is overshot as in most production cars, will wind up to some extent. When the outboard spring has more S bend and windup than the inboard spring, the axle must skew—with the outboard wheel moving forward and the whole axle assuming a toe-in condition with respect to the corner—thus causing roll understeer on corner exit and sticking the back end—which is a good thing if we can control it.

As in so many areas, the stock setup probably has too much of a good thing in the roll understeer department. First of all, under the influence of three times the power that the car was designed for and racing tires, the springs will deflect too much. The axle will then skew too much and too suddenly, breaking the footprint and upsetting the car. Secondly, forcing the leaf springs into unnatural positions and conditions stores large amounts of kinetic energy in the springs which must eventually be released. When it is released, the shock cannot dampen this energy as it is pointed the wrong way and we have the dreaded axle tramp under acceleration—which will effectively limit the acceleration.

The Hot-Rod Store solution to the problem in street cars is the Traction Bar, which is a simple rod clamped to the axle and paralleling the leaf spring to some sort of a forward mounting point. This creates a sort of Japanese equal length and parallel trailing arm setup with the spring as one arm. This works reasonably well and very cheaply at the Stop Light Grand Prix, but when corners are introduced to the situation, the traction bar and the leaf spring fight each other and the axle hops around. Of the many such devices on the market, the best (and the simplest to install) is the type that bolts below the spring saddle and clamps to the main spring leaf behind the eye.

The best solution for road racing is, however, the simplest. What is needed is a spring with minimum windup and in which the majority of the springing action takes place behind the axle while the forward portion does the locating. This means that most of the arch in the spring must be behind the axle, that the front spring eye must be centralized and that the leaves forward of the axle must be very tightly clamped together. I make my own clamps out of .093" mild steel and weld the clamp overlap seam while it is red hot. The clamp then shrinks as it cools and is really tight. This makes the front portion of the spring into an effective trailing arm and works just fine as a locator without causing tramp due to the release of energy or hopping due to geometric binding. The ultimate in leaf spring location is a tapered single leaf spring with centralized forward eye, but the cost is too high for the small advantage to be gained.

Often ignored is the simple fact that, in order for a leaf spring to work at all, the rear shackles must be slanted down and toward the rear at all times—otherwise the shackles will not swing and we get unpredictable oversteer. I run very soft rear springs—typically in the 200 to 225 lb/in range—and I run a lot of spring arch.

COIL SPRINGS

Coil spring beam axles are located by either two or four trailing arms. If the arm geometry is correct, about all that you can do is get rid of the rubber pivots. I prefer to use trailing arms only for longitudinal location and to use a Panhard Rod or a Watts Link for transverse location—I consider that the GM style of inclining the arms toward the CL of the

car and using them for lateral location as well is too complex and unpredictable as well as too highly stressed.

AXLE TRAVEL

The beam axle requires ridiculous amounts of travel—probably because of its excessive weight. Three inches of bump and four of droop are absolute minimums—I prefer to allow five each way and use lots of silasto bump rubbers.

PINION SNUBBERS

With road racing power to weight ratios I do not us pinion snubbers—either mechanical or hydraulic. If the pinion angle is somewhere near right and the axle is well located, they are just not needed. Further, unless the snubber geometry is perfect—which is difficult to arrange as the ideal forward pivot location always ends up somewhere in the gearbox—a mechanical bind between the snubber and the drive shaft will result. Lastly, I believe that the type of rocking axle tramp that the snubber is supposed to eliminate is actually vertical tramp caused by either too much rear brake bias or improper shock absorber characteristics—in each case accentuated by the mass of the axle itself. This sweeping statement leads us to the perplexing question of how to control the antics of this very heavy axle which naturally wants to spend all of its time hopping up and down. Two methods are available—lighten the damn thing and use trick shocks.

AXLE WEIGHT

Anything that can be done to pull weight out of a beam axle is a big plus. Unfortunately there isn't much that we can do except to use an aluminum diff carrier—which will drop the diff temperature a quick 20° F and make diff changes less unpleasant as well. So we end up with the shocks as the only available method of controlling the mass of the axle—simple, you say, "use stiff shocks." Wrong again. If we install stiff shocks to control the wandering axle, we will end up with wheel hop under both acceleration and braking, and the car will be slow. What we need is very little damping at low displacements and piston velocities. We can achieve this by opening up the rebound leak on the rear shocks at the end of some ride control.

So that is the basic sedan—the rest is tuning.

AERODYNAMICS

Since sedans feature about an acre of frontal area, drag reduction becomes critical. The first step is to make all of the bodywork seams as close fitting as possible—including the windshield seams. If you can get rid of the rain gutters and increase the windshield rake, do so. Next figure out some legal way to exhaust the high pressure air from the front and rear wheel wells and from the engine compartment. The latter will be a lot easier to do if you have closed off the front of the car except for the radiator, oil and brake cooling ducts—you may also be able to clean this area up with clever headlight covers.

Where the regulations permit, it is all too easy to get so much front downforce on a sedan that you cannot balance it at the rear with legal spoilers. The BMW and Porsche type airdams are sometimes too effective. The best bet is to get the most available rear downforce and then balance the front by extending the airdam toward the ground.

Probably the most critical part of sedan aerodynamics lies in ensuring an adequate supply of the coolest possible air to the engine inlet. This always works out to be a rearward facing inlet air duct which picks up its charge as close to the windshield as possible and which is sealed onto a large inlet plenum which in turn insulates the inlet system from the high under hood ambient temperatures. With the popular Holley carburetors, the use of a pre-smog air cleaner as a diffusor (the biggest one that you can find) will even out the inlet distribution and make for a happier engine.

PRACTICAL TUNING

The problems inherent in tuning sedans are the same as those found in any other racing car—they are just compounded by the mass of the vehicle and the lack of adequate downforce. We must kill the understeer on corner entry or the understeer is going to kill our overworked front tires. We do it by rational camber curves, maximum front track widths and the lowest front wheel rates we can get away with—and by smooth driving. To get the bite coming out of corners, we run the lowest rear wheel rates we can get away with, put as much static weight on the rear wheels as we can and run most of the roll stiffness at the front. Far more than pure racing cars, sedans respond to offset front camber settings (more on the outside wheel in the predominant or critical corners) and weight jacking (heavy on the inside rear). Vehicle balance is super critical because the cars are typically badly undertired, and an unbalanced car will very quickly kill the tires at one end or the other. For the same reason the cars, to be fast, should be driven on rails. Sideways doesn't get it done—in any form of pavement racing. With a sedan, it takes a lot of work and a lot of driver discipline to achieve smoothness—but it will be worth it when the act is all together.

Use a lot of front bump and not much rear—prop up the tortured corner with shocks and let the car squat and go off the turns without allowing it to fall over on the outside rear tire. Have fun.

CHAPTER FIFTEEN

RACING IN THE RAIN

RACING IN THE RAIN

Every so often the road racer finds it necessary to race in the rain. No one likes it. In the whole history of Motor Racing no Team Manager, Car Owner, Mechanic, Official or Race Promoter has ever been heard to utter one good word about racing in the rain. Some drivers say that they like it, but they are lying. The very best that one can hope for is to be uncomfortable for as short a period of time as possible.

Contrary to popular opinion, racing in the wet is not necessarily more dangerous than racing in the dry. It is, however, much more difficult and infinitely less enjoyable. One of the reasons why it is more difficult is that virtually no one ever tests in the wet and so very few operations know what their hot setup for wet conditions is. Despite the discomfort and the mess involved, every team should test in the wet at least once each year. When it does rain, if you know what the hot setup for your car is—and no one else does—you will have a *real* unfair advantage. Before you charge off to get miserable testing, let's take a quick look at the changes in the operating conditions caused by wet race tracks.

SEEING IN THE RAIN

To my mind, the major problem facing the racing driver in the wet is his inability to see well. At times, flying spray makes it impossible to see at all. When this happens, I feel that the Chief Steward of the Meeting has a moral obligation to stop the race until conditions get better. Even under normal wet conditions, however, helmet visors have a nasty tendency to fog on the inside which is not good at all. The condition is due to moist air, heavy breathing inside the helmet and lack of air circulation. What is needed is a defrosting system. Two are available. The first is an electrically heated visor. This device features wires imbedded in the visor and a small battery in the driver's pocket. It is available from several sources and it works well. Every road racing driver should own one. The second method, homemade, also works. It involves the use of two normal visors, spaced about 1/8" apart with weather stripping foam. A series of slots or holes is then punched or cut in each visor in such a way that they do not impinge on the driver's vision and so that the slots in the front visor are not in line with those in the rear one. This will allow air to circulate between the two visors and inside the helmet, but will not allow the direct passage of water drops—which feel like bullets at speed. No matter what de-misting system is used, it should be augmented by an application of Bell Helmet's anti-fog solution. Some drivers prefer to use open-faced helmets and goggles in the wet. Anyone who wears an open-faced helmet

in this day and age needs his brains tested. The time for the driver to start figuring out how he is going to see out of his Bell Star in the wet is well before the need arises. During a race is no time to test visors.

THE DYNAMICS OF THE WET RACE TRACK

By definition, a wet race track is a slippery race track. This simply means that the tires—even the best of the rain tires—will not be able to develop anywhere near as much traction, in any direction, as we had in the dry. In turn, this will cause less load transfer—in all directions—and less chassis roll to be generated. Because of the reduced load transfer values, the car that is set up for dry conditions will have too much front brake bias, too much damping, too much roll stiffness and too high ride rates in the wet. Additionally, we will have too much brake cooling, the cockpit air vents will become water hoses and everything electrical will get wet and tend to short out. We will also want all of the aerodynamic downforce that we can get—we are not going to worry about drag when it is wet.

So the directions in which to move to set the car up for rain are pretty obvious. Softer springs, softer bars, softer shock settings, more rear brake bias, more wing at both ends, softer brake pad compounds, and block off the brake and cockpit cooling ducts. The question is how far to go and that is why we must test in the wet. How far to go varies from car to car and from driver to driver. If you are stuck and haven't tested, cut the shock settings in half, go down one size on both bars, crank two turns of the bias bar onto the rear brakes, go for maximum balanced downforce and go racing. Remember that the car will basically behave just as it did in the dry—only more so. If it was understeering in the dry, it will still do so—only worse in the wet. Of course, any car will lean more toward power oversteer in the wet and so a gentle right foot is a necessity. The racing car which exhibits strong understeering tendencies will be undriveable in the wet.

DECISIONS

If it is raining at race time and you are sure that it will continue to do so, there is no decision. You put on the rain setup and go racing. If it is raining at the start and you feel strongly that the rain will stop and that the track will dry, don't change the springs, and make damned sure that you can make the car driveable in the dry during a tire change pit stop—the brake ratio is a problem here unless it is driver-adjustable. How far to go in changing to the full rain setup under these conditions is a matter of judgment and luck.

If the weather is "iffy" before the start, wet or dry will be a last minute decision—and often it will be anything but a clear-cut one. The whole process is full of "what ifs." My tendency is to leave the car on the most probable setup until the last minute and then guess. This precludes spring and bar changes, but that is about all that it rules out—everything else is a pre-determined number of turns in one direction or another and can literally be done in a matter of seconds. The Stewards are presently exhibiting strong tendencies to dictate what tires we start the races on and this is probably a good idea—although I would prefer to make my own decisions. One of the great scenes in motor racing is a grid full of experienced and supposedly intelligent Drivers and Team Managers all staring at a very cloudy sky and asking each other if it is going to rain.

The real difficulty connected with rain comes up when we can't figure out what the weather is going to do, but must make a decision because they are about to start the race. There is nothing to be gained by agonizing, so just make up your mind once and do it—after all, there are only two basic ways to go. When the situation is in doubt, I almost always opt to start dry—optimism, I guess.

If it starts to rain while the race is in progress, the situation can become very difficult. If the Stewards have not decided beforehand that they will stop the race for tire changing (ask at the driver's meeting exactly what their intentions are in case of rain), then we have to balance the time lost in stopping, changing tires and getting back on the race track, against the time lost slithering around on drys for however many laps remain—wondering all of the time whether or not it will continue to rain. One of the very safe procedures is to do what the race leader does. I usually leave this decision to the driver unless he is very obviously doing it wrong. Do not take time during a pit stop for rain tires to do anything but change the tires—unless you have quickly (as in pip-pin) removable anti-roll bar links and/or wing adjustments. This advice does not, of course, hold true in long distance racing or if the Stewards have stopped the race.

The opposite situation occurs when you are circulating on rain tires and the track dries out. We know that, not only are the rain tires slow in the dry, but their very soft compounds will blister and chunk very quickly indeed as they become overheated by the dry race track. So once again we get to weigh the length of the race remaining, the time lost in changing tires and the time lost trying to nurse the overheated wets to the finish. This one should not be a driver decision unless he actually chunks a tire and has to come in. Drivers are too busy to do even elementary math, and running the wets in the dry is not an unmanageable or dangerous situation—just slow. Before a tire disintegrates, the driver will be able to smell it and to see it crowning, Again, following what the race leader does is not a bad plan. If your driver does come in with a chunked tire—change them all.

DEGREES OF WET

When running in the wet, most drivers seem to be totally unaware that the track is not equally wet in all places. Unless a deluge has occurred, there is almost always a line on every straight and through every corner that is less wet than the rest of the track. This line is visible from the cockpit and seldom has anything to do with the normal racing line. It will always be the fast line. Traction is what we are looking for and, even with rain tires, we are not going to find it in puddles. Conversely, when the track has dried and you are trying to nurse tortured wet tires home, drive through every damp patch you can find. Do not, however, carry this to extremes by driving through small lakes—lest you aquaplane off the road.

THE ELECTRICS IN THE WET

Water is a very good conductor of electricity. Unfortunately, water will never conduct electricity where we want it to go. Instead, it will short out switches across their poles, get inside distributors and cause the fire to go out and generally wreak havoc with the whole electrical system—unless you have taken comprehensive safeguards. The typical racer's trick of wrapping a plastic bag around the distributor is just not adequate.

All switches and electrical terminals should be thoroughly coated with one of the silicone di-electric compounds (not an aerosol spray, but stuff that comes in a tube). The distributor or magneto cap should be sealed onto its body with a non-hardening di-electric and then vented. Spark plugs which live at the bottom of wells in the cylinder head should be sealed with the same glop. Aerosol di-electric compound should then be sprayed over the distributor and high tension leads—which should be separated from each other. Having done all of this, you should then pray a lot.

THE GROOVING IRON

For many years, an electric tire grooving iron was part of every professional racer's track kit. The tire Engineers also carried them around, but did not advertise the fact. This was necessary because Akron seemed unable to grasp the fact that rain tires had to have adequate drainage in both directions in order to work. To make them effective we had to groove our own rain tires. Looking at the 1978 Goodyear rain tire I rejoice that this is no longer true. Unless you really know what you are doing, I do not suggest trying to make your own intermediate tires by grooving slicks—it can be done, but it is dodgy.

CHAPTER SIXTEEN

PUTTING IT ALL TOGETHER

PUTTING IT ALL TOGETHER

Hopefully, the preceding pages will have introduced some new ideas and helped you to clarify your thinking with regard to some old ones. None of this will help you to win races unless you can put the knowledge gained to practical use. Knowledge and ideas tend to be a bit like experience—nice, but not necessarily useful. Clear thinking, logical priorities and the ability to reason will beat bright ideas and unassisted experience every time. The key to success in this business is the ability to utilize experience—our own and other people's. Never forget that the first race car that Derek Gardner ever designed, after a short but intensive and very logical development program, won Jackie Stewart the World Championship.

The winning of motor races is a question of applying knowledge and of damned hard work. If the Battle of Waterloo was won on the playing fields of Eton, then Grands Prix are won on the test tracks. Planning, evaluation, reasoning and establishing priorities are all more important than brilliance—either behind the wheel or at the drawing board. Most of the above are management functions and this is a tuning book. From the tuning or development point of view, it breaks down to evaluation and the establishment of priorities.

EVALUATION

The evaluation process comes down to only two factors—what our package does better than the opposition and what it does not do as well. You will note that both are relative factors. Once we learn to use a stopwatch rather than the human eyeball, this part of the process is simple enough. As part of the process we have to figure out why the package is either superior or deficient and then decide how to improve it and in which areas to concentrate. While we are at it, we also have to determine whether the difference is due to the driver or to the machine. If we can get that far, the rest is easy.

PRIORITIES

There are many different types of priorities in Motor Racing, the first—not within the scope of this book—being how much you are willing to sacrifice in order to get to where you want to go. Within the realm of tuning and development, the priorities are twofold. We must establish priorities in terms of lap time to be gained from our efforts and in terms of feasibility within the limits of the resources available to us.

In terms of winning races, the very first priority is that the car must finish the race. Everyone knows that, but the number of racers who consistently forget it is astounding.

This boils down to the design of the engine cooling systems and the overall preparation of the race car. Until we have established reliability there is no sense at all in wasting time trying to make the thing go faster—which is why I wrote *Prepare to Win* first.

From the lap time point of view, the priorities in order of their importance to the winning of races are: vehicle balance and driveability, the ability to accelerate off the corners, the generation of cornering force, the generation of usable braking force, aerodynamic drag and the development of usable engine power. Obviously the engine power can rank anywhere from first to last on the list depending on how good or how bad what you have may be.

From the resources point of view, there are two things to bear in mind. The first is that success will never result from attempting a program or a project that is beyond our ability to accomplish. The second is that since time and money are both finite, we have to ensure that we are getting the most performance per unit effort. In other words, don't spend your budget on a "low drag" body when you will get more performance for less time and money by increasing cornering power.

DEVELOPMENT TESTING

We covered many aspects of testing in Chapter Eleven. I did not, however, mention what may well be the most important aspects of the whole procedure—the attitude of the crew and the driver and the conservation of track time. Most of the race car "testing" that I have witnessed—at all levels of competition—has been a waste of time, effort and money. The operation that goes to the test track without a plan, or that goes out so that the driver can motor around and enjoy himself, will accomplish nothing worthwhile. There are times, particularly early in a driver's career, when the greatest need is seat time for the driver. This is perfectly valid. However, once the driver has reached the point where it is possible to improve the package—and he had better reach that stage very quickly indeed—any aimless motoring must be very firmly discouraged. First we will discuss the wasting of time in general—racers are good at it.

Nothing is ever in such short supply at a race track as time. It doesn't seem to matter whether we are at the track for a race meeting or for testing—there is never enough time. This is, of course, particularly true at SCCA Regional and National events, but only more so. Time lost during practice or qualifying is lost forever and time wasted during a day of testing is expensive and frustrating. Especially at one of the $1,000 per day tracks.

It therefore behooves us to take some pains to make sure that we get the maximum utilization of our time at the track. Very few teams do.

This becomes, as always, a many faceted program. The first most obvious and least often held to part of the program is to get to the track on time and to be ready to run when you get there. If you can start running at eight o'clock, you had better be at the track by seven so as to be unloaded, warmed up and ready to actually run at eight. There is only one word for the operation that shows up to test at Riverside at 9:30, spends an hour unloading and then decides to bleed the brakes, set the timing, change the jets, hot torque the cylinder heads and fit the driver to the car. The word is stupid. This sort of operation will probably have to send somebody back to the shop after the sway bars. They will also bitch their heads off when the crash crews go home at five.

Next is to establish a program—before you get to the track. Unless the whole object of the exercise is seat time, there will be a series of things to be tried. Arrange them in logical order—not only from the learning progression point of view but also from the work point of view, and make sure that all of the various bits that you are going to need are indeed ready and packed.

No matter how many miles you have on a specific track, you are going to have to baseline the car every morning. This is not because the vehicle or the driver will have changed—it is because the track will be different. It has to do with the amount of sand, dust and oil on the surface, wind velocity and direction, how much rubber is down and the ambient temperature. There is nothing that you can do about any of these features except to re-establish your base line.

It is silly to go out onto a green race track with good tires. At least your first ten laps are going to be spent sweeping the track with the race car. It makes little sense to waste expensive tires in this exercise. It is, however, a reasonable time to bed pads. Once the track is reasonably clean, put good tires on (the driver will have pronounced the car undriveable on the track sweepers) and go to work.

Car owners, sponsors, drivers and rival race teams never fail to be impressed by operations that start on time and keep running. They are also impressed by cars that go faster at the end of a day of testing than they did at the start. Even if all your demon tweaks have been disastrous and slowed the car down, return it to base line before you quit. It will go faster than it did in the morning and there will be a lot less disappointment.

All of the above holds true at race meetings as well as test sessions. Considerably less time is available and the penalty for wasting it is more severe. Qualifying is no time to try demon tweaks and practice is not much better. Race meetings are for drivers and testing is for engineers and mechanics. The car should be geared within one or two teeth when you show up—if it isn't, someone isn't doing his job. Don't change gears in the middle of a session—change them between sessions. Your driver needs all of the track time that he can get. Along these lines, a lot of time can be saved by making sure during the winter that everything on the car that is supposed to be adjustable is easily and quickly adjustable. It is rather silly to have to go through a giant wing dismounting exercise to change gears—or to take the rear suspension apart to change camber because the constructor didn't use left and right handed rod ends. My favorite is to find out that I have to take the top of the shock off because I installed it with the rebound adjustment wheel hidden. I also resent finding out that the tools to do a particular job are in the truck or the garage. (For tools you can substitute spare wheels, air tank, sway bars, fuel, brake bleeding kit and so on.) The other thing that you had better have with you for testing is a bubble balancer for the tires. They're pretty cheap, any fool can use one, and should it happen that you lose some weights, or if your tires are out of balance, it can save your whole day. You had also better have a lot of tape and some odd bits of sheet metal, tubing, pop rivets and a welding set. It's a bit silly to have to cancel a whole day of testing because of minor damage which could have been fixed if you had had the stuff to fix it with with you.

THE RACING DRIVER AS A DEVELOPMENT TOOL

There was a time, not very long ago, when the race car was a relatively simple device. It did not feature very many adjustable components and the driver's task was purely and simply to drive the car that was given to him to the very best of his ability. This is no longer true. Test driving—or the development of the racing car—is now and will be forever more the most important contribution that the racing driver will make to the success of the operation. While there is always a shortage of good racing drivers, there is a vast shortage of good development drivers—even though the requirements are identical. It is a question of discipline.

Two things are of paramount importance for the development driver; he must be totally objective in his evaluation—and that includes being completely honest, both with himself and his crew—and he must drive the car to its limit. He must not only drive hard, he must drive consistently hard. If the driver's performance is not a constant—i.e., isolated from vehicle performance—then the only predictable result of the day's work will be confusion. If the driver is completely consistent and objective but is not driving to the limit, the day will be an utter waste and nothing of any value will have been accomplished. It is true that this approach will inevitably result in the odd corner getting knocked off the car—it may even result in a hangnail or two. This is particularly true in the case of young drivers who have not yet gained the experience and judgment necessary to consistently overstep the limits by recoverable amounts. Development testing can be both expensive and dangerous—but there is absolutely no other way to win motor races.

It is not necessary that the development driver be a qualified engineer. Very few are. Some of the best that I have worked with didn't know which end to put the big tires on. What he does need to be is willing and able to take the car deliberately into never never land, bring it back in one piece and then, very objectively, tell someone how it behaved on its way to the limit, while it was there, and on its way back. He must also be willing to believe the stopwatch rather than the seat of his Nomex. It is then up to the corporate staff to interpret his ravings or mumblings—and to ask the pertinent leading questions.

If it is the driver's responsibility to work with the crew in the development of the machine, then it is equally the crew's responsibility to develop both the car and the driver—

particularly if the driver is relatively inexperienced. It will do no good to wish that you had a better development driver—you will have to manufacture a good one from what you have. Ken Tyrell's success is at least as much due to his skill at developing drivers as it is to the quality of his race cars. Make no mistake about it, even today the driver is still the major part of the performance equation—his role has changed a bit—but he is still the ultimate key to success.

In chassis development, the most difficult thing for the young driver to sense is when the car is actually at its limit of traction—without falling off the road when it turns out that he was wrong. Hard work and seat time is the only way that I know of to learn. While it is absolutely true that it is not possible to be really fast without also being very smooth, star drivers do not start out smooth and slow and become smooth and fast. They start out fast and hairy and then, gradually, become smooth and truly fast. These are not patient men. Disciplined, yes, but patient, NO. During the hairy phase of the future ace's career, he is going to fall off the road and he is going to damage race cars—he may even damage his body. While this tendency must and should be discouraged, we must be careful not to dampen the fire that burns within the young would-be race driver. The smoothness is a product of awakening awareness of what makes the race car truly fast and of self discipline—it must come from within. Real progress is being made when the driver becomes capable of distinguishing between forward bite and side bite—when he can actually feel the tires working. About then he will lose his infatuation with sideways motoring and set about the business of becoming a serious racing driver. I find it very difficult to force this coming of age process—lots of explanations and much time spent wandering around race tracks hand in hand with the young hero and watching the performance of the super stars at close range seems to work best. Ranting, raving and bad mouthing the driver will not get it done!

So with all of this engraved on our minds, the car and the spares are ready and we are going testing. What, exactly, are we going to do when we get there? First of all we are going to drive around the race track removing debris and sweeping off the big piles of sand and pebbles. We had better get there early, because the track will be dirty and it is going to take time to make it runnable. Next we are going to unload, pressure the tires, adjust the shocks and warm up the car. While doing that, we can also set up our equipment—which includes making sure that there are enough fire extinguishers and tools to do some good already stowed in some sort of vehicle, parked in the pit lane, with the keys in the ignition and ready to go. We will also make sure that no one takes that vehicle for coffee and that someone, other than the driver, knows how to get to the nearest hospital. It is all very well to say that it is essential to have a paramedic in attendance, but no one ever does—except at those tracks where it is required as a condition of track rental or at tire tests. The rest of us are too optimistic, too cheap or too broke to spend the money.

Assuming that we are testing a new car—or one that is new to us—the first thing that we are going to do is to run in the ring and pinion, get the engine running right, make sure that the thing will cool, shift and do all of the other right things. We can also spend this time getting the driver comfortable in and fitted to the moving car as opposed to the stationary one to which he was fitted in the shop.

Having progressed thus far, put a set of reasonable tires on the car and let the driver drive it for a while. How long depends on him. If the car is driveable, don't make any changes at all to the chassis until the driver has settled in, the tires are hot and you have established a base line—of lap time and of segment times. When the pads have been bedded, adjust the brake ratio and do whatever gear changes are necessary.

What comes next is, of course, a question of how the car is behaving. The desired sequence is as outlined in Chapter Eleven—get the understeer/oversteer balance right by playing with roll stiffness at low speed and downforce at high speed. Then establish optimum roll resistance and downforce by going up and down with each. Only after all of this is done is it time to play with roll center height and roll axis inclination, bump steer, anti-squat and the rest. Don't worry about aerodynamic drag at all, except as related to turbulence which disturbs wings, cooling air inlets or the driver. Improvements in drag are the last thing you will play with because they will cost you the most money and gain you the least time.

This sounds all too simple to be true—and it is. I don't believe that it is possible to prescribe in any more detail because of the complexity of the exercise, the interaction of all of the aspects of performance and the multitude of variables. There are some general don'ts—and no do's:

Don't make more than one change at a time—at least in related areas.

Don't try to evaluate chassis performance on cold or worn out tires.

Don't try to evaluate chassis performance until you have established good throttle response.

Don't make any tiny changes until you are getting pretty close to optimum—one click of shock adjustment isn't going to tell you anything early on.

Don't be afraid to try changes—you can always go back to where you were.

Don't trust subjective judgments, or even lap times. Take corner and straight times and find out exactly where you are gaining or losing time—if you know where, it is a hell of a lot easier to figure out why. Once you have figured out why, you can start to do something about it.

Don't make or accept excuses. The familiar "We're a second slower than the lap record, but, if the engine were fresh or if we had new tires, or if the sun weren't in the driver's eyes, we'd be a half second under it," is nonsense.

Don't work with a physically or mentally exhausted driver. If he is not in shape to do a hard day's testing, then he is not in shape to drive a race car. If he is not in shape to do his job, then he is not living up to his responsibilities and he should be replaced. The time to find out is before testing begins. It takes time for the human body to get into condition.

It is not possible to test too much. It is usually not possible to test anywhere near enough because of the dollars involved. You will never run out of ideas to be tried—and if you ever run even a couple of laps testing without learning something, then someone is not doing his job. There are valid ways to cut down some of the expenses involved in testing.

The big expenses in testing are track rental, tires and

engine wear. A lot of basic testing can be done on worn tires—engine tuning and cooling—or aerodynamic drag work, for instance. You don't need a prime race engine to test with—you need a reliable lump with the same torque curve characteristics, but you can very profitably sacrifice the last percentage points of power for reliability. You don't need new brake pads, and you can use gears and dog rings that are a bit second hand—so long as they don't lead to missed shifts. Most of all, you don't need one of the expensive race tracks. Engine cooling and aerodynamic drag work can be done at a drag strip just as well as at a race track and Willow Springs or Sear's Point is just as useful as Riverside.

THE RACE WEEKEND

Assuming that everyone has done his homework, the race weekend is for the driver, not for the crew. Drivers being what they are, they will attempt to wear the car out before the race. This is OK if (1) you have the budget to replace whatever he wears out before the race, and (2) he is actually making progress. Under no circumstances should the driver be allowed to just drive around because he enjoys it—especially if he is stuck in traffic and unwilling to do anything about it—he can always slow down and let the traffic go away.

There are two approaches to setting up the car at the race track—spend all of your time trying to go fast or set the car up for the conditions under which it will be raced. Strangely enough, the approaches need not be mutually contradictory. Logic tells us that the car will be fastest with a very light fuel load, a very low ride height, soft tires, possibly with more negative camber than you can race with, possibly with more rear brake bias and less downforce and with shorter gears than you can race with. So qualify it that way—just make damned sure that you KNOW what the race setup is—and that the driver knows what the car feels like in race configuration.

THE IMPORTANCE OF QUALIFYING

I have heard a vast number of supposedly intelligent and experienced racers downgrade the importance of qualifying. I do not agree—for many reasons. First and foremost is the simple fact that if you start the race ahead of another car, you then do not have to pass him. Since the performance of today's race cars is very equal, it is very difficult to get by a competitive car on the race track—it can take laps. During the time that you are trying to get by someone who is only marginally slower than you are, the race leaders are disappearing into the distance. It is worth whatever it takes to qualify at the front of the grid.

Second is the boost in driver and crew morale and confidence that results from qualifying on the pole—it can make your whole day. The operation that is on the pole is going into the race in the best possible frame of mind.

Third, and something that no one ever seems to think about, has to do with the financial realities of motor racing. Qualifying gets the headlines in the Sunday papers. Race cars are nothing but moving billboards—for the sponsor or for the driver's career—or both. We have no way of knowing what will happen during the race, but if we can stick the beast on the pole, we have at least gotten all of the publicity that we can get out of Saturday's activities—sometimes there is even money involved.

It is never necessary to go out and do a whole bunch of consecutive laps to put the car on the pole. If the car and driver have been tuned to the point where the pole is within reach, they should be able to get it done in a very few laps. It is necessary to remember that the tires which are going to put the car on the pole are going to lose their edge after a very few laps—and if those laps are spent either in traffic or waiting for a miracle—it won't happen. It is, of course, perfectly valid to wait for the cool of the afternoon before making the big try—but you had better have put forth your best effort before the last half hour or you are liable to find oil on the track, or a session cut short—that is why I really like the USAC method of qualifying one car at a time. You don't get your choice of track condition or ambient temperature, but you don't have to worry about traffic, and the whole operation is fully aware that they have to get the job done—right now. Besides, it keeps you from wearing the car out and the crowd loves it. Other sanctioning groups please take note.

Once qualifying is over, it is essential that the car be prepared for the race—it's OK to qualify with the chassis scraping the ground, with the engine over-revving a bit and the inside edges of the tires burning away—but no way can we race under those conditions. In order to put the race setup on the car, we must know what the race setup is—and we had better have found out in practice. We had also better get the driver out in the car in race configuration to make sure that we are right and he had better drive it hard enough to find out. That is what the Sunday morning warmup session is for—it is not for bedding brake pads.

CHAPTER SEVENTEEN

EVERYTHING ELSE

EVERYTHING ELSE

This is going to be a very strange chapter. It will contain all of the stuff that I could not fit logically into the previous chapters —or which I forgot.

THE DRIVER ADJUSTABLE ANTI-ROLL BAR

Other than driver technique and prayer, the racing driver normally has no means at his disposal to allow him to change the oversteer/understeer balance of his car while he is driving it. Assuming that the driver in question has sufficient experience and sensitivity to use such a device intelligently, there are a great many situations where he could really use one. When practice time is limited, it is a lot quicker for the driver to perform minor balance adjustments than it is to stop and have the crew do it. During a race, changing track, fuel load or tire conditions can and do change the balance of the car—never in the right direction.

If the driver can readjust the vehicle balance, he is going to gain time—sometimes considerable time. The easy way to achieve this is to provide the driver with a cockpit adjustable anti-roll bar—either front or rear or, in a sedan, with a weight jacker. I usually do it at the rear because it is easier— there is less stuff in the way. The available methods range from complex and expensive hydraulics through mechanically operated cams to the simple push-pull throttle cable setup illustrated by Figure (95). I use the simple way and I adjust both sides of the bar. Many people do not believe in letting the driver adjust anything lest he jack himself off the race track. To my mind this is ridiculous—if you cannot trust your driver to adjust an anti-roll bar, you need a new driver.

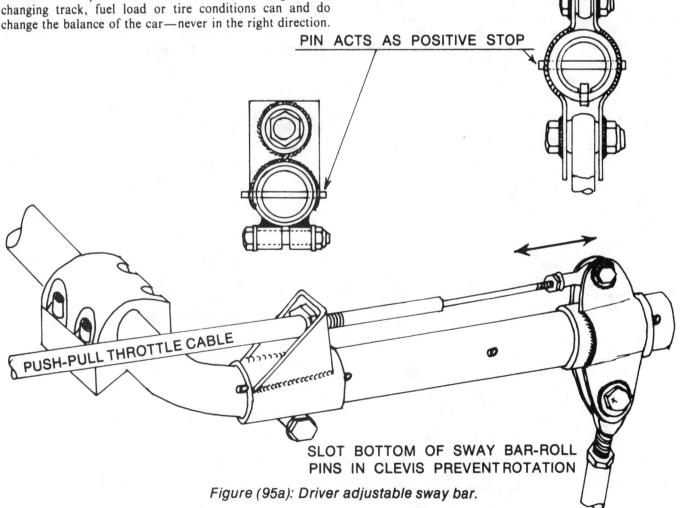

PIN ACTS AS POSITIVE STOP

PUSH-PULL THROTTLE CABLE

SLOT BOTTOM OF SWAY BAR-ROLL PINS IN CLEVIS PREVENT ROTATION

Figure (95a): Driver adjustable sway bar.

DRIVER ADJUSTABLE BRAKE RATIO

Everything that I just said about the advantages of a driver adjustable anti-roll bar also applies to driver adjustable front to rear brake bias—especially if the track gets wet—or even damp. Do not attempt to accomplish this feat with any kind of a pressure proportioning valve—it won't work. The easy way is a flexible cable attached to the bias bar at the brake pedal through a suitable coupling—good ones in straight and right angle configuration can be found at your local speedometer or taxi meter shop. Virtually any flexible control cable can be used to operate the device so long as a positive stop is employed at the cockpit end. Figure (96) illustrates.

SHIFTING WITHOUT THE CLUTCH

With the Hewland, or any other dog engagement type gearbox, there is no mechanical need for the driver to use the clutch when shifting—if he is skilled enough at synchronizing engine rpm, which he damned well should be. Eliminating the use of the clutch will not reduce the actual time it takes to shift, but it will eliminate a left foot movement which also takes time. This is one less motion for the driver to go through. More important, not using the clutch enables the driver to continuously use his left foot to brace himself in the cockpit. Since everyone is fallible, if my driver is not going to use the clutch, I grind about .020" from the top surface of every other dog on the dog rings—it makes for a bigger hole for the engaging dogs to fall into. I do not favor the use of the clutch by racing drivers, but I do not object to it very strenuously. It is, however, vital for every driver to develop the technique of shifting without it against the in-evitable time when he is going to lose his clutch actuating mechanism during a race. Any gearbox can be shifted without the use of the clutch and without damage to the box—although I will admit that it is difficult with baulk ring synchromesh.

THE LEFT FOOT BRAKE PEDAL

Most of the drivers who habitually shift without the clutch also use their left foot on the brake pedal. This both removes the possibility of getting the right foot tangled up in the pedals (don't laugh—it happens!) and improves both throttle and brake control. It also makes downshifting easier and more precise and does away with the amount of time wasted while moving the right foot from one pedal to the other. Since the steering column typically runs directly to the left of the brake pedal which effectively prevents the driver from placing his left foot on same, it is usually necessary to construct some sort of a sling shot or "Y" pedal. Make very certain that the extension is strong enough.

STARTER CABLES

Most of us don't use big enough starter cables. The usual villain in the "Damned starter won't work because it is overheated" situation is not the starter, but the cables. If you use standard automotive starter cable, when it gets hot—and it will—it often won't conduct enough current to spin the engine over—even with a good battery. I use either multi-strand aircraft cable or multi-strand welding cable—about 7/16 inch diameter. This becomes of considerable interest in those events where push starting incurs a penalty, and it becomes critical in long distance racing.

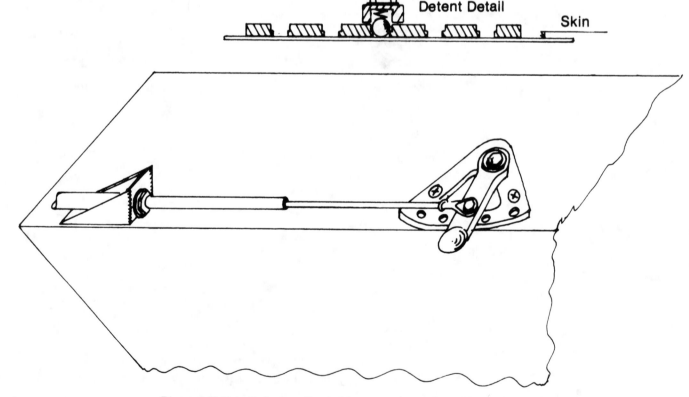

Figure (95b): Driver adjustable sway bar—cockpit end.

166

COMPOSITE MATERIALS

The aerospace industry has come up with pretty fantastic ultra high strength and ultra light weight materials called composites. These are composed of very thin filaments of either pure carbon or boron, woven together and bonded with exotic epoxiers. It is not going to be very long before clever people start making components such as connecting rods, pistons, hub carriers, wheels, flywheels, brake discs and who knows what else out of this stuff. The technology has been available for about a decade, but both material and tooling costs have precluded its use to date. The material cost is on the way down and it has to happen soon. Racing parts made from composite materials will be every bit as good as the engineering behind them.

BREAKING IN THE RING AND PINION

Most racers seem to believe that the proper way to break in a new ring and pinion is to do about ten very slow laps at a constant speed and low load. Wrong! The idea is to assist the two gears in getting happy with each other by removing the high sports in the tooth contact area and by physically moving metal around. The proper way to do it is to put a medium load into the gears for a short time to get some heat into the metal and then coast for a while to let them cool down. If the

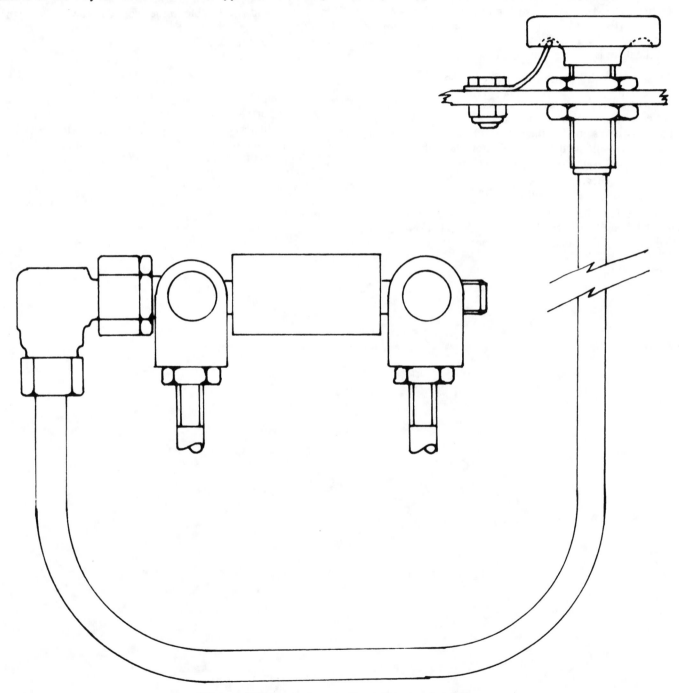

Figure (95b): *Driver adjustable brake bias.*

167

process is repeated for about ten laps of the average race track while the load is gradually increased, they will get happy in a hurry. Keeping a medium or low load on new gears generates too much heat.

NEW PARTS AND/OR NEW SUPPLIERS

Not a lot has changed in this department since I wrote *Prepare to Win*. There have been a few additions:

ROD END BEARINGS

The NMB range of superb rod end and spherical bearings is now available to the racer without the previous necessity of convincing NMB that you were going to use them on an airplane. Earl's Supply and Tilton Engineering are both distributors for the line. There is nothing better on the market and the price is as reasonable as that of any quality bearing.

THROTTLE CABLES

A new push-pull throttle cable is being manufactured by Cablecraft, 2011 South Mildred St., Tacoma, Washington. It is every bit as good as the previous best—American Chain and Cable—and considerably better than the ubiquitous Morse. It is cheaper than either.

OIL COOLERS

Earl's Supply has been appointed sole U.S. Distributor for the SERCK SPEED range of oil coolers. They are stocked in all sizes with both AN and BSP ports.

TILTON ENGINEERING

Mac Tilton has set up shop in El Segundo to solve a lot of the racer's logistic problems. Mac is both a good racer and a fine engineer. He is marketing a line of previously unavailable stuff that we had to make for ourselves—MacPherson strut hardware, high angle washers, really lightweight but structurally sound flywheels, brake bias bar assemblies, brake disc bells, production car hubs, wheel studs, etc. He is also THE stocklist for Borg and Beck clutches and Lockheed racing brakes as well as the Australian Hardie Ferodo racing brake pads. He is probably the only man in the country who really KNOWS about racing brakes and is available to the every day racer. Catalog is from TILTON ENGINEERING, 114 Center Street, El Segundo, California, 90245.

PLUMBING STUFF

Earl's Supply is now making their own line of competition plumbing parts—both hose and hose ends—in direct competition with Aeroquip. Earl's "Swivel Seal" line matches Aeroquip in quality and performance and comes in a whole bunch more configurations for the racer. A particularly nice feature is that the Swivel-Seal hose ends can be rotated with respect to the hose after it has been assembled. Catalog is $3.00 from Earl's Supply Co., 14611 Hawthorne Blvd., Lawndale, California 90260.

CHAPTER EIGHTEEN

THE END

That's it. I have said all that I have to say. If I have left anything out, or glossed over anything of importance, it is an error of omission, not of commission.

Judging from the number of letters that *Prepare to Win* generated, I suppose that our mail carrier will be moaning again. Sooner or later the right combination of driver and operation will inspire me and I'll go back to running a race team. When that happens I will have neither the time nor the inclination to answer letters which ask for advice—unless, of course, the problem interests me. So I will apologize here and now for not answering most of the letters that this book will generate. I will, however, read them—and appreciate them.

I hope that reading this effort has been as rewarding for you as writing it has been for me. It started out to be a pretty simple book, "to reduce understeer, soften the front anti-roll bar," and that sort of thing. I wasn't at all satisfied with that approach and *Tune to Win* has turned out to be a lot of very hard work. In the process of writing the book, I have been forced to re-evaluate my thinking in a lot of areas and to organize a lot of random knowledge and thoughts about the interrelation of various aspects of vehicle dynamics and performance. In that respect, the exercise has been good for me and will doubtless pay dividends in terms of racing successes down the line. If it does the same for you, the exercise will have been successful.

THE END

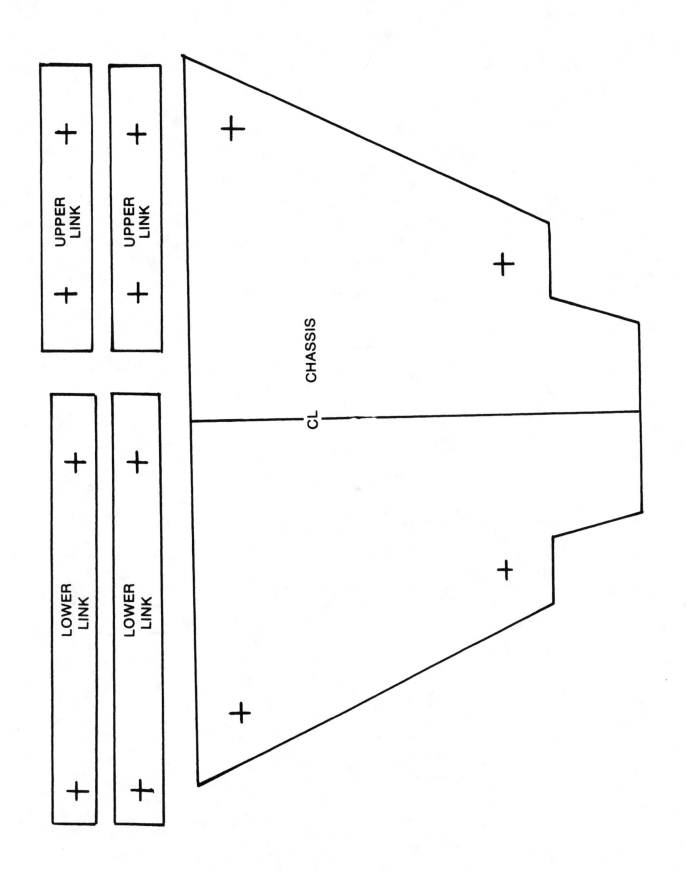

Upper Link (×2)
Lower Link (×2)
CL CHASSIS

APPENDIX — CUT OUTS FOR ¼ SCALE SUSPENSION GEOMETRY MODEL

171

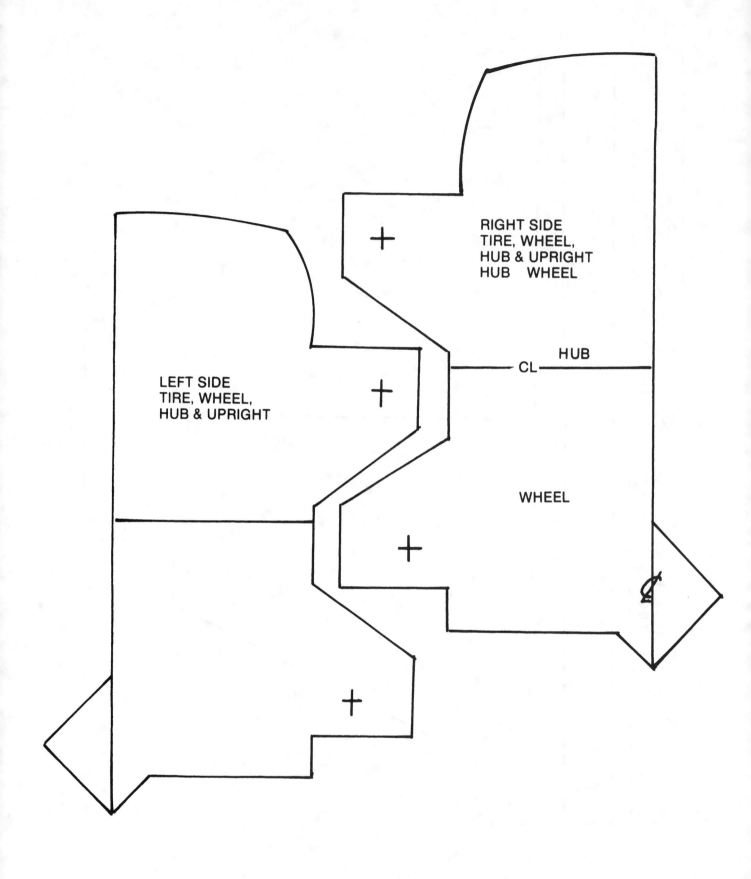

RIGHT SIDE
TIRE, WHEEL,
HUB & UPRIGHT
HUB   WHEEL

CL —— HUB

WHEEL

LEFT SIDE
TIRE, WHEEL,
HUB & UPRIGHT

*APPENDIX — CUT OUTS FOR ¼ SCALE SUSPENSION
GEOMETRY MODEL*